Comparative Cultural Studies and Latin America

Comparative Cultural Studies
Steven Tötösy de Zepetnek, Series Editor

Comparative Cultural Studies is a contextual approach in the study of culture in all of its products and processes. The framework is built on tenets of the discipline of comparative literature and cultural studies and on notions borrowed from a range of thought such as (radical) constructivism, communication theories, systems theories, and literary and culture theory. In comparative cultural studies, focus is on theory and method as well as application and where attention is on the how rather than on the what. Colleagues interested in publishing in the series are invited to contact the editor, Steven Tötösy, at <clcweb@purdue.edu>.

1. *Comparative Central European Culture*. Ed. Steven Tötösy de Zepetnek. 2002. 234 pages, bibliography, index. ISBN 1-55753-240-0.

2. *Comparative Literature and Comparative Cultural Studies*. Ed. Steven Tötösy de Zepetnek. 2003. 372 pages, bibliography, index. ISBN 1-55753-290-7.

3. Sophia A. McClennen, *The Dialectics of Exile: Nation, Time, Language, and Space in Hispanic Literatures*. 2004. 260 pages, bibliography, index. ISBN 1-55753-315-6.

4. *Comparative Cultural Studies and Latin America*. Ed. Sophia A. McClennen and Earl E. Fitz. 2004. 282 pages, bibliography, index. ISBN 1-55753-358-X.

Comparative Cultural Studies and Latin America

Edited by
Sophia A. McClennen and Earl E. Fitz

Purdue University Press
West Lafayette, Indiana

Printed in the United States of America

Library of Congress Cataloging-in-Publication Data

Comparative cultural studies and Latin America / edited by
Sophia A. McClennen and Earl E. Fitz.
p. cm. -- (Comparative cultural studies : 4)
Includes bibliographical references and index.
ISBN 1-55753-358-X (pbk.)
1. Latin American literature--History and criticism. 2. Literature, Comparative.
I. McClennen, Sophia A. II. Fitz, Earl E. III. Series.
PQ7081.C637 2004
860.9'98--dc22
2003027346

We dedicate this book to our families

Contents

Introduction

This volume of essays was first published as a thematic issue of *CLCWeb: Comparative Literature and Culture: A WWWeb Journal* 4.2 (2002): <http://clcwebjournal.lib.purdue.edu>, guest edited by Sophia A. McClennen and Earl E. Fitz and entitled *Comparative Cultural Studies and Latin America*. The genesis for this project stemmed from a growing conviction on the part of the editors that, given its vitality and excellence, Latin American literature deserves a more prominent place in comparative literature publications, curricula, and disciplinary discussions. As statistics compiled by Sophia A. McClennen in her article for this volume clearly show, the literatures of Spanish America and Brazil appear much less frequently in comparative literature journals worldwide than do works written in such languages as English, French, and German. That this situation exists at all in an age when the very future of comparative literature as an academic discipline is once again being questioned suggests to us that 1) there still exists, in some quarters, a lingering bias against literature written in Spanish and Portuguese and 2) that by embracing Latin American literature more enthusiastically, comparative literature would find itself reinvigorated, placed into productive discourse with a host of issues, languages, literatures, and cultures that have too long been paid scant attention in its purview. With this volume of essays, the editors are seeking to change this situation, to gain for Latin American literature the kind of respect and admiration that is routinely accorded other, more "canonical" national literatures. Believing deeply in the efficacy of the comparative method, and in its implicitly egalitarian approach to the world's languages and literatures, our intention, therefore, is not to weaken or diminish comparative literature as a politically potent and intellectually important form of literary study, but rather to strengthen it, to open it up to the authors, texts, and traditions of one of the world's most complex and challenging cultural conglomerates—Latin America. Our goal, in short, is to play an active role in the reenergizing of comparative literature by helping it adapt to changing times. Indeed, we would stress that, as the 1993 Bernheimer Report makes clear, the unique ability of comparative literature to respond to the rise of new languages and literatures constitutes one of the discipline's greatest and most enduring strengths (see Charles Bernheimer, et al., "The Bernheimer Report," American Comparative Literature Association, (1993): <http://www.umass.edu/complit/aclanet/Berheim. html.>).

Historically, comparative literature has always been best defined as an issue of methodology, of how and why select texts or aesthetic and intellectual issues are brought together for study, rather than as an issue of reading lists made up of certain works from certain "canonical" languages and literatures. We know that, in its incipient stage, comparative literature did deal primarily with texts written in certain European-based languages, and that, for some, these came early on to not only delineate the discipline institutionally, but also to establish the models against which all other literatures would have to be measured. And while we all agree that English, French, and German and other mainstream European nations have produced many wonderful works of literature, we also recognize that other languages and cultures have produced many outstanding works of literature as well. In our view, literary excellence is not the exclusive domain of particular languages at the expense of others. Consequently, it is imperative that the discipline of comparative literature (and that of comparative cultural studies) be understood, essentially, as a question of procedure, as a way of studying literature from an international perspective and as a rationale for framing its studies, rather than as a hierarchy in which some literatures, texts, and authors are always perceived to be at the top while others are automatically relegated to a secondary status. Understanding comparative literature and culture as an approach for the international study of literature and as a method for its even-handed commentary allows us to get beyond the rigid hierarchies that result from identifying the discipline with certain languages and national literatures and not others.

What Latin Americanists bring to this debate (in addition to several hundred years' worth of first-rate literature) is a great deal of experience reading their texts in the light of other, more "prototypical" texts, of constantly having to evaluate their authors in the context of standards and forms that, in far too many cases, render them inescapably and ineradicably "marginal" no matter how excellent their artistic and intellectual qualities might be. Borges, for example, had to be translated first into French and then into English before he gained an international following, and even then (in the beginning, at least), only because readers unfamiliar with him, his works, and the traditions out of which he was coming could, seeking ways to praise him, opine that he wrote as if he were "a French intellectual," a term that reveals a great deal about how Borges was received in the United States of the early 1960s. An even more egregious example of this sort of culturally dismissive attitude pertains to the case of the Brazilian author Clarice Lispector, whose extraordinary texts (and especially her 1973 "fiction," *Água Viva.* Rio de Janeiro: Artenova, 1973, translated as *The Stream of Life* by Elizabeth Lowe and Earl E. Fitz, with a foreword by Hélène Cixous. Minneapolis: U of Minnesota P, 1989) provided Hélène Cixous with the prototypes for her concept of "l'écriture féminine," but whose fundamental importance to this immensely influential reading strategy is rarely noted, much less commented upon, except by Latin Americanists. And what if we were to begin arguing that Machado de Assis, now recognized as "the premier nineteenth-century Latin American writer and one of the best of all time anywhere," was an inventive genius on the level of—or even superior to—"Flaubert, Melville, Hawthorne, and Poe" (Roberto González Echevarría, *The Oxford Book of Latin American Short Stories.* New York: Oxford UP, 1997. 95)? How would this be received by our more conservative colleagues in comparative literature? Are authors currently decreed to be the "best," or the most exemplary, forever to be enshrined in this exalted category? Or, given the nature of comparative scholarship (which seeks always to integrate new literatures and cultures into the mix), is it not possible that a writer from a very rich but widely ignored national literature (in this case Brazil) could be shown to be "superior" (however we would like to define that elusive term) to her or his European models? To be a comparatist (and a Latin Americanist) is to believe that the answer to this question is, unequivocally, yes; indeed, to us this is the essence of comparative literature, the heart of its intellectual integrity as a discipline. To answer this question "no," on the other hand, is to condemn our discipline to a slow and painful demise, one brought on by narrow-mindedness, an ill-considered embracing of exclusivity, and hypocrisy, qualities which are anathema to comparative literature but which, according to some scholars, all too accurately characterize the state of our discipline at the present time.

Although we do not seriously entertain the notion that alluring, but critically misleading, terms like "the best" have any eternal and unchanging value (except, perhaps, as abstract concepts), we do believe that there is much to be gained in reading a writer like Flaubert (or Joyce, Dante, or Kafka) in the light of a "marginal" writer like Machado de Assis. It is for this reason that, while we do advocate comparisons (albeit inverted) with the established models (European or otherwise), we do not wish to promote writers like Machado, Lispector, or Borges as automatically and forever more "the best," for to do so would be both simplistic and little more than the substitution of one form of hierarchical and binary thinking for another. Merely to replace one form of canon with another will surely lead to the same problems again and again in the future. Rather, we are calling for the kind of fluid, evolving approach often associated with René Etiemble, who long ago called for a truly "planetary comparatism," one that considers all literatures openly and equally and without the Eurocentric prejudices of culture (especially the warping pressures of coloniality), language, and prestige (see his *Ouverture(s) sur un comparatisme planétaire*. Paris: Christian Bourgois, 1988).

Frustrated by generations of feeling that they are the "poor cousins" of the literary world, Latin Americanists are now, at the dawn of the twenty-first century, in a position to revitalize the field of comparative literature. Moreover, they are in a position to do so by upholding, on the strength of their authors and texts, its fundamental commitment to international literary study, its flexible, open-minded approach to all literatures (even those long derided by some as "marginal," "derivative," or "inferior"), and its basic, conceptual belief that everyone should get a seat at the literary table, that no worthy text should ever be excluded, and most especially not because it was written in a supposedly "lesser" language or that it comes from a supposedly "lesser" culture. The great challenge now facing comparative literature is, precisely, whether it can accommodate this type and degree of change, whether it still has the requisite level of conceptual flexibility to do so.

Long practiced in the comparative method (and, by tradition, very favorably disposed toward it), Latin Americanists believe fervently that it does. Indeed, by virtue of their training and their sense of where their own authors stand in relation to the rest of world literature, Latin Americanists are, at their best, skilled and sophisticated comparatists in the truest sense of the term. Fluent, or, at least, competent, in several languages (including, very often, both English and French) and typically knowledgeable in their literatures, Latin Americanists nearly always possess the extensive linguistic and literary training that is the distinguishing feature of the comparatist.

Yet even today the training of the typical Latin Americanist is too often not what it should be, especially if our goal is to gain greater visibility in comparative literature journals and curricula around the world. In too many cases, doctoral students are permitted to complete a program in Latin American literature without ever studying much, if any, Portuguese or Brazilian literature, thus cutting out from their program a knowledge of the world's sixth most widely spoken language and one of the richest national literatures in the New World, one that (reflecting an ideal situation for the comparatist) has numerous parallels and points of contact with Spanish American literature as well as a great many differences and contrasts. Roberto González Echevarría, to cite one prominent scholar who has come to similar conclusions, writes, in fact, that "Brazil's is, with that of the United States, the richest national literature in the New World" and that "In the second half of the nineteenth century, Brazilian fiction was unequaled in the rest of Latin America in terms of production and quality" (*The Oxford Book of Latin American Short Stories*. New York: Oxford UP, 1997. xii, 15).

Because we believe that for a Latin Americanist of the twenty-first century such a lacuna is professionally untenable, we are strongly in favor of doctoral programs that require extensive training in both Brazilian Portuguese and Brazilian literature and culture. More than this, we advocate the inclusion of Brazilian texts on reading lists and in the dissertations that eventually evolve from them. In short, we recommend that the training of our future Latin Americanists extensively involve both "brasileiro" and Brazilian literature, even for students who wish to specialize in Spanish and Spanish American literature. For Latin Americanists concentrating on the Caribbean, however, or perhaps on Andean or Central American issues, it would, of course, be wise to consider making French, Dutch, or an indigenous tongue the second language. As a general rule, however, it seems to us that to have both Portuguese and Brazilian literature as part of our training not only enhances our teaching and research capabilities, it also provides the fledgling Latin Americanist with the tools necessary to do serious comparative work, and to do so in a way that is both methodologically rigorous and fully characteristic of the best of the comparative scholarship being done through other language combinations.

We therefore hope that this collection points to a number of productive avenues for the comparative study of Latin America, its literatures and cultures. Certainly, a key way to change the role of Latin America in comparative literature is through scholarly essays that exemplify this dynamic and diverse field. In addition to raising the visibility of comparative Latin American studies through publications, we believe that for real progress to be made it must begin in the classroom. We have both made concerted efforts in our teaching and curricula development to enable and facilitate comparative work on Latin American culture. Earl E. Fitz, while at Pennsylvania State University, initiated a series of courses in the Department of Comparative Literature dealing with inter-American literature. Since joining the faculty at Vanderbilt University, he has also made a course in comparative methods a requirement for all doctoral students in the combined Spanish and Portuguese Ph.D. program (see <http://www.vanderbilt.edu/AnS/spanport/grad.htm#PHDSP>).

And Sophia A. McClennen designed a Master of Arts concentration at Illinois State University in hispanic transatlantic cultural studies, where students concentrate on the cultural history of Spain and of Spanish America through comparative analysis of the cultural interactions between the regions (see

<http://www.foreignlanguages.ilstu.edu/graduate/reading_lists/>). Each of these pedagogical endeavors involves the application of comparative methods to Latin American culture. We believe that curricular initiatives such as these will help to foster and promote a new generation of Latin American comparatists, scholars trained in the methodological skills our profession demands.

As Latin Americanists look for increased participation in the world of comparative literary studies, two very promising possibilities come to mind almost immediately: inter-American literature and Latin American literature cast in a larger, more international perspective. By virtue of their languages and training, students of Spanish America and Brazil tend to be natural inter-Americanists. Because it is virtually impossible to read Latin American literature and culture without constantly referencing the United States, Latin Americanists are uniquely prepared to extend their areas of expertise and specialization to issues germane to the United States as well. Courses and research projects can easily involve both traditions and, in so doing, coherently expand and complement one's primary research area. A Latin American colonialist, for example, might well wish to begin to consider comparing and contrasting the colonial situations in Brazil and Spanish America (which are themselves far from identical) with the situation in English North America. Issues of race, religion, and sociopolitical organization immediately become apparent as sites of difference and, in some cases, of conflict as well. The question of relations between the European conquerors and the indigenous people is also one that Latin Americanists could easily develop into an inter-American perspective, as is the too often overlooked issue of the very different literary heritages brought to the New World by the English, French, Spanish, and Portuguese. How, for example, does the Latin American Baroque compare to the attitudes about creative literature held by the English Puritans? How do the poems of Sor Juana Inés de la Cruz and Gregôrio de Matos compare to those of Anne Bradstreet or Edward Taylor? Or how might we compare the sermons and essays of Bartolomé de Las Casas, Antônio Vieira, Cotton Mather, and Jonathan Edwards? We do not advocate that Latin Americanists abandon their primary areas of specialization to pursue inter-American connections, but, because we believe that Latin Americanists are in a particularly advantageous position here with respect to what is a very fast developing new field, we do urge students and scholars of Brazilian and Spanish American literature to consider at least some forays into the inter-American ken, developing this aspect of their professional portfolio as a closely related and inherently comparative secondary field.

Much the same can be said of our desire to take Latin American literature and culture into the larger, international arena. The integration of our texts into the European tradition is, of course, one that all Latin Americanists know well, although typically our experience with this effort means that our texts are inevitably judged to be the "lesser" ones, the ones that, though measured against the masterworks, always appear to be derivative and "marginal." Although this problem is endemic to the Americas, it has persisted in Latin America longer and more perniciously than it should have. It is time for a change. Keying on the originality of our works (an originality that often stems from the collision of the three great cultures that have formed Latin America: the European, the Indigenous, and the African), we need to learn to assert ourselves more in terms of these international comparisons; we need to learn to not be timid about arguing that very often it is our authors and texts that are demonstrating the most interesting formal and thematic innovations, and that these deserve much more attention than they have gotten. In addition to the inter-American project, we see other internationalist approaches, such as transatlantic, postcolonial, and comparative cultural analysis, as being especially productive for Latin American literature and for engaging comparative literature both imaginatively and restoratively.

Finally, a word should be said about the articles featured here. Our wish from the beginning was to bring together pieces from both new and established scholars that focused not merely on Latin American literature but on how Latin American literature might gain more recognition within the discipline of comparative literature. Given our loci as scholars working in the United States and Canada, we were especially interested in calls for disciplinary changes that would affect the comparative study of Latin America in U.S. and Canadian institutions, even though a number of the articles in this collection pay particular attention to comparative work and disciplinary innovations taking place in Latin America. We understand all too well that what we have proposed to do here is an immensely complex and contentious undertaking. We also understand that there are many important perspectives, positions, and discussions that are not included here, and for this omission we apologize to our readers. It was not intentional. Still, we firmly believe that the selections that are included all make important contributions to our overall goal, and it is our sincere hope that they will help initiate a dialogue the eventual outcome of which will be the heightened international and comparative recognition that Latin American literature so richly deserves. If, as you read these articles, you find yourself enumerating multiple possibilities for additional study not included in this volume, then we have achieved our goal. We hope, above all, that this collection will serve as a gateway to heightened dialogue, debate, and consideration of the scholarly potentialities that will arise from an increased interaction between practitioners of Latin American studies, comparative literature, and comparative cultural studies. While the organizational failings are ours alone, we hope our readers will join with us in thanking our contributors for allowing us to benefit from their stimulating thoughts and ideas. The essays selected for inclusion here range widely in terms of subject matter and argument, yet all provide new avenues for the comparative (cultural) study of Latin American literature. Thus, the concept of *Comparative Cultural Studies and Latin America* follows the principal aims and objectives of *CLCWeb*. Further, for a thematic issue related to the present volume of *CLCWeb*, see *Intercultural Negotiations in the Americas and Beyond*, guest edited by Barbara Buchenau and Marietta Messmer in *CLCWeb: Comparative Literature and Culture* 3.2 (2001): <http://clcwebjournal.lib.purdue.edu/clcweb01-2/contents01-2.html>. While the chapters in *Intercultural Negotiations in the Americas and Beyond* represent current European scholarship on the cultures and literatures of the continent, *Comparative Cultural Studies and Latin America* contains scholarship emanating from U.S. and Canadian scholarship.

The essays in *Comparative Cultural Studies and Latin America* are organized in alphabetical order by author, as follows. Gene H. Bell-Villada writes of how our concept of the "canon" has been affected by Hispanic literature (especially that of the Spanish American "boom" novelists of the 1960s), how Latin American authors are now beginning to replace European authors as an important source of influence on writers from the United States, and how the Comparatist/Hispanist must not allow the "canonical" figures of Latin American literature to be subsumed by departments of English eager to broaden their reading lists. Calling attention to the richness and diversity of our ancient Native American heritage, Gordon Brotherston and Lúcia de Sá discuss the importance of the Mayan *Popol Vuh* and demonstrate that the literatures and cultures of our "first peoples" lives on, throughout the Americas, as a vibrant and compelling, if too often overlooked, aspect of our New World existences. They argue that the rich legacy of Latin America's indigenous heritage is typically neglected in favor of seeking intertextualities and literary trends that link Latin America with Europe. They show, rather, that much European literature was influenced by contact with Latin American indigenous culture. Elizabeth Coonrod Martínez, in contrast, examines the experimental Spanish American novel of the 1920s and considers the many ways these texts exemplify certain aspects of the European avant-garde even as they express social, political, and intellectual problems germane to the Latin American experience. Linking these texts to the basic tenets of modernism, the author also argues that the experimental narratives of the 1920s should be acknowledged as important precursors of the "boom" novels of the 1960s and that they merit their own comparisons with the better known United States and European novels of the period. Román de la Campa reflects on the ways that Latin American literary study has changed since 1989. He suggests that the study of Latin American culture is entering a new phase where the intersection of political and economic change in the region coincides with increased attention to postmodern and postcolonial theory. Using the example of *testimonio* he compares its study in the United States (via the work of John Beverley) with its study in Latin America, particularly Chile (via the work of Nelly Richard). Ultimately, he calls for new comparative methods to be applied to the cultural production and academic study of Latin America.

Taking a theoretical tact, Earl E. Fitz argues that Latin American literature should always be thought of as including both the Spanish American and the Brazilian traditions, that Latin Americanists can easily expand their work as comparatists by engaging inter-American literature (an emergent field and one for which they are exceptionally prepared), and that the entire discipline of comparative literature is being redefined and rejuvenated by the inclusion of texts from Spanish America and Brazil. Moving us in a similar direction is Roberto González Echevarría, who, lamenting the current state of comparative literature as a discipline, challenges us, in our courses and in our critical studies, to make use of Latin American texts as the models against which the other texts have to be evaluated (to read Joyce only after reading Lezama Lima, for example) and, in so doing, to revolutionize comparative literature by displacing the stifling Eurocentrism that, in the early years of the twenty-first century, is preventing it from developing as naturally and as salubriously as it should. Summing up the profound changes that are characterizing Latin American literary and cultural scholarship at the present time, and arguing that Latin American literature is best (and most naturally) studied from a comparative perspective, Sophia A. McClennen offers us five very promising research areas or initiatives that conflate comparative literature, Latin American literature, and cultural studies and that demonstrate how, collectively and individually, these disciplines can benefit from heightened interaction. Alberto Moreiras turns his attention to Jorge Luis Borges, perhaps the most well known Latin American author among U.S. comparatists. Moreiras offers us a provocative intervention into the reading and interpretation of Borges, focusing on the "Tema del traidor y del heroe." Surveying some of the disciplinary changes that have taken place in U.S. and Latin American universities, Julio Ortega discusses the emerging field of transatlantic studies. Ortega describes the field as a dynamic and open-ended area of study that does not require a traditional canon or disciplinary configuration. Through her study of masculinity in Cuban American literature, Christina Marie Tourino argues that the massive flow of people within and beyond Latin America complicates comparative projects that focus on the national. She suggests that more productive comparative categories might track, for example, along lines of gender and sexuality and she provides a detailed comparative analysis of Cuban masculinity in Reinaldo Arenas and Oscar Hijuelos. Mario J. Valdés gives an account of the process of compiling the first history of Latin American literary culture. Describing the intricacies of the project, Valdés presents us with a theory of literary history which is comparative and informs, but which does not totalize, the object of study. Lois Parkinson Zamora adds to the debate about the role of Latin America in comparative study by focusing on globalization. Analyzing how comparative literature as a discipline illuminates key features of cultural production, Zamora highlights the central role that Latin American texts can play in such a project. Last, but not least, Sophia A. McClennen has compiled an extensive bibliography of web resources and published works that are representative of comparative Latin American cultural studies. This rich resource should serve as a useful starting point for further teaching and research.

We would like to thank Steven Tötösy de Zepetnek, editor of *CLCWeb* and series editor of the Purdue Series of Books in Comparative Cultural Studies and the advisory board of *CLCWeb* for their support of this project.

—*Sophia A. McClennen & Earl E. Fitz*
January 2004
The Pennsylvania State University & Vanderbilt University

The Canon is el Boom, et al., or the Hispanic Difference

Gene H. Bell-Villada

It is not too long ago—three or four decades, perhaps—that Hispanic literatures were considered a marginal player in comparative studies. The unofficial "Big Three" in the field were English, French, and German (in no particular order). Next came, say, Russian or Italian. Spanish stood a distant third. A novice twenty-something who chose to focus on the language of Spain and the other America might, from time to time, encounter polite doubts, puzzled looks, and raised eyebrows.

Things have changed, although not as much as we would actually like to believe. In dealing with this topic, I would like to take a brief look at the canon debates and other familiar polemics from the 1980s. But, with a difference, and this concerns the "Hispanic Difference" in the title of my essay. First, however, I must cite a revealing detail. Most readers of this essay are probably acquainted with a collection in the Graywolf Annual series edited by Rick Simonson and Scott Walker entitled *Multicultural Literacy: Opening up the American Mind* (1988). As its two-part title suggests, the volume comes in direct response to a pair of highly influential best-sellers from that decade, namely, Allan Bloom's *The Closing of the American Mind* (1987) and E.D. Hirsch's *Cultural Literacy: What Every American Needs to Know* (1988).

The final nine pages of *Multicultural Literacy* consist of a heterogeneous list of about six hundred items. It was conceived as a corrective to the famous long list included at the end of Hirsch's volume, which the Graywolf editors had deemed too exclusively centered on established, white-European or U.S. figures and concepts. Accordingly, the new list includes Salvador Allende, the Anasazi, Béla Bartók, and Bertolt Brecht, to pick a few entries from the first two letters of the alphabet. Well, among the names the editors deem essential for multicultural literacy are Pablo Neruda, Gabriel García Márquez, Manuel Puig, Jorge Luis Borges, and (of all people) Octavio Paz.

For those of us involved with Hispanic literatures, at least a couple of those names might come as a surprise. After all, within Latin America, Borges and Paz are the canon, the establishment, not the opposition or the counterculture. And yet, within the United States, even hallowed texts and artifacts from south of Texas can pose unsettling and even subversive challenges to the reigning mind and repertory of empire.

Let me say something so obvious that our jaded, professionalized sensibilities have too often taken blithely for granted. To wit: Over the past six decades, a rich, globally acclaimed, foundational yet contestatory prose literature has emerged in Latin America, a flowering comparable to that which had taken place in nineteenth-century Russia. Prior to that, moreover, there had occurred an efflorescence of great verse, both in the hemisphere and on the Peninsula. This historical fact well serves our best and most noble purposes as comparative Hispanists. Thanks to such a cultural moment (which is not yet done) we are able to teach "the canon" via major works that remain artistically fresh and intellectually provocative, and that—from the point of view of the ordinary reader enrolled in the classroom or on holiday at the beach—can be moving, exciting, subliminally informative, and often funny.

Texts such as these also help legitimate our cause as representatives of the culture of Latin America. As we all know, there is in this imperial nation (which the U.S. media have recently taken to referring to, simply yet inaccurately, as "America"), there is in this land a certain subtle condescension toward the people, products, and issues that are of Hispanic provenance. I can still remember my distant student days, when friends and acquaintances would ask me, "Gene, why are you in Spanish? Is there much Spanish literature worth reading?" More recently, in the early 1980s, conservative literary luminaries such as Anthony Burgess and John Simon dismissed the popularity of García Márquez as being scarcely more than ideologically motivated. And at a panel at the Modern Language Association of America convention that I happened to chair in the nation's capital in 1984, avant-garde novelist Ronald Sukenick dispatched Borges and García Márquez as mere imitators, respectively, of Kafka and Faulkner.

On a related note, in the early 1990s, I was looking for a publisher for my book *Art for Art's Sake and Literary Life* (published eventually in 1996). And at one point I got from University of Nebraska Press an extensive, detailed, anonymous report by a professor of comparative literature somewhere. The opinion was basically favorable, and it did in time lead to the manuscript's being accepted for publication. Still, he/she had a few reservations. One of them concerned my various sections dealing with Latin American authors with the modernista poets and, later, with the boom novelists. The outside reader found my discussions of "Spanish literature" (in the reader's words) to be "not very helpful." He/she suggested that I delete or cut them. And this scholar was a comparatist, mind you. In my reply, I argued, successfully, for retaining those sections.

The foregoing instances, however, stand for official opinion, *la historia oficial*, as the phrase goes. It is the older paradigm now facing challenges from and being replaced by a newer one. To shift age groups: now a few of our young students, both Anglo and Latino, start out blissfully unaware that there are such things as Hispanic Nobel Laureates, or indeed that the boom ever happened. And when these eighteen-year-olds encounter the likes of Neruda, Paz, and García Márquez, they pick up in the process a new respect for things Hispanic. Latino students, moreover, begin feeling a certain inchoate pride in the fact that such writing exists, and that it is written, moreover, in the language of their own households and perhaps even originates in the country where they were first born and raised. As a result of this reading, they are equipped with concrete answers to rebuke with if ever one of their Anglo peers might ask, "Is there much stuff to read in Spanish?"

From problems of attitude, I now move on to the larger, more intractable matter of the means of communication, of image reproduction—what Fredric Jameson aptly calls in his 1988 article "Postmodernism and Consumer Society" the "media society" (204). Our ear drums and eyeballs now live thoroughly surrounded and assaulted by a universe of man-made simulacra, of representations beyond counting, most of them as technically dazzling and skillful as they are ephemeral, ethnocentric, reactionary, silly, or just plain wrong. This highly seductive schlock is in turn gobbled up in all innocence by our young charges, who go on to internalize the world-view imparted by the media. With our modest pedagogical labors we can do our little bit to counteract media glitz and offer a more authentic, more complex, and yes, more truthful alternative vision of this country and its neo-colonies to the south of us.

And so, for instance, we can have our students read a long novel filled with love, sex, and war, in which the culminating chapters narrate a banana workers' strike against a U.S. agribusiness firm—an episode, incidentally, that adheres closely to the facts of a real such strike from 1928 (no need to mention the title of that now-classic 1967 book here). And we can expose our young minds to the historical experiences of race and racism through the poetry of Nicolás Guillén. We can introduce them to a world-system analysis that is as witty and passionate as it is informative in Eduardo Galeano's *Open Veins of Latin America* (1970). We can give them an immediate taste of U.S.-sponsored repression via Rigoberta Menchú's memoir (1983) and also the film *When the*

Mountains Tremble (1983)—this in spite of the campaign against her both from the thuggish right and the genteel, vital center. And we can provide them a vivid glimpse of 1960s student activism and show the repressive power of the Mexican State in Poniatowska's *La noche de Tlatelolco* (1971).

Political content aside, our engagement with such authors enables us to point our advanced students toward the Euro-American modernist classics. One of my regular assignments is to have my senior seminarians write a essay comparing García Márquez's *Cien años de soledad* with Faulkner's *Absalom, Absalom!* To many of them, it is their first encounter with Faulkner, and it provides an opportunity to acquaint them both with this astounding North American novel and with the techniques and resources of post-realist narrative. Another obvious instance is to lead them to Kafka by way of Borges, and in my survey course I assign a comparison between "La Biblioteca de Babel" (1941) and Kafka's "The Great Wall of China" (1931; it is worth noting that Kafka's text was translated by Borges into Spanish).

Other examples include having them read Nicolás Guillén, along with Langston Hughes's translations of the Cuban's poetry, or comparing Fuentes's *La muerte de Artemio Cruz* (1962) with Orson Welles's *Citizen Kane* (1941). This way they find out that there are indeed great U.S. films before 1981, some of them even in black-and-white, not to mention slow-paced (I'll never forget overhearing a bright undergraduate of mine observing casually that she liked watching old movies—from the 1980s).

In addition, in an advanced course, taught maybe in combination with a colleague from English, we can call attention to the formative influence that these authors have had on U.S. writing. For the first time in history, some of the key foreign influences on North American literature come not from England or France, but from Latin America. Borges's art helped redirect much of U.S. fiction in the 1960s and 1970s, as shown in the work of Barth, Pynchon, Coover, Barthelme, and John Gardner. The hand of García Márquez is clearly visible, and sometimes acknowledged, in the narratives and in the public statements of Paul Theroux, William Kennedy, Anne Tyler, Alice Walker, John Nichols, and again Robert Coover. These are impressive cultural realities and they can be conveyed to our students under the appropriate circumstances.

Finally, exposure to these authors and their biographies helps widen the ideological horizons of our students. It comes to them invariably as a surprise, and as a supreme absurdity, when I inform them that García Márquez spent more than three decades on the Immigration and Naturalization Service's official blacklist. And the left, in general, gains standing in their eyes when they find out that Neruda, Vallejo, and Guillén were Marxist activists, or that Carpentier was a staunch supporter of the Cuban revolution. The radical, left-wing consciousness of most Latin American authors may be something we lettered folks take for granted but, to most young students here in the empire, it will always be news.

Just a brief digression into popular culture: There is music, as represented in the most crucial work of Violeta Parra, Mercedes Sosa, Silvio Rodríguez, and Pablo Milanés. My friend Avi Chomsky has utilized their songs to good effect in her history courses at Salem State College, and listening to and singing along with *nueva trova* lyrics can prove a positive experience even in our language classes, whether the music be heard from an old-fashioned record player or in a high-tech, multimedia presentation. And then there is the political salsa music of Rubén Blades, himself a presence on the U.S. entertainment-industry scene and participant in many fine movies.

And of course, film, which by now is an integral part of our curriculum, though within a sobering, even alarming larger context. As we all know, foreign films are an endangered species in these United States where ticket sales for non-Hollywood items have hit rock-bottom. I am informed by Jerry Carlson, who teaches film studies in the CUNY system, that, in 1980, there were about a hundred foreign-language film titles shown on U.S. big screens. By 1990, the total figure had dropped to a mere twenty! That is very much of a collapse of an entire subculture. Even as I speak, excellent French, Italian, and German films are being rejected summarily by commercial movie-house managers and are relegated instead to campus or museum venues and to cinemathèque screenings.

And yet, once again there is that Hispanic difference. Carlos Saura's recent movies featuring dance have drawn good crowds and become standard reference points, notably his flamenco version of *Blood Wedding* (1981), an old friend within many of our syllabi. Gutiérrez Alea's last two works, *Strawberry and Chocolate* (*Fresa y chocolate,* 1994) and *Guantanamera* (1997), are classics in their own right among certain segments of the U.S. filmgoing audience.

Last but not least, there is Almodóvar, who utilizes the best and most significant aspects of world pop culture in movies that dramatize transgressive, postmodern sexual concerns, that garner international awards, and that, needless to say, are outrageous in their humor. Moreover, in one of his more recent works, the Oscar-winning *All about My Mother* (*Todo sobre mi madre*, 2000) Almodóvar intertexts with *All about Eve* (1950) and *A Streetcar Named Desire* (1951), and thereby furnishes us instructors an excellent pretext for leading our students to two quite disturbing yet firmly canonical U.S. works from fifty years ago—one of them even in black-and-white, and just right in that format. At this writing Almodóvar is barely fifty, and if he stays alive and holds on to his genius, he will continue enriching our canon and our course offerings.

Two more reflections before I close. I once watched a public interview with the great German moviemaker Werner Herzog in Berkeley, California. At one point a member of the audience asked him how he saw his role as filmmaker. I do not remember the exact words from Herzog's reply, but they were something to the effect that, in a world filled with facile, degrading, and misleading images, he feels called upon to offer images that are richer, more complex, and more reliable. From the drift of my essay, I think you can draw the analogy between Herzog's stated mission and our own.

My final point has to do with an aspect of academic politics with which I am sure readers of this essay will be familiar. I approach it by way of a personal anecdote. Back in the year 2000, a Chicano student wrote a letter to the editor of the Williams College student paper, protesting the absence of authors such as Borges and Isabel Allende in *English* department courses (note my emphasis). In a reply, I reminded him 1) that Borges and Allende are *not* Anglophone literary figures, 2) that the Department of English does not have among its duties the teaching of authors from Latin America or for that matter from Norway or Russia or Japan, and 3) that in our modest little Spanish and comparative literature programs we teach Borges and other such writers, both in Spanish and in English translation.

You all get my point: among students, there is this vague superstition, this falsely universalistic notion that all literary study belongs in and is to be found in English classes. Among professors of English, by the same token, there is the understandable desire to broaden their enrollments and reading lists by including Latin American texts. Nothing wrong with that, and a good thing for all concerned. The more the merrier, to quote some lesser-known if oft-quoted theorist. Still, we on our campuses should make it clear that the authors, musicians, and filmmakers I have been dealing with are *Hispanic* cultural figures and that their natural academic venue is in our classes. It is all too obvious, but one of the ongoing missions of us in the comparative-Hispanist fold is to ensure that we do not forfeit our canonical figures to the hegemony of U.S. English (pun intended), as has already occurred with writers such as Dante and Kafka.

Allow me to conclude with a reference to the theory of *dependencia*, allegedly now rendered obsolete and irrelevant by the triumph of neoliberal globalization. Among the notorious cultural effects of underdevelopment is that unfortunate tendency toward slavishly imitating foreign, metropolitan models at the expense of one's own local products. In our little academic rococo, we have our own *dependencia* in the attempts to follow the lead of the folks in English, and, for instance, to question the Latin American "boom" and the resultant canon (the pun here is accidental). I submit that, at this time in history, the canon, with all its related consequences, stands as the best we've got, and by and large it is a culture of challenge and opposition to the overall status quo. And that is why it continues to be worth teaching to our students.

Works Cited

Bell-Villada, Gene H. *Art for Art's Sake and Literary Life: How Politics and Markets Helped Shape the Ideology and Culture of Aestheticism, 1790–1990*. Lincoln: U of Nebraska P, 1996.

Bloom, Allan. *The Closing of the American Mind*. New York: Simon & Schuster, 1987.

Hirsch, E.D., Jr. *Cultural Literacy: What Every American Needs to Know*. Wisconsin: Turtleback Books, 1988.

Jameson, Fredric. "Postmodernism and Consumer Society." *Studying Culture: An Introductory Reader*. Ed. Ann Gray and Jim McGuigan. London: Arnold, 1997. 192–205.

Simonson, Rick, and Scott Walker, eds. *Multicultural Literacy: Opening up the American Mind*. Minneapolis: Graywolf P, 1988.

First Peoples of the Americas and Their Literature

Gordon Brotherston and Lúcia de Sá

With respect to the American continent, critics and historians of literature and culture have often proceeded along lines that, in practice, continue the great work of destruction, dispossession, and denial that began with the arrival of Europeans in 1492. Asserting or assuming (as many a celebrated academic has done) that the continent was devoid of literature before Columbus penned his log is like saying there was no philosophy either (see Maffie), which in fact was taken as the explicit premise of the 12th Inter-American Congress of Philosophers held in Buenos Aires in the monumental year of 1992. It also corroborates the ideologically charged term regularly applied to pre-contact America by a certain school of archaeologists: "prehistoric." In this view, despite having had demonstrably better calendrics than Europe, native America is allowed to join history proper only on the condition of being invaded and subjected. In the academic field of literature as such, the term "American" normally points back to the Old World in language and culture, just as "Latin American" invokes Rome. In these circumstances, simply to demonstrate the prior existence of literature in America and its continuities becomes a priority in itself. In what can be no more than a few indications here, we make use of concepts and terms standard enough in literary criticism and history generally, yet which are not so often applied to American literature. To begin with there is the indispensable notion of "classic" texts, major in scale and function ("foundational fictions," to use Doris Sommer's term), which are comparable among themselves. From any point of view such a grouping would be incomplete without the *Popol vuh*, the sixteenth-century Maya text which has aptly enough been dubbed the "Bible of America." Diachronically, these classics may then be seen respectively to define recognizable intellectual traditions, consciously sustained for periods readily comparable with those customarily back-projected into earlier phases of European literature. For its part, the *Popol vuh* categorizes itself specifically as a transcription and furthering of a prior Maya document of the same name, casting back to the origins of script and urbanism in Mesoamerica. A section in this essay highlights classic texts that indicate the extraordinary breadth of this literary heritage.

In turn, our project involves necessarily some consideration of medium and genre and an informed respect for pre-contact recording systems and scripts, especially in Middle or Mesoamerica, where books or codices were in use for many centuries before Hernán Cortés (see Boone; Brotherston, *Painted*; Boone and Mignolo). In the lowland Maya tradition, there is a clearly demonstrable, exact, and unbroken continuity, over nearly two millennia, between texts written in the phonetic hieroglyphs of the Classic period (300–900 AD; see Coe; Schele and Freidel) and the Books of Chilam Balam, which were being written and kept up in alphabetic Maya more than a thousand years later (see Barrera Vásquez and Rendón). The example of the Nahua and Aztec historians is similar, insofar as they transcribed pre-Cortesian annals into the alphabet, within the genre known in their language as *xiuhtlapoualli* ("year count"), examples of which extend back to the first millennium BC (as in inscriptions at Monte Alban, Oaxaca). Doing so led these native historians to question details of biblical chronology and to ask "Who entered whose history in 1492?" Such a perspective is certainly found in the chronicles of Chimalpahin, a citizen of Chalco in the Basin of Mexico, who wrote in Nahuatl around 1600. In the case of the *quipu*—the knotted string script of the Inca—the best approach to continuity has been that of ethnohistorians, who apparently take such literary criteria more seriously than literary scholars themselves. Marcia Ascher and Robert Ascher revealed the astounding conceptual possibilities of the *quipu* medium (1981), and Catherine Julien (2000) appeals ingeniously to the notion of genre with respect to *quipu* texts in order better to understand the Quechua and early Spanish colonial narratives that derive from them.

Clearly, none of this inquiry would be possible or practicable without the prior existence of good editions of key texts. This dissemination is a story in itself, one in which the role of native scholars and "informants" has been, with few exceptions, disgracefully downplayed. Just as Felipe Guaman Poma in Peru spent thirty years gathering information and transcribing *quipus* with the help of experts trained by the Inca in Tahuantinsuyu, so his contemporary the Nahua historian Ixtlilxochitl dedicated himself to salvaging what he could from the libraries burned by the Spaniards, reassembling a collection of books or codices that became a main reference for his and all future scholarship. In the native tradition, such a concern with text has tended to go hand in hand with the furthering and invigorating of literature, so that most authors writing today in their own languages do so aware of those who have already written and thought in them (see Montemayor; León-Portilla, "Yancuic"; Lara, *La literatura*). This kind of continuity exists, of course, within that of a larger idea of culture (see Burns; Harrison; McDowell; Lara, *Poesía popular*; Rowe and Schelling; Abercrombie).

To all this must be added some account of the huge impact that this precedent has had on literature in the Americas generally. It is the factor that distinguishes American literature written in imported languages like Spanish, Portuguese, and English, carrying it beyond the Old World paradigms inherent in those languages and cultures. Here the notion of intertextuality is no less decisive than it is, for example, with the great tradition that conjoins Petrarch, Dante, and Virgil, or Milton and the Bible. We will briefly point to the impact this rich native tradition has had on later literature in the Americas. Finally, so as to indicate the multiple effects that a classic or foundational text may have, we consider the *Popol vuh* as an exemplary case. The primordial authority perceived in or attributed to this local bible has come through in a variety of languages, literary genres, and media and has supported many particular readings of American genesis.

Classics

Foremost among the Native American texts that may fairly be considered "classic" stand those that deal with origins and first beginnings. Eminently comparable with each other in terms of scope and argument, these texts show that before its violent encounter with Europe, America had its own philosophy and understandings of genesis, similar in some respects to origin stories of the Old World, yet very different in others. Legible already in the pre-European books of Mexico, this tradition survives among many peoples who continue to live on the continent today. Although much variation can of course be observed over time and region, core beliefs and paradigms may be identified with respect to the origins of the world and humankind—beliefs that, as elsewhere in the world, may serve to define moral and social practice, and what may signify as knowledge. In this sense, American genesis can be seen to place different emphases on such notions as the feat of imagining and conceiving reality in the first place—the "authorship" of creation, as it were: the plurality of creation and the catastrophic endings of previous world ages; the articulation of time, with astronomical precision and over vast spans; the evolution and metamorphosis of life forms; the relationship between humans and other species; and, cumulatively, the achievement of agriculture. Between them, these American classics set up principles that diverge categorically from what became genesis in the Western tradition, especially with regard to all that concerns the plurality, time spans and agencies of creation, the place of humans among the other species, and the significance of agriculture. In American genesis—in many ways a blueprint for modern notions of ecology—it is hard to find an Adam fashioned in the image of God, who precedes woman and who is explicitly given dominion over other life forms. It is just as hard to find a first planter who is also the first murderer. The earliest of these classics in alphabetic form emerged from the Spanish invasion of the urban cultures of Mesoamerica (see Monjarás Ruiz; Recinos) and Tahuantinsuyu (see Ossio), and include the *Popol vuh*, the Book of Chumayel of the lowland Maya, the Nahuatl *Legend of the Suns* (see Bierhorst, *History*), and *Runa yndio*, the Quechua manuscript of Huarochiri (see Trimborn; Arguedas, *Dioses*; Salomon and Urioste). Today these narratives are supplemented by others from surrounding and intervening areas, like the Navajo *Diné bahane* from Anasazi, now the Southwest of the United States (see Zolbrod), the *Tatkan Ikala* from the Cuna islands off Panama's Caribbean coast (see Nordenskiöld; Kramer), and the Huinkulche narrative of the Mapuche homeland that straddles the Andes between Argentina and Chile (see Kössler-Ilg). From the rainforest, that last great bastion now under genocidal assault, come the Guarani *Ayvu rapyta* (see Cadogan), the Carib *Watunna* (see Civrieux), the Taria/Tupi *Jurupari* (see Medeiros, *Macunaíma*) and extensive narratives by the Huitoto, Desana, Shuar, and many others, all of them published for the first time in the twentieth century (see Preuss, *Die Religion*; Ribeiro; Pellizaro).

Comparing these American versions of genesis reveals important paradigms within and against which local differences may be the more finely gauged. Common to them, above all, is the scheme of world-ages, of plural creations that end in flood, eclipse, and other catastrophes. The emergence of our human species is posited as a late, though climactic, event in the story of life forms and is threaded particularly through the long and hazardous line proper to vertebrates (fish, saurian, bird, monkey) and epitomized in the plumed serpent of the tropical forest. Humankind's distinctive genius is to have learned how to feed itself, to have developed genetically the most nourishing and beneficent plants, first gourds and root crops like manioc and then beans and cereals. In the Anasazi and Maya texts, the cereal maize is even held to be the substance of human kind, according to the doctrine that you are what you eat. In the moral terms of this scheme, the encounter with Europe and the West is most often diagnosed as a regression to a less cultured age. While telling a story and naming their space in this way, these cosmogonies construct the world as they construct themselves. In other words they are complex literary artifacts, which reflect on their own beginnings, argument, and even ontology. And contrary to the positivist assumptions of earlier anthropology, this order of sophistication may be the greater, the more "primitive" its origin. Such is the case for example with the remarkable Huitoto creation, included in *Die Religion und Mythologie der Uitoto,* published by Konrad Preuss in 1921. Consciously and finely articulated, these texts have often gone through various modes of transcription and mediation before becoming statements on the alphabetic page. Several of the classics that emerged from the first moments of contact were written out by native authors themselves in the alphabet and in their own languages. Such is case with the Nahuatl and the highland and lowland Maya texts of the sixteenth century, which typically involved transcription from prior texts in native script, like the Aztec Sunstone (*Piedra de los soles*) and the Maya hieroglyphic books.

In the medium of speech an optimum example is the *Watunna* narrative of the Makiritare or Soto Carib, since the text may be considered an elaboration of highly condensed chants (*ademi*), unintelligible to the outsider. An idea of how this "verbal script" relates conceptually to Carib design (*timehri*) is given in the superb film version of the text narrated by Stan Brakhage. *Watunna* was brought before Western eyes as a result of the Franco-Venezuelan expedition that went in search of the true sources of the Orinoco as late as 1950, in the area that proved to coincide largely with Soto territory (see Lichy). Indeed, this geography is integral to the argument of the text, as it recounts the world ages centering itself on the western end of Pacaraima, the ridge that stretches from Roraima (the "botanical Eldorado" of South America as it has been called) towards Marahuaka, and the improbable Casiquiare canal that links the Orinoco and Amazon drainage systems. Then, once encountered, *Watunna* proved extremely difficult to transcribe and, in fact, parts and episodes are put together differently in successive editions in Spanish and English (Civrieux's *Watunna: Mitología makiritare,* 1970; *Watunna: An Orinoco Creation Cycle* 1980; and *Watunna: Mitología makiritare*, 1992). The differences resulted from continuing discussion between the editor, Marc de Civrieux, and the Soto authors, about how to resolve the problem of reducing to a single linear sequence a text whose structure depends originally on dense poetic language and on cycles of performance. Similar issues have also surfaced in editions of Desana cosmogony, the main point of reference in Gerardo Reichel-Dolmatoff's *Amazonian Cosmos* (1971), as well as studies by other Colombian anthropologists. Working with Berta Ribeiro, Umusin Panlon and other Desana shamans prepared their Brazilian version *Antes o mundo não existia* (1980) with the explicit purpose of correcting previous mistakes and misreadings.

Dissemination

In the 1880s, during the heyday of philology, the Philadelphian Daniel Garrison Brinton launched a scheme that he hoped would result in the publication of the chief texts or classics of Native American literature, from the continent as a whole, in their original languages and scripts and English translation. Brinton named his project the "Library of Aboriginal American Literature," and the ten or so volumes that appeared ranged from the *Iroquois Book of Rites* to such Nahuatl texts as the *Twenty Sacred Hymns* (entitled by him *Rig Veda Americanus*) and the *Cantares mexicanos* (*Ancient Nahuatl Poetry*, 1887; see Garibay; Bierhorst, Cantares). Chronologically, the texts included in the Library ranged from the earliest moments of contact and transcription from indigenous scripts to works of Brinton's own day, like the remarkable Central American dramatic dialogue known as the Huehuence (*The Güegüence: A Comedy Ballet in the Nahuatl-Spanish dialect of Nicaragua*, 1883). In *The Lenape and their Legends* (1884), he strove to match Ojibwa and Algonkian texts with the pictographic system developed by the Midewiwin society, a script form that incidentally prompted some of the better stanzas of Longfellow's *Song of Hia-watha.*

The first volume of the Library, *The Maya Chronicles* (1882), constitutes one of the earliest efforts by Western scholars to understand the workings of the lowland Maya Katun Count (*u kahlay katunob*), the cycle of thirteen lots of twenty years (*katuns*), which in post-Classic times regulated not only society but histories of the past and predictions for the future. In the larger panorama of Native American literature, the Katun Count provides perhaps the clearest case of continuity through transcription, first from the inscriptions of the Classic period to the post-Classic books or codices, and then to the post-Cortesian books named for Chilam Balam, which are written in alphabetized Maya. The continued vitality of this tradition, not least with respect to the centuries of resistance that exploded in the nineteenth-century War of the Castes, shows that continuity need not be synonymous with stagnation.

In the seldom-noticed story of how Native American texts came to be published and read outside their original context, Brinton's initiative remains a continental landmark. It is a first assembling of the classic texts of America, the terribly dispossessed "Fourth World" of Renaissance cartography, which culturally establish the continent's fundamental coherence. This much was certainly the understanding of that great Americanist, José Martí. Along with remarks on an early Central American translation of the *Popol vuh*, Martí's comments on Brinton's project in his essay "Autores americanos aborígenes" make up a key strand of the argument set out in his renowned *Nuestra América.* However, new styles of ethnography radiating from Berlin and typified in the United States by Franz Boas soon had the effect of making Brinton's Library seem overly literary, too little concerned with the actual circumstances under which texts were produced or performed.

This new anthropology, nonetheless, went on to produce its own corpus of texts, one that again remains seriously under-acknowledged for what it is. The Berlin cohort to which Boas belonged also produced such key scholars as

Eduard Seler, Theodor Koch-Grünberg, K.T. Preuss, Walter Krickeberg (famous for his anthologies of Native American *Märchen*), along with associates and successors like Kurt Unkel, Leonard Schultze Jena, Hermann Trimborn, and Karl Anton Nowotny. Reworking texts published by Brinton, Seler delved deeper into the process of transcription from codex antecedents, and went further than anyone in demonstrating the *patrimonium commune*, as he called it, of Mesoamerica. This was a line of inquiry closely followed by Schultze Jena in his translation of the *Popol vuh* and in his brilliant analyses of the visual language and logic found both on the pages of the codices and in ritual practice in Mexico today. In turn, Nowotny drew critically on Schultze Jena when he produced the indispensable *Tlacuilolli* (1961), to date the only comprehensive description of the codices, which respects their own system of genre classification and principles of reading (it has yet to be published in a language other than its original German). For his part, in South America Koch-Grünberg gathered and published a major Carib cosmogony in *Vom Roroima* [sic] *zum Orinoco* (1924), a Pemon forerunner of *Watunna*; and in his work Preuss did the same for the Kogi and the Huitoto of Colombia. Preuss also collected narratives by the Huichol and modern survivors of the Aztecs in west Mexico. Just before World War II, Trimborn produced the first serious translation and edition of the major seventeenth-century Quechua narrative *Runa yndio* from Huarochirí (1939—later José María Arguedas's source) while, adopted by the Guarani under the name Nimuendaju, Unkel was entrusted with their creation narrative; this major text was complemented by León Cadogan's edition of *Ayvu rapyta,* the "Origin of Human Speech." Later in the twentieth century, these German-language antecedents served as the richest resource for a number of U.S. scholars, among them John Bierhorst (*Four Masterworks of American Indian Literature*, 1974), and Jerome Rothenberg, whose reworking of Preuss's versions of Huitoto occupy a key position in his *Technicians of the Sacred* (1968). Rothenberg's reworking typifies an important formative strand in the ethnopoetics movement which, broadly considered, has produced an array of classic native texts in English translation: the *Popol vuh* in versions by Munro Edmonson (1971) and Dennis Tedlock (1985), the Zuni *Finding the Center* (Tedlock 1972), Paul Zolbrod's *Diné bahane: The Navajo Creation Story* (1984), and David Guss's English versions of *Watunna* (1980; 1992).

Historically speaking, Brinton's Library continued and much amplified a curiosity about Native American texts that begins more or less with the first European invasions of the continent. Hence the echoes of Iroquois stories in Rabelais, the Tupi songs quoted by Montaigne, and the codex pages printed as wood blocks in Samuel Purchas's *Pilgrims* (1625; *The Mendoza Codex*; see Berdan and Anawalt). In his *Essays*, Montaigne also reproduced, via Francisco López de Gómara and certain Nahuatl historians, a transcription of the story of the world ages or suns that is inscribed on the Aztec Sunstone. Like his English contemporary Christopher Marlowe, who via Heriot quoted Algonkian accounts of creation, Montaigne did this in a spirit that questioned the Biblical orthodoxy of the day, in which genesis happened thanks to one all-powerful (male) creator, and, following the seventeenth-century theologian James Ussher, not that long ago. In this, and indeed in many other details, the story of the plumed serpent and human vertebrates told in the *Popol vuh* can be seen having an impact on the quaint ignorance and limited intellectuality of Europe at the time of the first invasions. It was not until the late eighteenth century that Europe, held back by the sedimentarian bias of the Bible, first recognized igneous rock for what it is, stumbling upon a geological understanding of world formation already explicit for many centuries in the American world age story. In each of the empires they invaded, Aztec and Inca, Europeans found not just theories of origins, but also traditions of historiography, although unfortunately, they also chose to burn almost all the texts in question. In Mexico, these were the codices; while in the Inca Tahuantinsuyu, they were the knotted strings or *quipus*; indeed, whole libraries (*bibliotecas*) of *quipu* texts were reported to have been consigned to the flames. Nevertheless, Guaman Poma, Blas Valera, and others managed to transcribe some *quipus* into alphabetic Quechua and Spanish. Although *criollo* history has little to say about it, these textual antecedents, cosmogonical and historical, were seminal along the road to political independence in America. As we learn from eyewitness accounts by Ignacio Borunda and his disciple Fray Servando Teresa de Mier, the unearthing in 1790, in the heart of Mexico City, of the Sunstone that told the story of Mesoamerican genesis, had an unsettling effect on the Spanish viceroyalty, literally undermining its Old World authority. In the Andes, Independence was the cause, in Spanish eyes, of the *tupamaros*, that is, those who followed Tupac Amaru II's heroic attempt to restore Tahuantinsuyu in the uprising of 1780, continuing the *quipu* chronicle of Inca rulers that had been cut short with the assassination of Tupac Amaru I in Cuzco in 1572.

Impact on Later Literatures in the Americas

In the American continent, recognition of the native palimpsest was there already before Independence and certainly was an ingredient in the Americanism that typified above all the literature of Brazil in the nineteenth century. Yet the intellectual consequences of this recognition have taken longer to make themselves felt, in a process which has intensified over the last half century or more, especially in Latin American narrative and poetry. Already by 1930, the Brazilian Mário de Andrade and the Guatemalan Miguel Ángel Asturias had each published narratives which drew crucially on native originals, respectively, *Macunaíma* in 1928, and *Leyendas de Guatemala* in 1930. As Gerald Martin notes in *Jour-*

neys through the Labyrinth, this pair of works marked a definite turning point in Latin American narrative, in Portuguese and Spanish, with respect to both its sources and its formal development (146). Asturias went on to win the Nobel Prize with his novel *Hombres de maíz* (1949), which draws profoundly on the *Popol vuh*, along with other Maya and Nahuatl texts.

In the narrative genre, Andrade's and Asturias's works initiate a substantial corpus of novels which share indigenous textual roots. Rather than writing about or on behalf of the Indian, these texts provide a thorough intellectual immersion in native philosophy and ways of understanding the world. Other salient examples include *El zorro de arriba y el zorro de abajo* (1971), by the Peruvian José María Arguedas; *Yo el supremo* (1974) by the Paraguayan Augusto Roa Bastos; and *Maíra* (1976) by the Brazilian Darcy Ribeiro. In each case before and while writing their novels, the authors became deeply involved with the language and context of the native works they drew on: Asturias, Arguedas and Roa Bastos respectively translated and adapted the *Popol vuh*, *Runa yndio*, and *Ayvu rapyta*, and in the process they also transformed their earlier views of their continent, along with their way of writing about it. Arguedas wrote in Quechua, Roa Bastos in Guarani (see Lienhard; Rowe, *Mito*). Many others have since followed their path, some going in ideological directions of their own, like Abel Posse and Mario Vargas Llosa. The Guatemalan Mario Monteforte Toledo has written his most recent novel in Quiche and Spanish, *Utukel ulew re ri ch'ichi' / La isla de las navajas* (2001); moreover, in so doing he initiates a "dialogue with the Inca" of continental proportions. In all, as Arguedas argued, this indigenous engagement deserves to be more fully recognized as a key factor in the larger story of Latin American narrative, in particular of the *new novel* which in turn has had such an impact worldwide. It is no accident that the main example of a novel of this kind to have emerged from English-speaking America, Leslie Marmon Silko's *Almanac of the Dead* (1991), directly recalls the Latin American precedent. In Silko's novel, as we move out through the space of America we go back through its time, finding ever earlier examples of its "almanac," which regress from a colonial manuscript to a codex written in black and red characters.

As for poetry, the story is similar, though it starts earlier and has fewer main characters. A striking feature of the two nineteenth-century works which strove to become the epic of the continent is that they both highlighted its imagined heartland, in the domain of the Muisca or Chibcha in what is now Colombia; and both did so with the help of Alexander von Humboldt's panoramic *Vues de cordillères* (1803). In "Alocución a la poesía," one of the two fragments of the epic *América* (1828) that he actually completed, Andrés Bello retells the story of Bochica as a would-be foundational fiction, recalling how the cultural hero, Bochica, brought agriculture to Cundinamarca and highland

Colombia (see Brotherston, *Latin American Poetry*). In the case of the copious twelve cantos of Joaquim de Sousa Andrade's *O Guesa* (1888–1902), the frame, principal cultural reference, and the title itself come from the same source. Chibcha legends, ritual and calendrics provide a constant reference for this early Brazilian work by Sousa Andrade (or Sousândrade), as it ranges over the whole continent in space and time, correlating Inca empire, rainforest, Patagonia, Caribbean and Wall Street (see Campos).

Easily the best-known epic of the continent is Pablo Neruda's *Canto general* (1950), which achieves its coherence thanks principally to its Marxist model of history, in which native America has sadly little to say. Nonetheless, there is a perceptible tension between this mainstream argument and native testimony, one visually set out as such in the two illustrations included in the first edition of the poem, the first by Diego Rivera which depicts American genesis as a "Domingo pre-hispánico," and the second by Siqueiros, which celebrates human redemption through modern technology. In *Canto general*, the native voice can be heard in the continuing struggle typified by Cuauhtemoc in Mexico and Tupac Amaru in the Andes. Perhaps the most powerful moment in the whole poem comes during the chant that celebrates, in the first-person plural, Valdivia's defeat at the hands of the Mapuche and the communal eating of his heart. From this perspective, Ernesto Cardenal's *Homenaje a los indios americanos* (1969) can be better appreciated as the response to Neruda that it is explicitly stated to be, all within the larger idea of the necessity of a truly American revolution. For here the native voice is allowed far more space. Indeed, it becomes the principal means of exposition in the poem. Using techniques of collage and juxtaposition learned from Ezra Pound, Cardenal uses native testimony as the basis for each of the poems that make up his continental epic. These include such classics as the *Cantares mexicanos*, the Books of Chilam Balam, the *Tatkan ikala*, Guaman Poma, *Ayvu rapyta* and so on, in all a powerful polyphony that demonstrates the much-neglected strength of native imagination. Even at the level of sheer poetics, the interaction between Cardenal's own text and their originals remains the richest subject for a critical analysis. Such analyses presumably have been so seldom attempted due to uninterest in those originals. At the same time it has to be said that, like Neruda before him, Cardenal has his own thesis to urge, in his case a Christian one. In several poems this leads to a certain interference, in the name of Liberation Theology, which makes proto-Christians of Maya and Guarani alike. In 1982, a genre of documentary history, at once poetic and highly politicized, was pioneered by the Uruguayan Eduardo Galeano in his trilogy *Memoria del fuego* (1982), which has the whole continent as its scope and uses collage techniques reminiscent of the *Homage*. To set his plan in motion, Galeano similarly turned to Native American texts. In this way, pages from *Watunna* and other classics provide a foundation for his argument, becoming an indispensable first term of reference (see Palaversich).

No comprehensive account of the impact of native texts on later American literature has ever been published and it is clearly impossible to offer one here on the grounds of space alone. Rather, some main lines of connection may be noted which stem from and rely on the sort of cultural geography that native source texts themselves suggest, notably with respect to the Andes, Mesoamerica, and Amazonia. Of course this short list is very far from comprehensive. For example, the Chibcha who inspired Bello and Sousândrade reappear in Cardenal's *Homage* as the Cuna of Panama as well as the Talamanca in *Asalto al paraíso* (1992) by the Costa Rican Tatiana Lobo. In its continental purview, the *Homage* is also notable for its inclusion of what is now English-speaking America: indeed, it takes texts by Iroquois, Pawnee and Sioux in order to expand and strengthen the revolutionary thesis of the work as a whole. A brief overview follows of how native texts from these geographical areas—Andes, Mesoamerica, Amazonia—has an effect on later literature, not least via Cardenal's continental statement in *Homage*.

Thanks chiefly to the *Comentarios reales* of El Inca Garcilaso, the Inca had an astounding impact—still to be catalogued as such—on Europe, from Montaigne's essays to the magnificent *fêtes galantes* staged at Versailles. With Independence, this line was carried back to America, through such poets as Bello, José Joaquín Olmedo, Sousândrade, and Joel Barlow, author of the U.S. epic *The Columbiad* (1803), particularly with respect to the genre of Inca hymns and sagacious law making which are attributed to Manco Capac. Dismembered now between the Andean states of Ecuador, Bolivia and Peru, Tahuantinsuyu, the "Four Districts" of the Inca Empire, is reconstituted through an anatomy still alive in Quechua, which places the brow in Quito, the uterus in Titicaca and the navel in Cuzco. Politically, a similar anatomical logic makes the Inca head grow back into its body, in the legend of Inkarri, better known thanks to José María Arguedas's 1956 publication. In the first edition of Cardenal's *Homage* (1969), "Economía de Tahuantinsuyu" centers on Cuzco, node of South America's "broken roads," and the yearly round of the calendar detailed by Guaman Poma, where the emperor himself digs the first furrow. Occluded through invasion like the sun eclipsed at midday, *chuapi punchapi tutayaca*, as the Quechua quotation puts it, this order or cosmos is held out in hope, like a *quipu* thread or maize kernel clutched in the mummy's hand. Twenty years later, following the defeat of Velasco's Peruvian Revolution, *El secreto de Machu-Picchu* traces the voice of resistance more intimately, through the long-secret "prayer in stone" of that city (which features so prominently in Neruda's *Canto general*). A leitmotif of this poem is found in the

Quechua songs that tell of love and which also encode the summons to defend it militarily, invoking "the white mountains" of Antisuyu and the redoubts of Ollantaytambo, Vilcabamba and Paititi, and hence the resistance that extends from Tupac Amaru I (killed in Cuzco by the Spanish in 1572), via Tupac Amaru II (who rose up in 1780) to today's *tupamaros*. Among the Inca, similar songs had served to distinguish the leader and the sage, in the fashion of the riddles of the Maya katun. This discreet continuity also characterizes the living Quechua drama woven into the poem, like the tragedy of Atahualpa's death (see Lara, *Tragedia*).

Guaman Poma, the pilgrim scholar who wept over the outrages suffered by Tahuantinsuyu's former subjects at the hands of the Spaniards, is the object of particular homage in Galeano's *Memoria del fuego* and in Abel Posse's novels, where he reappears as Huaman, a constant sage and guide. First published as late as 1936, Guaman Poma's testimony impinges directly on the centuries-old debate over the nature of Inca power and hence the appropriateness of Tahuantinsuyu as a modern political model. On this point, Cardenal differs from Neruda's Marxist doctrine, explicit in the Machu Picchu section of the *Canto general* that deems the Inca state despotic and slave-based ("El Inca era dios/ era Stalin"). Like Galeano and Posse, Cardenal aligns himself less with Stalin and more with the planetary anti-colonialism of César Vallejo, whose poem "Telúrica y magnética" makes the millennia of achievement in the Andes the base for social justice and Indian identity alike (see Brotherston and Gómez). Perceived and named as Guaman Poma's modern counterpart in the work of Cardenal, Galeano and Posse alike, the Peruvian José María Arguedas gathered and translated Quechua texts besides being a novelist and poet in his own right. Arguedas also wrote in Quechua in correspondence with the *guerrillero* leader Hugo Blanco, and in his homage to Tupac Amaru (*Tupac Amaru Kamaq Taytanchisma: Haylli-Taki*; 1962), the recurrent hero of revolution in Peru. Grappling with the violent dichotomies of modern Peru he turned to *Runa yndio* of Huarochiri, which he had translated and which supplies the framework of his last work *El zorro de arriba y el zorro de abajo* and its two principles of authority. This line in Arguedas's work was carried forward in Manuel Scorza's *Garabombo el invisible* (1972), part of the quintet devoted to honoring the Quechua massacred during the Pasco uprising of 1962, which likewise draws on *Runa yndio* and the Inkarri legend (see Crumley).

As a geographical and cultural area, Mesoamerica is defined as the land of books, or screenfold codices of skin and paper, annals that tell of the plumed serpent Quetzalcoatl, Tula and the ancient migrations, Moctezuma and Nezhualcoyotl the "poet king" of Texcoco. Along with alphabetic transcripts like the opulent collection of *Cantares mexicanos,* these became the sources of poems in *Homage*. The ground text of no less than three long pieces, whole lines and stanzas of the *Cantares* are taken from the Spanish translations by Garibay gathered in his *Poesía nahuatl* (1965–68). Profoundly influential on Mexican poetry from Paz to Pacheco, Garibay's versions much enhanced understanding of the Nahuatl "flower song," "in xochitl in cuicatl," and the heightened sense of life variously expressed in its "planting," "orphan," and other modes. In particular, they raised the question, also asked by fellow Christian Cardenal, of how far earlier interpreters, among them the nineteenth-century U.S. historian Prescott, had given an ideological twist to the "laments" of the poet-king Nezahualcoyotl (1402–72), seeing in them a covert yearning for Cortés and his religion. Historically, like the archeology that discovered earthly paradise in the murals of Teotihuacan, these revised *Cantares* form part of the massive reappraisal of indigenous culture brought about by the Mexican Revolution.

Through another subgroup of Mesoamerican poems likewise interwoven with both the Maya calendar and current archeology—"Oráculos de Tikal," "Mayapan," "Ardilla de los tunes de un katun," "Katun 11 Ahau," and "8 Ahau"—the *Homage* traces continuity in lowland Maya consciousness, from the Classic inscriptions to the Chilam Balam Books, drawing moral lessons from calendar structure, and rescuing for the scribe-poet the honor of intuiting the true cause of eclipse. As a result, attentive to the katun revolutions of the lowland Maya, the poems implicitly argue their political cause, as does Abreu Gómez's novel *Canek* (1940), which similarly is couched in katun logic and the Zuyua language of the Chilam Balam Books. Moreover, transcribing the hieroglyphs of Quirigua and Copan, these poems make the decisive link between their millions of years and the beginnings of earthly time recounted in the highland Quiche-Maya *Popol vuh*, charting the vast scope of its evolutionary story. In Mesoamerica generally, native historiography has continued into modern narrative. For instance, Patricia Amlin has made the world-age story into a film that draws ingeniously on the Borgia Codex. By basing himself on native histories and above all the codices, Carlos Fuentes contrives to recreate imported and local time perspectives in Part I and II of his *Terra nostra* (1975). A version of how acute the distinction between them became at the dawn of Independence in Mexico can be seen in the cult of Guadalupe and the long local history attributed to her. An informed, if satirical account of this moment is given in Reinaldo Arenas's novel *El mundo alucinante* (1969), which draws on Fray Servando Teresa de Mier's autobiographical account of his association with the Mexican and pioneer Mexicanist Ignacio Borunda. This novel recounts how Borunda learned to interpret the world-changing message of the Sunstone and to read the codices as vindication for the idea of throwing out intrusive Spaniards. Updating just this heritage with respect to the modern megalopolis and its cosmic fate, Homero Aridjis likewise casts back to the Sunstone in his *Leyenda de los soles* (1993).

Still under siege today, Amazonia and the tropical rainforest of Brazil continue to supply culture in its highest forms, like air, vegetal food, and vision: the native texts which record that vision play a major part in the continental works of Galeano, Posse and Cardenal. Memory, in Galeano's trilogy, begins with the Carib creation recounted in *Watunna*, chief among the texts that stem from the Pacaraima ridge common to the Amazon and the Orinoco. This is the privileged literary territory sought by the hero of Alejo Carpentier's *Los pasos perdidos* (1953), the foundational novel whose cosmogonical reference extends to the codices and to the *Popol vuh* and the Chilam Balam books: quotations from these Maya works provide epigraphs that are critical to the novel's overall argument and structure. Sharing the same Carib source, the story of the Caroni river told in *Canaima* (1935), by the Venezuelan Rómulo Gallegos, likewise follows a native course. The Carib term of this novel's title, defined in *Watunna* as the madness that white invaders induce, also resonates with a short story by Guyanese Wilson Harris, whose novel *Palace of the Peacock* (1960) in turn traces an ascent to Roraima through the stages of the Medatia vision recounted in *Watunna*. Said to be "without character," the hero of Mário de Andrade's novel *Macunaíma* (1928) is in fact born and named in the geographical domain of *Watunna* and is formed by just that Carib belief system: descending the Uraricoera and crossing the Amazon, he travels to São Paulo, traversing all the space and time of Brazil, only to return to a landscape of ghosts and stars, which he ultimately becomes. With agility and humor, the narrative makes clear that its life is that of its palimpsest or life source, in this case the account of the Carib hero Makunaima which Mayuluaipu, a Pemon Indian, gave to Koch-Grünberg; and in so doing it anticipates the argument of the other novels that have emerged from the same biosphere (see Sá, "Germans and Indians").

Along with the poems in Raul Bopp's *Cobra Norato* (1928), *Macunaíma* best exemplifies the "anthropophagist" tendency of the Brazilian *modernistas*, and their Manifesto, which expressed interest in the Tupi and Carib as well as the cannibal revolution (*a revolução caraibe*). In being philosophically shaped by native sources, these works by Andrade and Bopp expose the fallacy of describing Brazilian "antropofagia" as a fanciful outgrowth from the line of purely Western thought begun by Jean de Léry's and Montaigne's reflections on cannibalism. In Brazil, the *modernistas* had remarkable predecessors in the nineteenth-century Americanists whose involvement was chiefly with the traditions of the Tupi-Guarani (Treece); at that stage, Tupi was still widely spoken as lowland South America's lingua franca (*língua geral*). A Tupi-Guarani theme taken up already then and present still in Posse's *Daimón* is that of the earthly paradise, the *Yvy mara ey*. These and similar beliefs are consistently opposed to biblical cosmogony in Posse's novel, and in novels by Roa Bastos and Darcy Ribeiro. In Roa Bastos's case, growing familiarity with the Guarani classics enabled him to set the endurance of that people, and the reason behind it, into the dialogues and dialectic of *Yo el supremo* (1974). This work also explores such local concepts as dual autogenesis and the blue jaguars of solar eclipse, concepts that reappear in Darcy Ribeiro's *Maíra* (1976). At the same time, *Maíra* considers the fate of Brasilía, ominously sited as it is in the Tupi cosmic landscape. Tupi-Guarani traditions are incorporated in Cardenal's *Homage*, which in "Los hijos del bosque de las palabras almas" goes to the root concepts of *Ayvu rapyta*, the "origin of human speech." Another poem, "La Arcadia perdida," traces back the story of Paraguay's *República guaraní* not just to the Jesuit missions but to Tahuantinsuyu ideals previously brought down from the Andes and translated into Guarani legends. The same link with the Andes is acknowledged by Arawak groups like the Campa and the Machiguenga some distance to the northwest, on the uppermost Amazon, and consequently surfaces, though to very different effect, in *El hablador* (1987), the novel by the Peruvian, Mario Vargas Llosa. In his egregious engagement with Peru's Amazonia, Vargas Llosa follows Machiguenga accounts of creation closely and suggests how the very survival of the Machiguenga depends on their speaking their own history and their own place in the universe. Yet at the same time he perversely introduces concepts of his own making in order to portray them as scattered nomads who are intellectually unable to defend themselves (see Sá, "Perverse tribute").

Author of the major study *A expressão amazonense* (1978; see also Pereira), Márcio Souza was the first writer to successfully bring rainforest literature to the stage. In *Dessana, Dessana* he shows how knowledge of the cosmogony published by Berta Ribeiro can transform perceptions of Indians seen on the streets of Manaus. In *Jurupuri,* he offered a feminist reading of that Tariana text. In staging both plays, he worked closely with members of the groups in question (see de Sá, *Rain Forest Literatures*). Cardenal, in his "Epístola a Monseñor Casaldaliga" (also in the *Homage*) and more recently in *Cántico cósmico* (1989), brings out the significance that rainforest cosmogony has for Liberation Theology, and for the revised notions of genesis that have been developed by theologians like Casaldáliga and Boff (who has published his own selection of victims' voices from 1492 to 1992). Cardenal's epistle-poem focuses particularly on the way that in Xingu beliefs shared between different languages and groups have helped to form the basis of wider resistance, a strategy that is echoed in Antonio Callado's remarkable novel *Quarup* (1966; now also a film). In this, thanks to his immersion in native thought, Cardenal anticipates what journals like *Ixtus* (Cuernavaca) have announced in the last few years as *teología india,* in which genesis for Christians is no longer the sole preserve of the Old Testament.

Popol vuh: An Exemplary Case

As the "Bible of America" the *Popol vuh* has been translated into most of the world's major languages and has increasingly become the focus of critical attention (see Carmack and Morales; Mary Preuss; Himmelblau; Chinchilla; López). It has found ever-greater resonance in the work of modern writers, artists and intellectuals and it has been the source of a long line of textual borrowings by Latin American authors. In its early stages, this story includes foundational figures of Spanish American Modernismo, like José Martí (see above), and Rubén Darío, who celebrated the Maya Quiche and their sky-heart deity "Hurakan" in "Momotombo" (*Cantos de vida y esperanza*, 1907). Going in another direction (perhaps to avoid the harsh Indian reality of his homeland of El Salvador), Salarrué used the Quiche text to support an Atlantis fantasy in *O-Yarkandal* (1929). In "Visión de América" (1948) and *Los pasos perdidos* (1953), Alejo Carpentier quoted from Asturias's translation of the *Popol vuh* when developing his ideas of a deeply rooted autochthonous American culture ("lo real maravilloso americano"), and the world-age scheme of creation that warns against mindless use of the machine. Even the Argentinean Jorge Luis Borges, hardly indigenist by calling, turned to the same world-age account, quoting it in the climactic moments of the Jaguar Priest's vision in "La escritura del dios" (1948). The political force of the Quiche text comes through in the Guatemalan Virgilio Rodriguez Beteta's *Los dos brujitos mayas* (1956) and the Mexican Rosario Castellanos's *Balún Canán* (1957), and it inspires the consciousness-raising plays produced by the La Fragua group in Honduras in the 1970s (see Burke and Shapiro) and the Lo'il Maxil group in Chiapas in the 1990s.

In *Hombres de maíz*, Asturias depicts the reality of his hero, the *guerrillero* Gaspar Ilom, in *Popol vuh* terms as he leads an uprising in Cuchumatanes, the heartland and source of the first maize agriculture in highland Maya cosmogony. The whole episode is based on an actual Maya uprising of 1900. Politically, this corresponds to the fact that engaging as a translator with the *Popol vuh* and other Maya classics actually transformed Asturias's view of his own country and of those who constitute its majority, curing him of an inherited minority white racism. "Gaspar Ilom" is the name assumed by his son Rodrigo as a guerrillero commander fighting for Maya rights in Guatemala's necessary revolution. The decisive encounter that Asturias had when translating the *Popol vuh* in 1927 (with Georges Raynaud's help) had an earlier effect on his *Leyendas de Guatemala* (1930), a highly innovative text that also draws on images from the codices, which he actually inserts into his prose. As a novel of specifically peasant resistance that is sustained by the cosmogony of the *Popol vuh*, Asturias's *Hombres de maíz* has been updated, this time with reference to twentieth-century El Salvador, in Manlio Argueta's *Cuzcatlan, donde bate la mar del sur* (1986). Argueta's powerful narrative succeeds in tapping the memory and deep imaginative root common to the Maya *Popol vuh* and the Nahuatl spoken by most of his country's people, at least before the unbelievably atrocious massacres ordered by ruling whites in 1932. In a comparable Central American narrative, the *Popol vuh* helped Mario Monteforte Toledo to recreate the world invaded by Columbus in *Llegaron del mar* (1966).

In poetry, the allusions to the *Popol vuh* seen in the Maya poems in Cardenal's *Homage* have been echoed in Pablo Antonio Cuadra's long poem "El jícaro" (1978), which uses the *Popol vuh* story of the Twins' mother Ixquic to foretell the overthrow of Somoza's bloody tyranny in Nicaragua. Over many decades, the *Popol vuh* likewise supported the fine revolutionary intelligence of Luis Cardoza y Aragón, a compatriot of Asturias who translated Quiche literature (*Rabinal Achi*) at more or less the same date, early in his career. From Central America and Mexico, this understanding of the text has spread to Chicano and Latino writing in the United States, especially writing by women, for whom the figures of Blood Woman (Ixquic) and Xmucane have become archetypal. Recently Dolores Prida published her "Heart of the Earth: A *Popol vuh* Story" in the Latina anthology *Puro teatro* (see Sandoval-Sánchez). The *Popol vuh* also sustains Silko's argument in *Almanac of the Dead,* especially with regard to its concern to reconcile revolutionary Marxism with Native American philosophy. It has also spread south, as in the case of Borges's "La escritura del dios." Similarly, in Brazil, Affonso Romano de Sant'Anna produced a "modern *Popol vuh*" which cross-references the Quiche work with the Guarani texts of his country (*A grande fala do índio guarani perdido na história*, 1978).

Gradually, the text and the concept of the *Popol vuh* have come to impinge on an ever-wider array of media. This work is now invoked and recast not just in the traditional literary world of narrative and poetry but in theatre, film, music, art, and even the electronic medium. In San Francisco, for example, it has become an interactive computer game (see González). It is the subject of the film by Patricia Amlin (1987), which is based on Edmonson's English translation and images taken from Classical Maya ceramics. Mediated by Asturias's *Hombres de maíz*, it also informs Gregory Nava's film *El norte*. Introducing the revolutionary spirit of La Fragua and Lo'il Maxil drama into the metropolis, Luisa Josefina Hernández's play *Popol vuh* has had several stage runs in Mexico City. In music, Edgard Varèse incorporated passages from the *Popol vuh* in his *Ecuatorial* (1961), following leads given by Asturias in his 1927 translation and in his *Leyendas de Guatemala* (see Medeiros). Meanwhile, as the seminal autobiography of Rigoberta Menchú shows, the knowledge embedded in the *Popol vuh* never left the Quiche people who authored it. Collaborating closely with Quiche elders and scholars has from the start been the constant privilege of translators of the text into other languages, from the time that Francisco Ximénez first produced a translation—into Spanish—in the early eighteenth century, and C.E. de Brasseur de Bourbourg followed him in French in 1856. Over the last half century this has continued to be the case with Dora Burgess, who jointly with Domingo Xec published the Spanish translation of 1955 that then became a principal point of reference for Munro Edmonson's version, and he in turn is reported to have worked with Eleuterio Po'ot Yah (1971). In producing the second direct translation from Quiche into English (1985) (Edmonson's being the first), Dennis Tedlock relied heavily on Andrés Xiloj of Momostenango. For their part, Quiche scholars and writers like Sam Colop and Víctor Montejo (who admires Edmonson's version) have produced *Popol vuh* editions of their own. Thanks to this growing native scholarship, translations are now also being made from Quiche into other Maya languages, among them Kekchi (Rigoberto Ba'q Q'aal), Tzotzil and Tzeltal. These projects are part of the pan-Maya move towards recovering and re-inventing a fragmented and demeaned heritage.

Conclusion

Precisely because it corrects a defect in most understandings of what is literature, the comparative method is indispensable for any approach to Native American texts. A comparative approach can also correct the widespread dismissal of interest in Indians as "romantic"—in the sense of undocumented and fanciful. Such an approach alerts us instead to beliefs and paradigms shared by cosmogonies and classics from all over the continent, establishing thereby a formal and philosophical premise that sets all subsequent American literature in due perspective. Only by acknowledging this shared precedent can there be adequate appreciation of the huge and ever-growing debt owed to the native literatures of the Americas by the widest variety of authors writing in the languages that Europe brought to America. In his novel *If on a Winter's Night a Traveler*, Italo Calvino also appears to be in sympathy with this approach, for through the character of the ancient Indian storyteller he insinuates that native America, especially its tropical heartland, could be the "primeval magma," an ultimate source for all the world's great narratives, among which he names the *Popol vuh* (Martin 306). In this essay, little or nothing has been said about mediation and transcription; nor about those authors who continue to write in their own languages, like the Nahuatlato Joel Martínez Hernández, Elicura Chihuailaf—who has also translated Neruda into the Mapuche language, and Kaká Wera Jecupé, who wrote his autobiography in Guarani; nor about the native impact on English-speaking America typified in its most widely read poem, H.W. Longfellow's *Song of Hiawatha* (1855); nor again about the impact on Old World literature, not just Montaigne and Marlowe but also Schiller and the

Rom-antics, Max Ernst and the Expressionists, Antonin Artaud and the Surrealists, and indeed philosophers like Jung (who took *Hiawatha* as a base for his *Psychology of the Unconscious*, 1916) and Ernst Cassirer, whose *Philosophy of Symbolic Forms* (volume 2) relies directly on Huichol thought (see Jáuregui and Neurat). It is thus to be hoped that, despite the myriad references and directions that we were unable to follow in this short space, what we have illuminated will be enough to indicate the complexity and richness of Native American literature and of the many transcultural processes associated with indigenous culture that remain seriously under-examined.

Works Cited

Abercrombie, Thomas. *Pathways of Memory & Power: Ethnography and History Among an Andean People*. Madison: U of Wisconsin P, 1998.

Abreu Gómez, E. Canek: *Historia y leyenda de un héroe maya*. 29th ed. Mexico: Oasis, 1975.

Amlin, Patricia. Popol vuh: *Sacred book of the Quiche Maya*. Videocassette. Berkeley: U of California Extension Center for Media, 1989.

Amlin, Patricia. *Popol buj*. Videocassette, dubbed in Tzeltal. Tuxtla Gutiérrez: Instituto Chiapanelp Yl'un kuxlejal, 1993.

Amlin, Patricia. *The Five Suns*. Videocassette. Berkeley: U of California Extension Center for Media, 1996.

Arenas, Reinaldo. *Hallucinations: Being an Account of the Life and Adventures of Fray Servando Teresa De Mier*. Trans. Gordon Brotherston. London: Cape, 1971.

Arguedas, José María. "Puquio, una cultura en proceso de cambio" 1956. *Formación de una cultura nacional indoamericana*. Mexico: Siglo XXI, 1975. 34–79.

Arguedas, José María. *Tupac Amaru Kamaq Taytanchisman: Haylli-Taki*. Lima: Salqantay, 1962.

Arguedas, José María. *El zorro de arriba y el zorro de abajo*. Buenos Aires: Losada, 1971.

Arguedas, José María. *Formación de una cultura nacional indoamericana*. Mexico: Siglo XXI, 1975.

Arguedas, José María. *The Fox from Up Above and the Fox from Down Below*. Trans. F.H. Barraclough. Pittsburgh: U of Pittsburgh P, 2000.

Arguedas, José María, ed. *Dioses y hombres de Huarochiri*. Lima: Museo Nacional de Historia, 1966.

Argueta, Manlio. *Cuzcatlan, donde bate la mar del sur. Tegucigalpa:* Guaymuras, 1986.

Argueta, Manlio. *Cuzcatlan*. Trans. Clark Hansen. New York: Vintage Books, 1987.

Aridjis, Homero. *La leyenda de los soles*. Mexico: Fondo de Cultura Económica, 1993.

Ascher, Marcia, and Robert Ascher. *Code of the Quipu: A Study in Media, Mathematics, and Culture*. Ann Arbor: U of Michigan P, 1981.

Asturias, Miguel Ángel. *Leyendas de Guatemala*. 1930. *Miguel Ángel Asturias: Cuentos y leyendas*. Ed. Mario Roberto Morales. Madrid: ALLCA, 2000.

Asturias, Miguel Ángel. *Hombres de maíz*. 1949. Ed. Gerald Martin. Madrid: ALLCA, 1992.

Asturias, Miguel Ángel, and J.M. González de Mendoza. *Los dioses, los héroes y los hombres de Guatemala antigua: O el libro del consejo, Popol vuh de los indios quichés*. Trans. Georges Raynaud. Paris: Editorial Paris-América, 1927.

Ba'q Q'aal, Rigoberto. *Popol vuh Kekchi*. Guatemala: CICM Ak'Kutan, 1996.

Bareiro Saguier, Rubén. *Literatura guaraní del Paraguay*. Caracas: Monte Ávila, 1980.

Bareiro Saguier, Rubén. *De nuestras lenguas y otros discursos*. Asunción: Universidad Católica, 1990.

Barrera Vásquez, Alfredo, and Silvia Rendón. *El libro de los libros de Chilam Balam*. Mexico: Fondo de Cultura Económica, 1948.

Berdan, F., and P. Anawalt, eds. *Mendoza Codex*. Berkeley: U of California P, 1992.

Bierhorst, John. *Four Masterworks of American Indian Literature*. New York: Farrar, Straus & Giroux, 1974.

Bierhorst, John. *Cantares mexicanos: Songs of the Aztecs*. Stanford: Stanford UP, 1985.

Bierhorst, John. *History and Mythology of the Aztecs: The Codex Chimalpopoca*. Tucson: U of Arizona P, 1992.

Boone, Elizabeth. *The Red and the Black*. Austin: U of Texas P, 2000.

Boone, Elizabeth, and Walter Mignolo. *Writing without Words*. Durham: Duke UP, 1994.

Brasseur de Bourbourg, Charles Étienne. *Popol vuh. Le Livre sacré et les mythes de l'antiquité américaine*. Paris: Arthus Bertrand, 1861.

Brinton, Daniel Garrison. *Library of Aboriginal American Literature*. 1882–90. New York: AMS Society, 1969.

Brotherston, Gordon. *Latin American Poetry: Origins and Presence*. Cambridge: Cambridge UP, 1975.

Brotherston, Gordon. *Book of the Fourth World: Reading the Native Americas through Their Literature*. Cambridge: Cambridge UP, 1992.

Brotherston, Gordon. *Painted Books from Mexico*. London: British Museum P, 1995.

Brotherston, Gordon. "Indigenous Literatures and Cultures." *The Twentieth Century Cambridge History of Latin America*. Ed. L. Bethell. New York: Cambridge UP, 1995. 10, 287–305.

Brotherston, Gordon. *La América indígena en su literatura*. Mexico: Fondo de Cultura Económica, 1997.

Brotherston, Gordon. "La herencia maya y mesoamericana en las primeras leyendas de Asturias." *Miguel Ángel Asturias: Cuentos y leyenda*. Ed. Mario Roberto Morales. Madrid: ALLCA, 2000. 511–24.

Brotherston, Gordon, and Natalia Gómez. "La poética del patrimonio: 'Telúrica y magnética' de César Vallejo." *Cuadernos hispanoamericanos* 548 (1996): 109–19.

Burgess, Dora, and Patricio Xec. *Popol vuj*. Quetzaltenango: El noticiero Evangélico, 1955.

Burke, Edward, and Ruth Shapiro. *Teatro!: Theater and the Spirit of Change*. Videocassette. New York: Filmmakers Library, 1989.

Burns, Allan F. *An Epoch of Miracles: Oral Literature of the Yucatec Maya*. Austin: U of Texas P, 1983.

Cadogan, León, ed. *Ayvu rapyta: Textos míticos de los Mbya*. São Paulo: U de São Paulo, 1959.

Cadogan, León. *La literatura de los guaraníes*. Mexico: Joaquín Mortiz, 1965.

Campos, Haroldo, and Augusto Campos. *ReVisão de Sousândrade*. Rio de Janairo: Editora Nova Fronteira, 1982.

Cardenal, Ernesto. *Los ovnis de oro / Golden UFOs: Poemas indios / The Indian Poems*. Bloomington: Indiana UP, 1992.

Cardoza y Aragón, Luis. *Guatemala: Las líneas de su mano*. Managua: Companic, 1985.

Cardoza y Aragón, Luis. *Rabinal Achi*. Mexico: Porrúa, 1975.

Carmack, Robert M., and F. Morales Santos. *Nuevas perspectivas sobre el Popol vuh*. Guatemala: Piedra Santa, 1983.

Carpentier, Alejo. "Visión de América." 1948. *Ensayos*. By Alejo Carpentier. Mexico: Siglo XXI, 1990. 13, 274–94.

Carpentier, Alejo. *Los pasos perdidos*. 1953. Ed. R. González Echevarría. Madrid: Cátedra, 1985.

Chihuailaf, Elicura. *Todos los cantos / Ti kom ül*. Santiago: Pehuen, 1996.

Chimalpahin. *Relaciones originales de Chalco Amequemecan*. Ed. Silvia Rendón. Mexico: Fondo de Cultura Económica, 1965.

Chinchilla Aguilar, Ernesto. *Breviario quiché-español del Popol vuh, para uso en la enseñanza de la lengua quiché*. Guatemala: Ministerio de Educación, 1967.

Civrieux, Marc de. *Watunna: Mitología makiritare*. Caracas: Monte Ávila, 1970.

Civrieux, Marc de. *Watunna: An Orinoco Creation Cycle*. Trans. David Guss. San Francisco: North Point P, 1980.

Civrieux, Marc de. *Watunna: Mitología makiritare*. 2nd ed. Caracas: Monte Ávila, 1992.

Codex Borgia. New York: Dover, 1993.

Coe, Michael. *Breaking the Maya Code*. London: Thames and Hudson, 1992.

Colop, Sam. *Popol vuj: Versión poética K'iche'*. Quetzaltenango: PEMBI, 1999.

Crumley, Laura Lee. "El intertexto de Huarochiri en Manuel Scorza: Una visión múltiple de la muerte en *Historia de Garabombo el invisible*." *América Indígena* XLIV (1984): 747–55.

Dzul Poot, Domingo. *Cuentos mayas*. Mérida: Maldonado, 1985–86.

Edmonson, Munro. *The Book of Counsel: The Popol vuh of the Quiché Maya of Guatemala*. New Orleans: Tulane U Middle American Research Institute, 1971.

Edmonson, Munro, ed. *Literatures* Supplement, *Handbook of Middle American Indians*. Vol. 3. Austin: U of Texas P, 1985.

Fuentes, Carlos. *Terra nostra*. Barcelona: Seix Barral, 1975.

Fuentes, Carlos. *Terranostra*. Trans. M. S. Peden. New York: Farrar, Straus & Giroux, 1976.

Galeano, Eduardo. *Memoria del fuego*. Madrid: Siglo XXI, 1982.

Garibay, Ángel María. *Poesía nahuatl*. Mexico: UNAM, 1964–68.

González, Servando. *Popol vuh: An Interactive Text/Graphics Adventure*. San Francisco, 1991.

Gossen, Gary H., ed. *Symbol and Meaning Beyond the Closed Community*. Albany: State UP of New York, 1986.

Guaman Poma, Felipe. *El primer nueva coronica y buen gobierno*. Ed. J. Murra and R. Adorno. 3 vols. Mexico: Siglo XXI, 1987.

Harrison, Regina. *Signs, Songs, and Memory in the Andes: Translating Quechua Language and Culture*. Austin: U of Texas P, 1989.

Hernández, Luisa Josefina. *Popol vuh; La paz ficticia; La fiesta de la mulata; Quetzalcoatl*. Mexico: Grupo Editorial Baceta, 1994.

Himmelblau, Jack. *Quiché Worlds in Creation: The Popol vuh as a Narrative Work of Art*. Culver City: Labyrinthos, 1989.

Hugh-Jones, Stephen. *The Palm and the Pleiades*. Cambridge: Cambridge UP, 1979.

Ixtlilxochitl, Fernando de Alva. *Obras históricas*. Ed. Edmundo O'Gorman. 2 vols. Mexico: UNAM, 1975–77.

Jáuregui, Jesús, and Johannes Neurat. *Fiestas, literatura y magia en el Nayarit*. Mexico: I.I.I, 1998.

Jecupé, Kaka Werá. *Oré Awé Roiru'a Ma / Todas as vezes que dissemos adeus*. São Paulo: Phgytoervas, 1992.

Julien, Catherine. *Reading Inca History*. Iowa City: U of Iowa P, 2000.

Koch-Grünberg, Theodor. *Vom Roroima zum Orinoco*. Berlin: Reimer, 1917–28. 5 vols.

Kössler-Ilg, Bertha. *Indianermärchen aus den Kordilleren*. Düsseldorf: Eugen Dieterich, 1956.

Kramer, Fritz. *Literature among the Cuna Indians*. Göteborg: Etnografiska Museum, 1970.

Krickeberg, Walter. *Märchen der Azteken und Inkaperuaner, Maya und Muisca*. Düsseldorf: Eugen Dieterich, 1928.

Lara, Jesús. *Poesía popular quechua*. La Paz: Editorial Canata, 1947.

Lara, Jesús, ed. *Tragedia del fin de Atawallpa*. Cochabamba: Imprenta Universitaria, 1957.

Lara, Jesús. *La literatura de los quechuas*. La Paz: Editorial Juventud, 1969.

León-Portilla, Miguel. *La filosofía nahuatl estudiada en sus fuentes*. Mexico: I.I.I, 1956.

León-Portilla, Miguel. "Yancuic tlahtolli." *Estudios de cultura nahuatl* 18 (1986): 123–69.

Lévi-Strauss, Claude. *Mythologiques*. Paris: Plon, 1964–71. 4 vols.

Lichy, René. *Yaku: Expedición franco-venezolana del Alto Orinoco*. Caracas: Monte Ávila, 1978.

Lienhard, Martin. *Cultura andina y forma novelesca*. Lima: Tarea, 1990.

Lienlaf, Leonel. *Se ha despertado el ave de mi corazón*. Santiago de Chile: Editorial Universitaria, 1989.

Lobo, Tatiana. *Asalto al paraíso*. 1992. San José: Norma, 2001.

Lopez, Têle Porto Ancona, ed. *Macunaima*. Paris: ALLCA, 1988.

López, Carlos M. *Los Popol vuj y sus epistemologías*. Quito: Abya-yala, 1999.

Maffie, James. "Truth from the Perspective of World Philosophy." *Social Epistemology* 15.4 (2001): 263–75.

Martí, José. "Autores aborígines americanos." *Nuestra América*. By José Martí. Ed. Juan Marinello. Caracas: Ayacucho, 1977. 334–56.

Martin, Gerald. *Journeys through the Labyrinth*. London: Verso, 1989.

Martínez Hernández, Joel. *Xochitlajtolkoskatl*. Tlaxcala: Universidad Autónoma de Tlaxcala, 1987.

McDowell, John. *Sayings of the Ancestors: The Spiritual Life of the Sibundoy Indians*. Lexington: U of Kentucky P, 1989.

Medeiros, Sérgio, ed. *Macunaíma e Jurupary: cosmogonias ameríndias*. São Paulo: Perspectiva, 2002.

Medeiros, Sérgio. *Popol vuh*. São Paulo: Iluminuras, 2004.

Menchú, Rigoberta. *Me llamo Rigoberta Menchú y así me nació la conciencia*. Mexico: Siglo XXI, 1985.

Monjarás Ruiz, Jesús. *Mitos cosmogónicos del México indígena*. Mexico: INAH, 1987.

Monteforte Toledo, Mario. *Llegaron del mar*. Mexico: Joaquín Mortiz, 1966.

Monteforte Toledo, Mario. *Utukel ulew re ri ch'ich' / La isla de las navajas*. Guatemala: Comunidad de Escritores, 2001.

Montejo, Víctor. *Popol vuh: A Sacred Book of the Maya*. Toronto: Douglas & McIntyre, 1999.

Montemayor, Carlos. *Escritores indígenas actuales*. Mexico: Terra Firma, 1992. 2 vols.

Montoya, Rodrigo, Edwin, and Luis. *La sangre de los cerros: Urqukunapa yawarnin*. Lima: Cepes, 1987.

Nava, Gregory. *El Norte*. Videocassette. Farmington Hills: CBS/Fox Video, 1983.

Neruda, Pablo. *Canto general*. Ed. E. Santí. Madrid: Cátedra, 1990.

Nordenskiöld, Erland. *An Historical and Ethnological Survey of the Cuna Indians*. Göteborg: Etnografiska Museum, 1938.

Nowotny, Karl Anton. *Tlacuilolli. Die mexikanischen Bilderhandschriften, Stil und Inhalt*. Berlin: Gebr. Mann, 1961.

Ossio, J.M. *Ideología mesiánica del mundo andino*. Lima: Prado Pastor, 1973.

Palaversich, Diana. "Eduardo Galeano: entre el postmodernismo y el postcolonialismo." *Indiana Journal of Hispanic Literatures* 1.2 (1993): 11–24.

Pellizaro, Siro, ed. *Tsunki: El mundo del agua*. Sucua: Mundo Shuar, 1979.

Pereira, Nunes. *Morongueta: Um decameron indigena*. Rio de Janeiro: Civilização Brasileira, 1967.

Popol vuh: Slo'il Sipakna / El cuento de Sipakna. San Cristóbal: Sna Itz Ibajom, 1990.

Popol vuh. Ed. Agustín Estrada Monroy. Facsimile. Guatemala: J. de Pineda Ibarra, 1973.

Posse, Abel. *Daimón*. Buenos Aires: Emecé, 1989.

Preuss, Konrad Theodor. "Forschungsreise zu den Kagaba-Indianer." *Anthropos* 14–22 (1919–27): 314–404, 1040–79.

Preuss, Konrad Theodor. *Die Religion und Mythologie der Uitoto*. Göttingen: Vandenhoeck and Ruprecht, 1921–23.

Preuss, Mary. *Gods of the Popol vuh*. Culver City: Labyrinthos, 1988.

Rama, Ángel. *Transculturación narrativa en América Latina*. Mexico: Siglo XXI, 1982.

Raynaud, Georges. *Les Dieux, les héros et les hommes dans l'ancien Guatémala d'après le Livre du Conseil (Popol vuh)*. Paris, 1925.

Recinos, Adrián. *Popol vuh: Las antiguas historias del Quiché*. Mexico: Fondo de Cultura Económica, 1947.

Recinos, Adrián. *Crónicas indígenas de Guatemala*. Guatemala: Editorial Universitaria, 1957.

Reichel-Dolmatoff, Gerardo. *Amazonian Cosmos*. Chicago: U of Chicago P, 1971.

Ribeiro, Berta. *Antes o mundo não existia*. São Paulo: Livraria Cultura Editora, 1980.

Ribeiro, Darcy. *Uira sai a procura de Deus: Ensaios de etnologia e indigenismo*. Rio de Janeiro: Colecção Estudos Brasileiros, 1974.

Ribeiro, Darcy. *Maíra, romance*. Rio de Janeiro: Editora Civilização Brasileira, 1976.

Roa Bastos, Augusto. *Las culturas condenadas*. Mexico: Siglo XXI, 1978.

Roa Bastos, Augusto. *Yo el supremo*. Madrid: Alfaguara, 1974.

Roa Bastos, Augusto. *I, the Supreme*. Trans. Helen Lane. New York: Knopf, 1986.

Rodríguez Beteta, Virgilio. *Los dos brujitos mayas*. Guatemala: Pineda Ibarra, 1973.

Rothenberg, Jerome. *Technicians of the Sacred*. Berkeley: U of California P, 1985. 2nd enlarged ed.

Rowe, William. *Mito e ideología en la obra de Arguedas*. Lima: Instituto Nacional de Cultura, 1979.

Rowe, William, and Vivian Schelling. *Memory and Modernity: Popular culture in Latin America*. London: Verso, 1991.

Sá, Lúcia de. *Reading the Rainforest: Indigenous Texts and their Impact on Brazilian and Spanish-American Literature*. Ph.D. Diss. Bloomington: Indiana U, 1997.

Sá Lúcia de. "Perverse Tribute: Mario Vargas Llosa's El hablador and its Machiguenga Sources." *Journal of Iberian and Latin American Studies* 4 (1998): 145–64.

Sá Lúcia de. "Germans and Indians in South America: Ethnography and the Idea of Text." *Myth: A New Symposium*. Ed. W. Hansen and J. McDowell. Bloomington: Indiana UP, 2002: 36–45.

Sá Lúcia de. *Rain Forest Literatures: Amazonian Texts and Latin American Culture*. Minneapolis: U of Minnesota P, forthcoming 2004. *Cultural Studies of the Americas*, 16.

Salomon, Frank, and George L. Urioste. *The Huarochiri Manuscript: A Testament of Ancient and Colonial Andean Religion*. Austin: U of Texas P, 1991.

Sandoval-Sánchez, Alberto. *Puro Teatro: A Latina Anthology*. Tucson: U of Arizona P, 2000.

Sant'Anna, Affonso Romano de. *A grande fala do índio guarani perdido na história e outras derrotas (moderno Popol vuh)*. São Paulo: Summus, 1978.

Schele, Linda, and David Freidel. *A Forest of Kings: The Untold Story of the Ancient Maya*. New York: Morrow, 1992.

Seler, Eduard. *Gesammelte Abhandlungen*. 1902–23. Graz: ADEVA, 1960–61. 5 vols.

Silko, Leslie Marmon. *Almanac of the Dead*. New York: Simon & Schuster, 1991.

Sommer, Doris. *Foundational Fictions*. Berkeley: U of California P, 1991.

Souza, Márcio. *A expressão amazonense: Do colonialismo ao neocolonialism*. São Paulo: Alfa-Omega, 1978.

Souza, Márcio. *Teatro 1: Dessana, Dessana; Jurupari, a guerra dos sexos*. São Paulo: Marco Zero, 1997.

Tedlock, Dennis. *Finding the Center: Narrative Poetry of the Zuni Indians*. Lincoln: U of Nebraska P, 1972.

Tedlock, Dennis. *The Popol vuh*. New York: Simon & Schuster, 1985.

Treece, David. *Exiles, Allies, Rebels: Brazil's Indianist Movement, Indigenist Politics, and the Imperial Nation-State*. Westport, CT & London: Greenwood P, 2000.

Trimborn, Hermann, ed. *Dämonen und Zauber in Inkareich*. Leipzig: Quellen und Forschungen zur Geschichte der Völkerkunde, 1939.

Unkel, Kurt (Nimuendaju). *Die Sagen von der Erschaffung und Vernichtung der Welt*. Berlin: Zeitschrift für Ethnologie, 1914.

Vargas Llosa, Mario. *El hablador*. Barcelona: Seix Barral, 1987.

Watunna. Dir. Stacey Steers and Stan Brakhage Narr. Berkeley: U of California Center for Media, 1987.

Ximenez, Francisco. *Las historias del origen de los indios de esta provincia de Guatemala*. Ed. Karl Scherzer. Wien: Academia Imperial de las Ciencias, 1857.

Zolbrod, Paul. *Diné Bahane: The Navajo Creation Story*. Albuquerque: U of New Mexico P, 1984.

The Latin American Innovative Novel of the 1920s: A Comparative Reassessment

Elizabeth Coonrod Martínez

The question might be asked: Did Peruvians, Mexicans and other Latin American writers create new fiction before the 1960s—the era the Latin American novel arrived internationally with what was called magical realism? Even comparative studies focus only on the second half of the twentieth century in comparing Latin American with U.S. and European works. In other words, there is no general critical concern with Latin American literary production during the early twentieth century. That historical era is one of rapid technological, scientific and political change that greatly affected and influenced literary creation. It is an era when the city became a focus of identity for the modern society, and emblematic of human existence. This is reflected in early twentieth century narrative fiction, whether in Europe and the United States, or in Latin America. As an example, although William Faulkner's influence on and compatibility with Latin American writers in the second half of the twentieth century is often noted, no comparisons have been made of Ernest Hemingway and Latin American authors during the early stage of his writing. Nor are there studies of the compatibility of Virginia Woolf and James Joyce with Latin American innovative writers of their era. More significantly, there exists an erroneous general view that novels produced in Latin America simply followed or imitated the artistic movements in Europe and the United States. Instead, many 1920s Latin American novels are creations of innovative structure and discourse arising out of the artist's own experience, which appeared simultaneous to new creative fiction elsewhere.

Modernism, the literary era of the first three to four decades of the twentieth century, enjoys a rich profusion of innovative artistic creation. Novelists and poets were influenced by quickly changing technology, science, ideological and philosophical thought, which forever affected contemporary poetry and narrative fiction. Innovative English-language writers include Joyce, Woolf, T.S. Eliot, Ezra Pound, and William Carlos Williams. While this is considered an important literary period and popular era for the English-speaking world, Latin American literary production for this same period goes largely unnoticed and receives little credit in the English-speaking world. In fact, Vanguardia—the title in Spanish for the same epoch as modernism—is only loosely classified and not as a literary period. For the English-speaking world, the starting point for the innovative Latin American novel is the boom—so dubbed because critics considered it to have exploded into existence only in the 1960s and early 1970s, to the acclaim of international readers. But the inception of a new style—in form and discourse—actually occurred in a previous generation, before the boom. This earlier movement highly influenced boom writers and the creation of novels such as Gabriel García Márquez's *One Hundred Years of Solitude*. Contemporary Latin American writers have begun to give tribute to their Vanguardia predecessors, but English-language critics still ignore (with occasional exceptions) Latin America's early twentieth-century innovative writers.

It did not help that the principal boom novelists declared themselves an "orphan" generation—with no universal Latin American "father" of influence (Donoso 20)—which supposedly emerged as the first generation of real Latin American novelists. Doris Sommer pinpoints the fallacy of this idea, showing that, while Mario Vargas Llosa says he sought to be "modern" and "different," he acknowledged that this desire fed from an existing tradition of experimentation (Sommer 3–4). Indeed, revolutionary style, a discourse on the (Latin) American experience and the technological era, and modernity are the obvious traits of the Vanguardia novels, and part of a tradition begun long before the boom's inception. The boom has been celebrated for its magical realism—a sense of an exotic *Other* (different from Europe), but has also been considered revolutionary for bringing historical and political contemplations to modern introspective creation. Each of these elements is evident in earlier twentieth-century narrative.

Eurocentric critics have generally considered that Latin American writers reacted to and were influenced by European and U.S. artists and writers in the early twentieth century. What was actually happening, however, was that the world was becoming a smaller place. Cities were becoming larger urban clusters and technology was speeding information throughout the globe. Artists not only influenced other artists with their antics and inspirations, they were all revolutionizing—brutally breaking with the realism and romanticism of the previous century and striving for a newness that explained the newly technological and rapid era—at the same time. Innovative narrative fiction published in various Latin American capitals is little known because these works were neither translated into English nor did they find an international venue (as occurred during the boom). Had it so occurred, we would know that, for example, Arqueles Vela (1899–1972) in Mexico was producing a new kind of narrative—with extremely short sentences, alternating with longer phrases, and short paragraphs—*before* and during publication of the Ernest Hemingway novels that won acclaim for their new brevity. Vela's innovative novel *El café de nadie*, which was written as early as 1922, was published in 1926, the same year as Hemingway's first novel *The Sun also Rises*. Vela's characters also demonstrate the impact of new science, specifically, the influence of Albert Einstein's early theories on relativity, i.e., that acceleration and deceleration create no apparent difference in a line or circle. Artistic creation, likewise, should not be hindered by direct flow or stops and starts, according to Vela's narrative fiction.

This study will explore Vela's novel as well as novels by three other Latin Americans—Ecuadorian Pablo Palacio (1906–1946), Peruvian Martín Adán (1908–1984), and Argentinean Roberto Arlt (1900–1942)—to demonstrate the innovative creative fiction of Latin American writers who are seldom considered in comparative studies on modernism. These four revolutionary Latin American novelists forever altered and renovated narrative form, and achieved a discourse little understood in their era. They are precursors to the boom, and to the so-called postmodern novel following the boom. Each of these novelists breaks with traditional content and structure when many other novelists were writing within the realist/naturalist tradition, popular in Latin America following its earlier surge in Europe. Because of the public's preference for mainstream writing, Vanguardia narrative was overlooked (and these novels remained out of print) until recent reviews of the period.

No other era had seen such an incredible burst of technology, thought and science, which simultaneously brought the nations of the world closer together while at the same time thrusting them into world wars. The initiators of the *new novel* in Latin America "transgressed boundaries, potent fusions, and dangerous possibilities"—notions of Postmodern theory (Haraway 154) which fit Vanguardia style surprisingly well. A less self-centered artist than his immediate predecessors (who were equivalent to the Parnassian/Decadent periods) or Romantic precursors, the Vanguardia artist construed his work as a form of activity in step with vigorous times. They synthesized the lyrical and the analytical into an artistically self-critical position, detached from and simultaneously critically engaged with the period in question. As noted by Vicky Unruh (who has published the first text in English focusing on Latin American narrative in the Vanguardia period), these novelists constructed complex, unfinished characters as central figures in their fiction in order to intellectually debate the modern artist's own creative paradox (82–83). Vanguardia artists were actively involved in their societies and responded to a call for universal social and political change. They recognized that a new type of narrative was needed to keep up with developments in science, philosophy, art, and politics that marked the new century. The Latin American Vanguardia extended from as early as the second decade of the twentieth century to as late as the 1940s, with principal works dating from 1922 to 1930. While the avant-garde novels are forgotten, fiction of this period is remembered mainly for its realism focused on specific regions for purposes of their development or civilizing process: Ricardo Güiraldes' *Don Segundo Sombra* (1926), Rómulo Gallegos' *Doña Bárbara* (1929), and the novels of the Mexican Revolution such as Martín Luis Guzmán's *El águila y la serpiente* (1928). In English-language criticism, the few studies on the Vanguardia movement have tended to focus on poetry.

Now, why would criticism on early twentieth-century Latin American literature focus principally on regional representations (using traditional form) of narrative fiction, and yet pick up innovative, revolutionary achievements in poetry? A likely reason is Rubén Darío's esthetic movement, which won literary acclaim in Spain in the late nineteenth century, when poetry was considered the highest form of creative innovation. This idea continued throughout the early decades of the twentieth century in Spanish-language art. Spaniard José Ortega y Gasset even warned against an indecipherable new form of novel in his influential study *Ideas sobre el teatro y la novela* (1925). If art is a deformation of reality and therefore incompatible with [supposed] realistic life, he declared, it would remove the reader from the cares of everyday life (76). Revolutionary novelists—more in number in Latin America than Spain—thought differently. They sought not to reject reality, or even universality as Ortega y Gasset feared, but instead to focus the new twentieth century reality by doing away with traditional components like the omniscient author and the elaborately contrived plot. Ortega y Gasset did not understand that many modern writers wanted to trust their readers' imaginations by having the readers complete the images in their novels. He and other early-twentieth-century critics paid no attention to the subtleties of parody and irony in the revolutionary writers' visions. Still, their observations influenced later critics. Even late-twentieth-century criticism has also focused on innovative Vanguardia poets such as Vicente Huidobro, César Vallejo, José Gorostiza, or Delmira Agustini, for their experimental language, while the Vanguardia novelists—who reinvented the novel—have been mostly ignored and forgotten. Theoretical premises on the novel, however, published mid- to late-twentieth century, have now provided the possibility of a review in hindsight to better understand early revolutionary narrative fiction.

Recent turns in literary theory offer unique opportunities to reevaluate narrative fiction in the early twentieth century for its influence on the contemporary Latin American novel and its place in literary history. New literary thought can aid recognition of Latin American literary influence and production before its "discovery" by U.S. and European critics (as with Christopher Columbus, this hemisphere's literature does not exist until it is discovered by the Europeans), and its evaluation alongside innovative works in English. For Mikhail Bakhtin (who began his critical writing in the 1920s, although little of it was published or translated until decades later and arrived in North American scholarship only by the 1970s), the novel was only born with the twentieth century. He considered that the novel is "the sole genre that continues to develop, that is as yet uncompleted," while other genres, such as the epic and tragedy, have been exhausted (3). Only the novel includes, ingests, and devours other genres without losing itself; it alone is "organically receptive" to new forms of perception or reading. In fact, the novel would "become for the contemporary world what the epic was for the ancient world" (10). In his essay "Epic and the Novel," Bakhtin notes that the rapid technological change and intense activity of the new century enhanced the novel's evolution: "In this actively polyglot world, completely new relationships are established between language and its object (the real world), and this is fraught with enormous consequences for all the already completed genres that had been formed during eras of closed and deaf monoglossia. In contrast to other major genres, the novel emerged and matured precisely when intense activation of external and internal polyglossia was at the peak of its activity" (12). Contemporary criticism has varying ideas as to the viability of the contemporary novel. While Bakhtin saw the possibilities, Harold Bloom says novels that revealed real-world (i.e., sociological or ideological) information would be "tarnished" (qtd. in Begley 34). The novels Bloom selects to form his *Western Canon* (1994) are valued only for their aesthetics. Another critic cites "Western thought" as preventing interpretations, because the critic's interpretation could be invented: "Can one look for structure without structuring?" asks Trinh Minh-ha in her study on postcolonial writing by women of color (141). The purpose of her book is to show that stories do not always have a specifically dictated beginning and closure as Western thought suggests: "Life is not a (Western) drama of four or five acts. Sometimes it just drifts along; it may go on year after year without development, without climax, without beginnings or endings. . . . In life, we really don't know when an event is occurring; we think it is starting when it is already ending, and we don't see its in/significance" (143).

For Ortega y Gasset and Bloom, literature must meet their perspective of "real life," but Bakhtin and Trinh Minh-ha see a less defined or encased possibility. It is likely that neither critic is right or wrong; instead, each opens additional perspectives. Vanguardia narrative identifies no beginning or closure in its search of the artist's inner depths in order to reveal artistic reality. Bloom would not have argued for the Vanguardia artist, whose creation does not follow the structure of Western drama or fiction. Nonetheless, early innovative prose writers in Latin America have influenced subsequent generations of writers whom Bloom has placed in his canon. The Vanguardia novelist sought to "reconstruct boundaries" much as the postmodern artist does presently (Haraway 181). And contemporary writers, like Mario Vargas Llosa, are beginning to acknowledge the ways Vanguardia narrative influenced them (Kinsella 33). According to Bakhtin, all cultural production is dialogic, in continuous struggle among several voices. If a revolutionary novelist writes to supplant previous voices, is the writer ideologically countering old masters or is he/she an artist of extreme individuality? A postmodern question is: how does one create a future that will acknowledge and incorporate the past without repeating it? This is also a question that concerned the Vanguardia writers. If the postmodern is a moment of extreme artistic self-consciousness, according to Lacanian thought, so was the Vanguardia; its challenge, however, was how to avoid the impasse of recuperation. In order to incorporate without repeating, parody and irony became essential to the dialogic Vanguardia process. Bloom thinks that the true artist must be removed from the world and its ideologies, but what of removing the artistic creation from master narrative control, in other words, resisting esthetic and traditional paradigms? The Vanguardia artist removes himself from the world, but he also defies tradition, thereby committing an ideological act. In the postmodern, this act is called a deconstruction of master European narratives or a loosening of the bindings of the traditional novel (Spivak 263). Therefore, the artist defies ideologies while implanting his own. Similarly, French deconstructionists separate the components of literary language and texts, and Marxists show how narrative has been used as an instrument of power to establish ideology (Kernan 212). Either the text has no meaning or it has scores of meanings. Avant-garde literature is only new if it seeks neither lofty esthetic goals nor ideological influences. It must exist for itself, creating its own influence. The Latin American Vanguardia novel's intention becomes clearer in light of contemporary theory.

Thus, there is a need to re-examine and reread those works overlooked by critics, and from new perspectives. This is the "ex-centric" position, according to postmodern theorist Linda Hutcheon. Postmodern theory does not invert, but uses the double paradox to critique the *Center* from both the inside and the outside. Now, in postmodern times, we perceive the boom as the Center, thus placing the Vanguardia on the margin. The Vanguardia novel wanted to be "a novel," but only if it could parody, both incorporate and challenge the novel as it had been: this is now defined as a postmodern trait (Hutcheon 251). While critics largely disagree on the inception of postmodern narrative—some deciding it begins in the 1970s and others suggesting it began immediately following the Vanguardia (modernism) period—there are strong arguments for the similarities between the postmodern and the Vanguardia. Jean-François Lyotard defines the postmodern as "incredulity" toward metanarratives, a direct product of progress in the sciences (72). Bakhtin says a variety of discourses on a textual space establishes a resistance to the dominance of any one (Lodge 22), and Hutcheon saw the need for modern fiction to parody master works in order to supplant them. Lyotard observes that postmodernism refines sensitivities to invent, to see differences, and to tolerate the incommensurable (73). Finally, theorist Donna Haraway states that postmodern language expresses an awareness of matter and imagination in continual interaction, and that only partial perspectives promise objective vision (190). Therefore, in the twentieth century the novel could only become *new* if it rebelled from traditional and master narratives, and revealed a variety of perspectives and states of awareness. During the literary periods of naturalism and realism, the artist sought to reveal a reality outside the esthetic emphasis of romanticism. In a similar manner, the Vanguardia artist—in Albert Einstein's generation—seeks a perspective that had not been revealed previously. His struggle is against "the one code that translates all meaning perfectly, the central dogma of phallogocentrism" (Hutcheon 175). The new novel—launched in the early twentieth century—would be a non-novel that defied master narratives.

The novels in this study represent a variety of Latin American countries, each attempting to reveal the new cosmopolitan identity of their respective cities. Each is a different voice with a similar goal of revealing specific Latin American identity in the new century. They have in common a lack of *structure*—their own particular creations of nonstructure—and a discourse that critiques the conventional novel and demonstrates the act of creating new fiction. Each was a first in their respective countries, for their abstract quality and outrageous defiance of traditional narrative. Each is also a highly achieved artistic creation. The creators of these novels were not hailed by their contemporaries nor by subsequent generations. It is only today that they can be saluted for showing twentieth century narrative the future of prose fiction. Arqueles Vela's *El café de nadie* (1926) is a novel in three parts, which can be seen as three different novels (since Vela completed and published two sections of the novel in 1922 and 1924 in literary magazines). Although unconnected in plot, the three similarly parody a passing era to present a new vision. The third section (which was written first), "La señorita, etc.," is the most technological in language and offers extremely short sentences, often alternated with average-size sentences, for example: "I was overcome by sleep. I felt tired. Her languishing form folded across my arms with the intimacy of a coat, for she had fallen asleep. It was natural. Six days of uncomfortable travel had made her lose her shyness. It wasn't for nothing" (Vela 77; my translation). In this last section of the novel, Vela's short sentences and paragraphs accelerate the pace, leaving memories behind and, by returning to the city, moving toward the *señorita*. The train movement produces her memory and the artist's thought process: "He is accustomed to living behind a door or in the groove of a window. Alone. Isolated. Misunderstood" (77; my translation).

The state of consciousness or thought process described by Vela's narrator is similar to James Joyce's narration in *Ulysses*. Both narrations vacillate between memory and physical presence. He leaves "her" to go in search of her memory—perhaps one artistic muse for another? It is a muse of mechanical images—"she" balances harmoniously on the handlebars of the trolley (81), and her breasts and my heart stayed trembling, exhausted, with that incessant sputtering of a motor that suddenly quits (87; my translation). The second chapter of this section begins with a countdown, from 1 to 26. The narrator considers whether it is a clock, then states this is not possible. So he considers a bell. Both images suggest urgency, a ringing to determine time, and a need to escape the village. He decides to return to the city with its telegraphic images, and stentorian and vociferous streets (79). Vela's brevity and descriptions extol the rapidity of the city and life being described, and provide tribute to Futurism (the first title used in Latin America for avant-garde artistic work). The number of pages in each of the three sections of this book shows no consistency or logic, and yet a search for numerical perfection is highlighted throughout the book. The first is 32 pages long, the second is 23 pages, and the third is 19. Literary critics like John Brushwood call the three sections "short stories" even though each section is separated into 10, 6, and 8 chapters (with short titles), respectively. But Vela was calling attention to a new, brief way of constructing the novel by insisting that each of the three parts were *novels*. The Italian Futurists used numbers in disorder to demonstrate the impact of technology and science. Vela's posthumous novel, *El intransferible* also relies on numbers—where disorder suggests a multipresence with the concepts of one and all (a human being and the universe). In the one-within-all are the notions of return, metamorphosis and transubstantiation, confirmed by a play of numbers (Picon Garfield 208–09). This insistence on numbers reflects the author's predilection for the scientific spirit and exact sciences of the new technological society.

The second section in Vela's book, "Un crímen provisional" is a parody of detective fiction and old logic. Vela's style of short phrases continues, although without repetitive descriptions, but the content of this novella is based on the analysis of a crime. This section is especially amusing. A "detective" who carries a flashlight inspects the blinds and imagines both the echo of compromising phrases and the trajectory of criminal footsteps. But he makes no conclusive deductions. The murderer, a "conquering and irresistible character in a light suit with large yellow checks" (60; my translation), says his only defense is the crime itself. The murdered victim turns out to be a mannequin, a fact that is simply stated, and the story goes no further. The crime here is against the detective novel—the prose of rationalistic philosophy by authors such as Arthur Conan Doyle or Edgar Allan Poe. This novel, or crime, is a precursor to another on the horizon (represented with sunset followed by sunrise in the section "El café de nadie"). The novelist is clearly stating that the novel must be different in the future (in order to survive, per Bakhtin). While Ilán Stavans gives Jorge Luis Borges and other Latin Americans the credit for "revising" detectivist prose (24), Vela is actually the first to parody, criticize, and bring attention to the need for revision. Vela's irony is effective for its humor, which Carlos Fuentes calls one of the most distinguishing traits in recreating Latin American language in the new novel (30). Vela engages humor, like the French avant-garde writers of the same era, as a device to alter the reader's expectations (Shattuck 172). Humor becomes a tool—for example the longing for a muse's inspiration, and the silliness of a false muse—that the Vanguardia artist uses to draw attention to the need for a new genre. Humor is also a tool for acknowledging complexity, a means of survival, and affirming life (Hutcheon 26). Just as irony comes into play because discursive communities exist, so humor reinforces existence—here the existence of a creative spirit—while exposing or subverting hegemonic ideologies.

Vela's three novellas (within a book) reflect various states of consciousness, all taking place in cosmopolitan life with access to modern technology. The first section of Vela's tripartite book is undoubtedly important as it carries the title of the novel itself. It contains a description of a café, with its two regulars, whose thoughts and actions seem to be joined, and an enigmatic woman whose name is Mabelina. The café itself is a landmark and symbol of the Vanguardia movement. *El café de nadie* was the name of a Mexico City café frequented by innovative artists (including Vela) of the radical *Estridentista* movement. The locale itself represents what the artists were attempting—breaking with tradition, belonging to no one. In the novella, the café serves as a metaphor of creative inspiration based on new theories, especially relativity. Futuristic images give the sense of an inevitability of mechanical creation. But the mechanical has a human feel—car honks that sniff the pedestrians' tracks—and nature fuses with manmade objects. Metafictionally, the artist is seeking inspiration in the new era. The last chapter consists of four short paragraphs, concluding the search within this text for a new muse. After a long, spiritual journey, the artist has discovered that his evocations are punctured by the muse's looks, like an ellipsis. The used-up muse (reflected in the person of a female character who has been with each of the male characters) steps outside the café as dawn commences; the café regulars have already left. Einstein's theories on relativity state that a ray of light from a distant star can, when passing near the sun, seem to be attracted to the mass of the sun and reflect the sun's own light. Mass and energy, according to Einstein, have equal value. But that mass has to act, that is, go toward the light or the sun's radiation. In order to create, the artist must abandon the old and move toward the light, hence the old muse departs the café. Vela demonstrates that artistic knowledge needs to move toward the sun or a new center of inspiration. Leaving the old behind required great risk. The women in Vela's three novellas represent the same illusory inspiration and artistic possibility—as well as frustration—that the novelist seeks and does not find in mechanical, continuous movement and logic.

The French Cubists held that tradition had to be destroyed, and only new creations were valid. Vela merges the old into and toward the new inspiration—a more scientific conclusion than the French artists. He sought no aesthetic goal in his creation; instead, his antimethodology—presented with three different examples—was to demonstrate mass moving toward energy, or the inspiration and first steps toward artistic creation. This opened avenues for novels such as Julio Cortázar's *Hopscotch* and García Márquez's *One Hundred Years of Solitude*. While Vela's peers were still encumbered by long sentences and paragraphs that led to interminable realistic descriptions, he created truly innovative prose and a discourse based on the influences of science. His writing style is similar to Hemingway's, but his intellectual range is much greater. Although the two were contemporaries, it is not very probable that Vela would have been aware of Hemingway's writings. (Vela did not travel to Spain until after he had written at least the early parts of *El café de nadie*. Hemingway, however, had been living in France and Spain since World War I and read Spanish. He could have read Vela's early publications in newspaper magazines.) Hence, Vela was a forerunner in rejecting old forms (long, realist images and sentences), and an artist who also attempted to adapt a new logic, based on new scientific discoveries, to narrative fiction.

In Ecuador, Pablo Palacio's short novel *Débora* (1927) demonstrated the rebellion of the traditional character, or, at least, the artist's rebellion in creating the character. The essential plot of *Débora* concerns a character that has not yet fully left the artist's head. It opens with a chapter labeled "Lieutenant" and the narrator saying, "You, go, I say, outstretching my arm as a pointer." Then, as the lieutenant tries to go about his development (or life)—getting ready in the morning, talking to a secondary character, visiting the seedy side of town, musing about his need for a girlfriend—he is regularly interrupted by the narrator's commentary on him. The novel ends because the narrator has the Lieutenant disappear (he is slashed by a paper cut), thereby neglecting traditional character development. Or so Palacio has the reader believe. While it includes sociopolitical commentary, and even political denunciation, Palacio's novel is a characterization of art and an attack on the romantic and realist novels of the previous century. His novel agonizes over the rules of logic of the traditional novel by having the narrator voice them as the characters are being shaped: "The realist novel hurtfully deceives. It abstracts the facts and leaves the field open to emptiness; it gives them an impossible continuity, because the veridical, what would be quieted, would not interest anyone" (72; my translation).

Enrique Anderson Imbert calls Palacio "an excellent monologuer," the artist choosing this technique long before other authors used it to reveal interior realities (262). *Débora* consists of two crisscrossing monologues, one is the character's and the second belongs to the narrator/author, who reflects on the novel in general and the process of creating the novel. It is an anguished narrative—anguish is felt by both the character and the author—with no final resolution. Palacio's novel is thus a characterization of art and an attack on literary style—novels—of the previous era. A Vanguardia artist, Palacio saw that new politics, science, and a modern society all precipitated the novel's need to change. The artist's labor-in-process, or contemplation of the work's creation, seems similar to that of a philosopher or scientist—a process to encourage thinking and discovery. His narrator pokes fun at the characters, but with a very serious intention: to remake the novel. Palacio's character should not be sentimental or romantic, but instead should reflect life in the present world (which is the premise for most artists during the Modernist period). *Débora's* discourse reveals that the matter is larger than the artist himself; our society tells lies and is not interested in the true reality of our lives. The Vanguardia artist wants to stop being subservient to a controlling system. Whereas the French Dadaists wanted to free words, Palacio sought to free his entire narrative from convention. Ultimately, Palacio includes an outright condemnation of traditional writers: "The shamefulness of those lies is that they say: I'm giving you a compendium of real life, this that I write is the pure and absolute truth; and everyone believes it. The only honorable thing would be to say: these are fantasies, more or less coated so that you can swallow them comfortably; or, simply, to not sugarcoat the fantasies and given them entertainment à la John Raffles or Sherlock Holmes. Liars! Tricksters!" (72–73; my translation). Even the "girl" the lieutenant character eventually courts is described as an ignorant, easy, and unbecoming young Indian woman. Palacio pinpoints societal and racial concerns that would later predominate in the Social Realist novel of international recognition (especially with Jorge Icaza's 1934 novel, Huasipungo): "The girl walked in. She was a little too much Indian with grossly thick hair. Her part (literally path for fleas) in the middle, separating the braids. But she was exuberant and had a juicy mouth" (Palacio 83; my translation). Neither the plot nor the characters in Palacio's short novel are fully developed, but the narrator/artist's presence is a constant. At first reading, it appears a fragmented novel needing to be completed, as some critics would soon state. But Palacio published this as his second new novel. Said instability or lack of completion was essential to Palacio's purpose—to mimic and parody the conventional novel and finally put it to rest as useless, to make way for the new novel in which the reader has a part to play. Patricia Waugh has noted that parody is an essential tool of metaliterature in demonstrating artistic style: "Parody of an earlier literary norm or mode unavoidably lays bare the relations of that norm to its original historical context through the de-familiarizing contextualization within a historical present whose literary and social forms have shifted" (66).

Jean Giraudoux wrote metafictional prose in the 1920s that required the reader to use his/her own imagination and participate in the novel (Nagel 78). Similarly to Giraudoux, Palacio does away with traditional components like omniscient author and the elaborately contrived plot. Giraudoux constantly reminds the reader to reflect upon the novel by revealing its conventions and disposing of them. Similarly, traditional fiction dies with Palacio's supposed-to-be romantic character. Susan Nagel's study explains how Giraudoux's subtle criticism of art and society was little understood by contemporary critics and much the same would be true for Palacio's novel with its subtleties and criticism of art and society. While nothing is sure in *Débora*, the plot is the least traditional; Palacio's plot is the remaking of the novel. *Débora's* structure is like a puzzle: it is a sequence of moments joined by the sole logic of fright or desolation, a grouping of strange meditations, and a coupling of the abstract and concrete (Fernández 319–20). If the story is about a Lieutenant with an unsatisfied wish, to whom nothing of consequence happens before death, then the structure coincides with the plot. The lack of structure and an empty plot filled with pessimism and social censure renders an empty novel. But Palacio's novel consists of much more than nothingness. His principal character, the pathetic, retrospective, sentimental Lieutenant, dies the death of the conventional novel so that in this "initial and final moment" (Palacio 90; my translation), a new creation comes into being. Palacio's discourse is an explanation of possibility and renewal in life, society, and art. The reader is offered two possibilities: first, the revelation of what is in his own conscience (in other words, that the reader and the author are a part of the internal world being articulated); and second, an outside, external point of view of the artist's conscience at work, as though someone were describing it (Jitrik 164). Thus, it is difficult for the reader to maintain distance, and, if he does, the reader still sees himself through the external viewpoint of the development and critique of narrative and society.

Martín Adán also foresaw the need for a new prose in the twentieth century. His discourse is based on the shifting forces of life that seldom remain the same except in memory, hence, the cardboard house of his title, *La casa de cartón* (1928; *The Cardboard House*, 1990). He documents the tangible and intangible realities of a coastal village on the outskirts of Lima. Through images, Adán demonstrates the sadness of an old way of life that is being lost—via a contrast with the modern—but one that at the same time reveals the Peruvian landscape and people. The village is a metaphor for Adán's art and his art a metaphor for Peruvian life: "Afternoons were white in winter, and in summer, a reddish gold. . . . But in March there was a Monday with a pink afternoon . . . and everyone was deeply moved by the pink afternoon" (*The Cardboard House* 44). Like Palacio, Adán documents the making of a novel; he cites and critiques modern and traditional writers, poking fun at conventional rules and structure as he writes his own kind of novel. Similarly to Vela and Palacio, Adán shows that life's shifting forces of political change and modernization have a correlative in the need for modernization in prose. There are no chapters in this novel. Instead, forty fragments of memories and images make up the text. Surrealistic techniques such as the absence of linear time, the blurring of identities, and an emphasis on the irrational provide for an esthetic series of metaphors. Irony and humor abound in the descriptions, making the purpose of the prose seem only to exalt the coastal village. But the impact of politics, outside wars and the world as a whole encroach in the pursuit of creation of a novel based on his region, just as the city of Lima is encroaching on this village.

There is no attempt to describe a reality behind the lives of the residents or visitors (who seem to represent new ideas and philosophies) to a specific vacation house in the coastal village of Barranco, or any sense of encounter between these people. On the one hand, *La casa de cartón* is rich in sensuous imagery that strives to convey myriad sensations and emotions underneath the surface reality of this village. On the other hand, the novel is limited by the subjective perceptions of a shy, sensitive youth whose consciousness filters the images. If the narrator is the artist's alter-ego, the house is his refuge and the place of artistic imagination, from which the author can gaze uninhibitedly at the Peruvian landscape. We are all images conceived during a calm, mule's trot, Palacio notes in one description, images that become foliated, plastered, and fenestrated (*The Cardboard House* 86–87). Art is life and therefore should reflect life. The plot of Adán's novel is no more than an ephemeral shell for his discourse. The characters, not fully developed, are essentially deconstructed as nonstereotypical characters that merge into the sights, smell, and plants of Barranco. Adán teases the reader with possible information that is never provided, choosing instead to take particular memories and develop them into a discourse. He does not overtly tell the reader about the constructions of the novel as Palacio does in *Débora*, but the narrator/author pretends to be describing life and Barranco while he develops his artistic theories. The narrator talks about an ice cream vendor's cart (the vendor's trumpet will open the last fragment of the novel) pulled by an old nag, an image that creates a confluence of new and old technologies. The vendor is representative of the Peruvian: "The rumble of the cart's wheels on the paving stones gladdens the sad waters of the fountain. The Indian—his cheeks the color of blood-soaked earth and his nose sprinkled with tiny, round drops of sweat—the Indian [driver] does not allow the cart to roll over the lawn of that meager garden" (*The Cardboard House* 5). In crisp, scintillating adjectives, Adán captures a moment in the hard life of a worker in this vacation town. He also makes note of Latin American racial and physical descriptions. In the fourth fragment, the narrator begins addressing a "you" which is the narrator's boyhood friend, who is said to look "more Negroid than ever" (*The Cardboard House* 10). While forging the new cosmopolitan identity of modern life, as with the other novelists in this study, Adán also reflects (as with Palacio) the racial/ethnic composition of his national identity—an early step in the issue of a search for identity that marks twentieth century Latin American literature.

Adán's narrator speaks to his boyhood friend, in his memory, about wrestling between conscious and subconscious states. Everything in life represents these opposites (*The Cardboard House* 90). In the final fragment, the artist can no longer be still, contemplating the "indoors or inner being of the subconscious" (*The Cardboard House* 103). The artist is a workman, not simply a creator (as previous literary generations thought); as a producer of texts, he must relate to the stimuli around him. He believes in the permanence of change and wants to keep his senses sharp to create along with change, or even ahead of it, if he is to be a nomadic intellectual. Adán's narrator also discusses literature with his boyhood friend, and creates metafiction that contemplates literature being published in the very era of the writing of the novel: "It might not be anything. Or perhaps it is a verse of Neruda" (*The Cardboard House* 59). His contemplation may thus be a verse by Pablo Neruda, who is one of the first writers to exalt a Latin American unique identity. The young characters also learn from characters in international writer's novels: "This is how we learned about the life of that poor Stephen Dedalus, an interesting man who wore glasses and wet his bed" (*The Cardboard House* 53). James Joyce's character in *Portrait of the Artist as a Young Man*, Stephen Dedalus, is only one of the fictional characters who influence Adán's narrator and his friends and, essentially, the artist. One critic calls Adán a Joycean, Stephen Dedalus-type (see Aguilar Mora 10). Adán most likely read the Joyce novel in translation as a teenager or in the 1920s when he began writing poetry. His narrator in *La casa de cartón* also cites Luigi Pirandello's play, *Six Characters in Search of an Author* (1920), which Adán must have read in the same period of time and which had a strong influence on him: "In this way we found out about the trick played on a good theater director by six characters, how they enticed him to write and then ended up not existing" (*The Cardboard House* 53). The narrator uses this fragment to suggest a new process for narrative fiction, which cannot follow the path of traditional narrative. Adán knows new fiction needs risk. He calls his European contemporaries Pirandello, Joyce, and George Bernard Shaw "idiots" (as he knows he himself will be called by critics), precisely for taking this risk. Then he makes a pronouncement on how he and his peers were educated: "All of us, except Raúl, were steeped in the Spanish and American moldy literary stew. For like on Sancho's Island of Barataria, it is the food of canon and rich men" (*The Cardboard House* 54). Making mention of Don Quijote's sidekick in Miguel Cervantes's famous novel, Adán slyly notes that the majority will simply follow tradition in order to be part of the canon, just as Sancho went along with Don Quijote's attempt to be part of an elite tradition. He continues to criticize members of the Spanish canon within the novel, subtly demonstrating the influences on his artistic spirit and others he chooses to discard.

Critics did not recognize Adán's work as incipient new narrative, instead relegating novels such as his to fragments of poetic words without structure (see, e.g., Lindstrom 71). Perhaps because Adán created this novel when he was only twenty years old, his work was not taken seriously. Curiously, García Márquez also wrote *One Hundred Years of Solitude* when he was twenty years old (in 1948, and twenty years after Adán's book), coming only years later to an understanding of its meaning (now called magical realism) and refining it for publication. In Adán's case, Mario Vargas Llosa has aided that reflection. He is greatly responsible for resurgence in the critical analysis of *La casa de cartón*, owing to two essays he published in 1965. Vargas Llosa considers Adán's novel a better representation of Peruvian reality than the highly acclaimed *El mundo es ancho y ajeno* (1941; *Broad and Alien is the World*, 1945), by Ciro Alegría. Vargas Llosa notes that Adán sacrificed clarity in plot and structure in order to reach into his inner depths and demonstrate the ambiance, character, color and anguish of Barranco (Kinsella 33). Adán's novel also prefigures the works of several Peruvian writers of ensuing generations, namely, Vargas Llosa, Julio Ramón Ribeyro, and Alfredo Bryce Echenique. Adán's lyrical novel revealed the meaning of new, twentieth century narrative fiction, which can now be discovered in English thanks to the excellent translation by Katherine Silver.

William Carlos Williams comes to mind for purposes of comparison here. While he published several works of poetry and prose in the early Modernist era, his work was overshadowed by the attention T.S. Eliot's *The Wasteland* (1922) received. In fact, Williams felt that Eliot and Ezra Pound were too attached to European culture and tradition. It was only in the 1950s and 60s that he began to receive deserved recognition for his efforts to invent an entirely fresh—and singularly American—poetic, centered on the lives of the common people. This is even evoked in the titles of his prose, *The Great American Novel* (1923), and *In the American Grain* (1925). Williams's epic poem "Paterson" centers on the poet's relationship to a modern city. The poet-protagonist wanders about the city, perceiving its present, remembering its past, and meditating upon his own life in it, until he is able to experience and understand all aspects of the city, and, in a sense, to become the city. Williams's narrator, like Adán's narrator in *The Cardboard House*, seeks to understand modern life. The past is gone, and the present must be reconciled. Adán's lyrical prose is very similar to the language of Williams's long poem, seeking to express the poet or artist's voice but speaking in a collective sense for his society. Pablo Palacio and Martín Adán, like William Carlos Williams in the United States, are attempting to portray a consciousness and reality native to the Americas—whether the Ecuadorean, Peruvian, or U.S. urban reality. Their work was produced in the same era, but may have been overshadowed by other artists' works because these Americanists were not more European-focused, and that world was not yet ready for a distinctive "American" (as in the continent) reality.

A final example is Argentina, which in the early twentieth century had several prominent writers who sought to reveal a true Argentine reality in its prose, namely, Ricardo Güiraldes, Jorge Luis Borges, and Eduardo Mallea. None, however, broke radically with tradition as Roberto Arlt did. He not only changed narrative structure and strategy, but also produced a discourse on artistic pursuit and the modern dilemma of man. Curiously, only since the 1970s have critics begun to study his influence. For example, David William Foster includes Arlt as a forerunner with Mallea, Ernesto Sábato and Julio Cortázar in his study *Currents in the Contemporary Argentine Novel* (1975). Arlt sought to express the experience of life in an alienated society by creating a chaotic but artistic text. Arlt's expressionistic milieu—grimy eateries, brothels, bars and their customers—stand out in his narrative, but it is his novels' structure that marks him as innovator. In fact, his "fragmentary, disjointed presentation and difficult-to-specify narrative data are features that later distinguish the Spanish American new narrative of the boom years" (Lindstrom 79). Arlt focuses on the alienation of technology and twentieth century society in his novel *Los siete locos* (1929; *The Seven Madmen*, 1984). The protagonist, Erdosain, is a madman, but his madness is neither political nor eccentric; instead, it is a complex human reaction to a crazy world. His narrator is an anarchist who believes a return to a simpler, rural society is the only effective solution, and that the solitude of nature will help man regain a sense of identity (Franco 304). His friends and those around him plan to control the world. The overt political message of Arlt's novel is the condemnation of fanaticism, be it political or religious. According to Foster, the key to understanding *Los siete locos* is to see Erdosain as an anguished soul who could be Everyman (28). A byproduct of an exploitative urban society, he is identified early in the novel when he is fired from his job for petty embezzlement and will be prosecuted unless he repays the money immediately. Interestingly, however, he has not spent the money on bettering his own life—with the exception of buying some meals in expensive restaurants, where the food and wine, he states, was not interesting to his palate. He gave most of the money away to waiters and those who appeared in need. He does not even buy himself a new pair of shoes.

In *Los siete locos*, Erdosain is elevated to the level of a martyr figure who thinks he will save his soul and all mankind through his commitment to the new order, even though it involves murder. This gives meaning to Erdosain's otherwise empty existence. For Arlt and possibly for the reader, society is simply a cruel fascist hoax to exploit the helpless, all of which points to the ultimate irony, that is, the tension between the knowledge of the reader and the lack of that same knowledge by Erdosain. Resolution, for the reader, comes in knowing the futility of transcendent orders, the paradox of the human quest for them, and the inescapable truth that if they do not exist (as with God), society will create them (Foster 37), this being a concept developed by Bertolt Brecht in his plays of the late 1920s. Irony, a key aspect of *Los siete locos*, is a powerful, apolitical tool wielded against authority (Hutcheon 27). Arlt, like the other novelists of this study, achieves the duality of sociopolitical commentary and demonstrating the way toward new narrative strategies. In his novel, Arlt resorts to shifting points of view, chaotic monologues, and alternations of time and space, or Bakhtinian chronotopes, such as meeting/parting (separation), loss/acquisition, search/discovery, recognition/nonrecognition (Bakhtin 97). Although supposedly chronological, it is not clear whether some events are imagined. It is often confusing as to who narrates—an omniscient narrator, a commentary on Erdosain's oral and written confessions, Erdosain's own voice, or his wife Elsa's thoughts. In addition, every few pages, the narration stops for a footnote (as part of the fiction) or makes reference to what is contained in an unwritten future novel. This technique can cause confusion, and some critics during Arlt's time, expecting a linear structure, were baffled by the contradictions (not realizing they were purposeful) within the text. For some, Arlt did not know how to structure his writing, and he was judged to be grammatically incorrect. This is still believed in 1960s criticism: "That askewed novelistic eye seems to belong to one of the lunatics in the novel. The prose is awkward and at times illegible" (Anderson Imbert 301). Throughout, several items are never clarified:

who exactly are the seven madmen? Does the Astrologer finally explain to Erdosain that he did not have Barsut—who was held for ransom to finance the Astrologer's plan to control society—killed after all? (Erdosain assumes he has seen his enemy Barsut's dead body.) The Astrologer is untrustworthy as the reader has already discovered. Erdosain, while sitting in a café, observes a man at another table. Soon he hears a shot and glances back to see the man slumped over the table. He mentions this to the Astrologer, who later contests his impression of the same: "By the way, where did you get that story about the suicide in the café? I have looked at yesterday's afternoon papers, and this morning's edition, and none have any news about this incident. You must have dreamed it." Erdosain then says, "Nevertheless, I could show you the café." "Well, then you dreamed in the café," the Astrologer says. "Could be, it's not important," Erdosain responds (238; my translation). Not even his friends are supportive. Finally, will Erdosain go to jail as he believes when he hides with the Commentator and tells his story? If these things do not matter, is the purpose of the story to get the reader to think—to see himself as Erdosain, neither a madman nor a savior, but a complex human consciousness?

The world in *Los siete locos* is a labyrinth without an exit. Anguish arises form the concept of existence in the universe, but it can also arise from the artistic act of devouring and replacing the previous artistic/creative generation. That is Arlt's anguish. Parody and irony are essential to the dialogic process; expressing dislocation or distortion is only a part of that process. The realization of the overwhelming role of irony in the novel and the particular form that this irony assumes is ultimately what the critics did not grasp. That is why, decades later, Argentine novelist Ricardo Piglia (in his novel *Respiración artificial*, 1980; *Artificial Respiration*, 1994) thought it necessary to make this point for postmodern literature: "Any grade school teacher, including my Aunt Margaret, Renzi said, could correct one of Arlt's pages, but no one could write it, except him" (Piglia 132). Structural participation in the action invited doubts as to Arlt's competence as a writer (Foster 44). If Arlt's novel were only a statement on the unacceptable circumstances of the lower classes, and their need for a belief in transcendent promises, *Los siete locos* would be a social realist novel. But it is much more innovative. Erdosain is not simply a disenchanted Everyman seeking escape from the urban, political world; he is the creative product at the hands of a perhaps maniacal artist seeking ultimate expression. There is no better "artist" than the Astrologer to make such a statement (44). The artist (Astrologer) offers the character (Erdosain) a "new order," and the hope of new meaning (in the genre). In Arlt's new order, the character finds a greater sense of life by seeking to establish meaning in his existence. The artist controls that expression, losing it occasionally to the character, that is to say, to artistic expression itself. Further, Arlt is in some ways reminiscent of Upton Sinclair, with his novel condemning the abuse of the urban worker, *The Jungle* (1906). It is easy to see that the challenges brought to city life and its populace by the new speed and technology of the modern era became a ready discourse for the writers of this era in any country. Even the film *Metropolis* (1926), by director Fritz Lang, expresses the robotization of the worker under a new capitalist mindset. All avant-garde artists were influenced by the quickly changing technological society, which made people more aware of and dependent on each other. The turn of century brought several key developments: the internal combustion engine, the diesel engine, and the steam turbine; electricity and petroleum as new sources of power; the automobile, the tractor, the telephone, the typewriter, and the tape machine—all of these established a rapid city life. Modern bus systems appeared in major cities during the first decade of the twentieth century, joining streetcars and trolleys, soon to be followed by subway systems. Orville Wright's 1903 debut in the air led to the manufacture of warplanes, while the first modern battleship appeared in 1906. These developments, together with the new ideologies, such as Fascism and Marxism, scientific theories such as Einstein's, and Sigmund Freud's *Interpretation of Dreams*, were impressive influences on artists who sought to develop a new poetics and discourse that revealed their new reality.

The Latin American artists considered here are as talented and innovative as those of the Modernist era in Europe and the United States, but they have been overlooked by a Eurocentric world that did not choose to "discover" them. This is why Roberto Fernández Retamar calls attention to the Latin American and especially Caribbean voice of Caliban the savage of Shakespeare's play *The Tempest*, who is "tamed" by Próspero, the European, and taught his language, but who later transforms that language to his own purposes. Latin American Vanguardistas are not imitators and they did not seek to completely destroy the past as other international avant-garde poets suggested; instead, they transformed their art from "hispanophone" to the evocation of specific Latin American identities. They sought to reveal their respective cosmopolitan identities, the anguish of their societies and their artistic consciousness. With their creations, they sought the exploration of continuity and change in the new scientific era, that is, they sought the formulation of a new discourse. Arqueles Vela, Pablo Palacio, Martín Adán, and Roberto Arlt are certainly not the only innovators or precursors to the Latin American boom novelists. Argentinian Jorge Luis Borges has long been cited as a precursor to boom fiction (although he never wrote a novel), and more recently Chilean María Luisa Bombal (her two novels and short stories were published in the 1930s and early 40s) has been hailed as another significant influence (Agosín

28). This study has attempted to show that the creative work of Vanguardia novelists, in their specific sociohistoric situations, laid the groundwork for the narrative production that followed. It also demonstrates that Latin American writers of this era were as revolutionary in their ideas as European and U.S. writers of the same era, while also seeking to express their *American* (continental) experience. The novels cited herein provide a foundation for rereading other novels of this period, often deemed only fragments or experiments by critics. With the close of the twentieth century, there is a need to examine why critics and novelists cite the boom as the first flowering of a Latin American new novel. We can repair that mistake by reevaluating early twentieth century Latin American novels, and making comparisons of these with works by American and European novelists and poets of the similar Modernist period.

Works Cited

Adán, Martín. *La casa de cartón*. Lima: Editorial Juan Mejía Baca, 1971.

Adán, Martín. *The Cardboard House*. Trans. Katherine Silver. Saint Paul: Graywolf P, 1990.

Agosín, Marjorie. "María Luisa Bombal: Biography of a Story-telling Woman." *Knives and Angels: Women Writers in Latin America*. Ed. Susan Basnett. London: Zed Books, 1990. 26–35.

Aguilar Mora, Jorge. *Martín Adán: El más hermoso crepúsculo del mundo*. Mexico: Fondo de Cultura Económica, 1992.

Anderson Imbert, Enrique. *Historia de la literatura hispanoamericana II*. Mexico: Fondo de cultura Económica, 1966.

Arlt, Roberto. *Los siete locos*. 6th ed. Buenos Aires: Editorial Losada, 1985.

Bakhtin, Mikhail. *The Dialogic Imagination: Four Essays*. Trans. Caryll Emerson and Michael Holquist. Ed. Michael Holquist. Austin: U of Texas P, 1981.

Begley, Adam. "Harold Bloom: Colossus among Critics." *The New York Times Magazine* (25 September 1994): 32–35.

Carrión, Benjamín. "La literatura más atrevida que se ha hecho en el Ecuador." *Recopilación de textos sobre Pablo Palacio*. Ed. Reinaldo Castilla. Habana: Casa de la Américas (1987): 29–46.

Donoso, José. *Historia personal del "boom."* Barcelona: Seix Barral, 1983.

Fernández, María del Carmen. *El realismo abierto de Pablo Palacio: En la encrucijada de los 30*. Quito: Ediciones Libri Mundi, 1991.

Fernández Retamar, Roberto. "Apéndice o Post-data al primer Calibán." *Plural* 245 (February 1992): 48–56.

Franco, Jean. *An Introduction to Spanish-American Literature*. New York: Cambridge UP, 1969.

Fuentes, Carlos. *La nueva novela hispanoamericana*. 1969. Mexico: Joaquín Mortíz, 1980.

Haraway, Donna. *Simians, Cyborgs, and Women: The Reinvention of Nature*. New York: Routledge, 1991.

Hutcheon, Linda. *Irony's Edge: The Theory and Politics of Irony*. New York: Routledge, 1994.

Jitrik, Noé. "Destruction and Forms in Fiction." *Latin America in Its Literature*. Ed. Ivan A. Schulman. New York: Holmes & Meier, 1980. 155–80.

Joyce, James. *Ulysses*. Ed. Hans Walter Gabler, et al. New York: Random House, 1986.

Joyce, James. *Portrait of the Artist as a Young Man*. New York: Penguin, 1981.

Kernan, Alvin. *The Death of Literature*. New Haven: Yale UP, 1990.

Kinsella, John. "Realism, Surrealism, and La casa de cartón." *Before the Boom: Four Essays on Latin American Literature*. Liverpool: Centre for Latin American Studies of the U of Liverpool, 1981. 31–39.

Lindstrom, Naomi. *Twentieth Century Spanish-American Fiction*. Austin: U of Texas P, 1994.

Lodge, David. *After Bakhtin: Essays on Fiction and Criticism*. London: Routledge, 1990.

Lyotard, Jean-François. "The Postmodern Condition: A Report on Knowledge." *A Postmodern Reader*. Trans. Geoff Bennington and Brian Massumi. Albany: State U of New York P, 1993. 71–90.

Minh-ha, Trinh T. *Woman, Native, Other: Writing Postcoloniality and Feminism*. Bloomington: Indiana UP, 1989.

Nagel, Susan. *The Influence of the Novels of Jean Giraudoux on the Hispanic Vanguard Novels of the 1920s–1930s*. London: Bucknell UP, 1991.

Palacio, Pablo. *Un hombre muerto a puntapies y Débora*. Santiago de Chile: Editorial Universitaria, 1971.

Piglia, Ricardo. *Artificial Respiration*. Trans. David Balderston. Durham: Duke UP, 1994.

Picon Garfield, Evelyn, and Ivan A. Schulman. "La estética estraVASANTE de la InNegAusencia o la modernidad de Arqueles Vela." *Nueva revista de filología hispánica* 29.1 (1980): 204–12.

Shattuck, Roger. *The Banquet Years: The Origins of the Avant-Garde in France*. 1955. New York: Vintage Books, 1968.

Sommer, Doris. *Foundational Fictions: The National Romances of Latin America*. Berkeley: U of California P, 1991.

Spivak, Gayatri Chakravorty. "Three Women's Texts and a Critique of Imperialism." *'Race,' Writing, and Difference*. Chicago: The U of Chicago P, 1985. 262–80.

Stavans, Ilán. "Detectives en Latinoamérica." *Quimera* 73 (1988): 24–27.

Unruh, Vicky. *Latin American Vanguards: The Art of Contentious Encounters*. Berkeley: U of California P, 1994.

Vela, Arqueles. *El café de nadie*. Xalapa: Ediciones de Horizonte, 1926.

Waugh, Patricia. *Metafiction: The Theory and Practice of Self-Conscious Fiction*. London: Methuen, 1984.

Comparative Latin American Studies: Literary and Cultural Theory

Román de la Campa

Latin American studies today comprise an array of discourses barely recognizable from the perspective of traditional frameworks. The same could be said for other areas study, but perhaps not to the same degree. In terms of Latin American literary analysis, as practiced in the United States and a few significant pockets of higher learning in Latin America, the field constitutes a site of production in constant revision, less moved by literature itself than by the unsuspected link between conceptual and marketing impulses. This growing nexus —often thought to constitute the basis from which cultural studies evolved in the United States—has also been a driving force within Latin American literary studies in the past two decades, a discipline bound to continuous redefinition as precondition for sustaining its academic status.

One should note that this period of time also coincides with the expansion of poststructural theory, in its many guises and applications, a thoroughly acknowledged body of work that kindled the extraordinary reach and ambition of contemporary humanistic endeavors. But less attention is paid to the specific ways in which concurrent marketing pressures have changed the place of humanist intellectuals in research universities, and have perhaps even influenced theory itself. One could cite the proliferation of critical anthologies devoted to postmodern, postcolonial and subaltern Latin American studies as a primary symptom of this new market. Nearly all of them are published in English, with a few exceptions, such as *Cultura y tercer mundo*, edited by Beatriz González Stephan, which provides an important register in Spanish as well.

To a considerable degree, most influential strands of contemporary Latin American literary and cultural studies still converge around the question of postmodernity. Even the postcolonial turn ultimately finds definition in response to it, no doubt due to the extraordinary influence of Borges and the new Latin American novel ("boom") in the early mapping of postmodernism as a global enterprise. But after a few decades, the postmodern turned into a fertile matrix of theoretical and applied work that has been defined in many different and disparate ways. Boom, post-boom, neo-Baroque, magic realism, *testimonio*, feminist writing, mourning theory, and various other discourses have claimed Latin American postmodernity at some point or another, each doing so by deploying their own combinations of epistemic indeterminacy, unremitting de-signification and ludic textuality, a nimble archive of theoretical metaphors especially able to adjust to current ebbs and flows in the new market of theoretical production. After 1989, the stage of production changed once again, following the near absolute demise of left-wing state projects and the subsequent onset of neoliberal order throughout the continent. Since that time, Latin American postmodern literary studies, originally armed with the ambitious arsenal of semiosis, deconstruction and meta-narrative critiques that Roland Barthes, Paul de Man and Michel Foucault had theorized far beyond the realm of literature, suddenly found itself caught in a discursive vacuum it had never quite imagined.

The postcolonial turn, with its own set of editorial offshoots and by-products, offers a most specific example of academic realignment following the neoliberal moment just described. (The original debates on the postcolonial topic published in *Latin American Research Review* [Mignolo, 1993], remains highly informative. See also my discussion of the problems and possibilities of postcolonial studies in my essay "Latinoamérica y sus nuevos cartógrafos: Discurso poscolonial, diásporas intelectuales y miradas fronterizas.") Postcolonialism (within Latin American studies) began as a radical questioning of the postmodern apparatus constructed around a few boom novelists—generally all male—from a predictable set of nations whose indigenous past was either minimally regarded or totally repressed. A postcolonial understanding of Latin America required much more attention to coloniality as a logic that lingered past the onset of modernist aesthetics and developmental models designed by social sciences. But the postcolonial has since subdivided in various ways around the topic of subalternity. One strand, closer to social science than literature, has attempted to place coloniality as the center of Latin American studies, with a special emphasis on race and ethnicity largely drawn from Andean and other Amerindian cultures. Another strand, closer to deconstruction, looks upon modern Latin America through the theoretical lens of "negative alterity," a critique imbued by notions of "impossibility" and "ungovernability" which are not meant to articulate new social or political programs but rather to capture the course of coloniality as a persistent, long-lasting logic of discourse production. This approach often includes literary sources, but more as negative model than privileged discourse. Moreover, it understands that writing, particularly in Latin America, no longer sustains neat generic distinctions.

The two strands share a point of convergence in their unconditional critique of the Latin American modern paradigm, even though they also contain different presuppositions. One leads to colonial history, the other to deconstruction proper; both move away from the exemplarity of literature. Together they provide a window into the inner workings of theory as much, if not more, than into any aspect of Latin America, particularly during the past decade or so. We know there is theory in every text, but perhaps we should also pay attention to the storylines, drama, and lyrical force attendant to theory itself. One of these narratives, perhaps the most telling, pertains to *testimonio*. The genre's early dawn takes place in the 1960s, with texts such as *Autobiography of a Runaway Slave* by Miguel Barnet, and then steadily rises throughout the 1970s and 1980, reaching worldwide attention after the publication of *I, Rigoberta Menchú* in 1984. Since then, a series of theoretical paradigms have overshadowed it. Its texts were first read as a sign of promise, not within the canon, but rather as an articulation of socialist literary alternatives to modern state formation. Now, after the Cold War and under the negative alterity paradigm, the same texts stand as intricate registers of theoretical impossibility, both in literature as well as in Latin American state formation.

Testimonio may have promised a realist alternative to the boom by Latin Americanist critics in the American academy, but the enthusiasm for such a reading waned considerably after the demise of the Central American revolution. A surprising irony comes about at that moment, as *testimonio* criticism turned to deconstructive theory, the very theoretical source that had nurtured boom criticism. The turn came, in part, by way of the subaltern studies approach of Ranajit Guha, which had already linked poststructuralism to a critique of British colonial history. Working from the suppositions of John Beverley, a noted example, Latin American *testimonio* moved toward Guha's construct, at times buttressed by the deconstructive insights of Alberto Moreiras, at times by the focus on Andean indigenous gnosis of Walter Mignolo. Roughly speaking, these divergent notions of subalternity came to be understood as a post-humanist corpus capable of opening a new left-wing stance on postmodernity through a complex fusion of critical and theoretical strategies. The first full iteration of this approach came in *Literature and Politics in the Central American Revolution*, co-written with Marc Zimmerman. Needless to say, the scholarship on *testimonio* is both vast and varied. I am here placing a special focus on the ongoing evolution of the subaltern perspective since the early 1990s, which later evolved into a subaltern critique of the state, within which there are many different, at times even opposing, perspectives often conflated as one. Among its basic tenets, the following stand out: a) deconstruction in the 1990s needed to move beyond literature proper to focus on the pervasive colonial relationship underlying modern Latin American state formation and modernist aesthetics; b) these two elements collude in the formation of a now defunct modern new world Creole utopia; c) subalternity offers the only mode of discursive resistance in the face of that tradition or writing.

This story, once again, emerged at a moment of exhaustion for Latin American revolutionary movements, a tradition fully committed to the early political ramifications of *testimonio* literature, including jingoistic representations. The subaltern reading consequently demands a series of valuations in the space of postmodern theory and Latin American studies. Politically speaking, the role for *testimonio* as third world literature vanished, a bitter insight that brought about a re-reading of all Latin American literature as the failure of the state and its intellectual classes. Theoretically speaking, Latin Americanism regrouped through negative alterity, an anti-aesthetic of impossibility applicable to all Latin American state projects, regardless of whether they emerged through coups, electoral regimes, or revolutions. (An important register in this context would be "On Zapatismo: Reflections of the Folkloric and the Impossible in a Subaltern Insurrection," by José Rabassa.)

The deeper literary issues pertaining to subaltern *testimonio* bear closer attention, given that this approach negates and reaffirms the importance of literature at the same time. Subaltern studies deconstructs official literature, particularly the boom period, but by extension the entire modern tradition, thereby consigning *testimonio* to a "post-literary" form. The once frequent debates on the literary nature of the genre gave way to a reflection on its indigenous historicity, understood as colonial practices, flows and traces forgotten or ignored by the state and its modernist aesthetics, which included the self-referential postmodernity of the boom. A counter-position has been articulated by Roberto González Echevarría, who argues that *testimonio* amounts to a step backward in comparison to the boom as far as Latin American literary development is concerned. Indeed, he sees its return to a realist domain as closer to earlier literary moments, such as the *novela de la tierra* of the 1940s, thus finding *testimonio* potentially more naïve (221). It also seems pertinent to note that the subalternist position shifts the weight of Latin American textuality from a literary to a culturalist matrix, say from Gabriel García Márquez to Rigoberta Menchú, or from Juan Rulfo to Gloria Anzaldúa. As such, its immediate frame also shifts somewhat from a Latin American context to the curricular debates in the United States, a nation-state whose modernity is hardly in question, even if it must also continuously grapple with the historical negation of its own indigenous history and the growing presence of cultural, racial and ethnic minorities.

It should surprise no one to find that scholars in Latin America grasp postmodernity, *testimonio* and subalternity in radically different ways, not to mention the fate of the state and its literature, even if these critical frameworks find just as much pertinence there as here in the United States. One major reason may be that postmodernity in Latin America has not been mainly articulated by literary scholars, nor has multiculturalism been tailored by a global marketing interest caught in an American binary of ethnic assimilation and minority contestation. This is not to say that concepts such as *"mestizaje"* and "transculturation" have not lent themselves to racialist myths promulgated by privileged Creoles in Latin America, but rather to suggest that a simultaneous critique of the "melting pot" and the "construction of whiteness" found in the United States seldom comes into play as we deconstruct the links between modern aesthetics and state formation in Latin America. European and North American modernities, due to the relative strength of their institutions, seem more capable of resisting theoretical shortcuts that link literary studies and state formation. (For a broader exploration of this problematic link, see my essay "Split States and Global Imaginaries.")

A comparative critique of racial imaginaries across the Americas remains relatively absent from subaltern perspectives, even though the latter rely on principles of racial difference, and in spite of the long tradition of African-American and U.S. Latino scholarship on these subjects. For instance, the recent issue of *Nepantla* (v. 4, issue 2, 2003), dedicated to the work of Cornel West, begins an important dialogue. The issue includes a number of essays on the subject, among them, Eduardo Mendieta's "What Can Latinas/os Learn From Cornel West?" and my "On New American Subjects." On the other hand, one should recognize that subaltern theory does actively engage, in some respects, U.S. Latino cultural forms—literature, film, music, and gender critique—with their attendant ethnic and diasporic thematics. The Latino constellation, a century-old migratory flow of multitudes towards the United States, has reached extraordinary dimensions during the past two decades. It therefore embodies a profound indictment of the modern Latin American state, a process of dispersion that provides ample material for the subaltern studies critique. But Latino presence raises many questions for American (U.S.) nation-state identity as well, an aspect often neglected by subaltern Latin Americanists. Comparative theory should therefore question these positions. It certainly cannot advance with simple here vs. there, autochthonous vs. foreign binaries, or state vs. anti-state proclivities. Difference will not be served without recognizing differing sites of production, consumption and legitimation that simultaneously claim Latin America.

It is not difficult to find imaginative books on Latin American postmodernity based on Argentinean or Cuban literature, for example, or new postcolonial critiques based on Bolivian or Ecuadorian cultural traditions, but few map Latin America transnationally with sufficient rigor to account for different modern traditions within each area. The stakes have risen for Latin Americanist scholarship, yet one-nation, or one-region specialists, by and large, continue to drive production—even in feminist research, a paradigm that by definition cuts across all others. If there is a common theme in many of the new approaches discussed thus far, perhaps it can be found in their multifarious—at times perhaps even capricious—attempts to accommodate deconstructive theory, which turned into an anchor of sorts for subaltern critiques after the socialist debacle. Obviously, the sense of closure that came upon utopian thinking after 1989 had its impact, but the pre-eminence of poststructural theory in the humanities, established prior to 1989—particularly in literary studies—also required important readjustments.

Neoliberal logic and subaltern insights now seem to converge, unwittingly, in their dismissal of modern Latin America. After all, global capital has come to look upon the nation-state structure as an obstacle, and its cultural imperative replaces the formative role of literature with a radical dimension of audiovisual performance and wired subjectivity. As stated earlier, the subaltern critique of literature may have been aimed less at literature than at widening the reach of deconstructive insights, initially confined to postmodernism in its strict artistic sense. Later it became more ambitious in its approach to cultural studies. One wonders, however, how negative alterity, or colonial historicity, will map the future of the masses as global capital unleashes its own process of de-centering at a time devoid of national emancipation narratives. Will the neoliberal utopia converge or silently collude with a subaltern critique content to elaborate the exhaustion of, if not an end to, the possibilities of the modern nation-state? Will the call for a postnational theory of Latin America respond to subjects who harbor hopes for national reconstruction?

The storyline I have drawn thus far, limited no doubt by its exclusions and oversights, as all stories tend to be, envisions a new Latin Americanism whose ways of mapping the area's literary and cultural referents must increasingly respond to transnational dimensions. The latter have been deeply felt in North American academia (the U.S. and Canada, although in different ways) not only through *testimonio* and the Latino diaspora, but also by the contestations of feminist approaches to the field. In Latin America, the unraveling or splitting of modern states has become the norm rather than the exception. Many different types of crisis have enveloped the area—Chiapas, Colombia, and Argentina, for example—not to speak of what it means for more than ten Latin American nations to have permanent communities of considerable size residing in the United States, whose remittances to their countries of origin constitute a leading line item in their former nations' respective economies. In short, Latin American texts, literary and otherwise, evidence an array of postnational entanglements that demand our critical attention and that call for more thorough ways of reading, theorizing and representing the region as an object of study.

These concerns have yet to fully capture the attention of many literary and cultural specialists. *The Real Thing*, a widely quoted anthology of essays substantially dedicated to *testimonio*, provides a telling example. A significant number of its entries offer a complex understanding of Latin American literary postmodernity, while others comprise an imaginative register of the practice of Latin Americanism in curricular debates within the United States. One should note, however, that few venture into the comparative terrain of cultural differences within Latin America, or how such specific knowledge would affect subaltern theoretical models largely framed in the United States, rather than the other way around. Indeed, the notion of "posthumanist" literature, together with the subaltern remapping it encompasses, seems to beg for a specific awareness of how it applies to the widely different cultures that pertain to this object of study. Without that level of specificity and without the onus of a comparative optic, Latin America easily folds into a synchronized global domain in which negative alterity becomes readily applicable to all nations and regions from a distance, perhaps signaling an unwitting return of the universalizing principle traditionally associated with modern aesthetics.

In their aforementioned book on the literary politics of the Central American revolutionary movements during the 1980s, Beverley and Zimmerman observed that Rubén Darío, a turn-of-the-nineteenth-century poet of refined, if not aristocratic tastes, took on a completely new meaning for the peasants involved in the Nicaraguan insurgency. Following the logic of these uncertain allegorical destinies, one might be therefore tempted to question any attempt to consign the symbolic value of writers like Gabriel García Márquez to the dustbin of modern, failed, Creole, Latin American discourses. Indeed, one could surmise that such a wide-sweeping brush stroke inadvertently engenders its own subaltern object—the existing masses of *mestizos* and Creoles in Latin America, who continue to identify themselves as such. Indeed, such identification, while subject to critique, communicates a cultural and political reality as well as an understanding of literature. These effects—as with Darío's poetry, or Borges's aesthetics, may be subject to change, but they continually resurface as unexpected combinations and contradictions.

To declare an end to the symbolic order, as with calls for an end of ideology or history, underscores a symptom of global capital filled with symbolism. If modernity equated state formation with national literature, postmodernity (along with its postcolonial shadow) equates the post-national with post-literature, perhaps privileging the globalizing tendencies of those few states that are able to absorb, and often promote, epistemic crises from a position of relative stability seldom found in regions like Latin America. That difference may be one way to understand the lingering, and perhaps untheorized, distinctions between First and Third World—different modernities caught up in myriad categories such as globalization, post-coloniality, postmodernity, maquiladora states, etc, that compete with each other in the markets of symbolic capital.

An interesting, albeit unsuspected, example of post-national literary anxiety, revealed itself with Harold Bloom's call for a new "Western" literary canon, a global model in which English and the American institutional apparatus of research universities function as the only exchange currency capable of reconstituting literary values. Bloom's speaks of preserving the Western canon from the onslaught of cultural studies, but beneath that concern lies the deeper question of the links between literature and the nation-state. In this case it materializes not as a critique but rather as nostalgia for the primacy of aesthetics within English and the United States. For that reason, his widely acknowledged proclamation for a new canon suggests the need for further thinking into the role of literature and criticism during global re-ordering, all the more so for languages other than English and states with less stability.

Calls for a new literary order, itself a symptom worthy of study, would therefore require many clarifications and distinctions. One major example corresponds to the literature of the Argentine master Jorge Luis Borges, for many a model of the post-symbolic imaginary. His short stories first conveyed the deepest challenge to literary conventions held by early twentieth-century traditions accustomed to surrendering individual texts to the tedium of literary history. Towards the end of the twentieth century his oeuvre took on a new symbolic meaning, as Bloom's inclusion of Borges in his new Western canon suggests. Indeed, Borges became a primary point of reference for late modern official aesthetics, a restoration of sorts within literary values that aims to reach beyond Western to perhaps global appreciation. The universally recognized mastery of Borges may thus lie precisely in having taken literature to an aesthetic plane that knows, or values, only how to probe its own making, a state of immanence eminently capable of renewing its own metaphysics. (Alberto Moreiras makes an impassioned argument for the centrality of Borges and post-symbolic theory in "Pastiche, Identity and Allegory of Allegory.")

It therefore seems pertinent to ask what kind of mapping evolves from an undifferentiated critique of modern meta-narratives inspired by negative alternity. Is it only a symptom of disillusionment that overcame a segment of Latin Americanist critics—many of whom lived and worked in the United States—after the demise of revolutionary projects in Latin America, or has it become a constitutive element of deconstructive work as a whole? One could also ask if the changing relationship between nation, literature and culture across the Americas might profit from a more differential body of theory. As I understand it, these questions obviously don't have singular answers, but they correspond to a more comparative framework than the one currently prevailing in Latin American literary and cultural studies. In order to illustrate this point and develop it a bit further, it might be useful to explore a different reading of *testimonio*, in this case derived from a Latin American site of theoretical and literary production. I will therefore turn to the perspective offered by Nelly Richard, formulated within the context of the Chilean post-dictatorship cultural scene, and especially in her article: "Bordes, diseminación, postmodernismo: Una metáfora latinoamericana de fin de siglo."

Richard has argued that privileging *testimonio* as a model of postmodern literature relegates Latin American texts to a use-value imposed by metropolitan centers (read United States) of academic power. The critique invokes a bit of the old center-periphery debate, but her primary concern lies elsewhere. She aims to unveil the hierarchy of values within postmodernism, particularly the obvious pull of institutional frameworks whose extraordinary influence cannot help but totalize knowledge production, even while they claim a theoretical commitment to de-centering. Richard has developed an approach that deploys deconstruction within Chilean culture, while questioning its use in the United States, almost suggesting that the latter's institutional power can't help but overwhelm, if not vitiate, that body of theory. Her elaboration of these premises begins in 1980s with *La estratificación de los márgenes*, followed by *La insubordinación de los signos*, and the more recent *Residuos y metáforas*. Together they encompass feminism, literature, and visual arts—indeed a significant slice of the Chilean post-dictatorship national imaginary. Yet, the grounds of Richard's mapping of *testimonio* as metropolitan use-value seems to overlook the earlier codification of Latin American postmodernism based on the boom novel. This was, and continues to be in many respects, a much more influential and perhaps even more hegemonic paradigm; indeed, it could be argued that the subaltern proposal, at least in its initial stages, was nothing but a direct response within literature.

One can't deny that the cultural wars in the American academy revolved, to a considerable degree, around Rigoberta Menchú's *testimonio*, but the post-NAFTA indigenous rebellions in Latin America, beginning with Chiapas in 1994, also find pertinence in the symbolic order conjured by that particular text. In that sense, there is another side of the *testimonio* story that pertains to Latin America in the deepest sense, even if Richard's otherwise acute critique leaves it unmentioned. By now, we have all grown accustomed to using Benedict Anderson's metaphor of imagined communities to explain nationalism in general, but I believe it can be further specified in terms of the relationship between intellectuals and their objects of study, a *patria chica* of sorts. In that sense, it would be easy to argue that scholars in Latin America are necessarily bound to imagine Latin America from the pull of their respective national communities, but what about the "national" among Latin Americanists in the United States? Diasporic Latin Americans may naturally continue to work the field from their own national frameworks, but working in the United States, regardless of national origin, also leads to a predictable set of interests, such as the conception of the field as a community of discourses able to absorb difference through theoretical paradigms. As Richard suggests, all contexts have their internal forms, needs and perhaps even use values, even if her own understanding of the United States as a "metropolitan" center excludes a greater awareness of the pulls that effectuate comparative Latin Americanism.

Richard's work does not seem particularly concerned with Latin American indigenous texts and cultures, nor with the wide-ranging impact of Latin American diasporas in the United States, yet I would argue that her Chilean-based critique has broad implications for Latin American and perhaps even American studies. That relevance comes from the specific deployment of "metropolitan" theory—deconstruction and negative alterity—with a distinctly local Latin American perspective. Her work aims to unhinge the metaphors that sustained Chilean national culture from their discursive foundations, be they military, economic, political, or, most importantly, academic, given the close relationship between disciplinary discourses and the pursuit of epistemic power. (See her "Signos culturales y mediaciones académicas.") All of this gains force due to its capacity to theorize the local in imaginative ways, perhaps even more so because Richard's discourse does not issue directly from academia, but rather from a cosmopolitan cluster of scholars, writers, visual and performative artists to which she belongs. Their work, in that sense, suggests a different understanding of cultural studies, something closer to cultural critique, which involves theory but remains close to artistic forms, rather than reducing art to just theory, or submitting it to a cultural studies domain indistinguishable from the logic of mass culture.

Richard's refusal to harbor a nostalgic look for the Allende period, or any earlier moment of Chile's national past, constitutes another important aspect of her critique, even though its focal point concerns the Pinochet regime and, most particularly, its aftermath. Her approach to national deconstruction specifically comes into play in her reading of *El padre mío*, by the Chilean novelist Diamela Eltit. Richard reads this text as a counterexample to the model of subaltern *testimonio* inspired by Rigoberta Menchú's life story. Eltit's protagonist is a deranged, apparently incomprehensible homeless man, whose life story hardly seems to inspire anything but nausea and disgust. But his insanity somehow provides a very clear picture of national unraveling. His speech acts are filled with proper political names, key historical periods, and well-known public figures, but they are all mingled, precisely because his aphasia prevents him from placing them in their "proper" order. He cannot speak about any topic differently, no matter how trivial the circumstance. The decomposition of Chilean history and grammar thus comes before our eyes in the words of this loathsome paternal figure, a most disturbing, yet articulate critique, one eventually offering a different understanding of subalternity not bound to specific subjects or specific claims to redress but, rather, to the differential possibilities of theoretical discourse itself.

The contrast with the traditional subaltern hero could not be clearer, but Eltit also seeks distinctions in terms of form. The customary *testimonio* preface, in which the role of recorder, transcriber, and compiler of the Other's story is revealed, gets a complicated, if not disturbing treatment in *El padre mío*, for Eltit declares a different object-subject relationship between herself as editor and her informant, with whom she eventually loses contact. She claims not to understand him or even know how to find him again. Her carefully drawn distance from her informer even suggests the possibility of a total work of fiction, or a way to replace anthropological conceits with those of literary theory. Indeed, her introduction, a highly stylized theoretical piece prefacing *El padre mío*'s "own discourse," tips its hat a bit when it explains that the only way of construing her protagonist's story as an image of contemporary Chile would be if it were seen as a negative. Of course, flirting with the possibility of total fiction may actually provide the ultimate deconstruction of *testimonio*'s claim to realist representation, particularly if one understands it as a canonical expression of Latin America in the United States, which, as I have argued, may be subject to further debate. Moreover, it should be said that Eltit's counter-*testimonio*, transgressive though it seems, could also be read as a return to a symbolic form of estrangement well established in contemporary literary history by such Latin American boom novelists as Severo Sarduy, whose body of work explored the limits of linguistic saturation and national de-signification since the 1970s, particularly in the dramatic context of dictatorship regimes. This Latin American context, however, does not factor in Richard's largely Chilean-based method of deconstruction.

Eltit's text may pose an even more important question: How does the Latin American scholar juggle such contrastive readings of *testimonio* as the two developed in this essay, one anchored in the U.S. academy, the other in Chilean cultural praxis, yet both, in their own way, imbued by the theoretical archive of negative alterity? It would be hard to find more distinct readings of postmodernity, subalternity, and the possibilities of literature at this moment of uncertainty for Latin American nation-states. How does the Latin American scholar—here, there, everywhere—approach the implicit disconnect between these and other valuable projects? One might expect the market to provide direction on this matter, given the growing number of theoretical monographs, critical anthologies and symposia on Latin Americanism during the past decade. Yet these differences generally coexist without clear definition or acknowledgement of disparity. Instead of discernment, the reader discovers the imperative of continuous production and promotion behind each group or paradigm, an energy mainly driven to sustain the market of symbolic capital with analogous products.

As I understand it, Latin American literary and cultural studies would be well-served by conceiving comparative frameworks able to approach the differential application of literary studies, postmodernity, feminism and cultural studies, as well as the growing disconnect between the humanities and social sciences. The question of difference seems paramount here. Latin American studies, particularly after the period of the Cold War that engendered area studies, requires a mapping of multiple contradictory textual and cultural practices difficult to encompass from national or regional paradigms. That realization, however, requires new thinking about national contexts, not their outright dismissal, a somewhat predictable approach for Latin American criticism within transnational centers of epistemic value. Postmodernity and post-coloniality in Latin America may thus require a deeper understanding of the relationship between literatures and cultures in the twenty-first century, without conflating the two, or dissolving their differences through colonial logic or theoretical immanence, a problematic that will not likely release scholars from the need to simultaneously study both *I, Rigoberta Menchú* and *El padre mío* in their contradictory richness.

Note: A brief discussion of the issues and authors discussed in this essay appears in my "Deconstruction, Cultural Studies and Global Capitalism." Here I attempt a more elaborate approach towards a comparative critique of Latin American literary and cultural studies.

Works Cited

Barnet, Miguel. Esteban Montejo: *Autobiography of a Runaway Slave*. New York: Random House, 1973.

Beverley, John, and Marc Zimmerman. *Literature and Politics in the Central American Revolution*. Austin: U of Texas P, 1990.

Bloom, Harold. *The Western Canon: The Books and School of the Ages*. New York: Harcourt Brace, 1994.

de la Campa, Román. "Deconstruction, Cultural Studies and Global Capitalism: Implications for Latin America." *Critical Latin American and Latino Studies*, Minneapolis: U of Minnesota P, 2003: 154–71.

de la Campa, Román. "Latin, Latino, American: Split States and Global Imaginaries." *Comparative Literature* 53.4 (2001): 373–88.

de la Campa, Román. "Latinoamérica y sus nuevos cartógrafos: Discurso poscolonial, diásporas intelectuales y miradas fronterizas." *Revista Iberoamericana* 176–77 (1996): 697–719.

de la Campa, Román. "On New American Subjects and Intellectual Models." *Nepantla*, 4.2 (2003): 235–45.

Eltit, Damiela. *El padre mío*. Santiago, Chile: Francisco Zegers, 1989.

González Echevarría, Roberto. *Myth and Archive*. Cambridge: Cambridge UP, 1990.

González Stephan, Beatriz, ed. *Cultura y tercer mundo*. 2 vols. Caracas: Nueva Sociedad, 1996.

Gugelberger, Georg M., ed. *The Real Thing: Testimonial Discourse and Latin America*. Durham: Duke UP, 1996.

Menchú, Rigoberta. *I, Rigoberta Menchú: An Indian Woman in Guatemala*. Ed. Elisabeth Burgos Debray. Trans. Ann Wright. London: Verso, 1984.

Mignolo, Walter. "Colonial and Postcolonial Discourse: Cultural Critique or Academic Colonialism?" *Latin American Research Review* 28.3 (1993): 1–30.

Moreiras, Alberto. "Pastiche, Identity and Allegory of Allegory." *Latin American Identity and the Constructions of Difference*. Ed. Amaryll Chanady. Minneapolis: U of Minnesota P, 1994. 118–40.

Rabassa, José. "On Zapatismo: Reflections of the Folkloric and the Impossible Subaltern Insurrection." *The Politics of Culture in the Shadows of Capital*. Ed. Lisa Lowe and David Lloyd. Durham: Duke UP, 1997. 399–432.

Richard, Nelly. "Bordes, diseminación, postmodernismo: Una metáfora latinoamericana de fin de siglo." *Las culturas de fin de siglo en América Latina*. Ed. Josefina Ludmer. Buenos Aires: Beatriz Viterbo, 1994. 240–53.

Richard, Nelly. *La estratificación de los márgenes*. Santiago: Francisco Zegers, 1989.

Richard, Nelly. *La insubordinación de los signos: Cambio político, transformaciones culturales y poéticas de la crisis*. Santiago: Cuarto Propio, 1994.

Richard, Nelly. *Residuos y metáforas (Ensayos de crítica cultural sobre el Chile de la transición)*. Santiago: Cuarto Propio, 1998.

Richard, Nelly. "Signos culturales y mediaciones académicas." *Cultura y tercer mundo*. Ed. Beatriz González Stephan. Caracas: Editorial *Nueva Sociedad*, 1996. 1–22.

Spanish American and Brazilian Literature in an Inter-American Perspective: The Comparative Approach

Earl E. Fitz

At the dawn of the twenty-first century, the place of Latin American literature within the discipline of comparative literature is both exciting and perplexing. On the one hand (as we all know), Latin American literature has a great deal to offer comparative literature; on the other hand, as statistics compiled recently by Sophia A. McClennen clearly show, Latin American literature is egregiously underrepresented in comparative literature journals worldwide (see McClennen in this volume). Why is this so, especially since, as Roberto González Echevarría and others have argued, Latin American literature has the potential to reinvigorate and even revolutionize the study of comparative literature (see González Echevarría in this volume; see also Pratt 63; Greene, "Generation" 152–53)? In answering this question, two issues must, I believe, be considered: first, there still is, I fear, a lingering bias, in some quarters, against the literary value of literature written in Spanish and Portuguese, though I also believe that this is fast waning; second, there sometimes exists among us, the Latin Americanists, an imperfect understanding of how, vis-à-vis the expectations of its professional journals, comparative literature tends to define itself, both as a discipline and in terms of the number of languages typically made use of in a critical study.

Historically, comparative literature has defined itself as the study of literature from an international perspective. Methodologically, this has meant that true comparative studies have to involve texts written in more than one language, this principle having firmly established itself (even in an age of interdisciplinary studies) as a *sine qua non* of the discipline. Thus, a study examining, say, the poetry of Sor Juana Inés de la Cruz and that of Góngora would, by the editors of most comparative literature journals, not be judged to be sufficiently "comparative," in the current professional sense of the term, to be included in one of them. Even though writers from two different countries were involved, and even though the working methodology might well involve comparisons of similarities and differences, the editors would likely conclude that the authors under consideration are still working in the same language and that the essay therefore would be more appropriate for a journal dealing with issues germane to Hispanic literature. In my several years as an associate editor for *Comparative Literature Studies* (a journal that, I am delighted to say, has been notably receptive to Latin American literature), this was a rationale often employed in evaluating manuscripts, and, given the way comparative literature continues to define itself as a distinctive academic discipline, I think it is an appropriate editorial policy, especially in certain cases. In considering the future of comparative literature programs across the nation, one can see, for example, that there is a very distinct disciplinary value to requiring comparison of works written in different languages.

Related to this policy tangentially, the "crisis" facing comparative literature today (to invoke similar concerns voiced by René Wellek back in 1958), however, is that, as a discipline, it is in danger of allowing itself to elevate certain languages and literatures to canonical (and therefore privileged) status and, in so doing, relegate others to lesser, or "marginal," status. This creeping and increasingly sclerotic hierarchism (which, if allowed to stand, is tantamount to sounding the death knell for comparative literature; for a brief discussion of this problem, see "The Bernheimer Report" 42) constitutes the discipline's real danger, and it may fairly be said that Latin American literature, long derided as "inferior," "secondary," or "derivative" by many traditionalists, offers it a chance for revivification, for regaining its original sense of mission, of relevance, and of egalitarianism, the very qualities that have long made it such an admired and important form of literary study (see Tötösy de Zepetnek, ed., *Histories and Concepts of Comparative Literature*).

Our problem, as Latin Americanists, is how to react to this situation, how to shape our essays so that they are more suitable for publication in comparative journals. In saying this, however, I do not wish to give the impression that I in any way advocate that, as Latin Americanists, we should "pull our punches," that we should feel obliged to prostrate ourselves in the face of the editorial practices of journals that we believe have discriminated against us in the past. If we wish to gain access to even the most conservative journals of the discipline, we must learn to present our authors and texts not as unworthy interlopers begging for admission into the "elitist" citadel but as great artists and enduring works of art, worthy in every respect of comparison with any others and, indeed, of serving sometimes as the model, or standard, against which these other, perhaps better known works should themselves be measured. We must dispense with the outmoded and self-defeating notion that, as Latin Americanists, we are somehow second-class citizens of world literature, that there is "nothing new to invent, no new books to write," and that our fate is "always to repeat what had already been done better in Europe or the United States" (Monegal, *The Borzoi Anthology*, vol. II, xiii). We must begin to assert ourselves, to argue with conviction that, at the present time, we are the ones to change the norms and parameters of comparative literature in the twenty-first century. Indeed, as Roland Greene has written, comparative literature is a discipline long *defined* by change, by being a field "permanently under construction, and that . . . this is how the Auerbachs and Spitzers would have wanted it" ("Reticence" 297). Long accustomed to being on the outside looking in, Latin Americanists are now the straw that stirs the drink (as Reggie Jackson once described himself), the catalysts for disciplinary renovation and growth. We must feel free to insist, for example, in our classes and in our scholarly work that the significance of Hélène Cixous and her theoretical apparatus should be considered only after a thorough reading of Clarice Lispector, and not vice versa, and that our understanding of the Renaissance epic is not complete until we have carefully read Alonso de Ercilla y Zúñiga's *La araucana* and worked it into discussions of the better known exemplars of this venerable form. We must no longer be timid about arguing that Brazilian concretist poetry is as energetic and sophisticated as can be found anywhere in the world or that a new genre, which we might wish to term the "Inter-American Novel," is fast arising out of recent work by such contemporary Latin American masters as Carlos Fuentes (*La frontera de cristal*), Isabel Allende (*El plan infinito* and *Hija de la fortuna*), Silviano Santiago (*Stella Manhattan*), and Alberto Fuguet (*Las películas de mi vida*). In short, we, as advocates of Latin American literature, must drop our traditionally mendicant posture and (politely but firmly) demand recognition as a vital part of the larger processes of globalization, democratization, and decolonization that, as Mary Louise Pratt has noted, are "transforming the way literature and culture are conceived and studied in the academy" (Pratt 59). As we can see, then, there are many things we can do to increase our representation in comparative publications (and in ways that stress the originality and vitality of our authors and texts), but I would like to call attention to three in particular.

First, and perhaps most important of all, is that, as Latin Americanists, we should all learn Portuguese so that the richness and diversity of Brazilian literature is open and available to us. This, of course, is not easy to do for those of us who are working in full-time positions, nor can it be done quickly. Nevertheless, it is worth doing, for to do so immediately gives us that all important second language that comparative literature journals so often require. More importantly, it does so without this second language having to be either English, French, or German, the languages that some academic conservatives still mistakenly regard as somehow "defining" the field of comparative literature, a discipline better understood as an issue of methodology, of *how* we seek to study the world's many languages and literatures, rather than as a pantheon of certain texts written in certain languages. Comparative studies involving Spanish American and Brazilian literature are "naturals" in terms of their legitimacy and in terms of their utility to us, and, although still not common, they unquestionably represent exciting new research opportunities. And because we, as Latin Americanists, understand quite clearly that they are essential to the healthy growth and development of comparative literature as a discipline, we should regard it as our duty to integrate Brazilian and Spanish American literature into it and to do so from a perspective not of inferiority but of strength. For those scholars who work on the Caribbean, French, or Dutch might be a more useful second language than Portuguese, but, in most cases, knowledge of Portuguese and Brazilian literature enriches our potential as comparatists.

A relatively early model of this type of study is Samuel Putnam's pioneering 1948 effort, *Marvelous Journey: A Survey of Four Centuries of Brazilian Writing*, which undertakes a comparison of Brazilian literature with that of the United States and which, in so doing, makes possible a number of later studies engaged in the same sort of inter-American work (see, for example, Wasserman and Cohn). Working in a similar mode are Stephanie Merrim's *Logos and the Word: The Novel of Language and Linguistic Motivation in Grande Sertão: Veredas and Tres tristes tigres* (1983), and Judith Payne and Earl Fitz's *Ambiguity and Gender in the New Novel of Brazil and Spanish America: A Comparative Assessment* (1993). In these latter cases, the Spanish American and Brazilian traditions are not discussed separately, as if they existed in isolation from each other (this being the old paradigm that dates back as far as 1942 and Torres-Ríoseco's groundbreaking *The Epic of Latin American Literature*, a work which, although it does deal with Brazilian literature, does so in only one chapter, not making any effort to integrate it into the corpus of Spanish American literature), but woven together into a single, comparative argument.

In our book, Judith Payne and I sought to use the advent of Latin American literature's "new narrative" in the 1960s to examine not just how it manifested itself in the works of such Spanish American masters as Borges, Rulfo, García Márquez, and Fuentes but also how the defining concepts behind this "new narrative" related to the production of Brazilian narrative during this same period. Our basic argument, which was based on a careful comparative consideration of key narrative works from both Brazil and Spanish America, was that although the Brazilian narrative tradition was much less known outside of Brazil, and although the term "new narrative" rarely appeared in Brazilian scholarship relating to this question, the Brazilian novel was, until the late 1970s, considerably more radical, in terms of style, structuring, and thematics, than its better known Spanish American cousin. Specifically, we found that if one includes Brazil in the mix, a "new narrative" first appears in Latin America in Brazil in 1880/81, with the publication of Machado de Assis's revolutionary novel, *As Memórias Póstumas de Brás Cubas*, and that, in the course of its development in Brazil, this Brazilian "new narrative" would come to be characterized by two qualities, both of which differentiate it quite distinctly from the Spanish American "nueva narrativa": its continuous and deliberate cultivation of metafictive ambiguity (this being a function of its concern with language as a very basic and inescapable problem of both ontology and epistemology and not merely as a mechanism by which reality can be described or represented) and, especially after 1944 and the publication of Clarice Lispector's first novel, *Perto do Coração Selvagem*, its steady cultivation of women, both as writers (Lispector, for example, or Nélida Piñon) and as strong willed, sexually charged, and socially iconoclastic characters. In terms of Latin American literary history, then, we can see that the year 1944, which, of course, also marks the appearance of Borges's world renowned—but radically different—*Ficciones,* is a very decisive moment; although the "nova narrativa" in Brazil had begun some sixty years earlier (with Machado, whom González Echevarría judges to be "the premier nineteenth-century Latin American writer and one of the best of all time anywhere" [*The Oxford Book of Latin American Short Stories* 95]), Lispector's extraordinary novel has as much influence on the way narrative would be written afterwards in Brazil as the Borges *Ficciones* had on the future of Spanish American narrative (see Fitz 1997, 1998). Thus, in what amounts to a revised sense of the genre's historical development, we can see that not only does the "new narrative" really begin in Brazil with Machado de Assis, it begins even then (first as very singular characters, then as authors) to make space for the participation of women.

Another example of this new, contrastive type of Latin American scholarship, and one that applies the comparative approach to the case of women in modern Latin American literature, is *Entre Resistir e Identificar-se*, a collection of essays organized by Peggy Sharpe and published in 1997. Stemming from a conference held in March 1996 at the University of Illinois, these studies, including several by such prominent Brazilian authors as Lygia Fagundes Telles, Nélida Piñon, Helena Parente Cunha, and Lya Luft, examine the numerous contributions that Brazilian women writers are making within the larger contexts of Latin America and the world. A recurring issue in the conference papers and in the discussions that ensued was how the work of Brazil's women writers differs from that being done by Spanish American women, how it compares and contrasts to that tradition. Although some of the pieces tend to focus more on issues of Brazilian culture and history, the overall thrust of the "encontro/meeting" and of the collection was therefore to identify and define Brazil's very powerful tradition of women's writing and to bring it to the critical attention of larger audiences worldwide. Perhaps the greatest lesson learned from the conference was that comparative approaches to Latin American women's writing constitute a new and growing field that offers tremendous opportunities for those linguistically and culturally prepared to perform the close textual analysis that is required.

Finally, mention must also be made of the 1998 thematic issue, *O Brasil, a América Hispânica, e o Caribe: Abordagens Comparativas* of the journal *Revista Iberoamericana*, devoted to comparative approaches to the literatures of Brazil and Spanish America (see Costigan and Bernucci). This important volume, edited by Lúcia Helena Costigan and Leopoldo M. Bernucci, was divided into five sections: "Agendas, Ciclos e Tendências da Literatura e da Crítica" (Agendas, Cycles, and Tendencies of Literature and Criticism); "Das Relações Culturais e Literárias na América do Sul (Of Cultural and Literary Relations in South America); "O Brasil em Diálogo com o Caribe e o México (Brazil in Dialogue with the Caribbean and Mexico); "O 'Entre-Lugar' da Voz e da Escritura Feminina" (The "In-Between" Place of Voice and of Female Writing); and "Resenhas" (Reviews). The titles of some of the essays give a good idea of the type of work that is being done in this fast-evolving and important area: "Global ou local?: O tropicalismo brasileiro e a presença da cultura de massa na narrativa da América Hispânica e do Caribe" (Global or Local?: Brazilian Tropicalism and the Presence of Mass Culture in the Narrative of Spanish America and the Caribbean), by Lídia Santos; "Machado, Borges e Clarice: A evolução da nova narrativa latinoamericana" (Machado, Borges, and Clarice: The Evolution of the Latin American New Narrative), by Earl E. Fitz; "A lua e o domador: símbolos literários e divisões sociais na poesia nacionalista de Cassiano Ricardo e Leopoldo Marechal" (The Moon and the Tamer: Literary Symbols and Social Divisions in the Nationalist Poetry of Cassiano Ricardo and Leopoldo Marechal), by Luiza Franco Moreira; "América Latina reinventada: Octavio Paz e Haroldo de Campos" (Latin America Reinvented: Octavio Paz and Haroldo de Campos), by Maria Esther Maciel; and "La subjetividad femenina en la metaficción feminista latinoamericana" (Feminine Subjectivity in Feminist Latin American

Metafiction), by Laura Beard. The importance of this entire project is aptly underscored by the closing words of the editors:

> The assembling of the essays published here, more than a simple editorial effort, constitutes one step more in the trek that we began some time ago, and that has taken a certain direction, in the sense of bringing together the two sides of the Continent. We continue, then, with this journey, whose primary goal is the reduction of the great distance that still separates the Brazilians from the other Latin American peoples. May the works included here serve as a point of departure for the new paths made into the field of Latin (and inter) American comparatism. Let us be comparatists!
>
> A reunião dos ensaios ora publicados, antes que um simple esforço editorial, constitui um passo a mais na caminhada que iniciamos há algum tempo, e que tem tomado uma direção segura, no sentido de aproximar os dois lados do Continente. Continuamos, por tanto, nesse percurso cuja meta principal é a diminuição da grande distância que ainda separa os brasileiros dos demais povos latino-americanos. Que os trabalhos aqui incluídos sirvam como ponto de partida para novas veredas no campo do comparatismo latino-(e inter)americano. Sejamos comparatistas! (12)

But if finding the time to become fluent in Portuguese is not really possible (and for many of us it simply isn't), then I would suggest that we try to use it as a reading language, as a language that most of us can, with the aid of a good dictionary, make use of at least to the extent that we could begin to work it into our studies. Moreover, I would not be averse to reading works of Brazilian literature in English translation first and then going back to the original for more careful stylistic exegesis. Although it is always better, of course, to be able to work with a text in its original language, in the case of Portuguese and Brazilian literature I firmly believe it is more advantageous for us, as Latin Americanists, to integrate these into our studies than to leave them out, a choice which, if made, weakens our case as comparatists at the same time that it cuts us off from one of Western literature's most engaging and surprising national literatures (see Bernheimer 44). Although, as Rodríguez Monegal pointed out over twenty years ago, "Spanish America and Brazil have always been separate and apart, since the first days of the discovery and conquest of the New World," and though history has thickened and hardened the line that has for so long separated them (Monegal v. 1, xiii), it is now time for us to cross that line and bring these two great Latin American traditions together in our classes and in our research. Thinking ahead, however, to the training of the next generation of Latin Americanists, we should insist that our graduate students study as much Portuguese and Brazilian literature as they can get. We must do this in order to prepare them as Latin Americanists in the most comprehensive sense possible, that is, as young scholars able to study and teach literature written in both Spanish and Portuguese (or, perhaps I should say, "Brasileiro/Brazilian," the very distinctive language of Brazil). If we are successful in this venture, we will be producing a new and more comprehensive type of Latin Americanist, one formally prepared to work comparatively in the literatures and cultures of both Spanish America and Brazil (see Rabassa and Merquior).

The importance of additional language instruction for Latin Americanists is not, of course, limited to Portuguese. Given its rich and diverse indigenous heritage, Latin American culture desperately needs scholars who are trained in such languages as Nahuatl, Quechua, and Tupi, just to name three of the most renowned. We would be well advised to remember the words of Oswald de Andrade, the *enfant terrible* of Brazilian modernism, when he famously declared, in reference to the direction the work of his modernist colleagues might take, "Tupi or not Tupi; that is the question." Oswald was right to call our attention to this issue; it would indeed be a travesty if we were to let these languages (and their cultural traditions) die out, for to do so would be to abandon an exceptionally vital and creative past that has given, and that continues to give, modern Latin American literature some of its greatest works of literature. Linguists tell us that, in their totality, our Native American languages are disappearing at an alarming rate, and while it is difficult to find a place to study these tongues, it is imperative that some of us, at least, make this a fundamental feature of our training as modern, comparatively inclined Latin Americanists. Once again, however, I would like to stress that I make this recommendation not as a form of ideological appeasement to the would-be guardians of the citadel but to the most venerable and ennobling standards of our discipline, those that seek to branch out, linguistically speaking, and connect the European tradition to other, non-Western literatures and cultures. Comparative literature has long championed the legitimacy of the oral tradition and so there is every reason to think that, if we can keep it alive in our work as Latin Americanists (and as inter-Americanists), we will be offering comparative literature journals scholarly studies in which they will likely have a keen interest, studies that their editors will view as having an invigorating and tonic effect.

Second, we can learn to think, at least part of the time, in inter-American terms, that is, in terms of courses and critical studies that compare and contrast the literatures and cultures of North, Central, and South America (see Fitz 1998). There can no longer be any doubt that inter-American literature is already well along in the process of establishing itself as a major new area of literary study, one that, as suggested above by Costigan and Bernucci, is custom made for Latin Americanists of a comparative bent. Studies of this type might, for example, look at the development of the novel as a form in, say, Brazil, Spanish America, Canada, and the United States, or at the various ways modernism, romanticism, or even the different colonial eras developed in the New World. Or they might examine how and why certain themes, miscegenation, the presentation of the Native American (including the nature of the oral tradition), the idea of "progress," or nature, for example, manifest themselves in the Americas. The possibilities for this type of scholarship are virtually endless, and the field, as important and full of potential as it is, remains wide open. Because inter-American literature is a vast and extraordinarily complex new field, one in which very few, if any, of us have any formal training, I do not recommend that we declare ourselves "experts" in all aspects of it. To claim this would be patently absurd, and would serve only to make us look foolish. But to claim, as well we might, that, as Latin Americanists we have a very special historical relationship with the United States, for example, and that we do indeed know a great deal about the literature and culture of the United States, is to make an argument for inter-American scholarship that is entirely reasonable and proper and that would be of considerable interest to many comparative literature journals. Indeed, it must be noted that scholars who work today with the literature of the United States, along with those concerned with American studies programs, are changing their views of what constitutes "American" literature and culture.

Another, more distinctly inter-American model is emerging, one that, as Paul Jay argues, involves "a broad critique of the narrow, nationalist conflation of the American and the United States," and that has, as a consequence, "sparked vigorous efforts to resituate the study of United States literature and culture in a hemispheric or Pan-American context" (Jay 45). Although Jay, who teaches English at Loyola of Chicago, does not discuss the importance for inter-American studies of this sea change concerning what it means to be "American" in the year 2002 (he says, still thinking only of English, that "Taking these new, innovative fields as models, we will be in a better position in our more advanced courses, and in our research and writing, to articulate how English has developed over time into a transnational mode of writing," Jay 45), we, as Latin Americanists, understand very well what is really at issue here. It might be said, in fact, that to train as a Latin Americanist is precisely to train as an inter-Americanist, and that this explains why, although an inter-American reconfiguration of literary and cultural study may seem a strange and unsettling new field for some students and scholars in departments of English, it is old (and, because of a history of racism, military intervention, and economic exploitation, sometimes painful) news to Latin Americanists.

The real point of contention, then, is that while Latin Americanists are, traditionally, conversant in both English and French and know the literatures that pertain to these languages quite well, our colleagues in these departments rarely, if ever, know Spanish or Portuguese or the literatures they have produced. The long standing hegemony of English departments, for example, and of their "American" literature sections (the term *American* being understood here in its traditional sense, as a synonym for the United States alone), within the academic and administrative structures of universities will thus be an obstacle that has to be overcome. And, indeed, it is. Stephen Greenblatt, for example, has written, of this issue, that while "It is easy enough to confuse globalization with American triumphalism and an insurgent English-language parochialism," "world culture does not depend on recent events or on the current strength of the English language" (Greenblatt 59). Although it is clear that English departments, concerned, at the dawn of the twenty-first century, about what they regard as the "globalization" of literature (an issue that Latin Americanists and comparatists have long embraced as an article of faith) and the changes this will necessitate in their programs, are beginning to recognize that other "Americas" exist all around them (see Porter, for example, or Mulford), their faculty and students are too often untrained in their languages, literatures, histories, and cultural differences.

In all fairness, however, it must be recognized that this situation, too, is changing, as more and more "Americanists," bilingual in both English and Spanish, are being developed, though, of course, French and Portuguese need to be cultivated as well. Recent work by Gregory Jay, Paul Jay, and Carolyn Porter, for example, should be lauded for its attempt to begin to comment on "Latin American" literature even though these same critics totally ignore Brazil, the largest nation in Latin America (thus rendering it, to paraphrase Ralph Ellison, "invisible" as a New World national literature) and even though much of what they are saying has long been common knowledge among Latin Americanists and inter-Americanists. Although I would not want to put too fine a point on it, this quite thorny problem of cultural (im)balance can be put in the following fashion: Latin Americanists, because of their training (both linguistic and literary), their cultural and historical experience, and the nature of much of their literature, tend to know much more about the literature and culture of the United States than, typically, students and scholars of United States literature know about Latin America. The one (Latin America) has, historically and culturally speaking, simply had to pay much more attention to the other (the United States), being forced, generation after generation, to measure its achievements against those of the other, an other (or "Other") that has never, until now, been much interested in its hemispheric neighbors. If inter-American studies is to succeed (as I truly feel it will), then this great cultural and academic imbalance, this near total ignoring of one side by the other, will have to be confronted and done away with, remaindered to the scrap heap of hemispheric history. González Echevarría, referring only to the relationship departments of Spanish and Portuguese have traditionally endured with respect to departments of French, tartly sums up the problem this way: "A Latin American intellectual would choose a slow, painful death over being caught short on his Mallarmé, and I have yet to meet one who did not know French. But I have never met a French intellectual or professor who knew Spanish [much less Portuguese, EF]. We, the 'colonized,' are cultural polyglots. . . . We 'know more,' yet have to constantly justify our membership in the field of comparative literature" (González Echevarría in this volume). And much the same could be said of departments of English and their relationships to departments of Spanish and Portuguese, to Latin American studies, and to inter-American literature generally.

Yet as inter-American study continues to grow and develop as a field, its impact on the definition and practice of comparative literature will be great (as will its impact on departments of English housing programs in American studies and American literature). It is no exaggeration, I think, to speculate that inter-American literary study, featuring, as it does, truly outstanding texts from several literary cultures rarely heard from (English and French Canada, Brazil, and the Caribbean, for example) will not only renovate but also revive comparative literature as a discipline. Of the future and importance of inter-American studies, J. Hillis Miller, for example, has recently written that "Going forward" with humanistic study in an age when "Manifold changes are making literary study more and more obsolete . . . means inventing courses and curricula that respond to the new situation and keep the teaching of reading and writing alive. Examples are new regional, transnational, multilingual, multiethnic programs (e.g., literatures of the Americas) and expansions of existing single-language programs" (Miller 2062), such as English, French, Spanish, and Portuguese. The real issue for Latin Americanists (and, indeed, the issue that lies, restively, at the heart of the entire problem) has to do with the question of whose books finally end up on the readings lists for our newly reconfigured courses in comparative inter-American literature. Will we have only Anne Bradstreet representing "American" colonial letters, or will we also be reading Sor Juana and Gregório de Matos? Will evaluations of the "new narrative" of the 1960s focus only on Spanish American writers or will it also include texts from Brazil, the United States and Canada (the Québécois novel of the 1960s is especially interesting in this regard)? Will discussions of individual authors, John Barth, for example, deal with his innovations in isolation in the United

States or will they take into account the influence such hemispheric cohorts as Borges, Cortázar, García Márquez, and Machado de Assis had on his work? In what ways, if at all, will Latino-American writers serve as cultural bridges between the United States and Latin America? These are the types of issues that Latin Americanists can raise as they enter into the inter-American fray and, equally important, as they begin to reconstitute the discipline of comparative literature for the twenty-first century. From our perspective, then, as Latin Americanists possessed of a larger, pan-American outlook, we will most likely agree with González Echevarría when he avers that "it is really the more recent canon that the struggle is about, the unstable edges where new membership is still being issued. . . . I believe that the issue is that many writers from areas not represented in the canon are *better* than those routinely included in the canon" (González Echevarría 97). Because, as we have seen, comparative literature is best conceived of as an issue of methodology rather than as a preordained list of "classics" from certain, select languages, it will respond positively to the introduction of artistically innovative and intellectually challenging texts from, for example, Latin America, an area we know to be rich in high quality literature and one that has myriad connections, culturally, intellectually, and artistically, with both the rest of the Americas and the rest of the world.

Deborah Cohn's recent book, *History and Memory in the Two Souths: Recent Southern and Spanish American Fiction* (Vanderbilt, 1999), is a good example of the type of innovative research that will speed this process along, as are Renata Wasserman's *Exotic Nations: Literature and Cultural Identity in the United States and Brazil, 1830–1930* (Cornell, 1994) and Stephen V. Hunsaker's *Autobiography and National Identity in the Americas* (Virginia, 1999). And, as we well know, many more works of this type are appearing every year (my own contribution, focusing on the development of narrative in Brazil and the United States, should appear, via the Modern Language Association, in 2004), a fact which tends to underscore something we already know: Latin Americanists are uniquely prepared to play a crucial role in the evolution of inter-American letters, an enterprise that is inherently comparative in nature and that will help immensely in what González Echevarría has identified as the decisive role Latin American literature can play in the formulation of "a new, redefined [and, one might add, re-energized; EF] comparative literature" (González Echevarría 96).

Finally, I would like to suggest that the third thing we can do to promote our work in comparative journals is to write studies of Spanish American literature and culture that clearly stress the often very great differences that exist between the various nations and regions of Spanish America itself. In undertaking these sorts of studies, we might, for example, emphasize such issues or topics as literary history, genre evolutions, and contrastive thematics and argue that while a writer from Buenos Aires and a writer from, say, Tegucigalpa might both work in Spanish, the many cultural, racial, historical, and even linguistic differences that separate them can justify a comparative approach. "Comparatists," as we read in the 1993 Bernheimer Report:

> should be alert to the significant differences within any national culture, which provide a basis for comparison, research, and critical-theoretical inquiry. Among these are differences (and conflicts) according to region, ethnicity, religion, gender, class, and colonial or postcolonial status. Comparatist research is ideally suited to pursue ways in which these differences are conjoined with differences in language, dialect, and usage (including jargon or slang) as well as with problems of dual- or multiple-language use and modes of hybridization. (Bernheimer 44)

For the editors of very traditional minded comparative journals, however, this will be a tough sell (since the texts studied will all be written in what is more or less the same language), but there is an intellectual validity to it and so it is an argument worth making. On the other hand, journals that emphasize cultural issues, like *Cultural Critique*, *Cultural Anthropology*, or *Hopscotch: A Cultural Review*, or that demonstrate an interest in issues of cultural studies might, as Steven Tötösy has suggested, be particularly receptive to this type of study (see Tötösy's "From Comparative Literature Today toward Comparative Cultural Studies").

A question that arises here, however, is the following: to what degree will studies of this type truly be exemplary of comparative literature? The study of literatures written (or spoken) in more than one language has long been *the* defining feature of comparative literature as a discipline, and so, if our primary goal is to see our work published in mainline comparative literature journals, perhaps we should be cautious about demanding that work done entirely in one language be regarded as truly comparative in nature, at least as the field has come to be defined by its leading journals. At the same time, perhaps we, as Latin Americanists, should feel that since we are well positioned to reinvigorate the entire field of comparative literature, we are also free to publish new, nontraditional work in new and nontraditional journals, especially those with some degree of a cultural studies orientation. If the discipline needs to change, we could argue, then let us be in the forefront of that change. Latin American literature, long vitalized by its historical concern with power structures, with social inequities and with issues relating to both political and economic justice, offers tremendous opportunities for culturally inclined criticism, more so, one might argue, than many industrial and postindustrial nations. In Brazil and Spanish America, hunger, disease, and poverty, for example, are still such widespread problems that, in some places, they threaten the existence of entire societies and populations. Literature, in such settings, cannot avoid having a powerful political dimension to it, and, indeed, this is one of Latin American literature's most venerable characteristics. As a result of this *engagé* aspect of its historical development, then, fiction, poetry, and drama in Latin America do not have such a great problem seeing themselves as "cultural texts" as opposed to elitist or belletrist literature. Although this tradition has, of course, existed in Latin American letters, the view that literary texts were largely, if not fundamentally, cultural documents imbued with very pronounced, and often deliberate, social, political, historical, and economic referents, has long been a vital one. In Latin America, real lives have often been dramatically affected by the literature that has been produced and consumed, and this makes it somewhat easier for the advocates of cultural studies to make their case for a closer working relationship with comparative literature, which, on many points, has a natural affinity with it (see Bernheimer 45).

Distressingly, however, the leading theoreticians of cultural criticism have, for the most part, ignored literary texts written in Spanish and Portuguese. Although this trend is slowly beginning to change, Spanish and Portuguese are still not the "preferred" languages for cultural critiques. Edward Said's hugely influential *Orientalism*, for example, "barely recognizes"—and then only in a footnote—"the existence of an earlier, much different form of Orientalism, in a Spain where Arabs were the dominant force for eight centuries" (González Echevarría 97) while Fredric Jameson's often cited introduction to the English translation of Roberto Fernández Retamar's "Calibán," seems "to ignore the fact that the essay is an answer to 'Ariel,' arguably the most important essay every written in Latin America," a critical omission that "reveals an overseer mentality that is much more that of the colonizer than of the would-be decolonizer" (González Echevarría 98; see, also, Pratt, 59). This sort of problem is indicative of the fact that Spanish (to say nothing of Portuguese!) is still not widely regarded as a language whose literary importance is sufficient for critics like Said and Jameson to bother with. But, as we have seen, the times are changing, and new studies, many of which are focusing on issues of inter-American literature and culture, that feature both Spanish and Portuguese prominently are appearing all the time.

One excellent example of this trend is Renata Wasserman's article "Mario Vargas Llosa, Euclides da Cunha, and the Strategy of Intertextuality," in which Wasserman argues that intertextuality, well known "as a condition for the existence of a text," can also be used "for the purpose of validating a cultural configuration, of asserting cultural power" (Wasserman 1993, 460). Using two twentieth-century Latin American texts as her examples, Mario Vargas Llosa's 1981 novel, *La guerra del fin del mundo,* and Euclides da Cunha's 1902 novel-like discourse on the bloody and wrenching 1896–97 revolt at Canudos (*Os Sertões*), Wasserman takes up the fundamental problem of cultural identity; what does it mean for the nations of Latin America, born out of European concepts and structures but grown into something quite different, when they are forced, as they inevitably are, to confront their American, or New World, realities? The issue of race, for example, is central to both works (as it is to New World literature generally), coming, finally, to demonstrate most vividly one of the most fundamental differences between European society and Latin American reality, with its mixed-blood population. The political issues that inform and circumscribe Latin America's troubled struggle for cultural identity constitute another key tie between the two books. While da Cunha slowly but inevitably comes to question whether he can honestly continue to attribute the noble qualities of the newly formed Republic, and of its European heritage, to "progressive," southern Brazil and "barbarism" to the interior of the nation (and specifically to the culture of Canudos), Vargas Llosa creates a fictional character, a European anarchist, Galileo Gall, whose espousal of "entirely coherent" but "completely irrelevant political theories lead him to interfere (destructively) in the American action and keep him from understanding it" (Wasserman 1993, 467). "Taken together," then, as Wasserman rightly asserts, "the two books create an inter-American intertextuality and affirm a kinship among American nations based on the recognition of shared problems that, even more than economic, are social and cultural, ontological and epistemological" (Wasserman 1993, 469).

What is especially effective in this study is that while the author clearly makes use of two literary texts to illuminate a larger historical and cultural issue, she does not fail to pay close attention to these same texts as objects of literature. Too often, in cultural studies, outstanding literary texts become lost, or neutralized, in the discussions of culture that they help germinate. Without denying the validity of one of the basic assumptions about cultural studies, that literary texts are always part of a larger social, political, and economic milieu and that, as participants in a culture's structures and practices, they are therefore never "politically neutral" (Saldívar 252), Wasserman manages to connect the "cultural" significance of *Os Sertões* and *La guerra del fin del mundo* to their literary, or textual, singularity. The result is a study in which the cultural importance of two seminal Latin American texts is clearly shown to derive, in large part, precisely because they are as powerfully and as effectively written as they are. Traditional literary analysis, in other words, enhances our ability to see the cultural impact these two works have. Although Wasserman's study makes use of texts from both of Latin America's two great literary traditions, its basis in the old problem of Latin American identity, in all its myriad forms and manifestations, amply confirms the unique value of cultural studies to nations like Brazil and its Spanish-speaking neighbors.

In thinking about the application of cultural studies to the situation of Latin Americanists, however, it is also interesting to consider how this term is understood when it is applied to Hispanic literature being written in the United States. For example, as José David Saldívar has written, "Cultural studies, as it is practiced in the United States, already seems to have taken its place as one of the established contemporary approaches to Chicano literature" (Saldívar 251). For Saldívar, however, who, in the beginning of his essay, critiques a study, "Ethnicity and the Post-Modern Arts of Memory" (see Clifford and Marcus, *Writing Culture: The Poetics and Politics of Ethnography*, 1986), on Chicano literature by Michael M.J. Fischer, the danger of cultural studies is that (as he believes happened in the Fischer piece) it can all too easily do little more than present the reader "with an overwhelming catalogue of ethnic textual 'data' with far too little discussion of local knowledge and local history" (Saldívar 253). While this danger seems more likely to exist in a predominantly English speaking but multiethnic nation like that of the United States, where anthropologists and literary scholars not seriously trained in either Spanish or Latino culture will find themselves led to make critical judgments about artistic production and consumption in cultures they do not really understand, it is much less problematic for professionally trained Latin Americanists, who, by dint of years of study, are fully prepared, linguistically, historically, and culturally, to speak both discerningly and authoritatively about Brazil and Spanish America.

Moreover, professional Latin Americanists who were born and raised in the United States possess two additional, and invaluable, skills, namely, their native linguistic competence and their experience as American citizens, both of which make them uniquely able to compare and contrast the cultures of Latin America with those of the United States. "Border studies" are particularly important here and they can serve as a kind of bridge connecting the United States and its hemispheric neighbors. As Greene has shown ("Generation" 152–53), much of the work of Rolando Hinojosa, Gloria Anzaldúa, and Carlos Fuentes exemplifies the possibilities inherent in this type of approach (I say this holding in abeyance the question of Canada and all it brings to the issue of "border studies"). Of course, it is also important to remember that native Spanish and Portuguese speaking Latin Americanists also have a lot of experience with "border studies" (as do English- and French-speaking Canada) and that these can and should be developed as important subjects for research. And cutting through all these European-based societies is the autochthonous tradition, the still powerful presence of Native America that, in ways both ancient and contemporary, binds us together by reminding us, sometimes painfully, that there are always borders within borders. Yet while it is easy and exciting to talk about the "expansion" of "American" literature and "American" cultural studies into the "Hispanic" sphere (even the language can sound imperialistic), certain crucial problems become immediately evident, the language question looming large among them. For those coming at this problem from the perspective of the literature and culture of the United States, real fluency in Spanish will be a necessity, at least if the scholar wishes to move beyond even a very important work like Anzaldúa's *Borderlands/La Frontera: The New Mestiza* (1987), which is written primarily in English with a few Spanish words and expressions embedded in it. The problem is that few, if any, doctoral programs in English and American literature currently require a student to be sufficiently fluent in Spanish (to say nothing of Portuguese) to read complex literary texts (and criticism) written in those languages. Thus, though a scholar might be able to work effectively with *Borderlands*, could she or he do so with untranslated Fuentes, Rulfo, or García Márquez? If she does not possess at least reading fluency in Spanish and Portuguese, how far can the American literature doctoral student's incursion into Latin American literature go? Once again, we see the unexpected advantage that Latin Americanists have in the application of cultural studies not merely to Latin America itself, with all its own diversity, but to the United States as well. At a time when the entire concept of "American" literature is being debated and rethought amongst scholars in English departments across the country (see, for example, J. Hillis Miller's enthusiasm for the development of programs that deal, in a more pan-American context, with the literatures of the Americas; see also Gregory Jay, Paul Jay, and Carolyn Porter), Latin Americanists must realize that they are suddenly in a position to forge ahead in the area of both Latin American and inter-American cultural studies, that they are uniquely prepared to make significant contributions to this important and fast-growing new field.

Since the 1980s especially, cultural studies has, as a movement, sought to analyze discourse, and discursive practices, as rhetorical constructs that relate directly to larger, sociopolitical issues of knowledge and power. While these goals are unquestionably germane to any culture, they are particularly important for Latin American culture, which, in so many ways, still suffers from dependency, exploitation, and discrimination. Cultural studies, "a border zone of conjunctures," as Saldívar argues, "must aspire to be regionally focused and broadly comparative, a form of living and of travel in our global borderlands" (Saldívar 264), an argument that is applicable to both Latino literature produced and consumed in the United States and to Latin American literature as it seeks to take its rightful place in the context of world culture.

In conclusion, then, I would like to repeat that I believe the best, long term solution to the problem we, as Latin Americanists, face with regard to our presence in comparative literature journals is for us to include Brazilian literature and culture in our studies (even if we have only a reading knowledge of Portuguese and even if we have to rely on translations to help us). In gaining competency in (Brazilian) Portuguese, we become more complete as Latin Americanists and we connect ourselves to a tremendously fecund field of literary and cultural study. Secondly, we need to think, at least part of the time, in terms of the larger inter-American issues, so many of which engage Brazil, Spanish America, the Caribbean, Canada, and the United States (see Morency) in ways that we, as Latin Americanists, can speak to with authority and generations of experience. The third approach I have suggested, the merging of comparative literature and cultural studies, will certainly generate legitimate scholarship but it may well elicit an adverse backlash, one that could be disadvantageous to our overall goal. We must never forget that, even as cultural studies teaches us to read literary texts as social and political documents, the greatness of writers like Machado de Assis, Borges, Guimarães Rosa, Clarice Lispector, Octavio Paz, Alejo Carpentier, and García Márquez resides in their abilities to change the ways we think about writing and about literature itself. Although cultural studies has much that will benefit Latin American literature, we must beware of reducing our greatest artistic and literary innovators to the level of popular culture. In entering the arena of world literature, we need to show our brilliance, not our commonality. We need to show, as González Echevarría puts it, how novels by Fuentes (or, I might add, Machado de Assis) can be used to read James and how those by Lezama Lima (or Guimarães Rosa) serve as perspectives from which we can better understand Joyce (González Echevarría 105).

In this same context, we should be developing ourselves as a "new class of readers," one "trained in the marginal literatures" and ready, willing and able to show, for example, how reading Clarice Lispector can teach us more about Cixous's concept of *écriture féminine* than we can glean from reading the French woman's texts alone, how, in other words, reading texts long relegated to the margins of world literature "mobilizes elements in the hegemonic texts that were previously inert, beyond the reach of criticism and theory" (González Echevarría 105). In any event, I firmly believe that Latin American literature, working in close consort with the development of inter-American studies on a variety of fronts, will inevitably transform not only the field of comparative literature but its very conceptualization. Of this I have no doubt. As we seek to make our literature better known among professional comparatists, however, and to increase the frequency of our appearance in comparative literature journals, we must never forget that the discipline of comparative literature is a profoundly humanistic, integrative, and inclusive approach to literary study, and, as Latin Americanists, we must seek always to strengthen and enrich it, and never to weaken or debase it.

Works Cited

Bernheimer, Charles. "The Bernheimer Report, 1993: Comparative Literature at the Turn of the Century." *Comparative Literature in the Age of Multiculturalism*. Ed. Charles Bernheimer. Baltimore: Johns Hopkins UP, 1995. 39–48.

Cohn, Deborah H. *History and Memory in the Two Souths: Recent Southern and Spanish American Fiction*. Nashville: Vanderbilt UP, 1999.

Costigan, Lúcia Helena, and Leopoldo M. Bernucci, eds. O Brasil, "a América Hispânica e o Caribe: Abordagens Comparativas." Thematic issue, *Revista Iberoamericana* 182–83 (1998).

Fitz, Earl E. *Inter-American Literature and Criticism: An Electronic Annotated Bibliography* (1998–): <http://www.uiowa.edu/~uipress/interamerican>.

Fitz, Earl E. "Machado, Borges e Clarice: A Evolução da Nova Narrativa Latino-Americana." *Revista Iberoamericana*, 64.182–83 (1998): 129–44.

Fitz, Earl E. "Metafiction in Latin American Narrative: The Case for Brazil." *Mester* 25 (1997): 43–69.

Fitz, Earl E. *Rediscovering the New World: Inter-American Literature in a Comparative Context*. Iowa City: U of Iowa P, 1991.

González Echevarría, Roberto. "Latin American and Comparative Literature." *Comparative Cultural Studies and Latin America*. Ed. Sophia A. McClennen and Earl E. Fitz. West Lafayette: Purdue UP, 2004. 89–104.

González Echevarría, Roberto, and Enrique Pupo-Walker. *The Cambridge History of Latin American Literature*. Cambridge: Cambridge UP, 1996. Vol. 3.

Greenblatt, Stephen. "Racial Memory and Literary History." *PMLA: Publications of the Modern Language Association of America* 116.1 (2001): 48–63.

Greene, Roland. "American Comparative Literature: Reticence and Articulation." *World Literature Today* 69.2 (1995): 293–98.

Greene, Roland. "Their Generation." *Comparative Literature in the Age of Multiculturalism*. Ed. Charles Bernheimer. Baltimore: Johns Hopkins UP, 1995. 143–54.

Jay, Gregory. "The End of 'American' Literature: Toward a Multicultural Practice." *College English* 53 (1991): 264–68.

Jay, Paul. "The Myth of 'America' and the Politics of Location: Modernity, Border Studies, and the Literature of the Americas." *Arizona Quarterly* 54 (1998): 165–92.

McClennen, Sophia A. "Comparative Literature and Latin American Studies: From Disarticulation to Dialogue." *Comparative Cultural Studies and Latin America*. Ed. Sophia A. McClennen and Earl E. Fitz. West Lafayette: Purdue UP, 2004. 105–130.

Merquior, J.G. "The Brazilian and the Spanish American Literary Traditions: A Comparative View." *The Cambridge History of Latin American Litera-*

ture. Ed. Roberto González Echevarría and Enrique Pupo-Walker. Cambridge: Cambridge UP, 1996. Vol. 3, 363–82.

Miller, J. Hillis. Untitled note on the state of the profession. *PMLA: Publications of the Modern Language Association of America* 115.7 (2000): 2062.

Morency, Jean. "Forms of European Disconnection in Literature of the Americas." Trans. Nicole Santilli and Barbara Godard. *Topia* 2 (1998): 11–21.

Mulford, Carla, ed. *Teaching Early American Literatures*. New York: The Modern Language Association of America, 1999.

Porter, Carolyn. "What We Know That We Don't Know: Remapping American Literary Studies." *American Literary History* 3 (1994): 467–526.

Payne, Judith A., and Earl E. Fitz. *Ambiguity and Gender in the New Novel of Brazil and Spanish America: A Comparative Assessment.* Iowa City: U of Iowa P, 1993.

Pratt, Mary Louise. "Comparative Literature and Global Citizenship." *Comparative Literature in the Age of Multiculturalism*. Ed. Charles Bernheimer. Baltimore: Johns Hopkins UP, 1995. 58–65.

Rabassa, Gregory. "A Comparative Look at the Literatures of Spanish America and Brazil: The Dangers of Deception." *Ibero-American Letters in a Comparative Perspective*. Ed. W.T. Zyla and W.M. Aycock. Lubbock: Texas Tech UP, 1978. 119–32.

Rodríguez Monegal, Emir, and Thomas Colchie. *The Borzoi Anthology of Latin American Literature*. New York: Knopf, 1977. 2 vols.

Saldívar, José David. "The Limits of Cultural Studies." *American Literary History* 2 (1990): 251–66.

Tötösy de Zepetnek, Steven. "From Comparative Literature Today toward Comparative Cultural Studies." *Comparative Literature and Comparative Cultural Studies*. Ed. Steven Tötösy de Zepetnek. West Lafayette: Purdue UP, 2002. 235–67.

Tötösy de Zepetnek, Steven. "From Comparative Literature Today toward Comparative Cultural Studies." *CLCWeb: Comparative Literature and Culture: A WWWeb Journal* 1.3 (1999): <http://clcwebjournal.lib.purdue.edu/clcweb99-3/totosy99.html>.

Tötösy de Zepetnek, Steven, ed. *Histories and Concepts of Comparative Literature.* Thematic issue, *CLCWeb: Comparative Literature and Culture: A WWWeb Journal* 2.4 (2000): <http://clcwebjournal.lib.purdue.edu/clcweb00-4/contents00-4.html>.

Wasserman, Renata R. Mautner. *Exotic Nations: Literature and Cultural Identity in the United States and Brazil, 1830–1930*. Ithaca: Cornell UP, 1994.

Wasserman, Renata R. Mautner. "Mario Vargas Llosa, Euclides da Cunha, and the Strategy of Intertextuality." *PMLA: Publications of the Modern Language Association of America* 108.3 (1993): 460–73.

Latin American and Comparative Literatures

Roberto González Echevarría

One has to wonder, in the wake of the radical critical revision of the past twenty years, and more important, the international recognition of writers from parts of the world not generally included in the curriculum, if comparative literature as a discipline has survived. Has there been a realignment of literary history parallel to the one in the international arena that calls for a fresh critical approach to the discipline, for a remapping, as it were? The debates sparked by the assault on the canon dramatize the urgency of such questions. Work on colonialism and literature is giving currency in literary studies—properly translated—to the linguistic dictum that a language is a dialect with an army. Many would now say that a literature is a body of texts with an army and an Alliance Française. It would probably be a shock to the founders of comparative literature, who acted to combat the scourge of nationalism, that the field is now seen as the reflection of only a slightly more encompassing kind of cultural arrogance: Eurocentrism. Even at its most liberal, when conceived as a study of literature transcending linguistic barriers, comparative literature compared literature to itself, meaning that it compared authors, works, and movements within the confines of the hegemonic powers of nineteenth-century Europe. This seems intolerable today and at odds with what should be the thrust of the discipline: to compare literature more broadly to texts not commonly considered literary, as well as to others coming from outside the confines of what were the imperial powers of the last century. In the current climate, there seems to be little future for comparative literature, unless a truly pitiless redefinition can be negotiated.

But what has occurred so far has merely been a prelude (one hopes), with very few real changes having taken place. In what follows I shall give my assessment of the situation, consider the place of Latin American literature in a new, redefined comparative literature, and close with a reading of a scene of Alejo Carpentier's *The Lost Steps* that may help in understanding how I think Latin American texts read the canon and how they can be "comparative." I will be expressing, for the most part, opinions based on personal experience rather than finely tuned and supported arguments.

Has the questioning of the canon really changed things, and has "theory" truly ventured beyond the canonical works? I am afraid not or, at least, not yet and not enough. The situation is, in terms of everyday experience, bewildering. On the one hand, Hispanists and colleagues in disciplines other than comparative literature, English, German, or French usually know, in addition to their language and literature of specialization, at least French and English, if not both, and they are conversant with the literatures of the hegemonic languages. But colleagues who specialize in those languages or in comparative literature rarely know ours. We know our literatures as well as our Proust, Dickens, or Schiller, but they have only the vaguest of notions, if any, about Lope de Vega, let alone Andrés Bello or Domingo Faustino Sarmiento. A Latin American intellectual would choose a slow, painful death over being caught short on his Mallarmé, and I have yet to meet one who did not know French. But I have never met a French intellectual or professor who knew Spanish. We, the "colonized," are cultural polyglots; they are generally conversant only with English, French, or German. We "know more," yet have to constantly justify our membership in the field of comparative literature. They can go around saying Valejo (as in "Valley Joe") for Vallejo, Borgés (as in "Boar Jess") for Borges, and Marqués (as in "Mar Case") for Márquez, but one would be loath to say Rimbaud (as in "tout"), Proust (as in "oust"), or Goethe (as in "pithy"). It would be foolish, of course, to fill ourselves with pride for our cosmopolitanism. They do not know our literatures for the very same reasons that we know theirs. Theirs are important, canonical, the core of the core curriculum; ours are marginal, exotic, frilly, not part of anyone's cultural literacy program.

Lest anyone be deluded, that core curriculum now being defended fang and claw by the far right is not a list of books handed down in a stone tablet on Mount Rushmore. It is the product of the nineteenth-century European imagination or, if you please, nineteenth-century European ideology. It is not the Greeks and Romans that we ought to read and revere but the Greeks and Romans as read, interpreted, and promoted in France, England, and Germany during the last century. The same applies to Shakespeare and the rest of the "great books" tradition. Yet I doubt that anyone is seriously challenging the value of Shakespeare, Dante, or Goethe. It is really the more recent canon that the struggle is about, the unstable edges where new membership is still being issued. Really, is it more important to produce one more study of Stendhal showing how he subtly got around contemporary definitions of sexual roles, which were constructed, needless to say, according to a Foucauldian model? Is yet another book on Sade, Bataille, Freud, and Lacan needed more than one on Jorge Luis Borges and the modern tradition? Do we have to read yet one more confession from a tedious academic who thinks the tribulations of his pathetic postmodern and presumably postcolonial ego are interesting? I do not think that anyone whose voice is worth hearing is seriously promoting abandoning oneself to a mindless relativism, with no value judgments allowed. On the contrary, I believe that the issue is that many writers from areas not represented in the canon are *better* than those routinely included in the canon. Should comparative literature invest in Smollet or in Sarmiento? Can comparative literature be seriously concerned with the relations between Latin American and French poets, rather than continue its obsessive study of U.S. and French poets? When will the Mallarmé-Stevens French connection ever give way to the Baudelaire-Neruda Latin one?

One should not be fooled into thinking that recent critical theory, even when allied to seemingly radical political agendas, has really strayed from the canon. It is very symptomatic that until *La Conquête de l'Amérique*, Tzvetan Todorov had devoted himself exclusively to the most French of the French, and the same applies to Julia Kristeva, whose *Théorie du roman* exhumes an obscure medieval French text, whereas the Spanish ones that would have been much more relevant to her arguments are relegated to a footnote. Has Kristeva ever heard of *Libro de buen amor* or *Celestina*? Kristeva's quaint and quiet *révolutions* of poetic language are tempests in the French teapot, easily absorbed by the Alliance Française because they never stray from the sacred texts. Where is Latin American literature in Jonathan Culler's reflective *Structuralist Poetics*? The same is true, alas, of Fredric Jameson and Edward Said, who have built their theories, for the most part, oblivious of Spanish. Said's *Orientalism* barely recognizes, again in a footnote, the existence of an earlier, much different form of Orientalism, in a Spain where Arabs were the dominant force for eight centuries (for a correction, from the field of Hispanic studies, see Kushigian). And only recently, and with what appears to be a very hastily acquired familiarity with the region and its texts, has Jameson finally begun to read Latin American literature as a projection of his political fixations. The field of Latin American criticism is so colonized and so terrorized by the fear of being politically unfashionable that a host of followers of Said and Jameson spring up immediately, willing to trail along, overlooking as minor flows their comprehensive ignorance of our culture. Said can go so far as to write things like "Central and Latin America," which on the pages of a State Department communiqué would cause wrath as well as mirth, yet feel that he has the authority to criticize Borges and Mario Vargas Llosa (215). Unless some geological upheaval, inevitably unleashed by California, has disconnected Central America from the rest of Latin America, Central America is and has always been part of Latin America. Another case in point is Jameson's introduction to the recent translation of Roberto Fernández Retamar's "Calibán." Jameson and his editors seem to ignore the fact that the essay is an answer to "Ariel," arguably the most important essay ever written in Latin America, published by José Enrique Rodó in 1900. It seems to me that boldness of this kind, which I am sure my truly admired friends Ed and Fred would not dare display when dealing with the French or the English, reveals an overseer mentality that is much more that of the colonizer than of the would-be decolonizer.

On the home front (that is, among Latin Americanists) there has not been a dearth of distortions, even when motivated by the best political interests. The effort in recent years to align Latin American literature with that of the so-called Third World has been a fiasco, unless it is understood simply as part of a political agenda with no basis in history. If by Third World it is meant countries that emerged from the debacle of modern empires in non-European regions of the globe, then Latin America, which was the creation of a much older and different colonialism, has to be a different cultural entity, with a different kind of literature. I am surprised and distressed by self-proclaimed Marxist critics who abandon all notion of the specificity of history to equate all imperialisms, and the cultural products of all colonial encounters, no matter when or where they took place. The burden of Latin American culture is a Western culture that reaches back to the Middle Ages, when the foundations of the Spanish Empire in the New World were set. Ours was from the beginning a culture of ostentatious viceregal capitals, surpassing in splendor cities of the Old World, often because they had to compete with magnificent urban centers constructed by the Aztecs, Mayas, or Incas. This urban quality of Latin American culture also obeyed Spanish Neo-Scholasticism, grounded on the Aristotelian notion that civilization was, as the etymology indicates, something proper to cities. Latin American colonial culture, in many ways medieval, is so distant from that of the United States that gross distortions and misreadings are bound to occur unless substantial study of it is required in the curriculum. For the time being, it seems as if the fate of Latin American literature in the American academy is to become the object of what Rolena Adorno calls "pop lit-crit."

The latest fad among a clique of Latin-Americanists has been to return to the old romantic yearning to read the West from outside the West, thereby aiming to redress all the injustices of colonialism. Either naive or in bad faith, these "critics," who call themselves postcolonialists but are thoroughly colonized materially [nearly all work in U.S. or British universities] and intellectually (they draw their ideas from Western thinkers), claim to work in favor of the marginalized by rejecting the aesthetic. Some are willing to dispense with Borges, Carpentier, Pablo Neruda, Gabriel García Márquez and Julio Cortázar and replace them with, one supposes, their own theorizing or the texts they rescue from oral traditions or popular culture. This fad will wind up, with "dependency theory," "theology of liberation" and "subaltern studies," in the junk-yard of ideological fantasies, while the authors mentioned continue to be read and cherished. Having just returned from the Bogotá Book Fair—April 2002—I can attest to the vigor and enthusiasm of young Latin American writers and their success with the public. Postcolonialists are not interested in literature, luckily for literature.

The question of the new is so poignant in Latin American literature because ours is such an old culture, back through our European roots and through those of the native and African cultures. The entire history of Macondo has been written in advance, in Sanskrit, by a wizard; it is a story that emerges from the very origins of history and writing. In those origins writing precedes history. The literatures of the Third World are recent; some have come into being in the twentieth century. Latin American writers find predecessors, within what they consider their own literature, in the sixteenth and seventeenth centuries. Octavio Paz's passionate and polemic literary biography of Sor Juana Inés de la Cruz is a case in point. There were Renaissance-style literary academies in Lima at the turn of the sixteenth to the seventeenth century, and hundreds of Petrarchan poets in seventeenth-century Mexico. If anyone should doubt this, he or she ought to read Alicia de Colombí-Monguió's *Petrarquismo peruano* and Irving Leonard's *Books of the Brave* and *Baroque Times in Old Mexico*.

A parallel, politically motivated effort that has, to my mind, met with failure is that of pretending that Latin American literature and culture are oral. The proliferation of "testimonial narratives," in which an informer "speaks" in the first person, is part and parcel of this movement. But Latin American culture is truly a culture of the letter, as Ángel Rama saw clearly in *La ciudad letrada*. There was a university in Hispaniola in the sixteenth century (called Saint Thomas Aquinas). A college at Tlatlelolco, near Mexico City, taught Latin to upper-class natives. Besides, the historical significance of the Discovery and Conquest of America was very much due to the invention of movable type. Only because of the disseminating power of the printing press did the Discovery have the impact it had on European history and thought. And only because of its ability to communicate through print was the Spanish Empire able to become a viable polity, through the issuance of the myriad laws that make up what is known as the *Derecho Indiano* (Laws of the Indies). Both the New World and its inhabitants gain legitimacy through writing, and polemical, literary, and historical writing proliferated in the New World. It was and is like a fine, resilient net from which it is very difficult to escape (see my *Myth and Archive: A Theory of Latin American Narrative*).

I would be the last to pretend that this primacy of the letter has not been accompanied by violence. "La letra con sangre entra" (Writing is taught by drawing blood), says the Spanish proverb, and there is no shortage of revolting examples attesting to its validity in Latin American history. But cruelty to the Other has also been perpetrated by oral cultures, if such a thing exists. More important, the preponderance of the written does not necessarily mean submission but a struggle from within that lies at the core of Latin America's most enduring works, like those of Borges, García Márquez, and Neruda. The oral does not bring about liberation. Latin American dictators—think for a moment what *dictator* means—have often been masters of oratory. Their dictates have been bravely contradicted by the written word—from graffiti to books—which does not require a physical presence that could lead to incarceration, torture, and death. Many Latin American liberators, from Simón Bolívar and José Martí to Che Guevara, have been writers, sometimes compulsive *grafómanos*.

Traces of the endurance of this culture of the letter are clearly discernible in Borges and García Márquez. Testimonial narrative could not be more revealing in this respect, but not in the way ideologues would wish (including some of their authors). By turning into writing the informant's account, the "lettered" observer enmeshes him or her into the world of writing. Rather than reinforcing the oral nature of Latin American literature, testimonial narratives reveal the very opposite to be true: that we are a culture of the letter. As Carlos Fuentes has written, "The Roman legalistic tradition is one of the strongest components in Latin American culture: from Cortés to Zapata, we only believe in what is written down and codified" (34). The resiliency of the old depends on this centrality of the letter, which I would be inclined to believe is not so crucial in so-called literatures of the Third World.

Because of its chronological depth, reading Ernst Robert Curtius and Erich Auerbach is as necessary to approach Latin American literature as it may be to study French or Italian literature. There is, for instance, a strain of classicism that reaches back to colonial Lima and wends its way to the present through nineteenth-century Colombia and modern Mexico. García Márquez has often said that among his favorite readings as a young writer were the Greek tragedies, and Carpentier used to repeat that there was, for him, no better novel than the *Odyssey*. This is indeed quite visible in *Chronicle of a Death Foretold*, whose plot is that of a tragedy, and *The Lost Steps*, which is, among many other things, a rewriting of the *Odyssey* (a book one of the characters carries in this journey through the jungle). José Lezama Lima knew patristic literature so well that he named his influential magazine *Orígenes* after Origen, and one need not belabor the debt of his major novel to medieval literature when its title is *Paradiso*. To overlook the solidity of Latin American literature's bond to the European tradition—not just the modern—is, as we say in Spanish, like trying to obscure the sun with one's finger.

The founders of Latin American literature as a self-conscious social and creative activity, a movement that coincided more or less with the process of independence from Spain, began their work in the early nineteenth century. They were diplomats, politicians, revolutionaries, from various regions of Latin America, who met for the most part in Paris and began to create a modern, continental literary awareness, a common sense of purpose, and cultural solidarity. This feeling of belonging to a linguistic and literary family was expressed not only by manifestos but by the editing of anthologies, like the famous *América poética*, published in 1846 by the Argentine José María Gutiérrez in Valparaíso, Chile, which included poets from all over the Spanish-speaking world. There were also books of criticism, literary gossip, manifestos, critical editions, prologues, which began to furnish Latin American literature with the kind of metatextual density modern literatures all but require. All of this happened much before the beginning of the twentieth century, and this explains why Latin American writers since then have considered Paris a kind of literary capital, a center that Mexico City, Havana, or Santiago could not always be, for geographical as well as political reasons. It also explains the depth of the French and European culture in general of contemporary writers like Carpentier and Cortázar, both eloquent defenders of the Third World but very different from writers nurtured in those regions, for whom the international arena could be foreign, menacing, and new.

The equation is simple. Literature as we know it and practice it is a Western concept and pursuit. If we posit that Latin America has a literature, then it has to be a part of Western literature, even if some writers deny it, because denying literature or the West is one of the components of the modern literature of the West. I repeat: once we proclaim the existence of a distinct textual field called Latin American Literature, we must accept that its being part of literature makes it inevitably part of the West, even and perhaps mostly when it pretends not to be so. Being Western, however, does not mean being like French, English, or even U.S. literature. What is, after all, that which makes Latin American literature distinct and apt to be compared? And how, in the final analysis, does it fit within that embattled and perhaps nonexistent field of comparative literature?

Paz has complained that, though modern, Latin American literature is missing a critical corpus to accompany its "creative" texts. This is true, but only to some extent, and has the deleterious effect of giving writers like Paz himself an authority as critics that smacks of collusion. This may be more harmful than the absence of criticism. But such an absence, if it indeed exists, is more than compensated for by the critical element that is so much a part of all major Latin American texts. What I mean by critical here may very well result from a lack of self-assurance, from a nagging question about its own legitimacy that leads to a searing self-questioning, a self-questioning that unsettles all elements of a text, from its linguistic foundations, to tradition, culture, and the very history of Latin America as a framing and supporting discourse. In this I follow Paz in another essay, in which he claims that Latin American literature is "a literature of foundations" (2–8). There are no certainties and no givens in a novelistic world such as Macondo's, where even the most ordinary things lack names and the very history of Latin America has to be retold, along with the novel, as if scaffolding and building, frame and picture, needed each other to exist as such. It is not coincidental that the major critical revision of the past twenty years in the West—structuralism and poststructuralism—has been accompanied, not by a similar process in Latin America, but by the emergence of literary texts by the likes of Borges, Lezama Lima, Carpentier, García Márquez, Fuentes, Augusto Roa Bastos, and Severo Sarduy. A case could be made that the same kind of critical activity is at work in those texts, some of which inspired critics like Foucault and Barthes. In Latin America, again, literature itself became the issue, but from within literature, not from the work of critics. At the height of the structuralist and poststructuralist controversies, French literature hardly felt the need to question itself, and when it did, in Sollers, for instance, hardly anyone paid any attention. Not so in Latin America, where such probing seems to be the spark that sets off the production of texts. Latin America's sense of belatedness may very well be what hones it into the cutting edge of literary production today.

If there is a difference between Latin American literature and that of the canonical West, it is one of degree, not of kind. And that degree of difference results from that foundational quality discovered by Paz. I would add that what this element brings to Latin American literature is an ability to be concerned in a rather impudent way with what I would call cosmic issues. The literature of the West, even the most modern or postmodern, is one in which major questions must be assumed to have been solved or are too cumbersome to present without embarrassment. Only in the most ironic or indirect way would a French, English, or North American novelist deal with themes such as the very foundation of history and culture of those societies. It is as if a French poet could write an epic about a certain battle at Roncesvalles and have a hero named Roland tell us a story of defeat and gallantry. Or as if an English novelist set out to rewrite *Beowulf* (*Macunaíma*, a modern Brazilian novel, has more in common with *Beowulf* than anything that I have read in English). The central constitutive idealization of Latin American fiction is that Latin American discourse emerged with the most significant historical break in the West since the birth of Christ: the Discovery and Conquest of America. This is why Carpentier can make Columbus and Queen Isabella, engaged in a sizzling love affair, the protagonists of one of his last novels, *The Harp and the Shadow*, and García Márquez can dare make Bolívar the protagonist of his *General in His Labyrinth*. Could George Washington or Thomas Jefferson play a similar role in a U.S. novel? In poetry, both Neruda and Paz have written in the epic mode in *Canto general* and *Sunstone*. In his poem, Paz, reaching back to Aztec mythology, is even more cosmic than Neruda. His poem links up with Aztec calendric and cosmological obsessions. Both *Canto general* and *Sunstone*, as well as several novels by Carpentier and Fuentes, are cast in a dizzying numerological mold that reaches back to Dante and a medieval conception of the organic nature of the cosmos. I don't find this in other modern literatures, except in James Joyce, whose relationship to the canon may very well be akin to that of Latin American writers.

There is a certain naïveté in this stance as well as an homage to the romantic origins of all modern literature. Carpentier was open in his debt to Blake and maintained that all modern Latin American literature was essentially romantic. It was his view that the task of Latin American writers was to name things for the first time, like Blake's Adam and like Columbus. This foundational element, this burning proximity to the origins of the modern tradition, is what distinguishes Latin American literature, what makes it different and hence capable of being compared with other literatures of the West. The question is how Latin American literature reads that tradition, how it incorporates it and incorporates itself within it.

One can safely say that the major conundrum in defining Latin American literature has been precisely how it deals with tradition, by which I mean received texts. Borges's idea is that it should be without superstition or reverence, and his disciple and biographer, Emir Rodríguez Monegal, claimed after reading Mikhail Bakhtin that all Latin American literature is parodic in essence. Borges writes in *Discusión* (Buenos Aires, 1957, 161): "Creo que los argentinos, los sudamericanos en general, estamos en una situation análoga (a los escritores judíos dentro de la tradición occidental); podemos manejar todos los temas europeos, manejarlos sin supersticiones, con una irreverencia que puede tener, y ya tiene, consecuencias afortunadas" (I think Argentines, Latin Americans in general, find ourselves in a situation analogous [to that of Jewish writers within Western tradition]; we can address all European topics, address them free of superstition, with an irreverence that can have—indeed, already has—

fortunate consequences). Belatedness and the anxiety of influence are overcome by means of an aggressive rewriting of the canon. I cannot accept Rodríguez Monegal's proposal completely because it condemns Latin American literature to a congenital secondariness and because parody tends to produce only minor works, with exceptions. Besides, one is hard put to read Neruda's *Canto general* as a parody of anything, and there is nothing carnivalesque in Borges himself. Moreover, how does the belatedness of Latin American texts differ from that of any other modern text and from the way tradition is wrought in the West?

Borges's idea seems more productive if we see it in relation to the Latin American obsession with historical beginnings and ends. In a sense what Borges claims is that Latin American literature *is* comparative literature, because dealing with the Western canon without superstition or reverence means to ignore the hierarchies and the chronological imperatives, not to take into account what is supposed to be most important or what came first. It means to read as if all of literature had already been written and were available to the Latin American writer in a kind of apocalyptic textual whirlwind where he or she could pick and choose at will. Latin American works often pretend that they are written at the end of history and contain all previous literature. These are what I call archival fictions, like *Terra Nostra* or *The War of the End of the World*, written precisely in an apocalyptic mode. Our anxiety about the beginning, about our beginning, leads us to posit (or to posture) that we are at the end, or better, that we are the end, the pregnant end of some new beginning that explodes out of the totality of history—a beginning as telling as the Discovery and Conquest of America. I realize that, taken to its ultimate consequences, this is not radically different from the stance of any modern text in the West, but as part of the cosmic disposition of Latin American literature discussed before, it is a founding fable different from any other one finds among contemporary literatures.

A redefined comparative literature could begin to use the reflections of European literatures in the "marginal" literatures as a way of remapping the field and rewriting the canon. In these literatures a more severe and rigorous test to the presuppositions of canonical texts may emerge than what obtains from the reflected self-analysis of much theory and speculation. The issue would then be one not of comparison but of rewritings. Such a process might lead back to literature rather than to criticism, and it is not a sure thing that it will yield a cogent theory or even a methodology in the way that we are accustomed. It will be more a guerrilla assault than a sustained siege in the grand manner. Perhaps what these marginal literatures teach us, after all, is the contingency of theory, its inapplicability beyond the self-enclosed textual subfield from which it emerges. Novels by Fuentes can be used to read Henry James and those by Lezama Lima to read Joyce. Again, the question will not be how these works agree but how they differ, how the reading and rewriting practiced from the margins mobilized elements in the hegemonic texts that were previously inert, beyond the reach of criticism and theory. This is criticism by fiction and friction. But to do this a new class of readers trained (not improvised) in the marginal literatures will have to appear. These critics and scholars will not read "peripheral literatures" always from the center, but will be capable of reading them also in their own context, with all of the philological care this demands. This is not an easy task when dealing with "untranslatable" works like those by Lezama Lima, but one worth attempting in founding a new comparative literature.

I would like to close by reading a passage of *The Lost Steps*, which may serve as an example of how Latin American literature reads the canon and how reading those readings can lead to new insights into both canonical works and those presently excluded. On their first night in the Latin American capital, Mouche and the narrator-protagonist of *The Lost Steps* go to the opera, "a falta de espectáculos de más color local" (for lack of more popular entertainment), as the latter apologizes (111, 43. Los pasos perdidos appeared originally in 1953 and *The Lost Steps* in 1956). They are playing Donizetti's *Lucia di Lammermoor* in a quaint theater adorned by busts of Donizetti himself, Meyerbeer, Rossini, and Herold. The whole atmosphere, according to the jaded and rather unpleasant narrator-protagonist, is romantic, filled with things "rescatadas de otro siglo" (111) (survivals from the past century, 43). The protagonist anticipates being put off by the ridiculous scene, but he is taken in by the powerful emotional appeal of the spectacle on and off the stage: "Pensaba divertirme con los ridículos de la ópera que iba a representarse dentro de las grandes tradiciones de la bravura, la coloratura, la fioritura" (111) (I had hoped to be amused by the extravaganzas of the opera presented in the grand manner of bravura, coloratura, fioritura, 44). "Me sentía dominado más bien por un indefinible encanto, hecho de recuerdos imprecisos y de muy remotas y fragmentadas añoranzas" (111–12) (On the contrary, I felt myself yielding to an indefinable charm, a fabric of vague, remote memories and partly remembered longings, 44). The protagonist's anticipated critical distance is replaced by an act of recall that pierces through what one might expect to be the many books he has read to a personal experience, allowing him to identify emotionally with his surroundings. The scene reminds him of a day in which he, alone in the house as a child, found a diary written by his great-grandmother:

> Una tarde que estaba solo en la casa, yo había descubierto en el fondo de un baúl el libro cubierto de marfil y cerradura de plata

> donde la dama del retrato hubiera llevado su diario de novia. En una página, bajo pétalos de rosa que el tiempo había vuelto de color tabaco, encontré la maravillada descripción de una *Gemma di Vergy* cantada en un teatro de La Habana, que en todo debía corresponder a lo que contemplaba esta noche. (112)

> One afternoon when I had been alone in the house I had discovered in the bottom of a trunk an ivory-bound book with a silver clasp in which the lady of the portrait had kept her diary. On one page, under rose petals that time had turned the color of tobacco, I found the ecstatic description of *Gemma di Vergy* sung in a theater in Havana that must have been the counterpart of the one I was seeing tonight. (44).

Things that "survived from the past century" are elevated by the displacement of the self involved in this process of remembrance, this "recherche du temps perdu." Much could be gleaned from the transformation of those rose petals into tobacco-colored leaves, but suffice it to say (if I may) that the patina of time has invested them with an intoxicating quality that suspends the protagonist's incipient disbelief and allows him to come closer to his surroundings.

The protagonist's reveries are cut short by Mouche, who insists on leaving the theater, bothered by the provincialism of the entire place. In her complaints she reveals the subtext of this suggestive scene: "Llegado el intermedio, Mouche se había declarado incapaz de soportar más, pues aquello—decía—era algo así como 'la *Lucia* vista por Madame Bovary en Rouen.' Aunque la observación no carecía de alguna justeza, me sentí irritado" (113) (At intermission time Mouche flatly stated that she could not take any more of it, for according to her, it might have been "*Lucia* as seen by Mme Bovary in Rouen." Although there was something to what she said, I felt suddenly irritated, 45). The narrator-protagonist's grudging recognition of Mouche's insight is one in a series of comments that show his increasing dissatisfaction with her (and indirectly with himself). She has come to represent a kind of mechanical agent of cultural translation that he wishes to exorcise. To Mouche, everything "aboutit au livre," whereas he fervently wishes to leap out of the book. Her obsession with finding literary and cultural allusions stands for an oppressive form of anteriority, a saturating tradition, a core of Western knowledge out of which it is impossible to find a way out. Of course, the book she discovers beneath the scene they are "living" could not be more appropriate or significant. *Madame Bovary* is, precisely, a text in which the saturation of life by literature is pushed to the extreme.

In *Madame Bovary* the scene recalled by Mouche is a savage attack on romanticism as well as a rigorous critique of representation as the projection of the image of an inner world of feeling. The clash in Flaubert is between the biting satire of the narrator and the identification of Emma with what she sees on stage. She is transported by the "lamentations mélodieuses" (the melodious lamentations) to the point where her own voice blends in with the music on the stage: "Emma jeta un cri aigu, qui se confondit avec la vibration des derniers accords" (224) (Emma gave a sharp cry that mingled with the vibrations of the last chords, 162). She is smitten by the figure of Lagardy, in the leading role, whose splendid life of adventure she tries to imagine. Like Don Quixote at Maese Pedro's puppet play—the subtext of Flaubert's own scene—Emma is oblivious to the distinction between fiction and reality. Her whole emotional life is projected onto the stage. To the narrator, on the other hand, Lagardy had an "admirable nature de charlatan, où il y avait du coiffeur et du toréador" (224) (an admirable charlatan type, in which there was something of the hairdresser as well as the bullfighter, 161). *Lucia di Lammermoor* has obviously been chosen because of its extremely melodramatic plot and the exaggerated displays of coloratura demanded of Lucia and Edgar, the "râles élégiaques d'une douceur infinie" (224) (the elegiac gurglings of infinite sweetness, 162), as the narrator describes their singing in mock-heroic terms. Emma, unlike Carpentier's narrator-protagonist, allows herself no critical distance, whereas Flaubert's narrator widens the gap between the character's feelings and the meaning of the language.

Emma's identification, however, is provoked not simply by the music but also by the plot, which she knew from having read Walter Scott's *Bride of Lammermoor*, on which the libretto is based. The theme of the bride who kills the husband to whom she has been married against her will and who then goes insane is close enough to her own situation to strike a chord within her. Charles, who is the Sancho Panza of the scene, is unaware of all this. He cannot follow the story because the music distorts the words. But Emma's memory of the book allows her to pierce through the music to the violence of the situation. She is not simply overwhelmed by the music. She is also drawn by the story, by the text. The story is alluring in a most personal and perverse fashion, a powerful invitation to murder, no less. It is Lucia's madness, therefore, that Emma focuses upon, because it is the model of her own, which is to live literature, to live representation; it is to live, in other words, beside herself in the other who is the mirror-image of her desires. In her madness Lucia imagines that she is being married to Edgar, that the fairy tale she desires is actualized. This is the most famous scene of the opera, a "holiday of coloratura," as a critic has called it (cover notes, *Highlights from Donizetti's "Lucia di Lammermoor"* (London Records, 1976)). What are the florid decorations of coloratura if not a nonsignifying utterance, a deviation from the linguistic and even musical code that suspends meaning, that does violence to it? It is the language of madness. Emma's fascination with the spectacle of *Lucia* is more significant than even the narrator suspects in his smug satire of romantic expression. The projection of feeling is mediated, in Emma's case, by the passion for literature that also afflicts Flaubert, by that text that her memory brings forth through the nondiscursive part of the spectacle. This passion is akin to Lucia's coloratura, a language of madness, of pure representation, that dwarfs the ironies of the narrator. The richness of this scene is to be found, precisely, in the resilience of Emma before the assault of the narrator.

Carpentier's scene takes up this dialectic. Mouche's reading of Flaubert is apparently superficial, but it indicts her as a Bovarist herself. She has really opened a textual Pandora's Box. She can only see the ridiculous and outdated elements of the scene around her, appearing to side with Flaubert's narrator. But by reacting with such alacrity, she is clearly allowing herself to be ruled by Flaubert's fiction. Yet Mouche is the agent that shatters the narrator-protagonist's delusion, his journey back through memory to his great-grandmother's diary, now fatally mediated by Flaubert's work. Carpentier's reading emerges from this confrontation, and it strikes in both directions: toward himself and toward *Madame Bovary*. It is only proper, perhaps, that a female figure be the one to call the attention of the narrator-protagonist to the fact of his own Bovarism. Mouche, the object of scorn, is nevertheless the critical element. She is on Flaubert's side.

We must not disregard the other female figure evoked in the scene: the great-grandmother who wrote the diary. While rewriting Flaubert, Carpentier has feminized his literary lineage, recognizing perhaps the strength of Flaubert's character, her strength before the onslaught of the narrator. But the female lineage could also be a strategy on Carpentier's part to neutralize the European tradition, one that is curiously bound to fail because Flaubert himself is, after all, the one who made his strongest character a woman. Neutralization at that level entails a different kind of Bovarism: confusing the character with her creator. It is clear, in any case, that both the narrator-protagonist and Carpentier are hopelessly entangled in writing and in the book. Reaching back to that personal, pristine moment of childhood inscribed in memory leads to a book, with very solid ivory covers and a firm silver clasp, to a memory that is as enmeshed in literature and literary tradition as the subtext that Mouche has uncovered.

Flaubert, on the other hand, is indicted for having created an inverted kind of Bovarism, one in which emulation of his narrator leads to a persistent refusal to give in to representation, while yielding to it by the very process of imitating his stance. Flaubertism is also a form of Bovarism, one from which

Carpentier seems incapable of escaping. The reach of the literary is thus widened; its capaciousness now also includes irony and doubt. Mouche's Pandora's Box is the *mise en abîme* of all modern perceptions of literature, one that is as voracious as the Quixotic quest to live representation. The scene in *The Lost Steps* reads, it seems to me, this double bind. Mouche is, in the last analysis, Flaubert. No less. True, Carpentier has not escaped tradition, but his text has tested the limits of tradition by reading it from one of its confines.

Note: A first version of this paper was delivered, at the invitation of Rodolphe Gasché, as the first Eugenio Donato Memorial Lecture, before the Department of Comparative Literature, State University of New York at Buffalo, 12 October 1990. I would like to thank Professor Gasché for the opportunity to honor the memory of our admired friend.

Works Cited

Carpentier, Alejo. *Los pasos perdidos*. Ed. Roberto González Echevarría. Madrid: Cátedra, 1985.

Carpentier, Alejo. *The Lost Steps*. Trans. Harriet de Onís. New York: Knopf, 1989.

Colombí-Monguió, Alicia de. *Petrarquismo peruano*: *Diego Dávalos y Figueroa y la poesía de la miscelánea austral*. London: Tamesis Books, 1985.

Flaubert, Gustave. *Madame Bovary*. New York: Garnier Classics, 1961.

Flaubert, Gustave. *Madame Bovary: Background and Sources, Essays in Criticism*. Ed. and trans. Paul de Man. New York: Norton, 1965.

Fernández Retamar, Roberto. *"Caliban" and Other Essays*. Trans. Edward Baker. Minneapolis: U of Minnesota P, 1989.

Fuentes, Carlos. "A Despot, Now and Forever (Review of Augusto Roa Bastos' *I the Supreme*)." *New York Times Book Review* (6 April 1986): 34.

González Echevarría, Roberto. *Myth and Archive: A Theory of Latin American Literature*. Cambridge: Cambridge UP, 1990.

Kushigian, Julia A. *Orientalism in the Hispanic Literary Tradition: In Dialogue with Borges, Paz, and Sarduy*. Albuquerque: U of New Mexico P, 1991.

Leonard, Irving. *Baroque Times in Old Mexico: Persons, Places, and Practices*. Ann Arbor: U of Michigan P, 1959.

Leonard, Irving. *Books of the Brave: Being an Account of Books and Men in the Spanish Conquest and Settlement of the Sixteenth-Century New World*. Cambridge: Harvard UP, 1949.

Paz, Octavio. "A Literature of Foundations." *The Tri-Quarterly Anthology of Contemporary Latin American Literature*. Ed. José Donoso and William A. Henkin. New York: Dutton, 1969. 2–8.

Rama, Ángel. *La ciudad letrada*. Hanover: Ediciones del Norte, 1984.

Rodríguez Monegal, Emir. *Borges: A Literary Biography*. New York: Dutton, 1978.

Said, Edward. "Representing the Colonized: Anthropology's Interlocutors." *Critical Inquiry* 15.2 (1989): 205–25.

Comparative Literature and Latin American Studies: From Disarticulation to Dialogue

Sophia A. McClennen

Because of the sheer breadth of these fields and because of their complex histories, any investigation into the critical intersection between Latin American studies, cultural studies, and comparative literature must by necessity be partial, provisional, and heuristic. Such a project, imperfect as it must be, is worth undertaking today for a number of reasons. First, the recent revisions and reconfigurations of these fields suggest significant potential for critical collaboration. Second, understanding the intersections between these scholarly areas of inquiry helps overcome the pitfalls of disciplinary insularity. While the overlapping of these three areas is noteworthy in much scholarly work (for instance, "culture" is often favored over literature, demonstrating ways that cultural studies has affected both Latin American studies and comparative literature; or Latin America figures more prominently in comparative literature and cultural studies), without paying careful attention to the implications of such disciplinary promiscuity, these changes run the risk of failing to alter the traditions they seek to challenge. My third reason relates to the threatened state of humanities scholarship in U.S. universities: if the humanities are to survive, then we must find a way to strengthen the ties across humanistic disciplines and also between the humanities and the social sciences. Collaborative scholarship and intellectual exchange will help challenge the academic division of labor that threatens the future of the humanities. What I am proposing, then, might be usefully applied to other cross-disciplinary collaborative frameworks.

Before beginning an overview of the current state of these fields, I would like to clarify my range of focus. The arguments that follow relate specifically to the case of Latin Americanists who study the literary, intellectual and cultural production of the region, leaving aside for the purposes of this study those who work in the social sciences. My principal interest is in tracing the historic disarticulation between humanistic studies of Latin America and the traditional practice of comparative literature while paying attention to the ways that cultural studies has influenced contemporary practice in both areas. The changing shape of these fields suggests that this is an opportune moment to investigate the role of Latin America in comparative literary and cultural studies. If we use the *2001 MLA Job List* as an indicator of shifts in disciplinary configurations, we find many more positions in comparative literature for scholars working on non-Western cultures and Latin America than jobs requesting specialization in Europe or the United States. Moreover, job announcements for Latin Americanists increasingly emphasize desiderata in cultural studies and cross-cultural analysis. They also favor "generalists" with knowledge of a vast array of national cultures over scholars who focus on the culture of only one nation. A significant number of jobs request Latin Americanists who work in inter-American studies or transatlantic studies. According to the academic market, comparative approaches, cultural studies and Latin America make sense together. Román de la Campa has noted the increasing prominence of Latin Americanism in U.S. research universities, and he points out that Latin American, Hispanic and Latino studies continue to be central areas of growth in the nation's top research institutions, attracting both research dollars and students. He explains, in the introduction to his book *Latin Americanism*, that "current critical debates about gender representations, theoretical shifts, modes of periodization, and *new comparative frameworks*—indeed, all the paradigms brought to bear on canonical literatures within the Euro-American academy—now incorporate Latin American literature without exception" (1; my emphasis).

The comparative study of Latin America is further strengthened by a number of scholarly projects that overlap in comparative literature, cultural studies, and Latin American studies. A significant growth area in comparative approaches to Latin America is in inter-American studies. In 2000 Djelal Kadir convened twenty-two scholars who founded the International American Studies Association, which will promote interdisciplinary dialogues about American culture and society, within the international scholarly community. Kadir also edited a special issue of *PMLA* on *America: The Idea, The Literature* and he asks: "How has the idea of America been defined, appropriated, embodied, incorporated, and used for literary ends?" Earl E. Fitz's annotated online bibliography on inter-American literature and criticism provides a rich resource for scholars working in this area. In 2001, *CLCWeb: Comparative Literature and Culture* published a special issue: *Intercultural Negotiations in the Americas and Beyond*, edited by Barbara Buchenau and Marietta Messmer with a number of articles by European scholars who work in inter-American studies. In addition to inter-American studies, transatlantic studies is a further cross-regional angle of comparison that has been gathering increased scholarly attention. A key center for this research is the Transatlantic Project on cultural interactions between Europe, Latin America, and the United States organized and initiated by Julio Ortega and hosted by Brown University. Treating Latin America as a region that requires the use of comparative methods, Mario J. Valdés and Kadir co-edited the *Oxford Comparative History of Latin American Literary Cultures*. According to the editors, the three-volume set "explore[s] a group of contingent, shifting problems which have arisen across national borders, geographic regions, time periods, linguistic systems, cultural traditions—and which, therefore, must be treated comparatively" (see also Valdés in this volume). In 1998 *Revista Iberoamericana* published a special issue on *O Brasil, a América Hispânica e o Caribe: Abordagens Comparativas* (see Costigan and Bernucci), which includes articles by well-known Latin American comparatists like Tânia Franco Carvalhal, who works in Brazil. The journal issue focused on comparative approaches to studying Latin America, which emanate from the specific cultural context of the region. Richard Slatta, a Latin American historian, has recently called for greater use of comparative methods in studying frontier history and is editing a special issue of the *Journal of the West*. These examples demonstrate three key areas of comparative work on Latin America—inter-American, transatlantic and inter-Latin American—and they represent only a sampling of recent scholarly endeavors that bridge comparative approaches and the study of Latin American culture.

These academic initiatives have been accompanied by structural changes to university organization in addition to adaptations in institutional priorities, which reflect greater dialogue between cultural studies, comparative literature and Latin American studies. In the spring of 2001, Princeton created a new Department of Spanish and Portuguese Languages and Cultures indicating "that the department will enrich its curriculum with an increasing attention to the extraordinary plurality of high and popular cultures found in the Spanish- and Portuguese-speaking world" (<http://www.princeton.edu/~spo/>). Other departments, like SUNY Albany's Languages, Literatures and Cultures, have changed their names to reflect greater interest in culture. Additionally, numerous departments have dropped Languages and Literatures from their titles, designating themselves as departments of Romance Studies, as in the case of Duke. Not only do we find changes in the names and foci of departments of foreign languages that teach Latin American literature and culture; departments of comparative literature have also been restructured to emphasize an interest in culture. The University of Minnesota's program in comparative literature is in the Department of Cultural Studies and Comparative Literature and includes a recently added major in Cinema and Media Culture. The University of Pennsylvania's Department of Comparative Literature and Literary Theory offers an undergraduate major in comparative literature, culture, and theory. Ohio State's Department of Comparative Studies offers undergraduate and graduate degrees that encourage "comparative perspectives on a wide range of cultural and historical discourses and practices: literary, aesthetic, folkloric, technological, scientific, religious, political, material" (see <http://comp-studies. ohio-state. edu/>). One of their specific areas of interest is in Latin American and Latino studies. There are also a few programs that take a comparative and interdisciplinary approach to area studies. Duke University offers a major in comparative area studies to students "interested in the interdisciplinary study of societies and cultures of a particular region of the world, complemented with a concentration in a second world area and comparative study of international issues" (see <http://www.duke.edu/web/CAS/>). One of their central regions of study is Latin America. Perhaps the program which signals the most innovative bridge between area studies and comparative literature is Columbia University's Center for Comparative Literature and Society, which was founded in 1998 "to promote a global perspective in the study of literature, culture and its social context" (see <http://www.columbia.edu/cu/ccls/>). The Center includes faculty and programs formerly affiliated with comparative literature, in addition to faculty from other disciplines: "we bring a literature-focused study of language and culture to the area studies as they rethink their mandate; and, conversely, we try to give substance and recognition to those directions in comparative literature that can benefit from the breadth of knowledge produced by a reshaped area studies." The Center acknowledges the need to innovate both area studies and comparative literature, while also recognizing the ways that both fields can productively engage in scholarly dialogue and exchange.

Despite these exciting developments, it remains the case that Latin America has historically been marginalized in comparative literary studies and dialogue between the fields has been minimal. Even though scholarship on Latin American literature has steadily risen since the 1960s, articles treating the region rarely appear in the most respected, traditional journals of comparative literary study. For instance, a five-year sample (from 1996–2000) of the comparative literature issue of *MLN* yielded only one article on a Latin American author. Surveys of well-respected comparative literature journals, such as *Comparative Literature* and *Comparative Literature Studies*, from the same time frame also produced few examples of comparative literary approaches to Latin American texts (recently, the fall 2001 issue of *Comparative Literature* on "Globalization and the Humanities" includes an article by Román de la Campa on the complexities of Latin American and Latino identities). Alternatively, students of Latin American literature and culture in Ph.D. programs are routinely expected to be familiar with the literary production of, at minimum, eight nations (and often as many as twenty) and many programs require students to study both Spain and Latin

America, yet these students are rarely, if ever, expected to be familiar with comparative methods. As I will explain shortly, the lack of familiarity with comparative methods, especially those that treat the intersections between national cultural developments and those that cross national borders, weakens graduate student preparation and scholarship in Latin American literary/cultural studies. So, just as traditional comparative literature has often ignored Latin American culture, comparative methods and approaches have been virtually absent from curricular requirements in Latin American literature programs.

Susan Bassnett states that "comparative literature in one sense is dead" (47), Roberto González Echevarría asks whether "comparative Literature as a discipline has survived" (see his essay in this volume, page 89) and Steven Tötösy calls directly for comparative literature to move towards comparative cultural studies (1999, 2002). Clearly, the comparative literature programs of the 1960s and 1970s have undergone significant revision and transformation. These changes were formally recognized in "The Bernheimer Report on Professional Standards" written for the ACLA in 1993, which called for a move away from Eurocentrism and an exclusive focus on the literary. In the introduction to the report Charles Bernheimer and his colleagues provide a brief evolution of the discipline in the United States and they outline the major arguments of the two previous ACLA reports on standards: The Levin Report (1965) and the Greene Report (1976). One of their key observations is that there has long been a disconnection between certain elitist notions of comparative literature and the actual practice of the discipline: "The anxieties about change articulated in the Greene report suggest that, already in 1976, the field was coming to look disturbingly foreign to some of its eminent authorities" (41). In the introduction to Bernheimer's edited volume, which includes his report and a number of responses to it, Bernheimer suggests that comparative literature has been plagued perennially by anxiety over change, over defining comparison, over finding a common methodology, over selecting objects of study, etc. These "anxieties of comparison" make it extremely difficult to define the theory and practice of comparative literature (1–3). In fact, many have argued that the one defining characteristic of comparative literature is that it escapes definition. Notwithstanding, the scholarly positions taken in the volume, according to Bernheimer, clearly present two main camps. One the one side are those scholars who worry about the departure from the literary and are troubled by too much attention to historical and cultural context: "These critics argue that the work of comparison involves first and foremost a reflection on the aesthetic phenomenon of literariness in a cross-national context" (10). On the other side are those critics who support the arguments of the Bernheimer Report, which calls for a multicultural studies perspective and a rejection of the discipline's historic Eurocentrism. Those who hold the latter position also accept the inherent "messiness" or "disorder" of comparison and contrast those scholars who are incessantly concerned with defining and containing the practice of comparative work. Clearly, the Bernheimer Report was and still is quite polemical. What is most significant for those of us who engage in comparative study of culture from Latin America is that the Bernheimer Report, appearing as the ACLA Report on Professional Standards, signifies an *official* articulation of a new phase of comparative studies. This new era, the "age of multiculturalism," where work is more global in perspective and more contextual in method, is, as I will argue, not new for many Latin Americanists. What is new, though, is the fact that the former margins now occupy a more visibly central space in the field.

As the study of comparative literature moves towards the study of culture in all of its forms as it appears all across the globe, it coincides with a similar trend in Latin Americanism. Scholars of the region have also shifted focus from the "great books" to culture and they increasingly consider Latin America in a global context (see Beverley; de la Campa; Larsen; Mignolo; Moreiras). John Beverley argues in favor of the subaltern studies approach to Latin American culture, since such an approach allows us to understand relations of power and how they are represented (*Subalternity* 1). In order to do this, though, we have to take a global perspective: "This critique cannot itself be contained within the territorial space the idea of Latin America designates" (3). His earlier book, *Against Literature*, specifically pointed to the need to abandon the "high" literature of Latin America and replace it with cultural texts produced from the margins. Such practices, perhaps best exemplified by scholarly interest in the testimonial, highlight a move from literary to cultural study (see Gugelberger). Graduate reading lists include, now more than ever, previously excluded literary and cultural forms—like the testimonial, women's writing, and film—uneasily balanced with the traditional "canon." De la Campa suggests that, in addition to our attention to new cultural forms, new methods are also necessary. Referring to the attention paid to the testimonial, he states: "What is still missing from the debate, in my view, is a comparative analysis, with perhaps some empirical work on reader reception, of how Rigoberta Menchú is read in different parts of Latin America itself" (*Latin Americanism* 23). As a further example, Neil Larsen's *Reading North by South* considers the ways that Latin American texts have been read and consumed by the U.S. academy. Alberto Moreiras's *The Exhaustion of Difference* argues for a radical deconstruction of Latin American studies by pointing to the epistemic systems and global developments that have shaped the field. Our attention is increasingly drawn to the ways that Latin American culture is affected by globalization and transnationalism. Latin Americanists have a long history of considering global relations of power as they play out on cultural terrain. Colonialism and neocolonialism, exile and immigration, national sovereignty and foreign intervention have frequently been at the center of debates about Latin American cultural developments. Even so, subaltern and postcolonial studies as well as calls for comparative studies of globalization point to new critical epistemologies that have been used to frame extraterritorial considerations of Latin American culture.

In considering the interactions between Latin American studies and comparative literature, it is worth noting that the field of comparative literature is especially vibrant in Latin America. Long-standing programs, such as the Program in Literary Theory and Comparative Literature (founded in 1961 at the University of Saõ Paulo in Brazil) or ABRALIC: Brazil Comparative Literature Association (founded in 1985) are now accompanied by newer programs like the Association of Comparative Literature in Argentina established in 1992 (see Franco Carvalhal; Dornheim; Nitrini). Sandra Nitrini provides a history of comparative literature in Brazil in her article "Teoria literária e literatura comparada." In Mexico, the Universidad Autónoma de México (UNAM) has had a graduate program in comparative literature dating back to 1989. Bassnett explains that, simultaneous to a crisis of comparative literature in the West, the field has witnessed significant growth and development outside of Europe and the United States (see also Tötösy for more on the development of comparative literature programs outside of the traditional U.S., French, and German centers). These programs tend to approach the study of comparative literature from a position that links questions of national identity and those of cultural value (Bassnett 9). Such postcolonial approaches stress "the politicization of literature and [reject] the formalist approach completely" (Bassnett 37). The affinities between this approach and the position of the Bernheimer Report should be obvious. Bassnett explains that comparative literature as it is practiced outside of its traditional center is a "political activity, part of a process of reconstructing and reasserting cultural and national identity in the postcolonial period" (39). Even though her comments here refer to the work of the Indian Comparative Literature Association, I believe that they are also applicable to comparative literature in Latin America. Zulma Palermo argues in her survey of comparativism in Argentina that comparative literature as it is presently practiced in Latin America can enable a reconsideration of a number of institutional paradigms which have affected the way that the region "conceives itself in these times of economic and commercial globalization, times when the peripheral societies return to a problematicization of their autonomy and identity from an 'alternative' theoretical position" (212). Lisa Block de Behar recounts the history of comparative literature in Uruguay and she emphasizes the ways that Uruguayan literary study, beginning with the work of Carlos Real de Azúa at the end of the nineteenth century, has always depended on comparative methods. After many years of hard work, she was able in 1988 to host a Latin American comparative literature seminar, which led to the founding of AU LICO: Uruguayan Association of Comparative Literature. The work of these Latin American scholars in comparative literature and the proliferation of programs, associations, and seminars dedicated to the topic adds a key dimension to our consideration of the connections between Latin America and comparative cultural study.

The strength of comparative approaches in Latin America, however, does not necessarily translate into the practice of Latin Americanism in the United States. The exchange and interaction between Latin American scholars of Latin America and those in the United States has a history of conflict and tension, as well as collaboration and dialogue. Moreiras attended the 1996 ABRALIC conference and he relates that the conference was fraught with divisions between advocates of literary studies and cultural studies, where cultural studies was considered to be a hegemonic approach imposed from an imperial center (6–8). Consequently, the growth of these programs should be read in the context of their complex intellectual terrain.

It seems clear, then, that these fields are in an important transition phase and that this is a moment of heightened critical intersection between them. I believe that greater interaction will strengthen the scholarship and training of Latin Americanists and comparatists provided that we are mindful of the historical marginalization of Latin America from comparative literature. Even though comparative study is in a process of change, many comparatists, especially Latin Americanists, are wary of associating themselves with the field because of its traditional legacy. This isolation was highlighted in the Bernheimer Report:

> In this unstable and rapidly evolving sociocultural environment, many of the scholars involved in rethinking the field of comparison have an increasingly uneasy relation to the practices called "Comparative Literature." They feel alienated because of the continued association of these practices, intellectually and institutionally, with standards that construct a discipline almost unrecognizable in the light of their actual methods and interests. (42)

Such alienation and disaffection has led many scholars to pointedly deny any affiliation with comparative literature, despite the fact that their work often bears key identifying characteristics of comparative methods. For instance, a number of scholars I contacted in relation to this current project and whose work I considered exemplary patently rejected the idea that they worked in comparative literature. The following analysis outlines the well-founded skepticism towards comparative literature held by a number of Latin Americanists. After explaining briefly some of the central reasons why some Latin Americanists disregard comparative literature, I focus on a number of key areas where greater dialogue would benefit scholars working in these fields.

Comparative Literature's U.S.-Eurocentrism

The U.S.-Eurocentric history of comparative literature is well known and well documented (see, e.g., Bassnett; Chevrel; Tötösy). From C. L. Wrenn's statement in 1967 that the "only proper object of study for comparatists . . . is 'European languages medieval or modern'" (Bassnett 20) to Henry Gifford's comment in 1969 that "whole continents are becoming articulate—South America yesterday, Africa today" (78), comparative literature has a long history of dismissing the culture of the "peripheries" as unworthy of study. When we combine the traditional Eurocentrism of comparative literature with its early emphasis on major authors, great books and universal literature, i.e., the highest of high culture, we find the combination of elitism and cultural imperialism that has contributed to the stereotype of comparative literature as fundamentally incompatible with the study of postcolonial cultures, such as that of Latin America. It is worth considering the extent to which such problems over the privileging of U.S. and European culture are more about comparative *practices* than comparative *methods*. As early as 1969 Owen Aldridge registered the critique of comparative literature's equation of World literature with Western literature: "These objections are valid, but they should be applied only to inadequate applications of the theory of world literature rather than the principle itself" (2–3). Certainly, Aldridge is raising a contentious point, since many scholars specifically consider the study of European literature to be at the heart of comparative *methods*. For Latin Americanists, Eurocentrism is not a problem limited to primary sources. Not only do we note the bias against "peripheral literatures" as objects of study, but we also object to the imprudent use of European/U.S. theory as the sole critical base for understanding Latin American culture. Traditional comparative literature studies texts from Europe and the United States and it has historically taught methods and theories that emanate solely from these areas as well.

The Cultural Colonization of Latin America

The practice of comparative literature has been repeatedly associated with cultural colonization. Arguments about universal literature, literary value, great books, master writers, etc., all serve to create cultural hierarchies, where texts from the United States and Europe inevitably rise to the top (see Bassnett; González Echevarría in this volume; Tötösy). Bassnett explains that the question of universal value, at the heart of much work in comparative literature, reveals the colonialist viewpoint of many early comparatists (19). In this sense, the quest for literary universals and the desire to define World Literature (both common principles to traditional comparative literature) are gestures that only serve to reinforce cultural hegemony when the criteria for assessment always derive from a U.S.-Eurocentric center. This critique of comparative literature moves beyond the issue of *practice* to *method*, since the comparative method of seeking compatible objects of study often implies assumptions about cultural value. As a consequence, canonized writers from the "peripheries" are often read in ways that either strip them of their cultural context or that consider their cultural context as a marker of lesser literary value. Such practices reveal the cultural colonialism of traditional comparative literature. Bassnett argues that: "Cultural colonialism was also a form of comparative literature, in that writers were imported by the colonizing group and native writers were evaluated negatively in comparison" (19). This practice, perhaps best termed "the poor imitation syndrome," explains the transference of literary movements onto the non-U.S.-European "other" as a futile exercise that exposes the desire of the margins to be like the center. Such thinking is not limited to scholars and writers working in cultural "centers" but is found among writers working from the "peripheries" as well. Robert J. Clements, in *Comparative Literature as Academic Discipline*, refers to José Donoso's personal history of the boom when he argues that only with the boom are "Hispanicamerican writers no longer influenced by American [sic] and French authors" (103). Clements rests his analysis on a "native informant" who ratifies his argument that Latin American writing prior to the boom was merely "poor imitation." Those authors that do produce a body of work that merits inclusion into the comparative literature canon, like Jorge Luis Borges, are often read with no regard for their cultural context. In contrast, Latin Americanists are more inclined to be familiar with the complexity of Borges's relationship to Argentine national culture, especially as it is expressed in his essay "The Argentine Writer and Tradition." A further problem with the inclusion of "newcomers" to the traditional canon, according to Rey Chow, is that in many contemporary cases the traditional Eurocentric canon is replaced with simply another set of texts that repeat the same hegemonic practices of seeking masterpieces and master narratives in accordance with a European privileging of the nation-state. A new practice of comparative literature "must question the very assumption that nation-states with national languages are the only possible cultural formations that produce 'literature' that is worth examining" (Chow 109). A progressive program of comparative cultural study will have to question not only problems of practice, but also problems of method, particularly those methods that are attached to questions of cultural value.

As we consider the conservatism and colonialist impulses of traditional comparative literature we should bear in mind that Latin American studies, especially as it has been practiced in the United States, has a similar history of cultural hegemony. The Latin American Studies Association (founded in 1966) and the American Comparative Literature Association (founded in 1960) reveal parallel moments in U.S. academic developments after World War II. Latin American studies has historically been dominated by the social sciences and has frequently been associated with conservative political agendas (see Mignolo; Moreiras; Morse). Walter Mignolo connects the rise of Latin American studies with the increased global power of the United States during the Cold War (194). Richard Morse, writing in 1964, suggested that many U.S. Latin Americanists were unconscious of their own colonialist attitudes towards the region, and he claimed that their work often revealed a "subconscious hostility" towards their object of study (170). Mark T. Berger's *Under Northern Eyes* provides a history of Latin American studies in the United States; he argues that: "The professional study of Latin America is embedded in a long tradition of viewing Latin America through northern eyes" where "most Latin American specialists, like U.S. policy-makers, are estranged from Latin America" (19). Mignolo, Morse and Berger point out that Latin American studies, like any academic practice in the United States reflects prevailing discourses of power. Moreiras also describes this tendency in Latin-americanism: "Latinamericanist knowledge aspires to a particular form of disciplinary power that it inherits from the imperial state apparatus" (32). This conservative, reactionary form of area studies is concerned with containing and controlling the flow of information about Latin America. Moreiras, however, also points to a second tendency where "Latinamericanism works primarily not as a machine of epistemic homogenization but potentially against it as a disruptive force" (87). In this version, Latinamericanism challenges traditional knowledge structures and homogenizing cultural forces. Like the progressive side of comparative literature described by Bernheimer, Latin American studies also has a long history of politically oppositional practice of which Moreiras's "antirepresentational Latinamericanism" is a recent example. Adding another perspective on the issue, Larsen calls attention to the Marxist politics of Latin American studies in the 1980s and he underscores the leftist approaches which ground many studies of Latin America (*Reading* 18–22).

In short, regardless of our training, in comparative literature or Latin American studies or both, we cannot overlook the colonialist history of these disciplines. Any reassessment of our scholarship will have to address the unequal relations of power between the U.S., Europe, and Latin America, in political, economic, cultural and academic terms. Gabriel García Márquez, in his 1982 acceptance speech for the Nobel, condemns the colonial impulse implicit in much foreign scholarship of Latin America: "The interpretation of our reality through patterns not our own, serves only to make us ever more unknown, ever less free, ever more solitary" (n.p.).

The Problem of Language

When comparative literature originated in the nineteenth century at the peak of European nationalism, language and nation were tied together as important markers of culture. François Jost writes, in his very influential *Introduction to Comparative Literature* (1974), that in Europe since the seventeenth century political and linguistic borders have tended to fuse and that language has been central to nation-building (5–8). Comparative literature served a strange dual impulse: On the one hand, it highlighted the existence of national culture, and on the other hand, it demonstrated that literature was transnational, thereby emphasizing the existence of what Goethe referred to as *Weltliteratur*, but which was actually European literature. Yet, in postcolonial contexts, language often serves not as a mark of national autonomy, but rather as a constant reminder of its troubled past. In fact, in 1492, as Christopher Colombus was setting off on his first voyage to the New World, Antonio de Nebrija presented the first grammar of the Spanish language to Queen Isabel. In his prologue he explains that creating order and structure for the language will help in Empire building: "una cosa hállo y: sáco por conclusión mui cierta: que siempre la lengua fue compañera del imperio" (one thing I find leads me to a certain conclusion: that language was always the companion of Empire; n.p.). The history of the Spanish language in Latin America is intricately tied to the history of Spanish rule. Richard Morse explains that "In the New World the language-national genus equation was problematical. . . . This was particularly so in Spanish America, where nearly a score of countries shared the same mother tongue" (16). According to Morse, in post-Independence Spanish America, nation-building required an intellectual tradition detached from Spain that frustrated the question of national language: "Understandably, the intelligentsia of the new countries often preferred the term 'national language' to 'Spanish' or 'Castilian'" (17).

Struggles to find linguistic autonomy in Spanish America return again and again to the problematic legacy of Spanish. Consequently, the disavowal of comparative work that treats Spanish-language literature from two Latin American nations as not meeting the requirements of "authentic" comparative literature merely serves to perpetuate colonialist epistemologies. Latin Americanists who practice comparative methods might regularly work on five or six different Spanish-speaking nations, but their work is less likely to be considered "officially" comparative than a scholar who studies Germany and France. The assumption that one must work across two languages in order to do comparative work not only belies the legacy of colonialist thinking that plagues comparative literature, but also holds particular consequences for Latin Americanists. Unlike Africa, Asia and the Middle East where literature is published in multiple languages, only in Latin America do we find some twenty nations (including Puerto Rico and the United States) producing culture in the "same" language. Additionally, Spanish, unlike French or English, has been marginalized as an imperial language as well. Walter Mignolo explains that "Spanish language, in Latin America, was twice subaltern: it was no longer the Spanish of Spain, which itself became marginal to European modernity beginning in the seventeenth century" (306).

Most traditional textbooks of comparative literature do not actually require that students work across two languages. Instead, they call for work across two nations, which they often assume will mean two languages. Nevertheless, as Yves Chevrel points out: "The notions of literature, language, and culture are not identical or totally coincidental" (10). Chow agrees with Chevrel in her response to the Bernheimer Report: "we could also, within comparative literature, teach students how to be comparative within 'single' languages" (114). Such a proposal is no small task when the language is used to produce culture across a broad variety of geographical locales, as in the case of Spanish (or English). Any comparative approach to Latin America will need to move beyond the reductive connections between nation and language and will need to reassess the problems of linguistic hegemony.

While I believe that the repudiation of inter-Spanish American comparative work by traditional comparatists should come to an end, I do not want to diminish the importance of working across languages as an important part of our training and research. These are two separate issues: one is the colonialist legacy of undervaluing the comparison of Spanish language texts and the second is the need for comparatists to be trained polyglots who are sensitive to the linguistic varieties of global, especially in this case Latin American, culture. Mary Louise Pratt suggests that polyglossia should be comparative literature's "calling card" but, rather than learn only the language, she advocates that students also learn the culture: "Maybe we should link our endeavors to the need for deeply informed, culturally competent individuals in a globalizing world" ("Comparative" 62). Pratt's point resonates with particular force when considering Latin American culture and leads to another language problem for Latin Americanists. Latin America is itself a region of polyglossia and the hegemony of Spanish in U.S. Latin American studies has often displaced Brazilian Portuguese and Amerindian languages. Our academic training rarely provides opportunities for students and scholars to gain even a minimal proficiency in indigenous languages and too few programs offer Portuguese. If we consider language learning to be at the heart of cultural knowledge, then we must recognize that Amerindian languages and Brazilian Portuguese should be central to our training and research. As Fitz argues, by engaging in comparative study between Brazilian and Spanish American texts, Latin American comparatists can avoid the problems of monolingualism (see Fitz in this volume).

What is more, familiarity with Brazilian literature provides a stronger comparative base for scholarship. For instance, Gregory Rabassa argued in 1978 that many scholars mistakenly consider Brazilian and Spanish American literature to track in parallel ways (119). Such unfamiliarity with Brazilian literature leads certain scholars to assume that Spanish American literature is the standard. A comparative approach to cultural study in the region would dispel such oversights. Regarding the importance of Amerindian languages and cultures, Mignolo contends that attention to subaltern languages is fundamental to any project interested in challenging colonialist epistemologies (261). "From the point of view of the Amerindian population, languages were critical in maintaining a sense of continuity from colonial times through the nation-building period, and up to the end of the twentieth century" (297). Consequently, polyglossia for Latin American comparatists might include Spanish, Brazilian Portuguese and Quechua as a productive array of linguistic proficiency. Nevertheless, few programs in either Latin American literature or comparative literature are prepared to train students in these languages and cultures.

The Problem of Approach

A fourth reason for the lack of dialogue between comparative literature and Latin American studies is a problem of critical approach and cultural theory. Comparative literature's affinities with positivism and its theoretical dominance in U.S. institutions by formalism and new criticism are incompatible with the dominant critical paradigms for the study of Latin America, which favor study of culture in political, economic, and historical context. Bassnett points out that the ahistoricism and formalism of comparative literature was a gradual process that eventually led comparatists, through the example of René Wellek, to eschew any socioeconomic or political aspects of literature (35–36). She maintains that "the crisis of comparative literature derives from a legacy of nineteenth-century Eurocentric positivism and from a refusal to consider the political implications of intercultural transfer, which are fundamental to any comparative activity" (159). Bernheimer also points to the legacy of formalist approaches in the practice of comparative literature ("Anxieties" 10–11). It is interesting to note, however, that there is also a long history of comparatists who have insisted that attention to sociohistorical context is essential for comparative work and that this tradition lives on. Jan Brandt Corstius wrote in 1968 that a foundation of comparative literature was the study of literature in its political, social, economic, cultural, and formal context (6) and more recently Steven Tötösy proposed the theory and method of the systemic and empirical approach where the notion of the systemic includes the historical, economic, cultural, political, etc., dimensions of a literature or of a text (see Tötösy, *Comparative Literature*). Although much of the history of comparative literature is fraught with overdetermined questions of cultural value, U.S.-Eurocentrism, and the persistence of imperialistic knowledge structures, there are aspects of the comparative approach that help illuminate the cultural history of Latin America. Moreover, because Latin Americanists have not considered their work as inherently comparative, they have not fully utilized comparative methods.

Next I would like briefly to point to five research areas that are strengthened by a combination of Latin American studies and a progressive revision of comparative literature that move toward comparative cultural studies.

Cultural Heritage

Comparative methods can provide useful critical approaches to the complex cultural heritage of the region. Latin America does not present us with one, unified cultural history. Instead, we find a combination of indigenous, African, European and U.S. influences, not to mention a variety of immigrant communities. Latin America has a rich and diverse indigenous culture with many regional variations. Spanish and Portuguese colonization, followed by U.S. neo-colonization, coupled with the cultural imperialism of Europe, especially France and England, has meant that Latin American culture has been influenced in intricate ways by Europe and the United States. Moreover, these influences have not been unidirectional; Latin American culture has also had an impact on the cultures of Europe and the United States (see Brotherston and Sá in this volume). Not only do cultural influences flow between the United States, Europe and Latin America, but foreign culture is often manipulated, transformed and hybridized upon arrival in Latin America. For instance, in his theory of transculturation, Ángel Rama argues that Latin America does not simply passively absorb foreign cultural intervention (33).

Unpacking these relationships requires careful attention to comparative methods for understanding cultural influence. Referring to the legacy of the European literary tradition Kadir explains that "Spanish America's literary culture engages most often and most virulently with its ancestral other" (*The Other Writing* 8). In addition, we must factor in the cultural effects of slavery, migration, immigration and exile (Palermo 216). Comparative approaches expose how these different cultural sources intersect, at times in conflict and at others in cooperation, within Latin America. One possibility is that comparative methods, inspired by anthropology and sociology—such as that found in the work of Néstor García Canclini, Pratt, Fernando Ortiz, and Rama—can be used to trace cultural influences and to identify cultural assimilation, dissimilation and transculturation. The strength of the comparative method in understanding Latin America's cultural heritage lies in the premise that cultural influences and movements track differently in different contexts. The comparative method of studying analogies, trends and influences provides useful tools for understanding the way a particular cultural form undergoes regional variations and displays a hybrid of cultural markers (see Jost). Such an approach, informed by postcolonial studies and comparative cultural studies, would yield more sophisticated readings of cultural hybridity in the region. For example using such a conceptual framework might help explain how the testimonial reveals a combination of complex narrative strategies. Doris Sommer's *Proceed with Caution* exemplifies this type of comparative work, as she argues for attention to the "rhetoric of particularism" that she tracks across a number of "minority" texts. Kadir's *The Other Writing* also provides a similar comparative model as he analyzes the tension between a number of "peripheral" texts that represent multifarious confrontations with the "mainstream."

Cultural Cartography

Many geographic parameters contribute to understanding the region designated as "Latin America." In the broadest sense, Latin America must be studied in relation to global history and across regions, as in the case of inter-American, transatlantic, or postcolonial studies. Another cultural map is that of the entire region of Latin America. The concept that all of the Spanish speaking countries of America plus the non-Spanish-speaking countries in Central and South America (occasionally including the non-Spanish Caribbean) all have common cultural connections is fraught with problems (see Mignolo chapter 3; Berger). Mignolo reminds us that the term "Latin America" came about in the nineteenth century and was imposed from outside the region (132). Frank Tannenbaum claimed, in the 1960s, that the countries of Latin America were more diverse than those of Europe and he "insisted that 'lumping them together' was a 'matter of convenience for literary purposes rather than a methodologically permissible device'" (Berger 244–45). Berger explains that the notion of Latin America as a single unit has been a common tendency in academic study and that it has typically been employed from a "colonialist" perspective. Linda Hutcheon, Kadir, and Valdés, in "Collaborative Historiography: A Comparative Literary History of Latin America," recognize the problematical premise that it is possible to comparatively study an entire continent: "Mapping has always been a way to make something exist for imperial eyes" (2). Nevertheless, the notion of a unified region of Latin America served as a key conceptual category during the struggles for Independence, especially through the efforts of Simón Bolívar. Regional unity has been the source of a number of Latin American cultural movements, such as the boom or the New Latin American Cinema. On the other hand, the notion of a unified Latin America has also been central to colonialism and neocolonial politics, like the "Good Neighbor Policy." Hutcheon, Kadir, and Valdés maintain that "the continent's culture and cartography have both been created in reaction to outside pressures and engendered in proactive and reactive ways" (6). Since the concept of Latin America as a single unit has served as both a tool of cultural colonization and as a source of cultural empowerment, scholars working on the region need to constantly reevaluate the notion of "Latin America."

Narrowing our map further, within Latin America we tend to assume that culture tracks according to inter-Latin American regions—such as Caribbean, Southern Cone, Central American, Andean, etc. It is generally accepted that each of these regions presents us with common cultural characteristics. In fact most Latin Americanists consider their area of study in regional terms, which relates to the way that the Latin American Studies Association (LASA) groups panels at their annual convention according to regional designations. Yet these regions should also be critiqued and investigated. They, too, are constructs that derive from discourses of power that employ universalizing tendencies and seek homogeneous cultural markers. For instance, what happens to Paraguay? Sometimes it is considered part of the Southern Cone and sometimes not. Paraguay is not included in the countries of focus for the LASA Southern Cone Studies Section and yet it is included in many other scholarly considerations of the region. The Caribbean poses a whole new set of problems, since it is multilingual and since its colonial legacies are so varied. Many Latin Americanists who study the Caribbean highlight only a few of the nations in the region. Clearly the regional designations are cartographic spaces that should be subject to scrutiny.

Narrowing still further from a conceptual map of inter-Latin American regions, the nation-state continues to be a site of supposed cultural commonality. We understand Latin American culture to develop along national lines. Chow writes that "comparative literature should remain the place where theory is used to put the very concept of the nation in crisis, and with that, the concept of the nation as the origin of a particular literature" (112). Pratt suggests that we should expand comparativeness to include comparisons within national cultures (60). Other axes of Latin American comparison do not conform to any of these spatial markers as in the case of indigenous studies, ethnic studies or the study of women's culture, etc. These practices might happen subnationally, as in the case of Chiapas, or transnationally, as in the case of Quechua culture. Rama characterizes culture as developing along Latin American, national and regional lines. He suggests that literature has many layers of geographic affiliation and that the common elements of culture often do not conform to national borders (58). Hutcheon, Kadir, and Valdés explain that their project focuses on "transnational zones of cultural interaction" since these cultural practices have been largely ignored (6).

In each case, comparative cultural work must be mindful of the geographic boundaries used to mark textual difference. Regional designations, such as Latin American, Andean, Peruvian, or indigenous, for example, chart a text's interpretive course. The text's context of reception is coded, at least in part, by its geographical affiliation, mapping the readers it will appeal to and the interpretive directions readings will take. We should be suspicious of the politics behind these types of cultural categorization. Moreover, these cognitive cultural maps are only guidelines and cultural developments may not always conform to these groupings. Comparative methods help disentangle all of these spatial markers that delineate patterns of cultural practice and they help us to critique these cartographic categories. Studying cultural developments in more than one context also helps draw attention to the values that we place on regional designations. Such a perspective helps explain why, for instance, a text by Borges might be understood as an example of Argentine, Southern Cone, Latin American, or universal literature depending on the context of reception and the politics of interpretation.

Translation Studies

A particularly strong point of recent comparative literary studies is in the area of translation studies (see Bassnett; Tötösy, *Comparative Literature*). According to Chevrel, "One of the problems to which comparatists should devote more space in their studies is how to read or study a literary text in translation" (8). The Bernheimer Report recommends more use of translated texts in comparative literature classes in contrast with the Levin and Greene reports' condemnation of the practice: "While the necessity and unique benefits of a deep knowledge of foreign languages must continue to be stressed, the old hostilities toward translation should be mitigated. In fact, translation can well be seen as a paradigm for larger problems of understanding and interpretation across different discursive traditions" (44). As we know, the issue of whether to encourage or dissuade the use of translations in classrooms has been a hot point of contention for comparatists. Yet, the Bernheimer Report moves the issue beyond the question of whether translation will hinder the language acquisition of students: "Comparative Literature, it could be said, aims to explain both what is lost and what is gained in translations between the distinct value systems of different cultures, media, disciplines, and institutions" (44). In this sense, comparatists have increasingly recognized that their training enables them to study the practice of translation and its theoretical and cultural implications for understanding the development and dissemination of literatures. A leading example is found in the work of Itamar Even-Zohar, who points to the complexities of translation as a cultural practice and the ways that translation is also about discursive and cultural power.

Most Latin Americanists agree that translation has been a powerful force in shaping the Latin American canon. It is well known that Rabassa's extraordinary translating skills had much to do with the literary importance of the Latin American boom (see Larsen; de la Campa). We are all well versed in the story of La Malinche, the region's first translator and the lover of Hernán Cortés, who embodied the inseparable cultural markers of language and identity. Bassnett explains that Malinche "is a figure that represents the Janus-face of translation" since she is depicted as both victim and traitor (153). Given that translation has marked Latin American cultural identity since the moment of the conquest, translation studies is an area where greater collaboration between comparatists and Latin Americanists would be especially productive.

Latin Americanists have repeatedly noted that once a text is translated into English and well reviewed in English-language newspapers, there is heightened interest in the text in its home country. Arguably, Latin Americanists can not avoid the issue of translation and the effects that it has on cultural discourse. The connections between translation and book culture, an area of study for progressive comparatists, are also of significance for Latin Americanists. Scholars who work on U.S. Latino culture are well aware of the ways that language, translation and book culture have all worked together to influence the development of the field. For example, Arte Público Press, affiliated with the University of Houston, was founded in 1979 in order to address the virtual absence of published Latino writers. Their program "Recovering the U.S. Hispanic Literary Heritage" is dedicated to publishing important Latino works in editions for the U.S. mainstream. A further example of the intersections between translation studies, the culture of the book, and Latin American literature can be found in the work of Ariel Dorfman. Since Dorfman is often a cotranslator of his works, I have found that on occasion he changes elements of the text in the process of translation (McClennen, "Ariel Dorfman" 106–19). These changes, especially noteworthy in his first novel, *Moros en la costa* (1973) translated as *Hard Rain* (1990), reflect Dorfman's newly imagined audience for the translated text as well as the shift in historical and cultural context between the original and the translation. Despite the rich potential for scholarship on these issues, we still find reluctance to consider translation as a serious area of research. Bassnett explains that comparative literature historically dismissed the study of the practice of translation (138). Nevertheless, the field is growing in both comparative literature and Latin American cultural studies. There is no question that dialogue and exchange between researchers in these fields would not only be useful, but necessary.

A Challenge to Exceptionalism

The exceptional quality of dominant Western culture can be challenged by the culture of the margins by showing that, in fact, the value placed on U.S.-European culture is predicated on an illusion that all culture originates in the United States or Europe. For instance José Carlos Mariátegui has been referred to as the Antonio Gramsci of the Americas (see at <http://csf.colorado.edu/mirrors/marxists.org/archive/mariateg/>). Yet both authors wrote at roughly the same time. Why is Gramsci not considered the Mariátegui of Europe? Progressive comparative methods can be used to explain and challenge this disparity. A founding principle of comparative literature holds that through the comparison of texts one can avoid reductive assumptions about cultural exceptionalism. And yet, comparative literature in its traditional practice was very exceptionalist, keeping careful guard of which texts and which authors were considered valuable enough to study. As Larsen suggests, the inclusion of literature from the non-Western and postcolonial world upsets the hegemony of U.S.-Eurocentric literature and theory (*Reading* 132). In this way, the arguments I have made about why comparative methods strengthen scholarship on Latin America and vice versa could be translated into similar arguments about Asian, African or Middle Eastern studies. Similarly, comparative approaches enhance research in Latin American studies and enable scholars to avoid unfounded claims of Latin American exceptionalism. Richard Slatta argues that "international comparisons serve as an antidote to exceptionalism, nationalism and xenophobia" (n.p.). A comparative approach that analyzes more than one cultural example across more than one context helps scholars to point out cultural specificities and also illuminates cross-cultural trends. In the case of Latin America, comparative approaches help identify regional particularities as well as point out transregional cultural elements. As mentioned above, the practice of comparative literature in the postcolonial world has often served to reconstruct and reassert cultural and national identity (Bassnett 39). Consequently, as evidenced by the work of Palermo and Block de Behar, we note that comparative methods may facilitate claims that "peripheral" literatures and cultures are valuable contributions to "world" literature through their unique dialectics between universalism and local specificity.

The Interdisciplinary Approach

Both Latin American studies and comparative literature are grounded in a belief that interdisciplinarity strengthens scholarship. In 1974, Jost described the interdisciplinary study of literature in relation to other cultural domains as one of the four main areas of research in comparative literature (viii). Latin American scholars, like Rama, working in roughly the same time frame, have also argued for the need to study literature in historical and political context. Rama finds it troubling that two currents of literary study put the context of the literary text at odds with its formal study. He argues that the literary text must be studied with its social-cultural context and also within its literary intertext (19). While interdisciplinarity in comparative literature has often meant the comparison of literature with philosophy or other art forms, for scholars of literature working in Latin American studies interdisciplinary work has increasingly meant the study of literature in terms of critical theory and historical-political contexts. Latin American interdisciplinary research, like that found in cultural studies, could serve to challenge the formalist, textualist and positivist tendencies in comparative literature. Dialogue across both fields, with added insight from cultural studies, would serve to create better methods of interdisciplinary research. In fact, the premise behind interdisciplinarity is that fields like comparative literature, cultural studies, and Latin American studies, which ostensibly, in and of themselves, constitute interdisciplinary approaches to research, are improved by greater scholarly engagement, collaboration, critique and intellectual challenge.

As many have noted, successful research in such broad fields of study requires collaboration, such as research teams (see Hutcheon; Tötösy). Not only should we make greater efforts to be aware of developments in each field, but we should also begin to break down the tradition of individual scholarly research. According to Pratt, "Facing the crisis of accountability and expertise will have the overwhelmingly positive consequence, one hopes, of clarifying the need for *collaborative* work in literary studies. Developing global perspectives cannot mean that each person must try—or claim—to know the whole globe" ("Comparative" 63). Instead of begging off the need for global awareness by arguing that such scope is beyond one's capabilities, scholars should relinquish their single-author mentality. (It is ironic that so many claim the death of the author, and yet in academia we continue to operate in a system where work is understood as the product of an individual creative mind.) Certainly the Oxford volume edited by Kadir and Valdés makes an important move in this direction.

Much Latin American studies scholarship is comparative. Arguably, because most Latin Americanists work across national boundaries their work is constantly considered within a comparative framework. Yet for some Latin Americanists comparative literature may appear so steeped in its conservative, imperialistic past that it is unable to be of much use. Nevertheless, the transformation of comparative literature away from traditional cultural practice and its growth as a field of study in areas like Latin America suggest that it has moved beyond its conservative past. Drawing on the comparative methods used in comparative literature as well as in other disciplines allows us to avoid what we might call a *com-*

parative unconscious, where scholarship displays elements of comparative analysis without direct attention to comparative methods. Alternatively, comparative literature has yet to fully embrace cultural works produced outside of the "mainstream," and this has crippled the applicability of research in comparative literature in a global context. Despite common concerns over nation, history, politics and cultural identity and common sources of critical theory, Latin American studies and comparative literature remain largely epiphenomenal. While these fields will continue to produce valuable research separately, I hope to have suggested a number of productive areas for collaboration. I do not wish to suggest, however, that these fields merge into one totalizing machine of cultural analysis. Rather, I hope to have argued that mutual awareness and recognition of intellectual developments in these fields would help us to avoid insularity and mistaken claims of exceptionalism. Moreover, despite a lack of interaction and dialogue, the fields have developed in strikingly parallel ways and they have often been influenced by similar trends in criticism. Perhaps increased interaction would enable sophisticated reflection on our research goals and the methods we use to attain them.

Works Cited

Aldridge, A. Owen. "The Purpose and Perspectives of Comparative Literature." *Comparative Literature: Matter and Method*. Ed. A. Owen Aldridge. Urbana: U of Illinois P, 1969. 1–6.

Bassnett, Susan. *Comparative Literature: A Critical Introduction*. Oxford: Blackwell, 1993.

Berger, Mark T. *Under Northern Eyes: Latin American Studies and U.S. Hegemony in the Americas 1898–1990*. Bloomington: Indiana UP, 1995.

Bernheimer, Charles, ed. *Comparative Literature in the Age of Multiculturalism*. Baltimore: Johns Hopkins UP, 1995.

Bernheimer, Charles, Jonathan Arac, Marianne Hirsch, Ann Rosalind Jones, Ronald Judy, Arnold Krupat, Dominick La Capra, Steve Nichols, and Sara Suleri. "American Comparative Literature Association Report on Professional Standards (Bernheimer Report, 1993)." *Comparative Literature in the Age of Multiculturalism*. Ed. Charles Bernheimer. Baltimore: Johns Hopkins UP, 1995. 39–48.

Bernheimer, Charles. "Introduction: The Anxieties of Comparison." *Comparative Literature in the Age of Multiculturalism*. Ed. Charles Bernheimer. Baltimore: Johns Hopkins UP, 1995. 1–17.

Beverley, John. *Against Literature*. Minneapolis: U of Minnesota P, 1993.

Beverley, John. *Subalternity and Representation: Arguments in Cultural Theory*. Durham: Duke UP, 1999.

Block de Behar, Lisa. "Uruguayan Comparative Literature: The Need for a Double Bet." *Comparative Literature World Wide: Issues and Methods / La Littérature comparée dans le monde: Questions et méthodes*. Ed. Tânia Franco Carvalhal. Porto Alegre: L&PM Editores, 1997. 149–72.

Brandt Corstius, Jan. *Introduction to the Comparative Study of Literature*. New York: Random House, 1968.

Brotherston, Gordon, and Lúcia de Sá. "First Peoples of the Americas and Their Literature." *Comparative Cultural Studies and Latin America*. Ed. Sophia A. McClennen and Earl E. Fitz. West Lafayette: Purdue UP, 2004. 8–33.

Buchenau, Barbara, and Marietta Messmer, eds. Intercultural Negotiations in the Americas and Beyond. Thematic issue, *CLCWeb: Comparative Literature and Culture: A WWWeb Journal* 3.2 (2001): <http://clcwebjournal.lib.purdue.edu/clcweb01-2/contents01-2.html>.

Carvalhal, Tânia Franco. "Dez Anos da ABRALIC (1986–1996): Elementos para Sua História." *Organon* 10.24 (1996): (n.p.).

Carvalhal, Tânia Franco. *Literatura comparada*. São Paulo: Editora Atica, 1986.

Chevrel, Yves. *Comparative Literature Today: Methods and Perspectives*. Trans. Farida Elizabeth Dahab. Kirksville: The Thomas Jefferson UP, 1995.

Chow, Rey. "In the Name of Comparative Literature." *Comparative Literature in the Age of Multiculturalism*. Ed. Charles Bernheimer. Baltimore: Johns Hopkins UP, 1995. 107–16.

Clements, Robert J. *Comparative Literature as Academic Discipline: A Statement of Principles, Praxis, Standards*. New York: Modern Language Association of America, 1978.

Costigan, Lúcia Helena, and Leopoldo M. Bernucci, eds. *O Brasil, a América Hispânica e o Caribe: Abordagens Comparativas*. Thematic issue, *Revista Iberoamericana* 182–83 (1998): <http://www.pitt.edu/~iili/lastri.html>.

de la Campa, Román. "Latin American Studies: Literary, Cultural, and Comparative Theory." *CLCWeb: Comparative Literature and Culture: A WWWeb Journal* 4.2 (2002): <http://clcwebjournal.lib.purdue.edu/clcweb02-2/delacampa02.htm>.

de la Campa, Román. "Latin, Latino, American: Split States and Global Imaginaries." *Comparative Literature* 53.4 (2001): 373–88.

de la Campa, Román. *Latin Americanism*. Minneapolis: U of Minnesota P, 1999.

de Nebrija, Antonio. "Prólogo a la gramática de la lengua castellana." *Gramática de la lengua castellana*, 1492: <http://ensayo.rom.uga.edu/antologia/XV/nebrija/>.

Dornheim, Nicolás Jorge. "La literatura comparada en la Argentina." *Boletín de literatura comparada* 3.1–2 (1978): 17–47.

Even-Zohar, Itamar. *Papers in Historical Poetics*. Tel Aviv: The Porter Institute for Poetics and Semiotics, 1978.

Fitz, Earl E. "Spanish American and Brazilian Literature in an Inter-American Perspective: The Comparative Approach." *Comparative Cultural Studies and Latin America*. Ed. Sophia A. McClennen and Earl E. Fitz. West Lafayette: Purdue UP, 2004. 69–88.

Fitz, Earl E. *Inter-American Literature and Criticism: An Electronic Annotated Bibliography* (2001): <http://www.uiowa.edu/uiowapress/interamerican/>.

Fitz, Earl E. *Rediscovering the New World: Inter-American Literature in a Comparative Context*. Iowa City: U of Iowa P, 1991.

García Canclini, Néstor. *Culturas hibridas: estrategias para entrar y salir de la modernidad*. Mexico City: Grijalbo, 1990.

García Márquez, Gabriel. "The Solitude of Latin America." *Nobel Lecture*. (8 December 1982): <http://www.nobel.se/literature/laureates/1982/marquez-lecture.html>.

Gifford, Henry. *Comparative Literature*. London: Routledge & Kegan Paul, 1969.

González Echevarría, Roberto. "Latin American and Comparative Literature." *Comparative Cultural Studies and Latin America*. Ed. Sophia A. McClennen and Earl E. Fitz. West Lafayette: Purdue UP, 2004. 89–104.

Greene, Thomas, Haskell Block, Nan Carpenter, Frederick Garber, François Jost, Walter Kaiser, Elizabeth Trahan, and Herbert Weisinger. "American Comparative Literature Association Report on Professional Standards (Second or Greene Report)." 1976. *ACLAnet* (2002): <http://www.umass.edu/complit/aclanet/Green.html>.

Gugelberger, Georg M., ed. *The Real Thing: Testimonial Discourse and Latin America*. Durham: Duke UP, 1996.

Hutcheon, Linda, Djelal Kadir, and Mario J. Valdés. *Collaborative Historiography: A Comparative History of Latin America*. Occasional Papers 35. New York: American Council of Learned Societies, 1996.

Jost, François. *Introduction to Comparative Literature*. Indianapolis: Pegasus, 1974.

Kadir, Djelal. "Call for Papers: 'America: The Idea, The Literature.'" *American Comparative Literature Association* (1998): <http://www.acla.org/opps_ann_upark.html>.

Kadir, Djelal. *The Other Writing: Postcolonial Essays in Latin America's Writing Culture*. West Lafayette: Purdue UP, 1993.

Larsen, Neil. *Determinations: Essays on Theory, Narrative and Nation in the Americas*. London: Verso, 2001.

Larsen, Neil. *Reading North by South: On Latin American Culture and Politics*. Minneapolis: U of Minnesota P, 1995.

Levin, Harry, A.O. Aldridge, Chandler B. Beall, Haskell Block, Ralph Freedman, Horst Frenz, J.C. La Drière, Alain Renoir, and René Wellek. "American Comparative Literature Association Report on Professional Standards (First or Levin Report, 1965)." *ACLAnet* (2002): <http://www.umass.edu/complit/aclanet/Levin.html>.

McClennen, Sophia A. "Ariel Dorfman." *The Review of Contemporary Fiction* 20.3 (2000): 81–132.

McClennen, Sophia A. "Cultural Politics, Rhetoric, and the Essay: A Comparison of Emerson and Rodó." *CLCWeb: Comparative Literature and Culture: A WWWeb Journal* 2.1 (2000): <http://clcwebjournal.lib.purdue.edu/clcweb00-1/mcclennen00.html>.

Mignolo, Walter. *Local Histories/Global Designs: Coloniality, Subaltern Knowledges, and Border Thinking*. Princeton: Princeton UP, 2000.

Moreiras, Alberto. *The Exhaustion of Difference: The Politics of Latin American Cultural Studies*. Durham: Duke UP, 2001.

Morse, Richard M. *New World Soundings: Culture and Ideology in the Americas*. Baltimore: Johns Hopkins UP, 1989.

Nitrini, Sandra. "Teoria literária e literatura comparada." *Revista Estudos Avançados* 22 (1994): <http://www.usp.br/iea/revista/>.

Ortiz, Fernando. *Contrapunteo cubano del tabaco y azúcar*. Caracas: Biblioteca Ayacucho, 1987.

Palermo, Zulma. "Cultural Articulation of the Comparative Literary Studies: The Argentinian Case." *Comparative Literature World Wide: Issues and Methods/La Littérature comparée dans le monde: Questions et méthodes*. Ed. Tânia Franco Carvalhal. Porto Alegre: L&PM Editores, 1997. 211–31.

Pratt, Mary Louise. "Comparative Literature and Global Citizenship." *Comparative Literature in the Age of Multiculturalism*. Ed. Charles Bernheimer. Baltimore: Johns Hopkins UP, 1995. 58–65.

Pratt, Mary Louise. *Imperial Eyes: Studies in Travel Writing and Transculturation*. London: Routledge, 1992.

Rabassa, Gregory. "A Comparative Look at the Literatures of Spanish America and Brazil: The Dangers of Deception." *Proceedings of the Comparative American Symposium* 10 (1978): 119–32.

Rama, Ángel. *Transculturación narrativa en América Latina*. Montevideo: Fundación Ángel Rama, 1989.

Slatta, Richard. "The Whys and Wherefores of Comparative Frontier History." *Journal of the West* 41.4 (2002): forthcoming.

Sommer, Doris. *Proceed With Caution, When Engaged by Minority Writing in the Americas*. Cambridge: Harvard UP, 1999.

Tötösy de Zepetnek, Steven. *Comparative Literature: Theory, Method, Application*. Amsterdam: Rodopi, 1998.

Tötösy de Zepetnek, Steven. "From Comparative Literature Today toward Comparative Cultural Studies." *CLCWeb: Comparative Literature and Culture: A WWWeb Journal* 1.3 (1999): <http://clcwebjournal.lib.purdue.edu/clcweb99-3/totosy99.html>.

Tötösy de Zepetnek, Steven. "From Comparative Literature Today toward Comparative Cultural Studies." *Comparative Literature and Comparative Cultural Studies*. Ed. Steven Tötösy de Zepetnek. West Lafayette: Purdue UP, 2002. 235–67.

Valdés, Mario J. "A Historical Account of Difference: A Comparative History of the Literary Cultures of Latin America." *Comparative Cultural Studies and Latin America*. Ed. Sophia A. McClennen and Earl E. Fitz. West Lafayette: Purdue UP, 2004. 178–97.

Valdés, Mario J., and Djelal Kadir, eds. *Oxford Comparative History of Latin American Literary Cultures* (1996–): <http://www.chass.utoronto.ca/lithist/latin.html>.

The Villain at the Center: Infrapolitical Borges

Alberto Moreiras

Life is but a walking shadow; a poor player that struts and frets his hour upon the stage, and then is heard no more

—*Macbeth* Act V, Scene 5

Paul de Man said that Borges's essays were just like *PMLA* essays, except that they were "a great deal more succinct and devious" (124). As proof of succinctness and deviousness de Man quoted the comment Borges made on Enno Littmann's German translation of *Arabian Nights*: "Incapable, like George Washington, of telling a lie, his work reveals nothing but German candor [probidad]" (qtd. in de Man 124). A literal and honest translation ends up yielding a literal and unimaginative world. Borges would have liked to learn of his extreme like-mindedness in these matters with Sherlock Holmes, for whom "there is nothing more deceptive than an obvious fact" (Conan Doyle 72). The somewhat alarming conclusion this juxtaposition permits is that *PMLA* essays, or their cousins, are the more deceptive the more honest and less devious they are; and, therefore, the less devious the more devious. Let us take *PMLA*-style essays on Borges: the critical effort of the last fifty years and more would depend one devious or deceptive way or another on "the ordering presence of a villain at the center" (de Man 124). But villains, when their villainy becomes explicit, end up revealing their fundamental candor. Is it not notorious candor to say "for Borges the literary exercise was a revealer of our possibilities. His literature speaks to us of what we are and cannot be, of failure, tragedies, uselessness. A literature that unconceals fragility, loss, fatigue" (Scarfó 83; my translation)? Or to say: "Borges defines the centrality of memory in the search for the crystal of memory and of his uncertain meaning, his dubious refractions" (Pimentel 164; my translation)? Nothing is more deceptive than the obvious. Thus, nothing more treacherous.

"The Theme of the Traitor and the Hero" comes to be written when "the date of the first centenary . . . was approaching" (Borges 143). It is true that the narrator means Fergus Kilpatrick's death, not Borges's birth, but the association is hardly avoidable today. The story narrates Ryan's story, who tells Kilpatrick's story and imagines or reveals in it a rare mimetic conspiracy: Kilpatrick signs a traitor's death sentence. His comrade James Alexander Nolan suggests "a way to turn the traitor's execution into an instrument for the emancipation of the country [*patria*; this is a bad mistranslation in this context] (145)." "Thus the teeming drama played itself out in time, until that August 6, 1824, in a box . . . draped with funereal curtains, when a yearned-for bullet pierced the traitor-hero's breast. Between two spurts of sudden blood, Kilpatrick could hardly pronounce the few words given him to speak" (145–46). The identity of the traitor and the hero becomes undecidable, but Ryan must decide. "After long and stubborn deliberation, he decided to silence the discovery. He published a book dedicated to the hero's glory" (146). The villain is at the center of this story by Borges, but he is also at the margins, since Ryan becomes a villain through his probity (and upright in his villainy). Ryan learns the truth and persists in falsity, in the name of a higher truth. Or conversely: Ryan learns a falsehood and persists in the truth. Nothing more deceptive. But Ryan is placed at the site of the critic, at the site of the *PMLA* contributor or of his Argentine cognate. Near the date of the first centenary, how can we avoid a meditation on the enigmatic relation between Borges and criticism that is prefigured in "Theme" as a step into, or a passage towards, undecidability? To advance into undecidability is, however, always a decision. And every decision is a cut into truth.

Paul de Man's essay was published in 1964, at the very beginning of the internationalization of Borges's writing. It is important to remember the central aspects of de Man's exegesis, also to the extent to which it has rarely been surpassed: "the artist has to wear the mask of the villain in order to create a style" (124); "whatever Borges' existential anxieties may be . . . they are the consistent expansion of a purely poetic consciousness to its furthest limits" (124); "the world [of his short stories] is the representation, not of an actual experience, but of an intellectual proposition" (125); "poetic intervention begins in duplicity, but it does not stop there. For the writer's particular duplicity . . . stems from the fact that he presents the invented form as if it possessed the attributes of reality, thus allowing it to be mimetically reproduced, in its turn, in another mirror image that takes the preceding pseudoreality for *its* starting point" (126); "by carrying this process to its limits, the poet can achieve ultimate success—an ordered picture of reality that contains the totality of all things, subtly transformed and enriched by the imaginative process that engendered them" (127); "all these points or domains of total vision symbolize the entirely successful and deceiving outcome of the poet's irrepressible urge for order" (127); "the success of these poetic worlds is expressed by their all-inclusive and ordered wholeness. Their deceitful nature is harder to define, but essential to an understanding of Borges" (127); "our 'real' universe is like space: stable but chaotic. If, by an act of the mind comparable to Borges' will to style, we order this chaos, we may well succeed in achieving an order of sorts, but we dissolve the binding, spatial substance that held our chaotic universe together" (128); "style in Borges becomes the ordering but dissolving act that transforms the unity of experience into the enumeration of its discontinuous parts" (128); "hence . . . his definition of his own style as baroque, 'the style that deliberately exhausts (or tries to exhaust) all its possibilities" (128); "the poetic impulse in all its perverse duplicity belongs to man alone, marks him as essentially human. But God appears on the scene as the power of reality itself, in the form of a death that demonstrates the failure of poetry . . . God is on the side of chaotic reality and style is powerless to conquer him. His appearance is like the hideous face of Hakim when he loses the shining mask he has been wearing and reveals a face worn away by leprosy. The proliferation of mirrors is all the more terrifying because each new image brings us a step closer to this face" (128–29); "although the last reflection may be the face of God himself, with his appearance the life of poetry comes to an end. The situation is very similar to that of Kierkegaard's aesthetic man, with the difference that Borges refuses to give up his poetic predicament for a leap into faith" (129).

With devious and duplicitous candor I take de Man's ordered vision of Borgesian reality as my point of departure. I oppose to it a contrary vision, which I admit can only be subjected, at least initially, to the treacherous mimesis of that which it denies: Enrique Pezzoni's, as it is given to us in some of the lectures recently transcribed by Annick Louis. And to the latter I will oppose a wicked, if succinct, essay by Raúl Antelo, "La zoología imaginaria como deslectura de las radiografías y los retratos de la nación en crisis." If at the end of this process we end up looking at Hakim the Dyer's face we will know it is not God's, but only Hakim the Dyer's—although nothing can be more deceptive than the obvious fact. Between the lines, to be completely honest and hide nothing, we may also fleetingly glimpse the image of another villain at my center, the later Heidegger.

Perhaps in despair at similar, if more abundant, verbosity Josefina Ludmer writes: "From where could one read Borges in order to leave him? From what reading position? I confess this is my recurring question since I arrived at Buenos Aires, in May, and I found the Centenary" (289; for this and all quotes from Ludmer, my translation). I suspect Ludmer carefully dissembles some of her tedium in order to not reveal the fundamental impatience she feels about the fact that Borges's centenary came and went, and with it sixty years of academic criticism on Borges, and we are still in Borges's presence like poor Borges himself was when he would come to visit at the house that sheltered the Aleph, and with it Beatriz Viterbo's atrocious revelation, and the world's: perplexed, jealous, bored, and with a Santafé *alfajor* hanging from a ribbon.

The proofs of our critical candor are innumerable, and we only have to check, say, the *MLA Bibliography* and other repertories for their precise enumeration. With few exceptions, like de Man's (and, partially, Ludmer's and, I will suggest, Antelo's), our relation to Borges mimetizes Carlos Argentino Daneri's relation to the universe: literal, if somewhat imaginative. We are lacking, grievously after so many years, a theoretical articulation of Borges's poetics; fundamentally, we are lacking a conceptual procedure that will allow us finally to move beyond the weariness that endlessly repeated clichés and truisms can only inspire. "These magical texts where a thousand luminous moments crackle" (Saer 31; my translation) (talking about the king of Rome) seem to have brought along little more than blindness, camouflaged in empty chatter about mirrors, memories, traditions, loss, and labyrinths. There is an aesthetic reading of Borges, perhaps the dominant one, that is precisely anti-aesthetic because it is only aesthetic pretension: in relation to Borges, we have never touched the aesthetic. Not having reached the aesthetic, not having conceived the possibility of conceptual labor, how can we think of exiting from Borges? Before leaving one must at least have arrived.

Enrique Pezzoni was a greatly reputed master of Borgesian literature, and a mentor for many. Those of us who only knew of him by fame would perhaps have expected a higher illumination than the one provided by the book that has been carefully edited by Louis, and that contains a number of class lectures given by Pezzoni at the University of Buenos Aires. I will focus on the class notes where Pezzoni concerns himself with "Theme." As I will show, Pezzoni hands us a snub, purely nihilistic, falsely subversive, metaphysical, and trivial Borges (with all my respects to the master I did not meet, but others met).

The distance between Ryan before his discovery and Ryan who makes the decision to write a panegyric is similar to the infinite distance between Miguel de Cervantes and Pierre Menard—it does not matter that, in the case of both successors, the text to be written would have been identical to the precursor's text. The deciding Ryan is not in symmetry with the initial Ryan, since the deciding Ryan is as fallen into the "theme of the traitor and the hero" as his protagonist. But the deciding Ryan repeats the critical position that Ludmer recommends on the basis of a brief commentary on Pezzoni. Here is Ludmer:

> Enrique Pezzoni writes in Sur in 1952 that after the first critical reviews and praise there occurs a fundamental revision of the opinion on Borges: 'what started to be discovered in him was his position

> regarding reality and culture, the latter conceived as a new reality at the same level as the former, and just as vast, as urgent.' I will retake this . . . because I believe it is crucial for us today, or at least for me: culture and reality, two realities with the same weight. I believe that without this premise I would be unable to read Borges. (Ludmer 292)

Two realities with the same weight: culture and reality. Between them, in some enigmatic manner, we must imagine literature: neither simply culture nor simply reality, but something else, perhaps the otherness that marks the possibility of that absolute separation or initial difference between culture and reality, but an otherness that becomes one only as it conquers, impossibly, absolute autonomy:

> [Borges] defined in Argentina a purely literary, modern literature, independent from other spheres, without spheres above it. He turned literature independent, or rather; he completed the process of autonomization that was open in 1880 with the establishment of the national State and the independence from the political sphere [sic]. He reduced everything to literature and wrote that philosophy was a branch of fantastic literature. (Ludmer 292–93)

Borges reduces everything to literature precisely through the same movement that allows him to create two radically heterogeneous orders of the real: reality, culture. In other words, upon discerning or absolutely deciding between reality and culture through his particular invention of literature, Borges paradoxically posits literature as an apparatus for the reduction of all difference between reality and culture. Such a trip is a parallel to the apotheosis of the modern State, which is constituted by the very autonomization of the political, and hence by the reduction of everything to the political (except, in a strong sense, the State itself): but with and through this reduction the State, like literature, also simultaneously, and aporetically, establishes an essential if enigmatic difference between the order of reality and the order of culture. "That is the fiction of the time of literature's autonomy and Borges' fiction, which is a machine that generates enigmas, that turns around the verbal decomposition of the legitimate truth and of perpetual ambivalence, of the undecipherable text, of the form itself of the secret in literature" (Ludmer 293–94).

What is this secret that Borges's fiction conceals and that the responsible critic, sincere and devious, must also conceal, like Ryan, into the perpetual ambivalence traitor/hero? This is Ludmer's second comment on Pezzoni:

> Borges may appear as a revolutionary writer in Argentina from the 1960s to the 1980s because textual ideology (the textual subject) can be opposite to the explicit ideology of the writer. And thus he appears, nihilistic and anarchistic, in Enrique Pezzoni's classes in the 1980s . . . Pezzoni reads Borges's procedure of the technical in-

> vention of series that deny each other successively, even as they absorb all kinds of other discourses. And he finds a textual subject that surpasses the division between pure literature and social literature. (294)

For Ludmer's textual economy, as I understand it, such a conception is precisely what must be abandoned. Pezzoni's "textual subject"—a subject that surpasses the distinction between pure literature and social literature, or the division between reality and culture—is a confused subject: in the first place because his supposed nihilism and anarchism absolutely coincide with the position of the State as subject, as state-subject. The textual subject that becomes autonomous in literature is in the same place as the state subject that becomes autonomous through the political, and both of them make a system, as Ludmer herself suggests when she says that Borges carries to "a fusion and a critical point" the history of the Argentine national-popular state after 1880 and the "history of literary autonomy (and with it the history of the idea of author, of work, of self-reference, and of fiction)" (292). Hence to abandon the state-national Borges is also to abandon the monumentalized and literary-autonomous Borges, and vice versa:

> Because, for me, to leave Borges, to take the name and the authority away from Borges does not mean not to name him, but rather to dissolve the organic unity of his work, to take away its stability and its monumentality. It would be to dissolve an autonomized organic unity and also to break the unity of his texts in order to build with his literature, with some fragments from his literature, another field that would no longer be a field ruled over by his name. (297)

It would appear that Ludmer is getting ready to mimetize the other Ryan, the Ryan of the alternative decision to deconstruct Fergus Kilpatrick against the foretold chronicle of the "emancipation of the fatherland." Borges, like life itself in Shakespeare's *Macbeth* (one of the recurring texts in the mimetic conspiracy Nolan orchestrates), would have come to be, in the future anterior of a new emancipation, the very possibility of an emancipation from Borges himself, now understood, somewhat resentfully, as "a walking shadow; a poor player that struts and frets his hour upon the stage, and then is heard no more." But such post-state or counter-imperial revelation remains merely imminent and never comes to fruition in Ludmer's text. Ludmer withdraws, against the real, towards the cultural, and proposes a field that is still a field ruled over by Borges's name, which is now the name of a suspect hero, a fallen hero who therefore needs the stage and the representation that Ryan, as a new Nolan, puts forth, or Pezzoni as a new Ryan, or Ludmer herself, since her critique of Pezzoni never radicalizes its own principle and thus never reaches its truth—or perhaps it does reach its truth, but in too succinct and devious a manner, and thus a manner that remains undecided regarding a necessary betrayal. Ludmer concludes:

> I would retain a Borgesian reading position regarding the use and critique of Borges. And I would transform Borges into a tradition. This irreverent tradition regarding Borges would be a critical tradition regarding national traditions and histories. Upon reading Borges as tradition, I would leave Borges from within, given his critical position regarding cultural traditions, which would make of this position a national tradition. (299)

Ludmer ends, against her own argumentation, by restoring the trap of a national Borges that Pezzoni's conception of the textual subject as a mediator between the heterogeneous series of reality and culture opens: in Ludmer the nation reemerges as the mediator between those two equal weights. But, after all, reality and culture do not have the same weight, just like a traitor and a hero do not weigh the same, and they are not the same thing. To posit their balance, which is what de Man or Borges never do, is a surreptitious wager on the superiority of culture, which will always have revealed its cards as a communitarian wager for cultural communion, in this and in so many other cases national communion, against the countercommunitarian rights that destabilize the real and follow a different fidelity.

Not so unexpectedly for a reader of Borges (or for deconstruction, itself an inheritor of Sophocles the detective-story writer), we can find in some words of Sherlock Holmes the secret of the dissymmetry between reality and culture that Borgesian criticism seems to have taken upon itself to keep and never to reveal. Says Holmes of the "ideal reasoner":

> [he] would, when he has once been shown a single fact in all its bearings, deduce from it not only all the chain of events which led up to it but also all the results which would follow from it. As Cuvier could correctly describe a whole animal by the contemplation of a single bone, so the observer who has thoroughly understood one link in a series of incidents, should be able accurately to state all the other ones, both before and after. We have not yet grasped the results which the reason alone can attain to. Problems may be solved in the study which have baffled all those who have sought a solution by the aid of their senses. To carry the art, however, to its highest pitch, it is necessary that the reasoner should be able to utilize all the facts which have come to his knowledge, and this in itself implies . . . a possession of all knowledge, which, even in these days of free education and encyclopedias, is a somewhat rare accomplishment. (Conan Doyle 105)

Given infinite knowledge, map and territory, reality and culture would infinitely coincide. It is the failure of knowledge, not the failure of reality, that unleashes the need for a figural or poetic consciousness, whose character in Borges is classically mimetic, but becomes baroque through its impossibility of stasis. Borges's poetic consciousness, as de Man notes, seeks to carry its expression to the limit, to exhaust its possibilities (which are then never exhausted). Borges's will to style is baroque tension inasmuch as it thematizes the fissure between reality and culture, territory and map. Far from positing a substitutive or compensatory possibility for the poetic artifact, far from thinking that the poetic series can bring the mimesis of the real to a point of closure (this is precisely what is most remote from Borges, what Borges never does, although his critics will not cease to betray him by attributing nothing else to him), Borges shows over and over again how the possibility of total vision is simply an illusion, an ideologeme that displaces and defers the real, the impact of the real, or the real as impact. De Man's ordering of chaos or Holmes's total knowledge are symptomatic formations and mere inversions of the Borgesian impossibility of closure for the real. Such an impossibility is the very name of the possibility of poetry—the very mode in which the poetic abandons truth as representation and enters an alternative theory of truth. In Borgesian aletheology the deceptive is the mark of a truth deeper than the obvious: hence the need for "the ordering presence of a villain at the center." In a context where truth as representation is revealed as a deceptive version of truth, deceitful representation—representation as deceit—points to a higher truth, a truth beyond representation. Every ordering act is a dissolving act. Only the villain can dissolve and (dis)order without threatening the substance of the mystery, since the villain understands the mystery from his finitude and does not aspire to infinite knowledge. With the villain, with the traitor, the goal of the poetic as finite is announced: poetry is finitude, and infinitude is pure cultural farce, pure (cultural) pretension of equivalence with the real. If there is a god in Borges it is the god of finitude, on the side of the real, and thus of the poetic, against every form of culture (including, most certainly, national culture).

Pezzoni's theory yields a nihilistic Borges because Pezzoni's Borges is a culturalist, so he is, nihilistically, against the real, which is (supposed to be) just another name for nothingness. The obvious inconsistency of this position does not keep Pezzoni from embracing it. In order to show this I will limit myself to Pezzoni's reading of "The Theme of the Traitor and the Hero" in the first part of *Enrique Pezzoni, lector de Borges*. Louis calls that first part "El sujeto Borges o la exhibición desaforada." It contains notes from classes 13 to 17, held between May and June 1988. Pezzoni's point of departure is summed up in the last class: "'Theme of the Traitor and the Hero' could be a kind of epitome of all Borgesian narrativity; and the game of the treason of opposites permanently under-lays Borgesian literature" (118). From this perspective, what Pezzoni determines in his lectures is good as a general statement on Borges's poetics, and should not be restricted to commentary on a single short story: the particular stands for the universal. First I transcribe some passages that I will then intersperse with paraphrases.

"['Theme'] questions the mechanisms commonly used to convey a real or fictitious fact, and how those procedures decisively and ideologically influence the vision of the conveyed real or fictitious fact" (30; my translation for this and subsequent quotes); "the Borges textual subject . . . is . . . a subject essentially subversive of institutionalized forms" (31); "a counterposition of two practices: the allegedly submissive practice of the documenter and the radically active, discursive practice of the one who proposes, invents documents—the core of ['Theme']" (37); "against the world, the best possibility is to propose alternative forms of ordering and schematizing the world" (40); "one could compose different biographies of a character, or a man, reordering the series of events in such a way that the re-reading of such a multiplicity of biographies would eventually show that all of them are the biography of the same subject" (41). Pezzoni imagines the existence of an "institutionalized form" that is a correlate of that which the "práctica sumisa del documentador" seeks. "Submissive practice" and "institutionalized form" sustain each other and constitute each other. Against that "submissive practice" he then imagines an alternative practice, "essentially subversive," another form of ordering of the world, but, curiously, an ordering whose referent is still "the same subject." We have a subject, and two different "procedures" "against the world." The subject makes an ideological choice between them. Borges would seem to opt, in every case, for the subversive practice, revealing in the process not only that whatever is institutionalized is ideology, but also that any subversive practice is also itself ideological.

"The Borgesian series, the series Borges makes up in his stories, like St. Thomas' series, also may never have existed. The difference is that, for St. Thomas, there is a first, noncontingent cause in the universe: God. The universe may never have existed, but it does. And its existence is explained through that non-contingent, non-aleatory, non-chance cause that is the divine. The Borgesian series is a series where somebody takes on the role of an absolutely contingent divinity—an aleatory and contingent divinity—invents an absolutely contingent divinity that initiates a series that, in effect, can never exist and that is absolutely contingent [sic]" (44); "Borges's ordering principle is absolutely contingent. So Borges's text and the series of events it presents is always unjustified. . . . The text always constitutes its own causality. . . . The text justifies with its proposed orderings the ordering itself. The world is like it is because the text suggests it is" (46–47); "they are ideological texts that conceive ideology not as content but as special forms, dynamiting forms, subversive forms, etc. In this sense, Borges is a kind of strange presence" (48);

"[Borges's] idea of the non-definitive text [is] an idea about the constant production of sense. Sense as production and not as search of something previous, reified, that already exists" (49). Contingency is then apparently subversive, but subversive of what? It can only be subversive of necessity, which somehow begs the principle. Borges is then a conventional atheist, that is to say, he is an atheist regarding the Western ontotheological convention according to which God is nothing but first unfounded cause and principle of sufficient reason. From that atheist or allegedly antimetaphysical, anti-ontotheological position Borges derives a simple parodic procedure: the text is placed in the ontotheological site, as a substitute for divinity. But since the text is written by Borges, Borges knows very well that there is no necessity, only contingency in his textual procedures. So Borges emerges as a villain god or false god, a demon or "extraña presencia" that subverts the ontotheological version of becoming, based upon the presupposition of a world-dominating, extratextual principle of sufficient reason. But how, precisely, does he subvert it? Whimsically, through the arbitrary, unjustified positing of ordering principles that yield disorder. For Pezzoni, this would allow us to understand that every act of creation is a proposal of meaning, and that there is no meaning except for the whimsical meaning given by any arbitrary form of ordering. I, Borges, upon assuming the creation of sense that had been supposedly a prerogative of divinity, realize that we can all make sense, so divinity is as ridiculous and false as I myself am. My sense is nonsense, unless it has the sense of showing that there is no sense, that there is nonsense.

"There is a kind of nihilistic and tremendously anarchistic ethics which prohibits falling into the temptation . . . of a transcending and founding cause, but at the same time [there is] the nostalgia for a transcending and founding cause" (50); "the absolute refusal to allow ultimate meanings that can impose themselves as true . . . the absolute questioning of any construction of sense as a sense that may transcend the very subjects that work with it" (53); "Borges exhibits procedure as form, as ideological form, that is to say, he shows ideology as form, as a form that proposes certain sense conceptions that destroy alternative conceptions" (61–62); "his ideological gesture consists of correcting history, of creating the possibility that universal history can be made anew, but at the same time, through a new nihilistic and anarchistic ideological gesture, he immediately devalues the new rigorous construction: that construction is false, it is not true. Truth is disseminated nowhere" (86); "history and literature continuously exchange their roles and devalue each other; the Borgesian ideological gesture is to destroy paradigms of knowledge. Epistemological paradigms are made to be destroyed, transformed, altered, ceaselessly replaced. There is no ultimate or final sense" (90); "his didacticism . . . would consist of showing literature as procedure, but at the same time of showing procedure as a way into ideological systems. That exaltation of procedure is also a degradation of procedure. In other words, it would correspond analogically to showing epistemological paradigms in order to discard them immediately through the emergence of new epistemological paradigms that are in turn discarded and of which only words remain" (96). And, of course, if my sense is nonsense, then nothing is true or false, and everything is relative, and so forth. I then declare myself a nihilist, since only nothingness exists, and an anarchist, because I do not even believe that my own capacity for ordering can give the world a principle of order. My procedure, which is not even a truth procedure any more, only a procedure of untruth, can only from now on take pleasure in the nihilist-anarchist hypostasis: I dismantle, I dynamite, and I make the word degenerate by showing that there is no more than word, that everything is (nothing but) word, and thus that even the word itself is nothing. Except perhaps for that vague "nostalgia" Pezzoni admits, and that he couples with the prohibition of the higher nostalgia for a transcendent, founding cause. Both of them, nostalgia and its prohibition, in their very dehiscence, insinuate a problem that can be shown to be the true "extraña presencia" in Pezzoni's interpretation, the villain at its center.

Beyond its tautologies, there is great probity in Pezzoni's interpretive proposal (I do not know whether it is Argentine probity in the same sense in which Littmann's was German). But it is, in any case, a treacherous probity: under the pretext of translating Borges's system literally, it betrays it by reducing it to nihilist triviality. Pezzoni would have in effect no reason to be surprised or bewildered by the fact that this Borges, his Borges, can end up serving as justification for the worst in the order of the political:

> Borges's work, eternally subversive, ideologically subversive regarding customary orders, with its great problem of the superimposition of the empirical subject and the textual subject . . . this tremendously subversive work, unfortunately, has served as support for conservative governments; in any case Borges's work has not shaken the order of military governments. (123)

The reasoning is simple: *if* there is (nothing but) nihilism, then order becomes the only possibility, that is, the absolute possibility of warranting a principle of immanence or stability for the social. Any order is preferable to disorder when disorder has no higher value than being a mere and vacuous alternative to order. The secret of anarchism, when anarchism is effectively nihilistic, is that it is essentially open to the worst forms of authoritarian totalitarianism: given that there is no order, let it all become an order. The great value of Josefina Ludmer's essay consists precisely in its reaction—a reaction that remains secret or unmanifested in the essay itself, but that constitutes its true possibility—against the intimate alliance between the system that proposes the total autonomy of the literary and the system that proposes the absolute autonomy of the state form.

We can now begin to understand the complicity between the twentieth-century avant-gardes and state totalitarianism, on which any possible conception of a communitarian nation ultimately depends. And we can now unleash the suspicion that the problem with Borges was not that he was a reactionary. The problem was the unintentional—but never innocent—reactionary-ism of Borgesian criticism, and not only on its Argentine side: we have created a national Borges, an anarchist-subversive and nihilist national Borges, whose dark shadow was necessarily the absolute apotheosis of the ontotheologism that underlies dictatorship as necessary state contingency and (final) principle of imanence of the social. In other words, Borgesian literature, in the nihilist-anarchist interpretation, created, or contributed to create, the ideological justification for the exceptional decision—the decision to rule on the exception—that is the very name of state sovereignty as the final principle of order-in-disorder.

We should remember the already-quoted words by Paul de Man: "if . . . we order this chaos, we may well succeed in achieving an order of sorts, but we dissolve the binding spatial substance that holds our chaotic universe together." One needs doves' feet not to fall into the ontotheological abyss, as Nietzsche, himself quite blind in key moments of his work to the complicity between metaphysics and nihilism, used to say. Pezzoni manages to create an "order of sorts" in the complex and subtle universe of Borges's work, but only at the price of dissolving its properly poetic substance, which is never of course merely functionalist and cannot therefore consist of the mere de-familiarizing astonishment regarding what is established, or institutionalized, or sanctified by a tradition radically compromised in any case by its complicities with state power and therefore with the history of political domination. De Man said "God is on the side of chaotic reality and style is powerless to conquer him . . . with his appearance the life of poetry comes to an end. The situation is very similar to that of Kierkegaard's aesthetic man, with the difference that Borges refuses to give up his poetic predicament for a leap into faith." If the poetic is fundamental awareness of finitude, because it depends absolutely upon its relation with the nonpoetic, with which it establishes a relationless relation to the extent that the nonpoetic absolutely resists the relation, then any leap into faith, whether ontotheological or anarchist-nihilist faith, is the end of the poetic and the betrayal, heroic or not, of the poetic as such. This is the treason that "Theme of the Traitor and the Hero" betrays absolutely by refusing all compromise in the infinite denunciation of the story's final words. Those words are:

> In Nolan's play, the passages taken from Shakespeare are the least dramatic ones; Ryan suspected that the author interpolated them so that someone, in the future, would be able to stumble upon the truth. Ryan realized that he, too, was part of Nolan's plot. . . . After long and stubborn deliberation, he decided to silence the discovery. He published a book dedicated to the hero's glory; that too, perhaps, had been foreseen. (146)

Conspiracy would seem exhaustively to coincide with the universe. Nolan occupies the site of the ontotheological god, lord and master of the disjunctive syllogism that will have foreseen and predisposed every possible variation in the historical plot ("either this, or this, or this") in such a way that any action by Ryan will end up proving his presence at the beginning of the ordering series as its noncontingent divinity or absolute lord of textual necessity.

By implication, then, also the writing of "Theme of the Traitor and the Hero" was foreseen. And this reading. But there is a crucial difference, repeatedly exposed in Borges's texts (let me just refer to the end of "The Lottery in Babylon," for instance), between what can be derived from understanding the possibility of conspiracy and understanding that understanding the possibility of conspiracy is a fundamental act of poetic freedom that presupposes—necessarily—the possibility of nonconspiracy, of the finitude of conspiracy. In other words, if understanding conspiracy and accepting its possibility is already to have fallen into the trap of the ontotheological reading of the world, to understand the possibility of such a trap is already to be open to an alternative history, to a nonontotheological relation to the world and to the real. Borges's text, in its baroque search for its limit-possibility, gives us over and over again, through its very acceptance of finitude, the open possibility of the mystery of the real, regarding which it is no longer a matter of positing the invention of sense, the proliferation of sense, the contingent construction of all sense, but the opposite: to understand the absolute limit of sense, to understand the radical insufficiency of any sense construction, and thus to receive the world and the real, as if by the first time, as an infinite gift and the total opening of sense. Regarding this alternative, which is, I insist, always literal in Borges, the positing of the textual subject as the dynamiter of sense in the theft of the ontotheological site of divinity is only the hypostasis of the textual subject, the author, and with them the entirety of the literary system, to a poor substitutive place that regards technical mastery as the only possible truth of art in modernity. But then art is the same thing as technology and state power.

Let me name that positing of the textual subject, which is endlessly repeated in the history of Borgesian criticism, "pathetic," using "Theme": when Kilpatrick enters Dublin on his way towards the theater where he will be assassinated (but already Dublin is the stage where the larger representation takes place), Borges says, "the condemned man entered Dublin, argued, worked, prayed, reprehended, spoke words of pathos [*palabras patéticas*]—and each of those acts destined to shine forth in glory had been choreographed by Nolan" (145). The textual subject, the critical subject are pathetic when they follow the ontotheological script and partake in conspiracy, that is, partake in the ideology of the infinite construction of sense as artifact or technique of conduct (or conduct of conduct, as it is precisely the Foucaultian notion of governmentality that is at stake here). Incidentally, this is the reason why Borges warns us that the quotations from Shakespeare that will be interspersed in those actions by Kilpatrick are the "least dramatic" passages in the events. Because those quotations, once recognized as such, are precisely what will allow us to understand the conspiracy as conspiracy: their function is essentially nonpathetic, as they make it possible to develop a nonconspiratorial vision of history. In other words, seeing the conspiracy for what it is already to enter the possibility of an alternative understanding—as with paranoia. With this, and crucially, Borges comes close to a theoretical proposal, that is, to a conceptual procedure that will allow us to confront the pathetic critical subject with a principle of "apathy" that constitutes the very center of the essay by Raúl Antelo I now comment upon.

The "apathetic" series defines in Antelo the possibility of a difference regarding "the dominant productions of sense that take life as their basis" (113; my translation, also in subsequent quotes). Departing from Giorgio Agamben's analysis in *Means Without Ends* according to which "the dominant biopolitical fracture in modern society" (113) is the difference between the popular and what remains outside it ("the popular is that which cannot be totally incorporated to the whole of which it is an inalienable part at the same time it cannot really belong to the whole to which, in spite of everything, it attaches itself" [113]), Antelo defines, from Borges, "pathetism" as precisely a discourse obsessed with the representation of the popular as a totality without division ("there is much of the pathetic manner of Spengler, Keyserling and even Frank, in Martínez Estrada's work" [Borges qtd. in Antelo 114]). The formulation of the possibility of an "apathetic version of experience" is of course identical to de Man's precision that the world of Borges's stories does not refer to "an actual experience, but . . . [to] an intellectual proposition." We should also recall here the early Walter Benjamin's notion, expressed in "On the Program of the Coming Philosophy," about the need to reform Kantian philosophy in favor of a more generous and less pedestrian conception of experience, where what is at stake is a critique of enlightened empiricism. The fundamental biopolitical fracture of modernity, between the popular and its remainder, between *bíos* and *zoé*, can also be represented as the fracture or the division between reality and culture. Both in de Man and Benjamin the revision of the Kantian notion of experience is crucial for a critique of the cultural as the site par excellence of the machination of modernity: in the split of the real between reality and culture experience is always on the side of culture, hypostatized into life, and metonymically into national or communitarian life. Within this division an appropriation of the real takes place whose categories suffer from a historical genealogy that is radically contaminated by the ontotheological modality of thought. "Life" becomes, for modernity, the sum of techno-economic machination and culture, where "culture" gathers the space of supposedly autonomous experience that techno-economic machination throws off as a mere residue. This is also the Heideggerian account in *Contributions to Philosophy*. If the apathetic series defines in Antelo something other than "the dominant productions of sense that take life as their basis," then the apathetic series is radically a-culturalist and a-constructivist, countercommunitarian, and counteraxiological, whereas the pathetic series, in Martínez Estrada's version, but also in Nolan's version, both motivated by the deluded teleology of "emancipation of the fatherland," like so many critical versions of Borges's work, seeks the establishment of a principle of experience disciplined or tamed into the production of a particular kind of sense: a sense always already contained within the parameters of the split reality/culture, always already relativized and hence destroyed by the unexamined weight of the cultural-communitarian instance. In other words, the pathetic series is the absolute beginning of a sentimentalization of life on the basis of the national-popular regime of rule and all its derivatives, including, by the way, the neoliberal regime of social control whose own brand of communitarianism goes under the name of multiculturalism.

The pathetic series is, therefore, the site of anarchism and of nihilism, where both of them figure as no more than the inversion of ontotheological sovereignty, thus totally dependent upon the latter: they are nothing but that sovereignty disguised as a villain, disguised as a traitor. Once ontotheological logic is accepted, once the pathetic principle of the real as division between noncontingent divinity and contingent series of events, between reality and culture, is absorbed, the mere negation of the first part of the division is also *ipso facto* negation of the second. And both negations, which are mutually supplementary and never counterposed, formulate the anarcho-nihilism whose very *terribilitá* is hardly dissociable from the conservative and apparently amiable benevolence that reveals metaphysical violence. Antelo's essay blows up such a tediously false polarity in a way that has rarely been accomplished in Borgesian criticism, and thus manages "exiting Borges with Borges," upon dismantling, among other things, the arbitrary and ill-advised split between textual subject and empirical subject, the apparent contradiction between textual subversion and reactionary politics that the Borgesian critical machine has done nothing but infinitely rehearse. In other words, Antelo's essay opens the possibility of a critical rupture by proposing the apathetic as a concept capable of turning Borges's literary practice into a theory of reading: a theory that will refuse national-popular pathetism, and thus every identitarian, subjectivizing, moving, sentimental, and statal formulation of the poetic apparatus. What is, then, the apathetic?

Liddell-Scott's Greek-English lexicon gives the following definitions of the word *pathos*: "anything that befalls one, an incident, accident . . . what one has suffered, one's experience . . . a passion, emotion . . . any passive state, a condition, state . . . in pl. the incidents or changes to which things are liable." The more limited Spanish Royal Academy *Diccionario de la lengua española* says under *"patético":* "what is capable of moving or agitating the mind by giving it vehement affections, particularly pain, sadness, or melancholy" (my translation). And under *"apatía"* "impassibility of mind . . . 2. Laxity, indolence, lack of vigor or energy." Antelo's essay, upon defining the apathetic's "line of flight" as the "fortuitous encounter that posits a new conception of experience that owes nothing to lived-experience [*vivencia*]" (115), moves in the sense of a modification of Liddell-Scott's first rendering: for Antelo the apathetic defines a modality of reception of the event not subsumable by lived-experience, or *vivencia*. *Vivencia* was a word invented by José Ortega y Gassett in order to translate the German *Erlebnis* in opposition to *experiencia* for *Erfahrung*. It is not necessary for us to go into deep philological labor, which would have to cross in any case the Benjaminian account of the difference between the two German words. It is enough to say that *Erlebnis* is on the side of biopolitical interiority and is therefore consubstantial with the difference reality/culture—*vivencia* marks what is pathetic in every literary appropriation. *Erfahrung*, by contrast, marks the apathetic series as an opening to the trace of the real. The apathetic is a radical opening to the sense of the real against the pathetic production of sense. In Antelo's words, "it marks . . . the in-between (a-synthetic and non-dialectizable) of sense, a sense where the value world circulates" (115). The world circulates through the apathetic sense, whereas the pathetic circulates intra-worldly. Apathy, which Antelo calls "acephalic" and "Minotaurid," "retrospectively rebuilds the ontological consistency both of individual *bíos* and of mass *zoé,* but it forces us, in exchange, to reassemble a labyrinthine world where the simultaneity of absolutely incompatible presents and the dissemination of not necessarily true pasts coexist side by side, giving a striated character to truth. It is therefore not a matter of evaluating reconstruction as restoration of the lived, but rather as a challenge for the creation of new ethical links through the potentialization of the false. In that series, whose virtue is the result of acting forces, truth, always differed and virtual, resides in the inactuality of all experience, in its unrepresentable void" (117). Apathy is, in other words, the opening to "truth present through its concealment, the truth of a narration that shows no truth but is ruled by it, to such an extent that its visibility duplicates the very fictional opacity that attempts to grasp it" (113).

If anarcho-nihilism is a response to a prohibition of nostalgia, then anarcho-nihilism is a form of self-repressing voluntarism and is therefore anything but anarcho-nihilism: the inconsistency of the difference between a Borgesian textual subject and an empirical subject starts there. If nostalgia, measured by its very prohibition, was in Pezzoni the anarcho-nihilistic ordering principle of Borges's text, and thus its uncanny guest and the axis of destruction of the ontological consistency in Pezzoni's critical proposal, Antelo's proposal for an apathetic critical practice enables the establishment of ontological consistency in the very displacement of ontotheology. Apathetic ontotheology seeks "the truth present through its concealment," that is, it seeks the infamous and villainous duplicity of a truth that is not exhaustible by representation, never subsumable in the production or machination of sense. That truth, the truth or nontruth of the mystery of the real, accounts for reality/culture at the same time that it displaces the horizon of interpretation beyond the biopolitical polarity towards an encounter with the face of divinity or the end of poetry and beyond the "emancipación de la patria," which is in any case always the entry of the fatherland into full domination, of the father, and of the name of the father, in the perpetual exclusion of that which the popular, pathetic name for the national totality of knowledge cannot account for. That is what "Theme of the Traitor and the Hero" gives us: the excess of the popular, a movement towards historical truth that coincides with the movement of the poetic drive towards its furthest limit, towards the truth of the social in its overwhelming immanence, which is the immanence or the infra-immanence of everything that ontotheoogy, including patriotic ontotheology, subalternizes. Borges's liter-ature, in its apathetic practice, is an infrapolitical literature against the biopolitical rapture of politics.

Works Cited

Agamben, Giorgio. *Means without Ends*. Trans. Daniel Heller-Roazen. Minneapolis: U of Minnesota P, 2000.

Antelo, Raúl. "La zoología imaginaria como deslectura de las radiografías y retratos de la nación en crisis." *Jorge Luis Borges. Intervenciones sobre pensamiento y literatura*. Ed. William Rowe, Claudio Canaparo, and Annick Louis. Buenos Aires: Paidós, 2000. 113–18.

Benjamin, Walter. "On the Program of the Coming Philosophy." *Selected Writings. Volume 1. 1913–1926*. By Walter Benjamin. Ed. Marcus Bullock and Michael W. Jennings. Cambridge: Harvard UP, 2000. 100–10.

Borges, Jorge Luis. "The Theme of the Traitor and the Hero." *Collected Fictions*. By Jorge Luis Borges. Trans. Andrew Hurley. New York: Penguin, 1998. 143–46.

Borges, Jorge Luis. "Los traductores de las *1001 noches*." *Prosa completa*. By Jorge Luis Borges. Barcelona: Bruguera, 1980. Vol. 1, 371–91.

Conan Doyle, Arthur. *The Adventures and the Memoirs of Sherlock Holmes*. London: Penguin, 2001.

de Man, Paul. "A Modern Master: Jorge Luis Borges." 1964. *Critical Writings 1953–1978*. By Paul de Man. Ed. Lindsay Waters. Minneapolis: U of Minnesota P, 1989. 123–29.

Heidegger, Martin. *Contributions to Philosophy: From Enowning*. Trans. Parvis Emad and Kenneth Maly. Bloomington: Indiana UP, 1999.

Ludmer, Josefina. "¿Cómo salir de Borges?" *Jorge Luis Borges. Intervenciones sobre pensamiento y literatura*. Ed. William Rowe, Claudio Canaparo, and Annick Louis. Buenos Aires: Paidós, 2000. 289–300.

Pezzoni, Enrique. *Enrique Pezzoni, lector de Borges. Lecciones de literatura 1984–1988*. Ed. Annick Louis. Buenos Aires: Sudamericana, 1999.

Pimentel Pinto, Julio."Borges, una poética de la memoria." *Jorge Luis Borges. Intervenciones sobre pensamiento y literatura*. Ed. William Rowe, Claudio Canaparo, and Annick Louis. Buenos Aires: Paidós, 2000. 155–64.

Scarfó, Daniel. "Borges y las literaturas imposibles." *Jorge Luis Borges. Intervenciones sobre pensamiento y literatura*. Ed. William Rowe, Claudio Canaparo, and Annick Louis. Buenos Aires: Paidós, 2000. 83–91.

Saer, Juan José. "Borges como problema." *Jorge Luis Borges. Intervenciones sobre pensamiento y literatura*. Ed. William Rowe, Claudio Canaparo, and Annick Louis. Buenos Aires: Paidós, 2000. 19–31.

Towards a Map of the Current Critical Debate

Julio Ortega
(Translated from the original Spanish by Sophia A. McClennen and Corey Shouse)

In the current post-theoretical scene, where what Ernesto Laclau calls a "contamination" between theory and the empirical is taking place, intercultural studies has acquired a distinctive role (vii). Laclau establishes a positivist solution to the current dilemma:

> The destiny of theory in our century is a peculiar one. On the one hand we are certainly witnessing the progressive blurring of the classical frontiers which made "theory" a distinctive theoretical object: in an era of generalized critique of the metalinguistic function, the analysis of the concrete escapes the rigid straitjacket of the distinction theoretical framework/case studies. But, on the other hand, precisely because we are living in a posttheoretical age, theory cannot be opposed by a flourishing empiricity liberated from theoretical fetters. What we have, instead, is a process of mutual contamination between "theory" and "empiria." (vii)

Probably the first characteristic element of the post-theoretical period is a prudence, even reticence, before the temptation to propose another theoretical model as superior, syncretic and summary relief. At the same time, there is a serious challenge to the critical possibility of a space of dialogue—a dialogue less determinate and vertical, where new reencounters come to play between reading, text, context and discursive genre. This time that interplay produces another object (a literary and cultural object conceptualized as process) that shows and demonstrates itself to be as porous as it is persistent, as dense as it is free. This rush to resignification is, moreover, in such a fluid state, that it casts a parodic emphasis over recent theoretical hyperinterpretation. We might conclude that, as the century drew to a close, the predominance of grand theoretical models was exceeded by their own conversion into a system of authority. But this would not have been possible without the intense questioning of the will to truth that these models exercised from their centralizing position; they wound up as current currency, mere academic power, and mediatic novelty.

Tilottama Rajan affirms in "The University in Crisis: Cultural Studies, Civil Society, and the Place of Theory" that "theory today has become an endangered species" (8). Cultural theory has been displaced in this age of economic predominance by cultural studies. The conceptual premise of cultural studies would be based, according to Rajan, on the notion of "absolute transparency" and on "total communicability." Rajan distinguishes between two types of "cultural studies": on the one hand, the tendency that comprises post-colonialism, gender, popular culture, and forms of everyday life; on the other hand, the tendency that includes technology, science, and conceives of itself as part of the process of globalization. The first dedicates itself to identitarian politics, the second to economicism. Both forms, ultimately, leave out literature and theory; they are a simulacrum of the social sciences from the humanities, and their "presentism" is grounded on the idea of an "end of history." Although this faith in cognoscente rationality seems to have taken to extremes the optimism of the legible that distinguishes semiology, it is also typical of the operativity of a contextualizing reading, whose principle of articulation presupposes the transparency of objects formed by a disciplinary field. The demonstrative lesson of this reading implies a political voluntarism (because it turns its demonstration into a norm) and privileges the heroic role of the subject among historied objects. But this perspective, characteristic of the social sciences, also carries nostalgia for a self-sufficient politics: it turned the document into the original scene of denunciation. In the rhetoric of denunciation, objects were converted into topics.

From the Latin American perspective, nevertheless, the crisis of the disciplines as methods of monologic reading has been forging the theoretical experience of critical reading. "Cultural studies," dedicated to the media and mass consumerism; "cultural history," dedicated to the social configurations of memory; and "postmodern" relativism, dedicated especially to placing in doubt institutionality, are some of the critical practices in tension with models from the academic Archive that, since the 1980s, illustrate disciplinary limits—limits, that is, of an objectivity overcome by the flux of signification of new objects and by liminal readings of the new. When disciplinary fields tried to reconvert themselves into an archive of genealogies or into the cultural field of markets and consumption, it was clear that the normative gaze of the disciplines had lost sight of the objects of anticanonical displacement and fluid mixing. Some new perspectives emerged from the boundary breaking produced by writing, from antimetaphysical philosophy, the ethnology of nomadism, and speculative psychoanalysis. It was demonstrated again that the disciplinary limits were not those of social experience and, moreover, that cultural objects could not be contained by the fields of reading. Disciplinary authorities shifted to "recycling" with the mediatic functionalism of the "market" or the identitarian politics of the "marginalized," but these functions were less explicable each time and more crossed by contrary and residual forces.

Dynamized by the new complexity of objects and the fluidity of subjects, intercultural studies soon distanced themselves from both positivist documentation and relativist constructivism; and they understood the instrumentation of some and the skepticism of others as situated readings between objects that were not always totally legible. This debate has circulated among a number of Latin Americanist journals interested in a revitalizing critique. Some examples are: *Journal of Latin American Cultural Studies* (London), *Revista de Crítica Cultural* (Santiago, Chile), *Revista de Crítica Literaria Latinoamericana* (Dartmouth and Lima), and *RELEA, Revista Latinoamericana de Estudios Avanzados* (Caracas). The latent promise of this transition corresponds, at the very least, to the eruption of new social subjects that were capable of forging strategies and cultural agencies during the exhaustion of dominant theories, which had begun to cancel even the notion of Subject. Excluded by institutional systems, with a cultural practice tested by regional discourses, migrations of every sort displayed the praxis of a heterogeneous identity—the position of the subject created in the interpolation of spaces. Identitarian politics were not enough to map these movements of desocialization. The question of the subject, its networks of negotiation, and its plots of association were foregrounded. It soon was clear that this was not only a question of the Other in its margins of exotic and remote otherness. It was a question of the immediacy of the transient, whose new language cast doubt on traditional ethics now that an urgent "you" seems to decide the moral fiber of the situated "I." The problem of the subject has been retraced by Enzo del Búfalo in *El sujeto encadenado* (1998), *Individuo, mercado y utopía* (1998) and *La genealogía de la subjetividad* (1991).

Certain groups of critics preferred to situate this Subject as "subaltern" among agents of social stratification; for others the Subject was cast as an actor of ethnic "resistance" among institutionalized powers; and in other cases, the Subject was understood as an "acculturated" victim between "colonial" and/or "postcolonial" forces. A rich bibliography recognizes the advances in these approaches, even if in certain instances they were willfully presentist, and on occasion they saw themselves taxed by the good professional conscience and liberal paternalism of symbolic compensations. The testimonies and indigenous literatures, in addition to the study of the popular imaginary, have contributed notably to overcoming purist autarchy and ethnological nostalgia in the name of the intense "de-urbanization" reflected by popular culture. The work of Martín Lienhard, William Rowe and Vivian Schelling, and Yolanda Salas are fundamental in this field; but this area still requires more comprehensive and articulated approaches that can provide a theory of the crisis and also illuminate the work of popular culture in processing everyday life—that is the community of the poor.

Other nuclei of scholarly work chose the uncentered horizon of "cultural studies," paying special attention to the costs of modernization, the role of the mass media in the social imaginary, and contemporary forms of mass culture. Groups inspired by postmodernism advanced the questioning of disciplinary tradition, at a time when the Latin American university, feeling threatened, on the one hand, by neoliberalism and, on the other, by new currents of contextual analysis, was becoming more disciplinarily conservative. Literary studies in Buenos Aires moved to emphasize the dramas of nation and nationality. History became documentary history and, in Brazil, self-sufficient discourse. Only in Santiago, Chile, after the dictatorship, did the university cross the disciplinary boundaries opened by theoretical practice. In almost every instance the most innovative research, interdisciplinary, and creative, took place in research centers within small critical communities. And although this is not meant to be a catalogue of all pertinent groups, it is important to mention at least those that opted to work on studies that focused on the border, contact, or hybridization (*mestizaje*) including bilingual literature, migratory sagas, and more contemporary forms of mixing as a creative space.

These and other parallel critical persuasions are characterized by their common empirical focus, their independent use of theoretical sources and models, and their methodic consciousness of academic borders. Fredric Jameson thought that cultural studies was a repoliticization of the North American academy, but in his enthusiasm he forgot that campus politics can only be classically liberal. In fact, the political dimension of criticism has been better suited to casting doubt on dominant models as well as debating institutional domestication and the conversion of the academy into a market. Also, it has been successful in providing readings that recover the critical radicalism of works and texts liberated from the museum of the canon and the archive of origin, returning them to the procedural power of their indeterminate and never-ending present. It should be noted that in the fields of Latin Americanism and Hispanism these contextualizing practices, despite some initial flirtations with authority, have contributed to renovating this dialogue, moving beyond the monolinguistic boundaries of recent jargons, autocratic convictions, and the consolation of areas of specialization. We no longer need concern ourselves with those who believe that vindicating personal inclinations demands a profitable philosophy.

The biography of the critical profession has yet to be written to include the militant "isms" of the powers that be, as well as the assimilation of minorities as second-class citizens through bureaucratic compensation—although this task probably belongs to the novel. The creativity of criticism is first and foremost in the strength of its self-critique.

Within this fluid and heterogeneous space, critical endeavor can today be conceived of as an open instrumentation defined by its dialogical capacity. If its protocol is that of resituated dialogue, then its relevance is operative, communicational, and its meaning the hypothesis of an articulation. It is because of this that diverse critical instrumentations have coincided, which, from philological genetics (based on the updated archive) to constructivism (de-based in the rhetorical construction), have sought to approximate one another. Not only has it been demonstrated that all disciplines are the daughters of their age—and oftentimes of the priorities of State reorganization—but also that artistic, literary and cultural objects say more about themselves when seen under the mediating light of a reading capable of breaching the borders of the object, both in terms of historical lineage as well as formal character. Disputes over interpretation are part of analytical operativity, but they are equally part of the cultural (and even political) history of such objects when reread. The relevance of this dialogical perspective has shown itself in the need to propose new readings of the articulation/intersection between social practices, symbolic production and narratives of identification and difference. Granting the circulatory hybridity of these objects it would be unproductive to propose a singular method for such an endeavor. Rather, it is more interesting to assume the creative opening of the field, broadened by transdisciplinary interactions. It is also important to recognize the exploratory will of a radical criticism freed of the fetishism of authorities of theory, transformed into a common currency by the highs and lows of academic power. Derrida has said that, having died, deconstruction would live on much like the ghost of the Freudian father, demonstrating an even greater presence in its absence. Perhaps more accurately, it could continue to do so as the theses of Marx and Freud have done, circulating as forms of modern—or given the case at hand—postmodern critical consciousness.

Even if these excesses might seem caricaturesque, it cannot be forgotten that only ten years ago, for example, it was widely taken for granted that the indigenous world of José María Arguedas was nothing more than an archaic and sentimental national myth. From this point there was but one step to suggesting that indigenous peoples could either enter modernity or disappear. This, however, was a step into the abyss of contradiction: this condemnation, in effect, proved the critical and moral bankruptcy of those who needed to penalize such excluded subjects in order to maintain their dominant discourse. Further, this was done through another myth, that of a West equipped with all forms of reason, including that of mortal sanction. Owing to its elaboration within theory, radical criticism today has become more pragmatic, realizing itself as such through the linking of cultural objects to both the contexts of their origin and their future. Symptomatically, Arguedas's work has, in effect, brought us "up-to-date" thanks to its migratory and fragmented saga of the modern, its sense of urgency as well as its enigmas. As Doris Sommer has suggested in *Proceed with Caution*, the bilingual cultural object is the most fragile and requires the greatest care. Alberto Moreiras, on the other hand, has provided a historiography of the distinct critical points of view of "Latin Americanism" that the North American academy has explored and in his book, *The Exhaustion of Difference: The Politics of Latin American Cultural Studies*, Moreiras dramatizes the contemporary importance of José María Arguedas as a heterodox paradigm (1).

Currently, intercultural studies seek to redefine the terms of this practice. For some work groups, this is undertaken as a repostulation of American studies to include the multiple languages of the continent, and a relocation of relationships of border, region and nation (what they refer to as the "postnational" as a means of freeing the dominant narrative from an abusive unity of authority). The discussion of community, nationality, citizenship, and the role of the mixing and hybridity of identities based not in similarity but alterity (Ricoeur), has, however, proven to be more complex, despite the simplification introduced by the project of "globalization." This redefinition of "globalization" as a producer of differences, is, by its own symmetrical contradiction, a theoretical necessity of reappropriation. For other groups, this has meant the reformulation of the long and unequal exchange between Spain and Latin America as a means of overcoming the regrettable division between the areas of "Peninsular" and "Spanish American" studies: having become a tired and fruitless practice, this has dulled and left barren the most relevant texts—precisely those texts which are best understood through their modern inclusivity and *mestizaje*. It is a painful truth that there are many experts on the Spanish Baroque, for example, who are completely unaware of its American origins. This is particularly problematic given the fact that the Spanish Baroque was stimulated by the abundance and wonder of the Americas, and cannot be understood without the gold, silver, chocolate, pineapple, birds, colors and flavors of the laboratory of the New World. And although the notion of a "Creole consciousness" transforms the object into a proof of itself, the practice of mixture (grafting, hybridism, intersection) can be called by many names, as long as these names don't domesticate the objects and their open process.

In this search for critical initiatives, which also includes teaching and methodology, transatlantic studies appears as a distinct possibility, free from the disciplinary genealogy and liberal *parti pris* that condemns the subject to the role of victim—colonial, sexual, imperial, ideological, etc. The transatlantic, then, is a map reconstructed amid its European, American and African currents, one that therefore redefines the monuments of civilization, modern institutions, and hermeneutics in debate. As such, more than historical it is intrahistorical time intersected by constantly updated narratives. Its discourse moves amid islands that reassign names and along coasts that exceed the process of cataloguing. Transatlantic studies brings to power distinct disciplines and different upheavals of the fields of social and humanistic studies. In England this approach designates at least two tendencies: studies of new internationality, which foreground postcolonial interlocutors; and Anglo-American studies, which now encompass a variety of ethnic and cultural minorities in the United Kingdom and the United States. Both appear fomented and supported by the principle (and perhaps the promise) to connect and broaden these spaces through the concurrent model of dialogue (what some of us know of others) and of the transatlantic (what we do not know from one to an/the Other).

An illustrative case of these reading operations, which in situating the object decide its status, is that of Caliban in Shakespeare's *The Tempest*. The latest readings of this work and the Caribbean subject (Caliban: Caribbean, cannibal) have been the terrain of postcolonial theory. In postcolonial studies the dominant hypothesis has been the political paradigm of imperialism and its symmetric notion of axis and periphery, as in the ideological diagram of master and servant, and the ethics of the Other and otherness. According to Edward Said in *Culture and Imperialism*, postcolonial studies critiques the notion of "a dominating metropolitan center ruling a distant territory" (9) and its symmetric notion of axis and periphery, as in the ideological diagram of master and servant, and the ethics of the Other and otherness. On the other hand, the postcolonial perspective also implies the historicist view of the colonial subject as deprived of identity by the brutal forces of the modern. Through a reductionist derivation, "dependency theory" would later deny that the Latin American subject had an authentic culture of its own, having been dispossessed of substance by the dominant culture. However, if we situate ourselves in an intercultural reading, we can demonstrate that the colonial subject does not always display such victimization, but rather that the colonial subject can, at times, negotiate its own margins. This subject is not always confined to the narrative of the Masters of the moment or to the archive of genealogies. Further, being a discursive construction first and a political construction second, it is not transparent to the social sciences. Similarly, we could demonstrate that in *The Tempest* Caliban does not learn to speak merely in order to "curse" as he himself says. Greenblatt argues persuasively that Caliban's "profit" here is his moral definition. In his book *Learning to Curse*, Greenblatt affirms that "Caliban's retort might be taken as a self-indictment: even with the gift of language, his nature is so debased that he can only learn to curse. But the lines refuse to mean this; what we experience instead is a sense of their devastating justness. Ugly, rude, savage, Caliban nevertheless achieves an absolute if intolerably bitter moral victory" (*Learning* 25). In truth, this would be a "victory" which would only confirm his dependent and subsidiary position. Instead, it is more interesting to demonstrate that in learning to speak, Caliban has become capable of naming. Consequently, he reappropriates the diversity of his own Island, recovering it from his owner, thanks to the fact that he, Caliban, knows better the fertility and abundance of the trees, fruits and flowing waters of nature, a nature which he rehabilitates thanks to language. That then is the shift in meaning: his passage is from "natural man" (slave) to "noble savage" (humanized by language). In the face of a postcolonial reading that would require the most monstrous of him in order to prove its denouncement, another reading could propose that Caliban is in the process of his own humanization.

This is the same colonial Subject that in Guamán Poma de Ayala's *Nueva Corónica* (New Chronicle) learns to write and in Inca Garcilaso's *Comentarios reales* (Royal Commentaries) learns to read. This reappropriated Spanish language is a tool for reconstructing cultural memory and reestablishing shared spaces. Our Subject is, therefore, constructed through the intense hermeneutics of exchange: European definitions are followed by American redefinitions. In a certain sense this suggests an allegory reborn from the "self-taught philosopher." Indigenous and *mestizo* intellectuals put this Subject to work not in the lost past but in the future-in-the-making—one of dialogue, difference and negotiation. As such, it can be demonstrated that the mestizo colonial world therefore constituted Spain's true modernity—a paradoxical modernity, in effect, that would soon become the political sign of the new.

Following the Seminario Iberoamericano, organized by Hispanists from Cambridge University (1995 and 1996), the Trans-Atlantic Project working group at Brown University has sought to raise this field of studies as a new exploration of intercultural history (see <http://www.brown.edu/Departments/Hispanic_Studies /Juliortega/ Transatlantic.htm>). The representations of the transatlantic subject and the re-writing of the colonial stage, the construction of the Other in voyage narratives, the hybridity of translation, and the crossings of exile and the avant-garde(s) are but a few of the nuclei of this debate. In the process of defining an agenda for this dialogue—which included Doris Sommer (Harvard), Alicia Borinsky (Boston University), and Beatriz Pastor (Dartmouth College)—the notion of the transatlantic was formulated as the theoretical-practical plot of intersections between Europe (especially Spain) and our Americas. The topics of study emerged from the interests of the group and, from the first instant, introduced the present of Spanish in the United States as a social and cultural mediating force between unequal spaces. In other forums—and in particular in the one dedicated to Spanish in the United States organized at the Casa de América in Madrid (1997) by the Trans-Atlantic Project from Brown—we explored the thesis that our cultural objects are best read by the light of both shores of language, in its constant voyage between the migrations of forms and the transformation of codes.

Colleagues from the University of Puerto Rico joined the working group and convened a colloquium on "The Trans-Atlantic Caribbean" that demonstrated the current state of this perspective in a region, which from its origins has been generated through the dynamics of this exchange. "Trans-Atlantic Mexico," a colloquium organized by the Brown Project and the Division of Studies of Culture at the University of Guadalajara in 2001, was held with the participation of colleagues from *UNAM* (Universidad Nacional Autónoma de México), *UAM* (Universidad Autónoma Metropolitana), El Colegio de México, the University of Guadalajara, and the University of Buenos Aires, in addition to the members of the base group. The thesis of these colloquia is that our countries are not only national creations, but that they are also the product of cultural interaction with the Atlantic world and its various branches of a Modernity which cannot be understood without the contradictory constitution of Latin America. In an age of globality these studies reveal the dramas of particularity and difference. Perhaps the best to come of these transatlantic studies—favored by "New History," which works memory like a fertile shore of the present—could be the fact that they do not require a set program or canon: instead, they are an open exploration and a proposal for the reconstruction of dialogue.

Works Cited

Greenblatt, Stephen J. *Learning to Curse: Essays in Early Modern Culture.* New York: Routledge, 1990.

Lienhard, Martín. *La voz y su huella: Escritura y conflicto étnico-social en América Latina, 1492–1982.* Lima: Editorial Horizonte, 1992.

Moreiras, Alberto. *The Exhaustion of Difference: The Politics of Latin American Cultural Studies*. Durham: Duke UP, 2001.

Rajan, Tilottama. "The University in Crisis: Cultural Studies, Civil Society, and the Place of Theory." *Literary Research / Recherche littéraire* 18.35 (2001): 8–25.

Ricoeur, Paul. *Oneself as Another*. Chicago: The U of Chicago P, 1992.

Rowe, William, and Vivian Schelling. *Memory and Modernity: Popular Culture in Latin America*. London: Verso, 1991.

Said, Edward W. *Culture and Imperialism.* New York: Knopf, 1993.

Salas, Yolanda. "Nuevas subjetividades en el estudio de la memoria colectiva." *Venezuela: tradición en la modernidad.* Ed. Carmen Elena Alemán and María Matilde Suárez. Caracas: Universidad Simón Bolívar y Fundación Bigott, 1998. 261–79.

Sommer, Doris. *Proceed with Caution, When Engaged by Minority Writing in the Americas.* Cambridge: Harvard UP, 1999.

Anxieties of Impotence: Cubans in New York City

Christina Marie Tourino

> *Cuba becomes more difficult to map than to situate. It may stand, for example, for the gaps that currently exist geographically, politically, and culturally between Cubas and Cubans.*
>
> —Ricardo Ortiz, "Reinaldo Arenas' Last Writing"

Industrialization, globalization, and U.S. economic and foreign policy have set unprecedented numbers of bodies in motion across national borders. Along with other dependent nations, tribes, and continents, Latin America has seen many of its citizens migrate, immigrate, and go into exile. As a result of such movements over the last century and a half, Latin Americans are dispersed in such a way that related but different cultural groups spring up in many parts of the world, many of them in the United States. These groups continue to evolve as increasingly complicated flows of subjects and their capital make ceaseless round trips in which "home" and "abroad" become harder and harder to name.

For critics of Latin American literatures, this state of affairs irreversibly complicates comparative literature projects. Comparative literature as a discipline has changed dramatically from its earliest moments in the nineteenth century, when its project was to search for literary influences and universal themes in European literatures of the Middle Ages. In the early twentieth century, comparative literature began to be invested in the definition of national characteristics. Projects compared European literatures across national and linguistic boundaries in an attempt both to unearth universal themes and to register national and linguistic specificities (see Bassnett 24). More recently, in addition to Europe, the United States and its literature entered the purview of legitimate comparative study. The complete upheaval of literary study in the 1960s and 1970s has resulted in an interest in postcolonial literatures, which has, in turn, demanded models of comparative literature that work across national boundaries within the "Americas" hemispherically considered. In the late 1980s and early 1990s, groundbreaking projects in this newly developing comparative field of "inter-American literature" or the "literature of the Americas" compared texts across an Anglo/Latin divide (often including Canada as well). Studies comparing the works of William Faulkner with those of Gabriel García Márquez, or Henry James and Joaquim Maria Machado de Assis exemplified this approach (Fitz; Pérez-Firmat; Zamora; Saldívar; Chevigny; Laguardia). Such studies sometimes undertook comparisons of modernist Latin American texts with "ethnic" texts from the United States in order to locate ways in which both groups challenged U.S. political and cultural colonialism.

Bilingual and bicultural critics have called into question the practice of pitting a text from "North America" against one from "Latin America" in ways that have continued usefully to pressure the field of comparative literature of the Americas according to the increasingly complicated inter-and intranational cultural migrations described above. In "We are *Not* the World," George Yúdice warns that even the most well-intentioned attempts on the part of U.S. intellectuals to "include" the "diverse" cultural productions of Latin America are restricted by uneven networks of dissemination and reception. That is, U.S. enterprises and universities mediate the flow of Latin American cultural products into the U.S. in ways that have no counterpart in Latin America. As a result, Yúdice explains, elite Mexican writers such as Carlos Fuentes are recruited as "representative" of underrepresented "Mexico," although Fuentes has very little to do with Mexico's nonhegemonic groups, and cannot be considered analogous to ethnic writers in the U.S. (Yúdice, 203–204). Recent studies have been more sensitive to the complications involved in comparing nonhegemonic writings of the Americas, and have even broken out of binary comparisons altogether. Still, each of these approaches depends upon the coherence of "national" or "ethnic" groups as the basis for comparison. In this essay, I would like to take seriously the increasingly complicated inter- and intranational cultural migrations described above, and consider another model for comparative literature of the Americas that jettisons "different" national or ethnic categories as a prerequisite altogether.

In his article "Latin, Latino, American," Román de la Campa argues that "global pressures foreshadow a new cartography of the Americas" (376) in which the category "Latinos" blurs almost beyond recognition the North/South divide as it is construed by American studies and Latin American studies. "Latino," according to de la Campa, does have a coherent referent, "an ontological plurality that comes from deriving an identity from more than one American imaginary, an aspect that has specific importance for all Latino groups, regardless of national, racial, or ethnic origin" (377). Still, he argues that "Latino" is itself a "split state," a permanent and distinct Latino/Latin American diaspora "nurtured by the constant flow of capital—human, symbolic, and financial—between the Americas" (377). I am suggesting that literatures between and among Latin Americans and Latinos, then, hail from such culturally heterogeneous sites and are made over by so many relocations that they call for comparative projects. Instead of the national or ethnic group, this essay takes as a point of departure the cultural divergences set in motion by the global flow of capital. Oscar Hijuelos's *The Mambo Kings Play Songs of Love* (1989) and Reinaldo Arenas's *El asalto* (1990) both descend from Cuba and are born in New York, but their authors come from groups that have migrated in response to very different pressures. Hijuelos is a second-generation immigrant of parents who came to the United States voluntarily. His protagonists, the Castillo brothers, also immigrated to New York voluntarily in 1949. Cubans of that generation were joining Cuban communities that had been established the century before. This group consisted of mainly Caucasian intellectuals, politicians, musicians, and others who had assimilated and escaped prejudice largely directed at other ethnics of color. In Miami, these early Cubans were wealthy and came as such a large group that they enjoyed quite a bit of economic and political power. They also continued to look forward to the possibility of a post-Castro return to the island. The Cubans who came during the 80s and 90s, in contrast, were often lower in class status and were part of a marginal ethnic or racial group (de la Campa 379). Arenas was in some ways the most marginalized of these: he fled Cuba on the Mariel boatlift in order to escape persecution by Castro's revolution both for his outspoken defiance of Castro in his writings, and for being gay (a "crime" for which he spent many years in a labor camp). Arenas's writings are often autobiographical and depict young gay Cuban men in similar dire circumstances. Hijuelos himself is conservative and straight; Arenas is nearly anarchistic and gay. Hijuelos lives and writes openly in New York; Arenas was censured in Cuba. Hijuelos is relatively independent, while Arenas was dependent upon the elites of both the United States and Cuba. In comparing these two works, I want to discover what persists in "Latin" culture despite transformations due to radical departures, dislocations, languages, and differing constructions of race, gender, sexuality, and class.

Anxieties of Impotence

> *"This denial of the continued resonance of national romances indicates a desire for literary self-generation that results from a particularly Latin American anxiety of influence. . . . It stems from an ongoing fascination with and anxiety over masculinity as the guarantor of regional independence and autonomy, legitimate leadership, and self-generation for citizens as well as for Latin American literature."*
>
> —Rebecca Biron, *Murder and Masculinity*

Hijuelos's *Mambo Kings* won a Pulitzer Prize and reviewers and critics highly praised it for nostalgically evoking a historical moment in New York when

Latin culture was glorified in the U.S. mainstream because of the sheer energy and beauty of its music (see Kanellos; Pérez-Firmat). Popular reviews of Arenas's *El asalto* emphasized Arenas's defense of individual rights, while academic critics cite the text as an example of Arenas's "irreducible liminality" and his "unmanageable body of difference . . . that refuses to comfort the reader" (Ávila 110–13). Whether in celebration of the "ethnic" or in rebellious assertion of unmanageable difference, these authors have been received as oppositional Latins in the Anglo world. Yet in the same way that boom narratives may have used magical realism to reinstate colonial relations between the elite intelligentsia and the masses (Colás), these "oppositional" narratives by Hijuelos and Arenas may be reinstating colonial relations themselves. Yúdice points out that within Latin America, beyond a shared repugnance for U.S. imperialism, there is often an interior colonization along other lines such as race, ethnicity, and sexual preference by those Latin American intellectuals with entrenched class privilege (203). What interests me here is the way in which both Hijuelos and Arenas narrate stories that depend upon a male colonization of women.

Despite differences in sexuality, politics, marginal status (immigration vs. exile), and language, Hijuelos and Arenas both posit a fantasy of excessive masculinity as the source of an all-male family that reproduces (or repeats) itself without women. This fantasy may function to compensate for the powerlessness that a marginalized man faces (to differing degrees) as an immigrant or an exile. In an attempt to assimilate and survive in the adopted country, immigrant men are often frustrated in the maintenance and reproduction of their patriarchal culture of their home country. For an exile, this alienation is even more extreme; for a gay man, already exiled from the nuclear reproductive family, it is more extreme still. Alongside this excessive masculinity, this fantasy also points to what is most "Cuban" in these characters. That is, Hijuelos and Arenas write the identities of these protagonists as masculine and as particularly "Cuban" at the same narrative sites. Although Hijuelos's protagonist is straight, and Arenas's is gay, both exemplify this "ethnic" and masculine excess. Hijuelos writes in English about Cesar Castillo and his brother Nestor, mambo musicians from Havana, Cuba, who immigrate to the United States in 1949 on the eve of the mambo heyday in New York. Hijuelos's characters suffer very few of the indignities facing most immigrants. They are talented, charismatic, and though they are meat packers by day, they quickly develop devoted nighttime fans, and soon Cesar is sleeping his way through every woman in the city. Arenas writes a dystopic novel in Spanish that imagines what a future under Castro might look like in which all citizens live with the threat of execution for the slightest intellectual or sexual deviancy. Arenas's unnamed narrator has managed to escape the total loss of humanity that plagues most citizens under the dictatorship; however, he poses as a devoted member of the revolution (complete with the violent murder of many "treasonous" Cuban citizens) in order to gain enough mobility to satisfy the alarming desire that drives the entire narrative—to find and execute his mother. Both texts are repetitious and episodic. Hijuelos's writes about a Don Juan who conquers women but never gets domestic with them; Arenas's narrator, though closeted, systematically slaughters one gay man after another. In both cases, the performance of Cuban masculinity in the face of its loss—a performance that accomplishes the repetition, if not the reproduction, of Cuban culture—is simultaneous with the (sometimes violent) exclusion of women. Biron describes a similar dynamic in terms of Latin American literary self-generation. She cites Sommer's argument that high modernist boom narratives must construct themselves as having been birthed without recourse to feminized and "popular" national romances (Sommer, *Foundational Fictions*). If, as Biron suggests, Latin American authors suffer from anxiety of influence in the face of lowbrow literature, many of their characters suffer from anxiety of impotence in the face of women's generative power. Whether erotic picaresque or despotic picaresque, these heroes live in an all-male fantasy of extravagant self-expansion that never has to take recourse to biological motherhood.

The bravado, freneticism, and exuberance of these all-male fantasies are fueled by a masculine anxiety that seems to appear repeatedly in literatures about men genealogically related to the Caribbean or Latin America. I do not mean to suggest that Latin men are more sexist (or uniquely so) than men found in other regions such as Asia, Africa, or North America. I do, however, see that sexism play out in a particularly exaggerated and performative mode. Before reading texts by Hijuelos and Arenas, I would like briefly to digress and consider a few other texts of Latin cultural heritage that are produced from widely varying degrees of social disenfranchisement and political investments that flesh out the "family resemblance" of masculine impotence that interests me here. These authors range from conservative to leftist, immigrant to exile, and gay to straight. Still, their texts all engage in narratives of masculinity, which appear in Hijuelos and Arenas as well, where men work out their cultural and masculine identities on a field of women. Recurring versions of this masculinity involve a love/hate relationship with the mother, impotence in the face of women, performances of self-birthing, and exaggerated sexual prowess.

In his short story "My Life as a Redneck," Cuban American Gustavo Pérez-Firmat gives voice to an anxious Cuban-born male living in North Carolina. His anxiety centers on mothers, a fear that he locates geographically in the threatening waters engulfing his homeland: "Cuba is a body of land, smaller than a continent, surrounded by mothers on all sides. Big mothers. Mean mothers. Total mothers. No Cuban is an island because we're all caught and connected in the great chain of maternal being" (223). "Mother" as it is invoked here is an obscene insult, pointing to something grotesquely outsized and hostile. The narrator overtly names male anxiety of entrapment, impotence and loss saying, "Cuba is a feeble phallic epiphenomenon awash in the endless mothering ocean" (224). Speaking of his own actual mother, the narrator says, "A mother she was, a real mother. Lovely and lethal and overweight" (223). The narrator's fear of Cuban mothers and the sexual inadequacy it invites leaks into his marriage and inspires a compensatory affair. The narrator's wife is a Cuban mother herself; and, in an attempt to escape their sexless marriage, he has an affair with his American secretary, Catherine. Everything about the affair is epic in proportion. Initially the narrator is so afraid that he fails to achieve an erection, the *atraso* that sets in as a result of protracted abstinence is "monumental" (227), and the sex, once successful, is nothing less than a vehicle for the narrator's cultural immersion: "Sleeping with her was like making cross-over dreams come true. I was bewitched, bewildered, and bicultural" (228). The affair even takes over his working life as an academic literary critic: "For several months, pheromones suffused the rarefied air around Cultural and Literary studies (Clit studies for short). I had finally understood what the pleasure of the text was all about. My life in theory devolved into the most frenetic kind of praxis" (232). Despite his obvious adoration of his secretary, she functions as a field on which the narrator acts out his sexual, cultural, and even professional exploits. Tail tucked between his legs, he goes back to his wife after a few months (he says that all Cuban husbands do), but he blames his own impotence for failing to make a complete break with the Cuban mother of his children. Even as a child, he overstayed his time inside his mother and, had he not been forcibly removed, he says that he would still be there, "softly boiling in Mami's ooze" (234). His wife receives him as the sea receiving driftwood, a metaphor that returns us to the overwhelmed "feeble phallic epiphenomenon" and aptly summarizes the narrator's sense of irrelevance.

Mexican American Richard Rodriguez also thematizes the threatening mother as metaphor for the country of origin in *Days of Obligation*. Although Rodriguez's subtitle is *An Argument with my Mexican Father*, and although his father is identified with a dark Mexican skepticism that Rodriguez is beginning to appreciate in his "American" self, it is the mother who appears over and over again in Rodriguez's arguments. Rodriguez tells us that his book is about California and Mexico, and then proceeds to set up a number of oppositions that describe the two places: comic and tragic, Protestant and Catholic, adoptive and parental, sterile and reproductive, future and past, public and private, masculine and feminine, even gay and straight. The measure of what he fears is a dangerous drift toward Mexico is the number of negative, ominous, and even sometimes sinister descriptions of the country. Rodriguez opens his book with a scene in which he literally vomits a Mexico that he simply cannot stomach: "bits and pieces of Mexico spew from my mouth, warm, half-understood, nostalgic reds and greens dangle from long strands of saliva" (xv). Mexico is female to the male migrant in Rodriguez' description of those who go north in search of better wages: "They were men without women. They were Mexicans without Mexico" (52). Mexico is also a prostitute: "Mexico laid down and the gringo paid in the morning" (88). She is the carrier of all that is foreign, dirty, disease-ridden, and chaotic (91). She is also embodied in a terrifying bewhiskered failure of femininity that tries to attack Rodriguez during his stay in Mexico: "An old hag with chicken skin on her arms grabs for my legs—extravagant swipes, lobster-like" (98).

According to Rodriguez, however, Mexico is more than anything an angry and abandoned mother who will return like the repressed: "Everything that America wants to believe about himself—that he is innocent, that he is colorless, odorless, solitary, self-sufficient—is corrected, weighed upon, glossed by Mexico, the maternity of Mexico, the envy of Mexico, the grievance of Mexico. Mexicans crossing the border are secret agents of matriarchy" (72). This fear of motherhood is mixed with a sense that for Mexico, adulthood is achieved by having children. Rodriguez describes an old beggar woman in Mexico, and understands her lack of grace as a result of her childlessness (77). Mother Mexico makes Rodriguez feel himself to be inadequate as a Mexican male not only because he has assimilated to American culture and language, but also because he is gay and has no children. Rodriguez narrates a scene in which he is sitting in a bar in Mexico City with five other Mexicans who are working on the film project with him. Among them is a Mexican woman who is the curator of the National Anthropology Museum. This woman scolds Rodriguez for his bad Spanish, and then impugns his masculinity, at once mimicking the embarrassment of Mexican Americans who can no longer speak much Spanish and suggesting Rodriguez' paltry manhood: "*Poquito, Poquito*" (74). She follows this by remarking on his childlessness, and the group decides to take him to a club where he can get some female attention. Again, Rodriguez fails to be manly. The singer approaches Rodriguez to sing to him during her act, inviting him to join. Although he writes earlier in the chapter that real macho Mexican men express their emotions most fully in song, here he sings grudgingly, just to get her to go away (77).

Chilean exile Ariel Dorfman, in his memoir *Heading South, Looking North*, rehearses the desire to flee the threatening mother and create oneself anew in a particularly guilt-ridden but clear way. Dorfman narrates a moment in his young life soon after arriving to New York in which he decides to refuse to speak Spanish and speak only English. He is provided with this opportunity because he suffers from an illness that requires a lengthy hospitalization and quarantine from his parents. He reflects in his memoir that he has been unable to access this turning point in order to discover why he rejected English as he did. Dorfman narrates this potentially benign frustration in a way that suggests rape: "We all desire to find out how we began, force the legs of memory open. . . . I thought I could . . . access what had been my second birth, the moment when I mothered and fathered myself . . . when I had created myself" (43). Later in his life, when he does an about face and decides to move back to Chile, speak only Spanish, and become part of the leftist community, his self-recreation again is inseparable from sex. Dorfman identifies Chile with his Chilean wife, and although he criticizes that move—he complicates it, he retracts it—it is, nevertheless, a starting point that he cannot resist narrating, and it is worth citing rather extensively:

> Ever since I had met her, Angélica had been confused, in my mind, with Chile . . . the hot sexual thought of a lithe *moreno* body under her dress. . . . How much of this I identified with the exotic Chile, the exotic Latin America that I had been secretly and transgressively hungering for all these many years, is anybody's guess. I experienced love through the metaphors available to males in Latin America—and elsewhere—at the time, no matter how suspect and gendered I may consider them now . . . the woman as the earth, the earth goddess to be excavated, a territory to be explored by a pioneer, a land in which to root your manhood like a tree—those were the images that surged inside me as we made love, I could never entirely rid myself of the feeling that I was somehow making mine something more than an individual woman, that I was making love to a community that was inside her. (178)

Like Pérez-Firmat's narrator who experiences sex as a way to become American, Dorfman writes that, at least temporarily, his marriage to Angélica is what allowed him to feel Chilean after his mysteriously self-imposed assimilation to the United States. In each case, women are more symbolic than real: mothers don't birth sons, and wives provide raw material that facilitates male ethnic self-making.

Masculine Excesses

The United States draws both Cuban immigrants and exiles with a promise of independence from poverty and political repression. Still, in the same way Rousseau's enlightenment philosophy allows for the continued subjugation of women through the theory of sexual complementarity, fictional freedom-seeking Cubans continue to exclude women from the Cuban ethnic/national group and the family through their constructions of masculinity. In both Hijuelos's and Arenas's novels, there is a complicated double ideology of masculinity at work. *Mambo Kings* presents two incompatible versions of proper Cuban

American male identity: the macho and the domestic. The macho is expected to bed as many women as possible, while the domestic is expected to be a loyal family man and provider. In the novel, a cost free resolution between these two competing masculinities is achieved through the exclusion of women that operates in both to solidify an all-male family. Similarly, *El asalto* also describes two competing male types: the macho and the *maricón*. The macho is a soldier in Castro's revolution, completely devoted to the state, and ready to kill. The *maricón*, in contrast, is the worst deviant possible to both the revolution and the heterosexual reproductive family. By macho logic, since the *maricón* is the passive partner in gay sex, he is feminized and thus corrosive to the macho group. As Hijuelos brought together the macho and the domestic, Arenas also reveals the macho and the *maricón* to be more similar than different. Arenas argues that all men in Cuba engage in gay sex (the only difference being that the machos are active and *maricones* are passive), and thus the Cuban machos and the *maricones* more similar than different.

These contradictory masculinities are joined in their exclusion of women and the formation of an all-male family. Hijuelos accomplishes this with seduction, Arenas with assault, but both resolve contradictions between independence and sexism. In *Mambo Kings* the all-male family is, first, the mambo band, and later a Latin nightclub called Club Havana. These fictional families are echoed in the real-life *Buena Vista Social Club*. Both the music group and the documentary film include very few women. Further, the *Buena Vista Social Club* exemplifies the complicated flow of capital mentioned in the opening section of this essay. These aging musicians not only revived the popularity of Latin music in the United States, their success in the United States caused them to begin playing again in Havana, where Castro's government pays them a salary to play in cafés because they bring in tourists, many of them probably from the United States. In this way, a Cuban male group reproduces Cuban culture. In *El asalto*, the all-male family is the army: Arenas's other works trace versions of the all-male families such as young revolutionaries, men in work camps, and a genealogy of gay male writers that nurture Arenas artistically.

These Cuban male groups are striking in their ethos of excess, both in terms of masculinity and cultural production (in this case, writing). In the most obvious and embodied site of excessive masculinity, each author narrates characters that describe themselves as having almost otherworldly organs. In *Mambo*, Cesar cavalierly acknowledges to the reader, "So I was led around by my penis, so what?" (53). For the Mambo King, sex is a form of cultural insertion that allows him to be successful in America without ever having to give up his Cuban-ness—in fact, it is precisely his charisma as a Cuban male that facilitates his sexcapades. Cesar compares the veins of his erect penis to the Mississippi River and its tributaries (19) and its head to a Cortland apple (20), mapping his member directly onto the U.S. landscape in a loving gesture of cultural conquest. Upon penetration, one woman "felt as if she were being occupied by a living creature the weight and length of a two-year-old cat" (299). Arenas's works also, *El asalto* above all, narrate the penis in an exaggerated, and often violent, way. In *Otra vez al mar,* Arenas writes a battle scene between Greeks and Trojans in which they use their penises to fight. In *El asalto,* the narrator, in an attempt to eradicate all gay men from the island, forms a team of soldiers to help entrap gays, but his choices obviously belie his own repressed gay desire: "I have chosen from the ranks of our agents those who are most physically fit and well endowed, those with long athletic legs, firm tread, and patent sexual endowment" (95).

Sexual excess, both literal and metaphorical, is central to both narratives. In Hijuelos's novel, Cesar's sex-drive is practically religious in the magnitude of its importance. In a footnote celebrating women's lingerie, Cesar speaks of panties as though they were the sacred objects of a sexual ritual invested with healing grace. Before his death, he performs a rosary-like recitation of the names of 57 women he has loved (394). He recalls, "A spectacular evening among so many spectacular evenings. How the rum flowed then, Jesus, how the bottles of booze multiplied along with the thick latex prophylactics and quivering female thighs like the miracle of fish and bread" (31). Here, Cesar revises Christ's miracle so that what is multiplied is not fish or bread, but booze, condoms, and female flesh. In Arenas's works also, sexual excess is the rule. In his memoir, *Antes que anochezca*, he reports that both in the Cuban countryside and among Cuban revolutionaries in the 60s most Cubans were sexually free and most men had sex with other men (19). Of Arenas's memoir, Sánchez-Eppler writes, "From the emplacement of late-1980s New York, every bit of ostensibly marginalized Cuban sexuality will be paraded as the most often practiced thing in the world. Out in Arenas's rural home, sex with animals and sex with cousins of all genders, and even sex with uncles, will be represented as frequent, hardly exceptional, matter-of-fact" (166). Concerning the revolution, he continues, "The bus- and truckloads of young bodies fueling the grand revolutionary mobilization turn into an ecstatic and uninterrupted homoerotic feast" (173). In *El mundo alucinante*, the narrator describes a group of men frolicking and diving in an entire pool of semen.

Sex takes on an exaggerated importance in *El asalto* as well, providing much of the novel's dark humor. The narrator decides that it is his patriotic duty to punish any gay "pervert" who even looks in the vicinity of a man's crotch. The punishment is "Total Annihilation," which means that not only is the criminal executed, so is anyone associated with the criminal. Arenas stretches this to impossible proportions. A group of agents send a request to the narrator that they be "allowed to wear special blinders to keep them from being able to look down" in order to avoid committing the crime of perversion. The narrator responds:

> El documento me encoleriza hasta tal extremo, que además de aniquilar a todos los que lo redactaron, garfearon, portaron, ojearon, etc., redacto un contradocumento que dice así . . . el hecho de haber propuesto llevar unas orejeras, demuestra tal debilidad ideológica, que lo descubre, ante cualquiera, como vil depravado. (94)
>
> That document so enraged me that besides Annihilating all the agents that wrote it, touched it, carried it, caught sight of it, etc. I drafted a counterdocument which read as follows . . . the fact of having proposed to wear blinders is *prima facie* proof of such ideological weakness that the proponent is revealed as a depraved and perverted criminal. (99)

This parody criticizes the hypocrisy implicit in Castro's absurdly sexually restrictive regime.

Although inflated sex organs and carnivalesque sex in these novels are outside of progeny and the hetero nuclear family, they are closely tied to the reproduction of culture. That is, while much of the sex talk in these novels is literal, the hypersex serves a more symbolic than physical function. This excessive Cuban masculinity is the way that these men at least repeat their culture, even if they cannot reproduce it. This obsessive repetition is both thematized in these novels, and mirrored in their narrative strategies. *Mambo* contains almost as many repetitive cultural forms as it does sex scenes. The mambo, itself a repetitive cultural form, is immortalized in a short piece of film that was shot at the opening of Cesar's nightclub, Club Havana. The club eventually folds because Cesar cannot meet its financial obligations, but he tells us what happened to the film in an extended parenthetical that is, I think, a central aside:

> And the film? The night's work resulted in only ten minutes of footage that would be shown at a festival in the Whitney Museum and included a brief interview with Cesar . . . he was saying, "I came here with my younger brother in the late 1940s and we had a little band, the Mambo Kings. I composed with my brother a song, 'Beautiful Maria of My Soul,' and this caught the attention of the singer Desi Arnaz, who asked us to appear with him on his TV show I Love Lucy, do you know it?" And that ran in the film in a loop, jerking back to a point where he's first saying, "Desi Arnaz, who asked us to appear with him on his TV show I Love Lucy." Jerked back, it showed about ten times in quick succession. Then it cut to the same kind of loop of Pablito dancing the pachanga with his wife, the same steps being repeated over and over again in a jerky manner. It was shown many times in the viewing room of the Whitney, and then later in France, where it won a prize. (319)

As a loop, the film literally repeats both Cesar's proud relation to Arnaz and the dancing expertise of Pablito and his wife. The film loop, along with the mambo music and dance, jerk around repetitiously in ways that mirror the novel as a whole. Hijuelos's narrative is also decorated with jerky flourishes of the mambo—Hijuelos's relentless return to the Hotel Splendour (which occurs no fewer than 35 times) is like a horn line in mambo music that becomes familiar through repetition. In novelistic repetitions of repetitions, the Hotel Splendour is a place where Cesar can re-live to relieve. He even re-lives moments of reliving themselves, such as being at Club Havana, "listening attentively and feeling pleased by the repetition of certain events" (329), or being grateful to his final lover, Lydia, for making him feel "as if he would be able to re-live and do certain things over again" (350). The real locus of this cultural repetition, and the axis upon which turn the film loop parenthetical and the novel itself, is the *I Love Lucy* show. The novel is anchored by an episode of the *I Love Lucy* sitcom in which the Castillo brothers were invited to perform (Hijuelos even repeats word for word, on pages 142 and 404, over a page of material that describes the night-club performance). If Cesar, despite his energetic sexual activity, cannot reproduce, he can at least re-run, as it is Desilu's re-runs that accomplish the repetition of Cuban American culture that Cesar is trying to achieve. Arenas's repetitions occur both within his works and among them. Because the manuscript was either lost or confiscated, Arenas was literally forced to rewrite *Otra vez al mar* three times before the third version was successfully smuggled out of the country. The five novels of his *pentagonía* are an extended fictional autobiography; scenes from these are repeated and revised in his memoir *Antes que anochezca*. Arenas also repeats two alarming themes throughout his works: a love/hate relationship between the narrator and the mother, and suicide. Sánchez-Eppler finds no fewer than twenty-seven separate mentions of suicide in *Antes que anochezca*, along with the suicide of the mother down the well in *Celestino*, and Héctor crashing his car at the mouth of the Havana Harbor Tunnel in *Otra vez al mar* (178).

El asalto contains many repetitions as well. First, the name of the Castro/dictator character is the "Reprimerísimo," as though he were not simply a dictator, but intensely so, over and over again. Arenas also repeats the idea that under a dictatorship, even language and memory are taken from the people, until they can only grunt repetitive phrases that frustrate their ability to communicate. For example, the people must memorize a "Diálogo Universal Autorizado" for delivery at the Great Assembly for the Represiversary. The dialogue repeats "gar" and "Viva el Reprimerísimo" and "viva" over and over again (102). The government also writes a version for children in which they repeat "¡Jiuuuuuu!" and "¡Jiaaaaaaaa!" several times (96). In one scene, the narrator bumps into a female who tries vainly to make a connection with him by appealing to a recent episode in which they had made eye contact, a rare and illegal occurrence under the regime. She tries to speak with him, and to explain the basis for her come-on. The narrator is disgusted by her: "*Y así sigue hablando que si yo al mirar ella mira que si me miró y yo la miré que qué sé yo qué al mirarla y ella mirarme. Y así que cuando tú me mirastes yo te miré . . . y sigue: cuando te miré me mirastes y al mirarnos*" (68) ["she goes on talking that way, saying that if when I looked at her she looked back then we looked at each other and if we looked at each other then I looked at her when she looked at me, and that if when she looked at me I kept looking at her, well then . . . and still she goes on talking: Because if you looked at me when I looked at you, and you kept looking at me even when I looked back at you"; 69–70]. Although dark, this evocation of the extreme and inane result of dictatorship is funny, and resonates with the film loop in *Mambo*. The limitations of context of the *Mambo* film—its short length, the poignantly absurd recognition in France—significantly deplete its meaning. In both Hijuelos's and Arenas's texts, the anxious work of constructing masculinity (the sexy macho, the repressive revolutionary, and the closeted gay man alike) is exposed as empty as empty can be.

This suggests a critique of a socially endorsed masculinity that betrays its failings for both men and women. Hijuelos's text is sometimes read as a sympathetic unmasking of machismo's pimples and warts. Most critics of Arenas's *El asalto* have taken it as a fiercely parodic undoing of masculinity and dictatorship (Biron) because Arenas depicts Castro's dictatorship as repressive, deadening, and grotesquely and hypocritically murderous. But in the case of both texts, this critique of masculinity surfaces only to be ultimately overridden by its complete remystification and redemption in the repetitive, performative, excessively masculine family. What is more, because this family depends upon the expulsion of the female, it cannot be benign. Instead, at the moment of the successful cohesion of Cuban culture under siege, colonial relations are instantiated anew vis-à-vis women.

In *Mambo*, Cesar invokes a cliché of misogynist advice in speaking to his nephew: "Women, boy, will ruin you if you're not careful. You offer them love, and what do you get in return? Emasculation" (223). In a few instances, female characters register their complaints against this macho all-male family. By and large, however, male relations with women in the novel are friendly; Cesar seduces his female conquests, who are grateful for his visitation (only once does he secure sex through rape). Machismo as the mystified standard of Cuban masculinity is more often justified by Hijuelos's female characters than challenged. Dolores, who despite being described as "a woman of intelligence and beauty literally trapped inside a crush of men" (170), still corroborates some of machismo's most deeply cherished maxims. Dolores is raped by an American man after a date, and she responds with anger, sadness, and shame. But even after she knows she will be raped, Dolores feels almost a fondness for the awkward ardor of her date. What finally disgusts Dolores, what betrays the pitiful character of the man, and what possibly even gives her the revenge of the last laugh (according to the novel) is the sight of the man's tiny penis: "And there it was, his member, slightly bent and wavering in the air. She thought, 'It's like a child's.' Something between a look of pity, mirth, and pure contempt crossed her face" (76). Dolores refuses to cooperate; her date ejaculates prematurely and must masturbate to help himself finish the job.

That Dolores can be endeared by her date's passion even in the context of a rape, and that she loses this feeling only upon seeing the size of his penis, suggests her acquiescence to a standard of masculinity that uses the penis as the ultimate index of measure. But it is Dolores's strategy for dealing with the rape that is most convincing on this point. She fantasizes about her own Cuban father's penis, a penis that is almost disembodied, its goodness not limited to the temporary realm of the flesh. As the rape progresses, she imagines it as she saw it one afternoon as her father lay sleeping naked, "his member, huge and powerful, an entity beyond the bodily weakness that would one day kill him" (76). Then, as the word "'virile' floated through her thoughts" (76), she began to flirt with a "sexual speculation about her father" (77). Dolores's response to the abuse of a tiny penis is to long for a huge and protective one, contrasting a pathetic, underdeveloped North American masculinity with an excessively male, and potentially saving Cuban machismo.

The final action of *Mambo* remystifies masculinity as well. Despite the physical death and failure of the literal all-male family, the all-male mambo band survives and self-replicates spiritually. At the novel's end, Eugenio (Cesar's nephew) is the only Castillo left. Eugenio's father dies in a car accident and his uncle Cesar commits suicide; abandoned and despondent, Eugenio goes to visit Desi Arnaz for some comfort. But Arnaz abandons him, too. Eugenio receives only polite hospitality, and he is painfully reminded that the kinship between the Mambo Kings and Desi was something scripted for a make-believe show. Eugenio is left without the male family he so desperately needs. But make believe begins to take on religious weight as it provides Eugenio with ecstasy, if not salvation. After Arnaz leaves him, Eugenio drifts into a religious reverie about the *I Love Lucy* show. In yet another repetition of the famous episode, Eugenio imagines it to be playing itself out right before his eyes. His dead father appears before him in the flesh (404), and, prayer-like, the text repeats word for word the Castillo's now mythic performance on Ricky Ricardo's stage. After the repetition of the rerun, Eugenio's vision continues in a religious vein as he imagines a mambo orchestra in the choir stall of the cathedral where his father's funeral is being held. The novel takes this fantasy seriously—the praxis of rehearsing the memory of the Mambo Kings on *I Love Lucy* reruns creates an all-male community by faith.

If women in *Mambo* are contained through seduction or ignored as irrelevant, in *El Asalto*, they are expelled in a far more obvious and more violent way. First, the narrator strangles to death the woman who made a pass at him. More powerfully, the end of the novel thematizes Arenas's love/hate toward the mother that appears in each of the books of the *pentagonía*. As I have said, the narrator has been searching for his mother during the entire book in order to kill her. Along the way, he has successfully slaughtered so many counterrevolutionaries that he is to be presented with a special award during the great ceremony in honor of the Represiversary. As the dictator himself approaches the narrator to bestow the award, the narrator sees that the dictator is his mother. Enraged, his penis begins to swell until it is literally a weapon with which he knocks off layer upon layer of her armor:

> Maniobrando detrás de sus monumentales nalgas, doy un salto, caigo de frente y la vuelvo a atacar. De un golpe mi pinga derriba su cuarto envoltorio. Y al fin puedo ver su cabeza, desprovista del casquete reprimero, su odiosa y cenicienta cabeza de vieja ladina, su gris pelambrera revuelta de chiva vieja flotando entre el sudor y la furia . . . Y ahora la veo, está ahí, con sus millones de manchas y arrugas; la inmensa vaca encuera, con sus enormes nalgas y tetas descomunales, con su figura de sapo deforme, con su pelo cenizo y su hueco hediondo. El miembro erecto, con las manos en la cintura, me quedo de pie, mirándola. Mi odio y mi asco y mi escozor, son ahora innombrables. (139–40)

> I scramble behind her, and under the cover afforded me by the mounds of her enormous buttocks I leap over her, land before her, and continue my attack. With one blow, my member knocks off her fourth coat of armor. And at last I can see her head without its protective helmet—that hated head of a cunning old hag, her ash-colored mat of hair like some stinking nanny goat's emitting a stench of sweat and fury. . . . Her huge buttocks and breasts, her body like some monstrous toad's, her ash-gray hair and her stinking hole are exposed for all to see. With my member throbbingly erect, and my hands on my hips, I stand before her, looking at her. My hatred and my revulsion and my arousal are now beyond words to describe. (144)

The narrator's rage is finally brought to the boiling point when she calls him "hijo." As the dictator, she is someone who both as mother and as nation threatens to steal his masculinity and make him impotent. The narrator proceeds to murder his mother by raping her:

> Mi erección se vuelve descomunal, y avanzo con mi falo proyectándose hacia su objetivo, hacia el hueco hediondo, y la clavo. Ella al ser traspasada emite un alarido prolongado y se derrumba al mismo tiempo que yo siento el triunfo, el goce furioso de desparramarme

> en su interior. Ella, soltando un aullido, estalla lanzando tornillos, arandelas, latas, gasolina, semen, mierda, y chorros de aceite. (140)

> My erection swells to enormous proportions, and I begin to step toward her, my phallus aimed dead for its mark, that fetid, stinking hole. And I thrust. As she is penetrated, she gives a long, horrible shriek, and then she collapses. I sense my triumph—I come, and I feel the furious pleasure of discharging myself inside her. Howling, she explodes in a blast of bolts, washers, screws, pieces of shrapnel-like tin, gasoline, smoke, semen, shit, and streams of motor oil. (145)

As a result of this murder, Cuban citizens are finally liberated and the narrator lies down to rest.

Some critics have argued that this scene is a parodic attack on misogyny and therefore no different from others scenes in the novel in which Arenas parodies violence or repression. Biron, for example, suggests that this scene critiques a cultural imperative for men to reject identification with women through violence, and exposes the poverty of a freedom that requires sexual attack (28). Yet, how can we be sure that this scene constitutes an exposé? It seems clear that scenes of violence against gays, or repression of language and artistry are critical because in those instances there are no outcomes that we recognize as positive. In this case, however, it is through the rape/murder of his mother that the narrator, and indeed, the entire island, is liberated and at long last at peace. Further, in each of the novels of Arenas's autobiographical *pentagonía*, the mother is tyrannically omnipresent, oppressive, and judgmental of both Arenas's artistry and his sexuality.

Ávila reads this scene as the narrator's only way to escape the hell of absolute control exerted by the dictator: "By killing the phallic couple embodied in the mother as *Reprimerísimo*, Arenas enacts the fantasy of overcoming the source of his abjection, the possibility of killing the ambiguous objects of desire who simultaneously lure him into the house and cast him from it" (114). Certainly, the *Reprimerísimo*, as both Castro/father and mother, is oddly transgendered. And the novel may point to the pre-Oedipal more than the Oedipal moment, before gender is even constructed, in which the parent exercises complete power over the child. Still, during the climactic moment of release, to call the *Reprimerísimo* a couple is to ignore the narrative fact that the dictator is embodied as the narrator's mother and that she inspires a male narrator's anxiety of impotence. This masculine anxiety is in fact dispelled through fantasy, but it is a specifically sexist rape fantasy. What is more, the body matters a great deal in the content of these passages: the mother shrieks, she stinks, she's a hag, she's an animal, her body is full of the abject and the industrial. Ávila wants to read Arenas as radically liminal, comforting no one. But I would suggest that there are readers for whom the rape/murder of the mother is comforting. Arenas certainly challenges many oppressive structures with this text and others, but with this scene he joins a male revolutionary family that resorts to the most excessive forms of masculine violence in order maintain the illusion of self-generation.

Excess, repetition, self-birthing male families: both Hijuelos's and Arenas's texts leave us with a version of masculinity that, despite its vigorous protestations to the contrary, fails to reproduce anything. We are left not with too much, but too little. Excess gives way, finally, to lack. Eugenio is stranded by the absence of father, uncle, and icon. Arenas's narrator, in staging an invasion of the site of his own origination, sullies his very source and invites his own death. These texts of masculine anxiety throw us up against a Cuba that is constituted by a series of gaps more than a location.

Charles Bernheimer describes, in his article "The Anxieties of Comparison," the anxieties felt by practitioners of comparative literature in "an age of multiculturalism"—over object of study, method, expertise, authenticity with respect to identity politics, and over the potential loss of our elite status among literary critics. The anxieties of impotence that I have placed under study here give rise to my own professional anxieties of comparison. I have said that for comparative literature really to reflect the current circumstances of globalization, we need to consider challenging the nation or ethnic group as the definitive categories from which we draw comparisons. In this way, we may open up the field of comparative literature to Latin American literature in ways that productively engage cultural groups defined in other ways—moment of migration, reason for migration, political affiliation, class status, sexuality. And yet, have I really successfully done without the nation or ethnic group here? Has Cuba really become more an absence than a presence, a split state? At precisely the moment in which I am trying to account for globalization and the way it is making categories such as "national" obsolete, my efforts resituate a characteristically Cuban (even Latin) logic of masculine excess.

Works Cited

Arenas, Reinaldo. *El asalto*. Miami: Ediciones Universal, 1991.

Arenas, Reinaldo. *The Assault*. Trans. Andrew Hurley. New York: Penguin, 1990.

Arenas, Reinaldo. *Before Night Falls*. Trans. Dolores Kock. New York: Penguin, 1990.

Ávila, Rubén Ríos. "Caribbean Dislocations: Arenas and Ramos Otero in New York." *Hispanisms and Homosexualities*. Ed. Sylvia Molloy and Robert McKee Irwin. Durham: Duke UP, 1998. 101–19.

Bassnett, Susan. *Comparative Literature: A Critical Introduction*. Oxford: Blackwell, 1993.

Bernheimer, Charles. "Introduction: The Anxieties of Comparison." *Comparative Literature in the Age of Multiculturalism.* Ed. Charles Bernheimer. Baltimore: Johns Hopkins UP, 1995. 1–17.

Biron, Rebecca. *Murder and Masculinity: Violent Fictions of Twentieth-Century Latin America.* Nashville: Vanderbilt UP, 2000.

Chevigny, Bell Gale, and Gari Laguardia, eds. *Reinventing the Americas: Comparative Studies of the Literature of the United States and Spanish America.* Cambridge: Cambridge UP, 1987.

Cohn, Deborah. *History and Memory in the Two Souths: Recent Southern and Spanish American Fiction.* Nashville: Vanderbilt UP, 1999.

Colás, Santiago. "Of Creole Symptoms, Cuban Fantasies, and Other Latin American Postcolonial Ideologies." *PMLA: Publications of the Modern Language Association of America* 110.3 (1995): 75–81.

Davis, Lisa. "An Invitation to Understanding Among Poor Women of the Americas: *The Color Purple* and *Hasta no verte, Jesús Mío.*" *Reinventing the Americas: Comparative Studies of the Literature of the United States and Spanish America.* Ed. Bell Gale Chevigny and Gari Laguardia. Cambridge: Cambridge UP, 1986. 224–41.

de la Campa, Román. "Latin, Latino, American: Split States and Global Imaginaries." *Comparative Literature* 53.4 (2001): 373–88.

Dorfman, Ariel. *Heading South, Looking North.* New York: Penguin Books, 1998.

Fitz, Earl. *Rediscovering the Americas: Inter-American Literature in a Comparative Context.* Iowa City: U of Iowa P, 1991.

Hijuelos, Oscar. *The Mambo Kings Play Songs of Love.* New York: Harper and Row, 1989.

Hunsaker, Steven. *Autobiography and National Identity in the Americas.* Charlottesville: U of Virginia P, 1999.

Kanellos, Nicolas. "Review of *The Mambo Kings Play Songs of Love*, by Oscar Hijuelos." *Americas Review* 18 (1990): 113–14.

Mirandé, Alfredo. *Hombres y Machos: Masculinity and Latino Culture.* Boulder: Westview P, 1997.

Ortiz, Ricardo. "Pleasure's Exile: Reinaldo Arenas's Last Writing." *Borders, Exiles, Diasporas.* Ed. Elazar Barkan and Marie-Denise Shelton. Stanford: Stanford UP, 1998. 92–111.

Pérez-Firmat, Gustavo, ed. *Do the Americas Have a Common Literature?* Durham: Duke UP, 1990.

Pérez-Firmat, Gustavo. *Life on the Hyphen: The Cuban-American Way.* Austin: U of Texas P, 1994.

Pérez-Firmat, Gustavo. "My Life as a Redneck." *Iguana Dreams: New Latino Fiction*. Ed. Delia Poey and Virgil Suárez. New York: Harpers, 1992. 223–34.

Rodriguez, Richard. *Days of Obligation*. New York: Penguin Books, 1992.

Saldívar, José David. *The Dialectics of Our America*. Durham: Duke UP, 1991.

Sánchez-Eppler, Benigno. "Reinaldo Arenas, Re-writer Revenant, and the Repatriation of Cuban Homoerotic Desire." *Queer Diasporas*. Ed. Cindy Patton and Benigno Sánchez-Eppler. Durham: Duke UP, 2000. 154–82.

Sommer, Doris. *Foundational Fictions: The National Romances of Latin America*. Berkeley: U of California P, 1991.

Sommer, Doris. *Proceed With Caution, When Engaged by Minority Writing in the Americas*. Cambridge: Harvard UP, 1999.

Yúdice, George. "We Are Not the World." *Social Text* 10 (1992): 202–16.

A Historical Account of Difference: A Comparative History of the Literary Cultures of Latin America

Mario J. Valdés

In his influential essay "Literary History as Challenge," (1982) Hans Robert Jauss makes the following argument: "The task of literary history is . . . only completed when literary production is not only represented synchronically and diachronically in the succession of its systems, but also seen as 'special history' in its own unique relationship to 'general history'" (39). My response to Jauss's third point—regarding literary history's own unique relationship to general history—will constitute the major part of this essay and in so doing I will outline my basic argument for a post-Foucault history of literary culture. In order to take up Jauss's challenge we must first establish the social basis for literature and, consequently, literary history. A community in the sense of the Greek polis cannot be made by a housing development or a city planner or by a religious leader of a utopian settlement. A community, like a language, grows out of human interaction and an open public life that will eventually encourage group identity. The foundation of community life is dialogue, the willingness of people to talk and to listen to each other, the expression of mutual concerns, a debate on differences of opinion. Above all, it depends upon a sense of belonging and therefore having a vested interest in the life of the community. The question that immediately arises is: How do we situate communities in a literary history without reducing the diversity and unique features that distinguish them? The answer—in any case, my answer—was to enlist the participation of social scientists: cultural geographers, linguists, demographers, social historians and anthropologists to map the foundations of the rich diversity of Latin American literary cultures (see the website of the project at <http://www.chass. utoronto.ca/lithist/latin.html>). This mapping constitutes the first section of Volume 1 of our *Comparative History of Latin*

American Literary Cultures (see Vol. 1 at <http://www.chass.utoronto.ca/lithist/1engdetail.html>).

Some of the key questions that pertain to the viability of a community are covered by the issue of who has the right to speak. Throughout history there have always been some persons who live in the community but who are excluded from debate. They have been prevented from participating for many reasons including religion, caste, race, and gender. The sense of belonging to the community, which is so central to its development, paradoxically has also been the basis for excluding those who are different from those who set the rules. People in authority in communities around the world and in all periods of history, including our own, have established rules of eligibility or citizenship, which regulate rights and privilege and which also attempt to control communal dialogue, but to no avail. There is no law that can get people to talk to each other with mutual respect when they do not already have it, nor is there any law that has been successful for long in silencing those who would speak in spite of being excluded. There is a political dilemma here. In ideal terms universal freedom to speak is a desirable goal, but governments cannot legislate mutual respect when there is inherited distrust of those who are different. Or, to put the dilemma in terms of Hegel's political philosophy, is it possible to have a community wherein everyday practice does justice to both particularity and universality? Northern Ireland has given us a prime example of the dilemma. The Canadian philosopher Charles Taylor has come up with the most lucid response to Hegel's paradox in his *Philosophical Arguments* (1995): "What seems to be emerging . . . is a hazy picture of history in which our understanding will be embedded. It rejects altogether the Hegelian single line of development, but it retains something like the notion of potentiality. . . . It does point us to a future of humanity in which the kind of undistorted understanding of the other aimed at by the comparativist enterprise will be increasingly valuable. . . . We can hope to advance in this direction, to the extent that the community of comparativists will increasingly include representatives of different cultures, will in effect start from different home languages" (164).

We live in a time of distrust in all aspects of life. Just as Cuba has lost its revolutionary self-confidence, so has the United States lost its self-certainty of empire. Foucault's recognition of the lust for power in all social organizations has become a fact of life at the end of the twentieth century. There is one universal truth today: a loss of faith in the human capacity to respect differences. If we turn to Jauss's thesis that literary history must be related to general history, we must deal with this central issue in historical terms—the inclusions and exclusions which literary history has itself practiced throughout its existence. General history does not select the participants and the events that have been designated significant within the tradition although individual historians may choose to revise the estimations of some. It is only in literary history that the process of selection is either openly ideologically determined or, in most cases, uses the notion of aesthetic quality and formal achievement to disguise what is ultimately inclusion on the basis of ethnic political conservatism. Is this not the crux of the matter? If literary history is to be given the same reception as general history, the process of exclusion must be examined closely.

Literary History After Foucault

Our response to this challenge was to establish two groups who examined literary histories in Latin America. One group addressed the exclusions on the basis of socioeconomic, racial, and ethnic factors and while another focused on perceptions of gender and sexual orientation (see Vol. I, Section 2 at <http://www.chass.utoronto.ca/lithist/1engdetail.html>). In *The Order of Things* (1994) Foucault argues that between the codes of perception and the reflexive knowledge by which we organize reality there is a middle region of the experience of order itself (355–66). I interpret Foucault's designation of experience as our quotidian practices of living in the Polis which revolve around agreement and disagreement, concord and conflict. We have words like "argument" that cover all disputes, but others, like "dialogue" and "debate," are specific social practices of presenting if not resolving differences. Other words, like "contradiction," "contrary," and "contradistinction," are more individual designations of difference, either attributed to the other person or to the arguments presented by the other. In all these words and their semantic derivations we are dealing with differences, with struggle, opposition, and tension, with or without resolution.

Let me review what I have taken from Foucault before going on to my hermeneutics. The codes through which we function in our social life should not be confused with rules of comportment or laws of civil regulation. These codes of perception and engagement govern the way we relate to each other within the community ranging from everyday greetings to sexual relations. These codes constitute the ways through which we explain our action, our intentions, and ourselves. These codes are embedded in our language use and in the social status implicit in language use. These codes put into practice the multiple preformed values of our social group. At the other end of the spectrum there emerge the various paradigms of order; these are the logical, rational means society and, especially, history have developed in the last four hundred years to control diversity. All forms of historical writing are paradigms of the creation of order out of diversity and, by the same generalizing token, all literature (in its basic function of mimesis) makes manifest the diversity of human perception; therefore, literary history is an attempt to organize the self-representation of life writers have given us. And in between the codes and the sense of order lies the irreducible reality of difference. In summary, writers start from within the shared codes of the community, but they are also under the constraints of modes of organization operative in the community, be they modes of religious, political or class distinctions. The tension between the writers' experience in the observance of life under social codes and the modes of order subscribed to by the cultural authorities leads to rebellion, opposition at all levels and, ideologically, contradiction. This dynamic view of literary culture is not easily described in a historical narrative. Our proposal for a hermeneutic approach to literary history begins by taking the historical perspective of difference as the problem to be addressed. A few additional remarks are necessary on what I have been calling the social codes through which we live in communities. First, it must be recognized that these codes all relate to interpersonal behavior that has been given or assigned meaning. Second, the transmission of these codes is accomplished by literature, cinema, television and, today, by electronic communication. Actions expressing both love and esteem are the most frequent in the behavioral repertoire of interpersonal relations (since we must recognize that the well-being of the individual takes precedence over goods and services) and they are also the primary topics of literature. But love that is unrequited and esteem that turns into envy are always implied. Amongst the multiple social symbolic codes that operate in our communities we can designate four general categories that encompass multiple codes expressed consistently and, primarily, through literature. They are: 1) all forms of *love* including self-esteem, regard for the other(s) and love of community which becomes a form of primary identification, as in nationalism, and the negation of any or all of these; 2) *status*, which includes standing in the community and related issues of ethnicity, class and gender and the underlying manifestation of authority; 3) *questioning* or the need to know, a category that includes education and self-learning as well as the drive for control over information; and 4) *participation* in *exchange systems*, which includes all forms of work and services provided and received in exchange for value. These codes have both a history of concrete realization and of symbolic expression; the former is the domain of anthropology; the *latter* is that of literature. Among the modes of order aimed at controlling the writers' use of social codes are all forms of direct and indirect censorship and, of course, school curricula (with the legitimizing status it gives), as well as the various forms of canonical domination. What interests us here is finding a model of literary history that will explain the tensional relation between the codes of symbolic action within a society and the organizing modes of order which always and without exception select and, also, exclude and marginalize those elements of the symbolic codes that do not subscribe to the ideological preformation of culture they support.

The relationship between the codes and the organizational modes of order is best characterized as a struggle that can be as destructive as it can be constructive of a literary culture. There are only two basic issues: what are the modes of order that have been imposed on the symbolic discourse of the community in question and how is it possible to avoid the necessary distortion of the exercise of power gained by the control of knowledge or, better yet, the knowledge-construct? Implicit in this inquiry is the question of responsibility. In his final works before his death in 1984, Michel Foucault revealed what, to most of his readers, even some of his most careful readers, was a consistent yet hidden line of thought on ethical responsibility. A retrospective reading of his major works brings to light an overriding will to unmask the very activity of philosophy in terms of moral responsibility. He was not interested in a code of conduct for philosophic writers and, much less, in setting up ethical models of conduct. But with increasing intensity, he questioned the ethical responsibility of intellectual inquiry itself. In this sense his ethical concern was shared by his contemporaries, Levinas and Ricoeur. The question of the ethical consequences for intellectual inquiry is never far away from the opening pages of Foucault's later works. But what, perhaps, distinguishes Foucault among his contemporaries was his oblique approach to the issues of responsibility. For example, instead of addressing the problem of how and by whom knowledge is constituted, he asked, what does it do? Knowledge in functional terms becomes that which one group has that gives them an advantage over those who do not possess it. Or, to give another example, instead of examining how the holders of power represent reality, Foucault moves ever so slightly to an oblique angle and asks us to look at what power constructs and purports to be reality. In terms of the history of philosophy he leaves behind the epistemological inquiry that had dominated Western philosophy since Kant and suggests that human institutions and the means of how we know the world are invented by the center of power in any social group. His concern was with the use of knowledge and the strategies to take advantage of information as power. If knowledge is reconfigured as power and power is a means of domination then the disclosure of these power relationships becomes an ethical necessity. Foucault realized that there was never to be an escape from the configuration of the knowledge-power relationship and thus, like a modern-day Don Quixote, he was unyielding in his declaration that there was no social relationship which was either necessary or unchangeable. The overwhelming nature of Foucault's challenge was to construct a literary history that effectively addressed the plurality of cultural discourse in Latin America. Our response was to organize this section on the basis of five related but clearly distinct units: 1) religious, scientific, and political discourse, 2) orality, 3) the diversity of discourses in theater and public theatricality, 4) popular culture, and 5) cinema (see Vol. I, Section 3: <http://www.chass.utoronto.ca/lithist/1engdetail.html>).

A History of Literary Culture: Texts, Poets, and Events

What if we were to change the historical focus from the traditional paradigm of the author and/or his works, to a concerted examination of the context in which they were written and received? How would we organize our inquiry? How could we cope with the multiplicity of the social codes on the one hand and the reductionist tendencies of the institutions of literature on the other? Obviously, we could lose the disciplinary unity of a biographical dictionary of poets and of the corpus of their work, but what we could gain would be a historical narrative of the poet's appropriation of his/her own culture and other cultures which he/she encountered and, on a deeper level, the role as a nodal figure in the development of literary culture. Even a cursory glance at this kind of material would reveal a series of tensional opposites, sometimes irresolvable contradictions and, at other times, points of conflict and encounter that would lead to historical ruptures. As comparative literary historians, let us begin by recognizing that the designation of Latin America is a completely artificial construct. Yet, by the same token, we must also recognize that there are areas of social and cultural dynamics throughout the continent that have become cultural zones of interaction. In undertaking the historical consideration of both the production and the reception of the cultural imaginary in Latin America, we are exploring an essential aspect of historical life—the way peoples imagine themselves and others—and we are also cutting across national borders, geographic regions, time periods, linguistic systems, and cultural traditions. Establishing the broader context, political, religious and social, in which literary culture flows is a challenge of some consequence to the comparative literary historian. But, above all, we must come to grips with syncretic cultural expression and mestizo cultural identity. Clearly, there can be no attempt to gain a comprehensive historical examination over such a vast and complex area with hundreds of years of conflictive history.

Latin America is too diverse and multifaceted to permit such synthesis. Nevertheless a comparative cultural history can, by focusing on connections, inform discussions of the historical problematics by insisting on foregrounding all aspects of inclusion and exclusion to legitimation, and by maintaining a reflexive self-questioning, one that is central to a hermeneutic approach. In order to anchor such vast cultural diversity and social variability, we have undertaken the transcultural examination of the centers of cultural production and of the institutions with control over this production. The texts and events of production thus enter the historical commentary, unfolding a richer contextualization that is open ended. Thus, the vast scope of the undertaking—an entire continent, living in numerous distinct languages both European and Amerindian over the last five hundred years—put enormous pressure on us not to lose sight of the narrative requirements of writing history. We had to tell the story of Latin American culture, but we were committed to not impose closure. Our solution was a second volume that brought together institutional modes and cultural modalities. This volume has three parts: 1) cultural institutions; 2) textual models and, finally, 3) the cumulative synopsis, the cultural centers of the continent (see Vol. 2 at <http://www.chass.utoronto.c/lithist/2engdetail.html>).

It is not by chance that today we have a widespread rejection of the validity of literary history and we retain only its most basic function, that of giving an initial orientation to students. The last quarter of the twentieth century has been characterized by a retreat, if not a withdrawal, from the horizon of expectation of literary history as historical knowledge. At the same time we have seen a drastic narrowing of the space of historical experience to biography and appreciation, equating it to that of personal testimonial of status and taste. On the one hand, some historians have gone so far as to say that literary history is not history but merely opinion with dates and, on the other, deconstructive critics have claimed that there is no authority in writing about texts from the past beyond our own testimonial of how we have read them. The first rejection of academic literary history, and still one of the most powerful, was Roland Barthes's 1963 *Sur Racine* (148). If Ralph Cohen in his "A Note on New Literary History" could state more than thirty years ago that literary history was rejected as scholarship, and if today we no longer bother to consider it to be more than an introduction to literary study (6), it is because we are in a time of major change in literary and historical scholarship. For many, expectation has given way to cynicism or to taking refuge in neo-Marxist or essentialist utopias.

Tradition has become the mausoleum of literature. But my position is that this critical juncture far from being an apocalyptic ending is a time of intense development of new directions. The task of writing what Ricoeur calls effective literary history is very much a part of the present critical period when all the assumptions of the past have been openly questioned, when not deconstructed. In hermeneutic terms, the dialectic between the expectation of knowing the past and the experience of knowing the text is translated into a creative tension of inquiry. A breakdown of the historical inquiry results if the expectation of knowing breaks off from the space of experience into a nondialectic opposition with no relation between them. This break of the horizon of expectation with the space of experience is best known to us today as essentialism, whether it be religious or gender related. Without using the hermeneutic terminology for the dialectic engagement I have been advocating, Homi Bhabha similarly argues in *The Location of Culture* (1994) that we may then "see how modernity and postmodernity are themselves constituted from the marginal perspective of cultural difference. They encounter themselves contingently at the point at which the internal difference of their own society is reiterated in terms of the difference of the other, the alterity of the postcolonial site" (196). This breakdown has already happened in some quarters of deconstructive literary criticism and what in North America is called cultural studies. Effective literary history draws upon the continuous dialectic between the horizon of expectation that demands explanation and the space of experience that recognizes the limitations of understanding. Most of the literary histories written in Latin America fall into two categories. On the one hand, we have written monumental literary history with its parade of genius and masterpieces. On the other hand, we have from time to time written antiquarian literary history which, abandoning the critical sense of the present, values everything that can be assembled from the past.

Monumental literary history decontextualizes literature by presenting ideas, styles of writing, and creativity in isolation from the social reality. Antiquarian literary history, by attempting an undifferentiated preservation of the past, reduces the past to nominalism: titles, but no inquiry into the writing. Today monumental literary history engenders hostility for its implicit totalization, but antiquarian literary history only induces boredom. The paradigm shift of effective literary history displaces the disembodied record of genius as well as the nostalgic reverence of everything from the past and turns to the communities whose literary culture is under scrutiny. The user, i.e. the reader, of effective history is thereby given accessibility to the past of literary culture. The demands of effective history of literary cultures are multiple and the proliferation of specialized information is so vast that this scholarship has been induced to follow the path, long used in the sciences, of collaborative research. The requirements for successful collaborative research in literary history are in fact the basic rules of operation in experimental science but they are quite new in literary history. Collaborative research demands a high degree of mutual involvement, dialogue, and a common adherence to the task of developing the conceptual model. Therefore, the imposition of any previously designed plan or a simple division of labor are procedures that do not warrant this designation of collaborative research. In many respects the example of Braudel's work is exemplary of the collaborative histories we have put together for Latin America and East Central Europe. As early as 1958 Braudel had recognized in his article "La longue durée" the importance of collaborative research: "There is a crisis in the human sciences today; they are all burdened with their own success. The accumulation of new knowledge has made it necessary to engage in collective research, for which it is crucial to have intelligent organization. All the human sciences whether its practitioners like it or not, directly or indirectly, are affected by the progress of the most able among them; this collective engagement is resisted by a retrograde humanism which can no longer serve as a research frame" (1958, 725; my translation).

The conceptual models of collaborative literary history can only come about through extended and intensive exchange of ideas in response to the historiographic problems that have been selected for study. Once the collectively designed conceptual model begins to take shape the pattern of research we call collaborative can begin. The requisites are the same whether we are talking about physics or literary culture. All the researchers must have a full and commonly held grasp of the model, and of the interface between specific areas of research. The over-all design must be clear at all times and the means for continual development and elaboration must be in place so that the conceptual model is not complete until the research project has been completed. Let us turn to David Carr: "To tell the story of a community and of the events and actions that make up its history is simply to continue, at a somewhat more reflective and usually more retrospective level the story-telling process through which the community constitutes itself and its actions" (177). With these words he begins his conclusion to his book *Time, Narrative and History* (1986). I cite it here as the point of departure for my basic thesis that de-objectifies literature and that removes it from the prevalent concept that it is only a cultural commodity. In philosophical terms, my thesis is that literature stands at the centre of a linguistic community's identity, with the all-important qualifier that language and, therefore, linguistic communities are not self-contained. How can we cope with the complex problem of writing a history of literary culture that captures the sense of identity of the diverse communities? Our solution was to engage Latin American identity as one that begins bifurcated by the violence of conquest and slowly develops through a discourse of melancholy to a search for legitimation, finally pouring forth in the multiple discourses of modernity. This is the first section of Volume 3 (see at <http://www.chass.utoronto.ca/lithist/3engdetail. html>).

In *Time and Narrative* (1986–88), Ricoeur gives us what is one of the finest expositions of his hermeneutic premise, one that culminates a mode of inquiry developed from 1955 to 1985. He writes that temporality is the structure of human existence and that it resides in language as narrativity. Language as a mode of living is constituted through narrativity and its ultimate referent is time. The claim is a strong one: that the nature of human time itself is narrativistic. Thus the argument is that historians do not impose narrative form on facts constituted as events that might be otherwise presented through non-narrative discourse, but rather, Ricoeur argues, that historical events themselves in the minds and memories of participants have the same structure as narrative discourse. It is, consequently, this narrative structure that distinguishes historical events from natural events. The presence of human agency which is central to a historical event can transform a natural event like an earthquake or a flood into a historical event. But not all narrative accounts can be accepted as history. For example, Ricoeur writes, journalistic accounts of events may be well informed and make sense of the facts of the case at hand. Yesterday's political speech may be well described, with a prudent distance of analysis, and still fall short of being history, and this is so because the journalist's story lacks the secondary referentiality of a story within a story within a story. The historian is not a reporter of past events; historians are mediators between events and certain experiences of temporality. Thus, there is a poetics of history and a professional critique of the methods of research and also of the ways of emplotting events. A history is a narrative account that reaches conclusions and can be taken as a whole and thus exceeds by far the sum of the sentences that it contains. To emplot a sequence of events transforms the writing from being only a chronicle of incidents into forming a story. This mediation is the ultimate task of the historian. Emplotment is therefore both necessary and always limited, open to question. But to say that one form of emplotment is flawed is not the same as saying that the historian could do without the construction of causality. The plot can be depersonalized and human agency can be deferred, but the presentation of an event is also the presentation of how and why the event happened. The meaning of stories is given in their emplotment. By emplotment a sequence of events is configured (grasped together) in such a way as to represent—symbolically—what would otherwise be unutterable in language, namely, the ineluctable aporetic nature of the human experience of time.

Historical discourse is a privileged instantiation of the human capacity to endow the experience of time with meaning because the immediate referent of this discourse is real, rather than imaginary, events. Historians cannot invent the events of their stories; they must find them. This is so because historical events have already been created by past human agents, who by their actions produced lives worthy of having stories told about them. The construction of the historical event is nothing less than the assignation of meaning to a configuration of data that surrounds human action. J.W.N. Watkins sums up the discussion in his "Historical Explanation in the Social Sciences" (1959) thus: "Every complex social situation, institution or event is the result of a particular configuration of individuals, their dispositions, situations, beliefs, and physical resources and environment" (505). This means that the intentionality informing human actions, as against mere motions, takes us to the creation of lives that have the coherence of emplotted stories. The creation of a historical narrative is an action exactly like that by which historical events are themselves created, but it is in the domain of narration rather than that of action. By discerning the plots prefigured in historical actions by the agents that produced them, and by configuring them as sequences of events having the coherence of stories, the historian makes history.

Literary History and Cultural History

Literary history as a part of cultural history, be it national, regional, or comparative, is the story of stories. In formulating emplotment literary historians have developed historiographic constructs as plotting scripts. The script favored in monumental literary history is the idea of "the tradition" or even "the great tradition" (see, e.g., Leavis, *The Great Tradition*; Menéndez y Pelayo, *Historia de las ideas estéticas en España*) and in comparative literary history the preferred device has been the literary movement (see, e.g., Balakian, *The Symbolist Movement in the Literature of European Languages*). While historical meaning is prefigured in the actions of historical agents, the agents themselves cannot foresee it because human actions have consequences that extend beyond the purview of those who perform them. This is why it is wrong for historians to limit themselves to trying to see things from the position of past agents alone, to trying to think themselves back into the mind or consciousness of past actors in the historical drama. They are fully justified in availing themselves of the advantages of hindsight. Moreover, they are fully justified in using the techniques of analysis developed by the social sciences of their own time in order to identify social forces at work in the agent's environment because these forces may have been only emergent in the agent's time and place and not perceivable to them. Human actions have consequences that are both foreseeable and unforeseeable, that are informed by intentions both conscious and unconscious, and that may be frustrated by contingent factors that are both knowable and unknowable. It is for this reason that narrative is necessary for the representation of "what actually happened" in a given domain of historical occurrence. A scientific historiography of the sort envisioned by the Annalists, which deals in large-scale, physical and social, anonymous forces, is not so much wrong as simply limited to telling only a part of the story of human beings at grips with their individual and collective destinies. It produces the historiographical equivalent of dehumanized drama that is all scene and no actors, or a novel that is all theme but lacking in characters. Such a historiography features all background and no foreground. The best it could provide would be a quasi-history comprising quasi-events, enacted by quasi-characters and displaying the form of a quasi-plot.

Once a human being is allowed to enter such a scene, inhabited only by forces, processes and structures, it becomes impossible to resist the narrative mode of discourse for representing what is happening in that scene. Even Braudel must tell stories whenever human beings, acting as agents, are permitted to enter, to appear against the background of those forces that he would describe solely in quantitative and statistical terms. Braudel's vehement opposition to historical narrative must be contextualized as a reaction to the excesses of French historiography in this regard, but, as every reader of his *Mediterranean* (1949) knows, there is a strong narrative line that tells the story of the shift in power from the Mediterranean to the Atlantic. The Braudel contribution cannot be overestimated. My work has gained greater insight because of his work. Braudel must tell stories in spite of the fact that it goes against his own conscious repudiation of narrativity as the principal impediment to the creation of a scientific historiography.

Ricoeur's insistence that history and literature share a common ultimate referent in human time represents a considerable advancement over previous discussions of relations between history and literature based on the supposed opposition of factual and fictional discourse. Historical narrative discourse alone is adequate to the representation of the experience of historicality in a way that is both literal, in what it asserts about specific events, and figurative, in what it suggests about the meaning of this experience. What the historical narrative literally asserts about specific events is that they really happened, and what it figuratively suggests is that the whole sequence of events that really happened has the order and significance of well-made stories. Narrative discourse does not simply reflect or passively register a world already made; it works up the material given in perception and reflection, fashions it, and creates something new, in precisely the same way that human agents by their actions fashion distinctive forms of historical life out of the world they inherit as their past. Thus conceived, a historical narrative is not only an icon of events, past or present, of which it speaks; it is also an index of the kinds of actions that produce the kinds of events we wish to call historical. It is this indexical nature of historical narrative that assures the adequacy of its symbolic representations to the real events about which they speak. The indexical aspect of the historical narrative consists of three interrelated features: the references to events in other places and other times must be fluid so that the contextual framework is in evidence; the accuracy in describing participants must be such that they can become the referential points in other historical narratives; and finally, the material circumstances behind the event must be as fully constituted as possible. It is in this third feature that the Annalists found the traditional historical narratives of the nineteenth century wanting. Historical events can be distinguished from natural events by virtue of the fact that they are products of the actions of human agents seeking, more or less self-consciously, to endow the world in which they live with symbolic meaning. Historical events can be represented in symbolic discourse because such events are already themselves symbolic in nature; the narrativization of action by human agents has preceded the actual constitution of the event.

Narrativization, following Ricoeur in *Time and Narrative*, is the basis of human temporality. Therefore, the reports and documents upon which the historical narrative depends are already narrativized (Vol. 3, 104–26). So it is with the historian's composition of a narrative account of historical events: the narrativization of historical events effects a symbolic representation of the process by which human life is endowed with symbolic meaning. Historical narrative which takes the events created by human actions as its immediate subject does much more than merely describe those events; it also imitates them, that is, performs them, performs the same kind of creative act as those performed by historical agents. The performance of the historical narrative is the enactment of the past intended to be presented with the utmost accuracy but, above all, it is the configuration of meaning. History has meaning because human actions produce meanings. These meanings are continuous over the generation of human time. This continuity, in turn, is felt in the human experience of time organized as future, past, and present (rather than as a mere serial consecution). To experience time as future, past, and present (rather than as a series of instants in which every one has the same weight or significance as every other) is to experience historicality. This experience of historicality can be represented symbolically in narrative discourse because such discourse is a product of the same kind of figuration as the events themselves; they have beginnings, middles, and ends just as the actions of historical agents who figurate their lives as meaningful stories. The meaning of history resides in its aspects as a drama of the human effort to endow life with meaning. This universal, human quest for meaning is carried out in the awareness of the corrosive power of time, but it is also made possible and given its distinctively human pathos by this very awareness. In this respect, that manner of being-in-the-world that we call historical is paradoxical and cannot be apprehended by human thought except in the form of an enigma. To sum up, prefigurative narrativity is the basis for temporality and, therefore, historical narrative offers us the only way to make sense out of past events. The historian's task is one of mediation between the events and the story of human agency that gives meaning to these events.

If the historian emplots events into a narrative account, we must now ask which events does the literary historian engage in the task of literary history, assuming that literary history is history. The assumption that literary history is history is so basic that it appears to be elementary, but if we examine the indexical nature of historical narrative we recognize that most literary histories fall far short of the mark in presenting the material circumstances of the event described. The reduction in narrative description of the material dimensions of production in literary culture is the principal cause for the separation of literary history from history (see Colebrook's *New Literary Histories* for an excellent review of the relationship between literature, literary history and history, 1–30).

Can the composition and publication of a book be considered an event, or must we include the reception by the author's contemporaries as part of the event? And, if this were so, can we account for vastly changing modes of reception of the same work? Can a history of production concomitantly deal with a history of reception? The direct answer to this question is that if literary history aims at historical textuality, it must bring together the historicity of production (including material circumstances) with the historicity of reception in which the work is completed (see Achugar's commentary on the power politics of critical reading in South America, 53–72). Every form of history by necessity is an approximation to the past and although literary history shares this limitation, it must consider that in addition to the historicity of production, the daunting history of reception is required (see Colebrook's discussion of Pierre Bourdieu's impact on literary history, especially with regard to the historicity of production, 90–111). This answer is obvious, but implementation is another matter.

If literary history is to regain its place within history, clearly all events of consequence in the development of a literary culture must be addressed. In our history an elaborate schema was created by our coordinator, Alberto Moreiras, that worked to bring out the fuller scope of the dominant ideologies behind the historical events; this second section of Volume 3 is organized in four historical phases: 1) lettered mediations; 2) peoples, communities and nation building; 3) the inversion of social Darwinism; and 4) modernization and the formation of cultural identities (see Vol. 3 at <http://www.chass.utoronto.ca/lithist/3engdetail.html>).

The Hermeneutics of Literary History

A hermeneutic historiography of literary history begins with the recognition of the essential problem of description of an event that must be constantly reconstituted. The reconstitution of the literary event differs from historical revision in that literary texts change in meaning from one climate of reception to another. The classic example is Don Quixote as the fool in the seventeenth century becoming the tragic hero of romanticism and the existential hero of the twentieth century. There is no question that the significance of past actions must first be understood in terms of their agents' own values and aesthetic perspectives and not in terms of our very different ones. But, on the other hand, to ignore the meanings of our own redescriptions of the events would be to play the fool. There are three preliminary tasks before us: to understand how our narrative form cannot escape our own value spectrum; to abandon the notion of a universal history; and to open up for scrutiny the concept of event itself. The cognitive function of the historian's narrative form is not a neutral compilation of a succession of facts and ascribed purpose and design; it is, above all, the making of a whole out of a number of interrelationships, which are not in themselves related by necessity but only by the historian's purpose of exposition. The assemblage of data used in the description of the historical event is never fixed because its make-up is not determined by physical necessity but rather by the demands of plausible exposition; thus it is that lists of foodstuffs stored in the royal palace could be, or not, part of the explanatory data depending on the direction the exposition takes. Narrative form is thus an artifice designed to represent a specific explanation for past activity. We would clearly expect that the narrative form used by a feminist, like Elaine Showalter, or a Marxist, like Fredric Jameson, would be the best instrument possible to further their historical ensemble as valid and presenting a general truth-claim. The identification of form with ideology should not be taken as negative. The point to be made is that every telling of a story is partial, limited and directed but that it is as valid as its telling allows for a debate with other versions. The debate amongst historians is a factor of the utmost consequence, for it is only through this conflict of interpretations that the historical event will be enlarged. In the case of literary history, the debate has been, for the most part, confined to the meaning of the texts and not the meaning of the historical event, but this is also changing rapidly with the return of literary history to history (see Cornejo Polar's *Escribir en el aire*, 11–24; also see "History as Theory" in Shapiro's *The Sense of Change: Language as History*, 114–19).

In literary history the designation of the aesthetic perspectives of the past, such as the baroque or romanticism, has been built up by a succession of literary historians, each revising or adding to the work of predecessors. A close examination of the principles and norms used to mark the beginning, apex and end of these perspectives indicates that the basis for the designation is in the narrative description of the differences between the idea of reality expressed in the texts and the idea of reality recognized by the historians as their own. The historian aims to make the aesthetic perspective as distinctive and well defined as possible as a cultural view that is different from both predecessors and successors, but the sense of difference is discernable only from the vantage point of the literary historian himself. Michel de Certeau has put it succinctly in his *The Writing of History* (1988): "The historian is no longer a person who shapes an empire. He or she no longer envisages the paradise of global history. The historian comes to circulate around acquired rationalizations. He or she works in the margins. In this respect the historian becomes a prowler" (79). Works of literature are, of course, historical in their composition, but they are also in history as long as there continues to be reception recorded. Certain works of literature are therefore generators of social discourse in the life of a linguistic community and catalytic agents of change in other communities they reach altered through translation. A history of literature that seeks to grasp together the many versions of the literary work must find new ways of organization.

If the work of literature, its production and reception (in the original language and in translation) is the subject matter of literary history, then the literary work must be recast as a historical event, but as an event that multiplies in time with continuities and discontinuities. If, following Benveniste, we define the present as the moment when speakers make their utterances, then an event is always a retrospective construct and, at the core of this construct, there is an axial moment that allows the historian to date the event. R.G. Collingwood recognized that the making of a historical event is the imaginative reenactment proposed by the historian (see *The Idea of History* 282–302). Although the production and reception are contemporary at the beginning, they bifurcate soon after, and commentary of reception rapidly exceeds commentary on the work's production. Both change with time; only the writing itself remains stable once it has been established as authoritative.

It can be said that by expanding the concept of historical event to include the vicissitudes of subsequent paradigms we have overloaded the argument and made literary history impossible. There is no doubt that by changing the concept of literary event to include reception we have changed the way in which literary history is written but, I would argue, we have also enriched the historical depth of the literary text. Not all literary works have a constant history of reception; most, in fact, have a very short time under critical scrutiny. Nevertheless, when a work from the past is brought into the historical record a number of different events are in play. When we include works, which come into the literary corpus in translation, a new event is introduced which is the rupture of recontextualization. Works can suddenly be plunged into a linguistic and cultural community that is different and distant from the context of origin with extraordinary and unpredictable results, which sometimes can return as aesthetic ideas to the community of origin. A good case for this phenomenon can be made with the Latin American literature of the 1960s, which swept through the non-Spanish-speaking world like a firestorm and has subsequently given rise to ideas of postmodernism that now return to Latin America as an aesthetic perspective (see, for example, Ortega's "Postmodernism in Spanish-American Writing" and Coutinho's "Postmodernism in Brazil").

What I have begun to sketch out is not so much a break with literary historians of the past, but rather a more reflective plan of operation and a rejection of the master narrative. I concur with David Perkins when he writes: "A text from the past embodies a lived experience, an aesthetic, a culture that is alien. Of course, it is not completely alien. Continuities and universals in human experience are the themes of antiquarian literary history and humanist criticism. But most literary histories emphasize the difference of the past" (184). However, I cannot agree with the either/or nature of his proposal when a few lines further he writes: "Here, incidentally, is why literary history cannot surrender the ideal of objective knowledge of the past. Though the ideal cannot be achieved, we must pursue it, for without it the otherness of the past would entirely deliquesce in endless subjective and ideological reappropriation" (185). His argument is that either we strive for objectivity or we risk getting caught in the morass of subjective relativity. Perkins concludes the paragraph with the telling statement: "A function of literary history, is then, to set the literature of the past at a distance, to make its otherness felt" (185). Indeed, but this function would be better served by a mode of interpretation that opened the past to the multiple varieties of present appropriations without closing the works or their context into a master narrative. My thesis is that the historical study of literature is the construction of a complex network of data, imaginative reenactment, and interpretation. One primary aspect of study with respect to the elaboration of textual meaning by the historian is the literary truth-claim as the determinate basis of the literary configuration. The truth-claim of a literary text is the injunction to the reader that certain statements are to be taken as valid or true. The issue is not whether such claims are true or not, but rather that they function as claims to be true in the reception of the work. There are many different kinds of truth-claims in literature ranging from the empirical fact, to historical data, belief claims in God, nation, etc., textual claims that certain events happened in the textual world itself, but what concerns me here is the historical weight of the truth-claim in creating a history of literature.

The historical significance of truth-claims has three principal factors to consider: the ways in which truth-claims are made in texts are a relatively conservative feature showing little change over the years; the generic forms which govern the use of truth-claims as discourse do change, but in an evolutionary process of gradual mutation; the aesthetic perspective which is always that of the historian looking at texts from the past is a relationship of difference and always alien to the text in spite of the historian's best effort to contextualize it. This is the difference between the historian's own sense of reality and that of the textual world, which is never the same as that composite construction of a historical period put together by historians. Thus there are three historicities at work in the aesthetic perspective: those of the historian, those of the text's emplotment, and the documentary reconstruction of what was purportedly the author's historicity. Major changes in aesthetic perspectives become evident perhaps two or three times in a century and as such present a history of textual commentary which must be inserted into both a history of reconstructions of the author's contexts as well as a history of reappropriations. Changes in aesthetic perspective have for the most part been absent in literary history; these changes in the conditions of reception have been primarily the domain of the cultural historian (see, for example, Henríquez Ureña's *Las corrientes literarias en América Hispánica*).

Although the way in which truth-claims are made does not change or changes slowly, the meaning of the truth-claim changes notably from one period to the next. This change is a change in the vantage point of successive literary commentators as each has a perspective necessarily determined by the ideas of reality generated by their own linguistic and cultural community. These changes in perspective are discernable through the examination of the difference in the present meaning of texts from their past significance. A good example is that of Stephen Greenblatt's *Shakespearean Negotiations* (1988), which constructs a context for his commentary of Shakespeare's works. Greenblatt does not claim this discursive context is directly attributable to Shakespeare himself, nor does he assert that his interpretation be final. Greenblatt offers us his study of Renaissance England as a time, place, and culture that are quite alien to us but that we can understand through the difference. The significance of Greenblatt's work has been recognized by contemporary criticism as the groundwork for "new historicism" (see Colebrook 198–219). Once again, I turn to David Perkins to state the argument for the other side, for literary history as a master narrative that imposes closure on the works of the past. Perkins continues: "But narrative literary history, intent on explaining the events it portrays, must leave the reader's imagination less scope. It does not and cannot give the whole story, as the examples we analyzed abundantly illustrate. But all that it does give must hang together. Events that do not cohere do not explain each other. Interpretations that are potentially open must be closed by argument" (48). I take issue with Perkins's description of the task confronting the writing of literary history. My disagreement is with his dismissal of alternatives to the closed literary histories of the past. A comparative history of Latin American literary cultures as effective history aims to be a history of pluralities joined together under the perennially contested designation of Latin America. It is not a straightforward record of books and authors from a determined place; it offers a provisional dialectic grid of inquiry to challenge the epistemological privilege of evidence by adding perspective. These are often presented in the interrogative form. Thus, among the new questions the history seeks to address are: Why a plurality of literatures? What are the parameters of Latin America as spatial and as human geography? What is meant by a cultural formation and, most pertinent to the case, why should the pursuit of literary history entertain such notions as cultural formations? The idea is to construct a history without closure, one that can be entered through many points and can unfold through many coherent, informed, and focused narrative lines. A history without closure would appear to be a contradiction in terms according to David Perkins. I disagree.

Closure is imposed on the historical narrative when the historian tries to circumscribe events and thus give a rational explanation to the way in which the past unfolded. An open history presents the events and delineates multiple consequences without closing off any, for history, as Foucault has reminded us, is not linear except in the fantasies of historians. There are multiple ruptures, new beginnings, and folds that juxtapose the distant past and the present. The twentieth century in Latin America has been a time of immense change alongside of a certain timelessness or a sense of repeating cycles of oppression and liberation. The last two sections of our history have mapped some of these ruptures, cycles, and radical change within the framework of the previous sections. Section 3 of Volume 3 focuses on the rise of new and the return of old literatures to the mainstream of engagement. First, we look at Amerindian literary cultures as a significant presence at the end of the twentieth century; we then turn to the emergence of Latino literary cultures in the United States. We conclude the long voyage that began with cultural geography with an overview of literary culture in Latin America's twentieth century as a time of rapid and radical change. There are three parts: 1) historic displacements; 2) modernity, modernisms and their avatars; and 3) ideologies and imaginaries. This is a history of hundreds of communities linked by language, history, or economic patterns. The material conditions of these communities will serve as the mapped background against which to examine the institutions and the literary culture they share. The value of cultural artifacts such as literature lies, in part, in the ways these expressions are held in common—in other words, their exchange value and the measure of their use. What do we aim to give our readers? A narrative by many hands about narratives as lived reality, then and now, or to put it differently, a literary history worthy of being considered history.

Note: A longer and more detailed version of the above paper is included in *Rethinking Literary History*. Ed. Linda Hutcheon and Mario J. Valdés. Oxford: Oxford University Press, 2002; and in *The Oxford Comparative History of Latin American Literary Cultures*. Ed. Mario J. Valdés and Djelal Kadir. 3 vols. Oxford: Oxford University Press, forthcoming in 2004.

Works Cited

Achugar, Hugo. "El parnaso es la nación o reflexiones a propósito de la violencia de la lectura y el simulacro." *Esplendores y miserias del siglo XIX*. Ed. Beatriz González Stephan, et al. Caracas: Monte Avila, 1994. 53–72.

Balakian, Anna. *The Symbolist Movement in the Literature of European Languages*. Budapest: Akadémiai, 1982.

Barthes, Roland. *Sur Racine*. Paris: Seuil, 1963.

Benveniste, Emile. *Problemas de lingüística general*. Vol. 1. Trans. Juan Almela. Mexico City: Siglo XXI, 1972. 179–97.

Bhabha, Homi. *The Location of Culture*. London: Routledge, 1994.

Braudel, Fernand. "La longue durée." *Annales* 13.1 (1958): 725–53.

Braudel, Fernand. *The Mediterranean and the Mediterranean World in the Age of Phillip II*. 1949. Vol. I. Trans. Siân Reynolds. 2 vols. New York: Harper & Row, 1972.

Carr, David. *Time, Narrative and History*. Bloomington: Indiana UP, 1986.

Certeau, Michel de. *The Writing of History*. Trans. Tom Conley. New York: Columbia UP, 1988.

Cohen, Ralph. "A Note on New Literary History." *New Literary History* 1.1 (1969): 3–6.

Colebrook, Claire. *New Literary Histories*. Manchester: Manchester UP, 1997.

Collingwood, R.G. *The Idea of History*. Oxford: Clarendon P, 1946.

Cornejo Polar, Antonio. *Escribir en el aire*. Lima: Horizonte, 1994.

Coutinho, Eduardo F. "Postmodernism in Brazil." *International Postmodernism*. Ed. Hans Bertens and Douwe Fokkema. Amsterdam: John Benjamins, 1997. 327–34.

Foucault, Michel. *The Order of Things*. New York: Random House, 1994.

Greenblatt, Stephen. *Shakespearan Negotiations*. Berkeley: U of California P, 1988.

Henríquez Ureña, Pedro. *Las corrientes literarias en América Hispánica*. México: Fondo de Cultura Económica, 1949.

Jauss, Hans Robert. *Towards an Aesthetic of Reception*. Minneapolis: U of Minnesota P, 1982.

Leavis, F. R. *The Great Tradition*. London: Chatto and Windus, 1948.

Menéndez y Pelayo, Marcelino. *Historia de las ideas estéticas en España*. Santander: Biblioteca Menéndez y Pelayo, 1985.

Ortega, Julio. "Postmodernism in Spanish-American Writing." *International Postmodernism*. Ed. Hans Bertens and Douwe Fokkema. Amsterdam: John Benjamins, 1997. 315–26.

Perkins, David. *Is Literary History Possible?* Baltimore: Johns Hopkins UP, 1992.

Ricoeur, Paul. *Time and Narrative*. Trans. Kathleen Blaney and David Pellauer. 3 vols. Chicago: U of Chicago P, 1986–88.

Shapiro, Michael. *The Sense of Change. Language as History*. Bloomington: Indiana UP, 1991.

Taylor, Charles. *Philosophical Arguments*. Cambridge: Harvard UP, 1995.

Watkins, J.W.N. "Historical Explanation in the Social Sciences." *Theories of History*. Ed. Patrick Gardiner. New York: The Free P, 1959.

Comparative Literature in an Age of "Globalization"

Lois Parkinson Zamora

I.

I have titled my essay "Comparative Literature in an Age of 'Globalization,'" trusting my reader to take note of the quotation marks around "globalization." This punctuation will suggest the exploratory nature of my project; in fact, there should probably be quotes around "comparative literature" as well, because the changes occurring under the sign of globalization may also be shifting some of the parameters of our profession. In the following discussion, according to good comparative procedure, I want to weigh seemingly unlike entities—the cultural processes of globalization on the one hand, and our own disciplinary processes on the other—to see whether their differences—and certain similarities—may prove instructive. I am, of course, well aware that globalization is a venerable process and that cultural contacts have operated globally since antiquity. Here, however, I will consider "globalization" narrowly, as a term referring to the changes in cultural conditions worldwide during the past ten to twenty years, and then test my generalizations against a number of Latin American literary texts. These texts are part a long tradition of cultural theorizing that addresses the nature and effects of cultural contact in Latin America, and thus the processes of globalization *avant la lettre*. I ask you, then, to join me in considering how (or whether) comparative literary study has changed, and how it should change in Latin America and elsewhere, given the effects of what we now routinely refer to as the globalization of culture.

No doubt most of us already have a working definition of this household word, and our definitions are likely to include a strong affective charge; most discussions of globalization, however academic, are value-specific, with *description* and *judgment* often interdependent and sometimes worrisomely indistinguishable. Here, I intend to avoid this tendency, because my concern is not polemical but pedagogical, and it is this: how are we and our students to engage critically the operations of globalization and their as-yet-undetermined outcomes? For my purposes, it is sufficient to refer to globalization as a complex of transcultural operations characterized by four factors: 1) the presence of new information and communication technologies; 2) the emergence of new global markets; and 3) the unprecedented mobility of peoples and levels of immigration, with their accompanying cultural displacements; and 4) the reconfiguration of space, both conceptually and experientially. The first two are causal, the second two are usually effects: that is, new information technologies and the emergence of new global markets impel immigration and other spatial displacements—indeed, more often force than facilitate them.

A general statement of the effects of globalization might be couched in terms of the "shrinking world" metaphor, which goes like this: societies are increasingly interconnected, so that events and information in one part of the world increasingly affect people and cultures in other parts of the world. The revision of spatial categories is fundamental to virtually all discussions of globalization, whether space is engaged metaphorically as shrinkage or mobility or distance, or discussed literally in terms of decentralization, deterritorialization, redrawing boundaries, or any number of other ways of signifying current global realignments. Once the presence of these characteristics has been recognized, most discussions of globalization move directly to comparative cultural questions. Anthropologists, economists, ecologists, political scientists all become cultural comparatists, weighing cultural differences against what is generally considered to be the inevitable function of globalization: the *leveling* of cultural difference. This comparative quotient runs inexorably, it seems, through discussions of globalization, and this should interest us as a profession, since our own most basic disciplinary methods are, of course, designed to recognize and interpret difference.

I think of my own work in comparative American cultures, for example, as moving along a spectrum between assumptions of basic cultural difference on the one hand, and literary examples of analogous attitudes and expressive structures on the other. I look for common contexts in order to ground my comparisons, but it is the differences that will matter most to my analysis. So a mirror image begins to emerge; whereas the literary comparatist may be said to value significant differences, and to study literature for what we may learn from those differences, the processes of globalization would seem to work in ways that are something like the reverse—toward a *leveling* of significant difference in favor of insignificant sameness. But this comparison, too, will need to be complicated, for homogeneity and heterogeneity are not necessarily antithetical and may, of course, operate in dialogic relationship.

Consider, for example, my third characteristic of globalization—unprecedented levels of immigration—a circumstance that suggests the following paradox: the processes of globalization may homogenize tastes and habits by means of new information technologies and global markets, but at the same time they may also generate configurations of striking difference as immigrants occupy new cultural and linguistic spaces. Nowhere is this truer than in the United States, where we are experiencing the greatest migratory influx of our history. Certain regions of the country are more illustrative of this than others, but let me say simply that my classes at the University of Houston are far more diverse culturally, linguistically, and ethnically than they were ten years ago—a comparative cultural opportunity that I feel, frankly, I have not yet fully engaged in my own teaching, and that our curricular and departmental structures have not yet fully responded to, either. For example, we have not adequately considered how to engage the new variety of linguistic competencies in our classrooms. As we wait for our students to reach a level in German or French sufficient to read Mann or Gide, we might try to engage their native command of Tagalog or Tamil or Tzotzil. Especially in Houston, Texas, where Hispanic students constitute a minority majority, we have the opportunity to engage our students' multicultural heritage in innovative ways. How to do so is a complicated question, and here I will state it in the most general terms: the globalization of U.S. culture is providing challenges and opportunities for comparative literature programs, and though our disciplinary strategies of engaging *difference* may be inversely aligned with some of the *leveling* effects of globalization, comparative strategies are nonetheless appropriate to the analysis of emerging patterns of global change.

There is another aspect of our disciplinary practice, though, that may *not* be usefully aligned, and that is our disciplinary dependence upon nation. National literatures and languages have long been the analytical units of our discipline, but the processes of globalization tend to detach cultural formations from national territories in ways that undermine the territorial coincidence of language, culture, and nation. This development involves the (re)conceptualization of space to which I have referred. Terms like "postgeographical" and "postnational" sprinkle discussions of globalization, and there is virtual unanimity on one point: the ratios of local and global are no longer clearly fixed, and familiar distinctions between "here" and "there" are unstable, if not gone. (The recent coinage "glocal," combining local and global, seems unlikely to catch on, but never mind: we can always recur the venerable term "cosmopolitan," combining "cosmos" and "polis," which John Stuart Mill coined in 1848 in his second volume of *Political Economy* to suggest the changing relations of local and global in his own time.) The forces of globalization are affecting regional and local cultures at the expense of national constructs—whether displacing them or, on the contrary, reinvigorating them. The impact or globalization upon regional and local cultures has particular importance for Latin America, where regional cultures differ greatly within national boundaries (the 2000 Mexican census counts thirty indigenous languages still spoken by ten percent of the population) and may have more in common across national borders than within them (related Maya cultures cross Mexican and Guatemalan borders, among others). In short, cultural spaces are increasingly mobile, volatile, virtual, fungible, and in many cases are becoming something like the opposite of the fixed spatial category of nation upon which comparatists continue to depend.

A moment of reflection on the ways in which the history of comparative literature as a discipline is tied to the conception of European nationhood will, I think, make clear the assault of globalization upon this particular area of our disciplinary practice. The nation-state is a modern Western construction, of course, and as the basis of comparative literature it was first and foremost connected to language communities, and to the cultures of those communities, a connection that had its most pertinent protagonist in Johann Gottfried Herder, to whom our basic conceptions of national "identity" can be traced. Richard Taruskin provides a useful overview of Herder's argument in his article on musical vernaculars during the nineteenth and twentieth centuries in Europe (Taruskin 2001). He begins with Herder's fundamental assumption that language is what distinguishes us from other animals, and since language can only be learned in communities, it functions to form each community's specific contribution to world culture. When the concept of language is extended to cover other aspects of expressive behavior—belief systems, dress, literature—these cultural characteristics, too, can be understood in terms of a collective national spirit or personality. Over time, national cultures come to be seen as a primary determinant of the individual's character and destiny.

Following Herder's conception of nation and national character, Taruskin points out that we may understand the history of nineteenth-century Europe as a progress toward the goal of having the political boundaries of nations coincide with the boundaries of language communities. If the Herderian ideal of the coincidence of nation and language unified European countries in the nineteenth century, in the twentieth century it generated aggression and intolerance as collective national identities became increasingly reified. And the drawing (or redrawing) of the European map continues along Herderian lines, most recently in the separation of Slovakia from the Czech Republic and the breakup of the multilingual Yugoslav Federation. Ironically, current processes of globalization may also conform to Herder's conception of linguistic nationalism in this way: the expansion of English-based electronic and mercantile cultures expands U.S. territory, though the territory in question is now virtual.

This summary of Herder's ideas is intended to suggest the historical bases of comparative literature's disciplinary emphasis on significant differences among national cultures, and it is also intended to suggest why this model may be less useful now than in the past. For one thing, the model has always excluded the Islamic world, in which nation is a subcategory of religion (ethnic and linguistic differences are subsumed under the presumptive sameness of religious culture) and states were defined by dynasties with shifting territorial frontiers rather than as fixed national boundaries. While I do not mean to say that there are no comparatists working on Islamic literatures and cultures, I do think that a more flexible set of spatial categories might encourage us to foreground cultural relations that are *not* nationally based, and encourage us to amplify our comparative discussion of other world systems that precede or parallel modern Europe. Examples are Immanuel Wallerstein's influential discussion of "world systems" and Enrique Dussel's more recent elaborations of that model. Furthermore, several leading comparative literature journals point in this direction in special numbers devoted to the subject of globalization: what it is and how it operates in literature and the teaching of literature.

If, then, nation is the basic constituent part of what comparatists have taken to be the global whole, how should we now consider adjusting the relationship of these parts to the whole? Most universities have already seen some de-nationalizing trends in literary study: in U.S. ethnic studies programs, which focus on intranational cultural relations; in border studies programs, which focus on the geographical contact points of cultures and nations; in area studies programs, where transnational cultural relations are foremost; and in gender studies programs, which may well abandon territoriality altogether as a basis for comparative cultural analysis. Indeed, with hindsight we may even perceive the poststructuralist revolutions of the 70s and 80s as the beginning of the deterritorializing of literary analysis in favor of transterritorial theoretical processes. Masao Miyoshi and others have written about the "decline of the nation state"; at best, they contemplate a diversification of spatial categories that offers us and our students new ways to think relationally.

Having said all of this, I should, perhaps, locate myself. I teach and write about a loose and baggy territory called *las Américas*, the Americas, and most often about the part of that category referred to as Latin America. This latter space includes nations, of course, but the demarcation is far more flexible because of its plural referent. The writers who inhabit this territory possess dual citizenship, for they are self-avowed "Latin American" writers at the same time that they are also Mexican, Argentine, Peruvian, Cuban. In fact, they are often deeply engaged in describing their own national cultures, and are far from ready to throw out the baby with the globalizing bathwater. Indeed, Mexico is a particularly interesting case of the use of nation as a defense *against* the leveling pressures of globalization—a nationalism of resistance, in Wallerstein's terms, rather than a nationalism of domination.

For example, the much debated NAFTA, the North American Free Trade Agreement—or the TLC, *Tratado de Libre Comercio*—opened Mexico's borders to American commercial onslaughts in the early 90s, but in cultural matters, the treaty encodes a very different attitude. The Free Trade Agreement contains an Annex that provides special protection to Mexico's cultural industries. Some of its provisions are as follows: 1) The use of the Spanish language is required for the broadcast, cable or multipoint distribution system of radio and television, except when the Secretaría de Gobernación authorizes the use of another language; 2) A majority of the time of each day's live broadcast programs must feature Mexican nationals; 3) The use of the Spanish language or Spanish subtitles is required for advertising that is broadcast or otherwise distributed in the territory of Mexico; and 4) Thirty percent of screen time of every theatre, assessed on an annual basis, may be reserved for films produced by Mexican persons either within or outside the territory of Mexico. Interestingly, it was originally Canada, not Mexico, which insisted on cultural industry protection clauses in the North American Free Trade Agreement.

In fact, cultural industry protections are common throughout Europe. France recently passed legislation requiring that French radio stations devote forty percent of airtime to French music, and Spain has also passed legislation requiring that one-fourth to one-third of all movies shown in Spanish theatres be of Spanish origin. And England has long protected its movie industry: the great film director Michael Powell got his start, as did other British directors during the thirties, making what were called "quota quickies." So, even as I suggest that comparatists may want to review our nationalist institutional and disciplinary structures in the light of global mobilities, nations continue to protect their cultures against those same forces.

II.

As a literary critic, surely my best source of information on "globalization" is literature, and I hardly need to say that this is the subject of a great many works of contemporary Latin American fiction. In fact, starting in the first decades of the twentieth century, *indigenista* movements undertook the challenge of addressing cultural (and racial) difference, contesting the cultural homogeneity imposed by European and U.S. colonialism; indigenismo valorized indigenous traditions and practices, and reconstituted the question of cultural inclusiveness. The movement was led by the Peruvian intellectuals José Carlos Mariátegui and José María Arguedas, with related discussions of transculturation and national identity by Ezequiel Martínez Estrada in Argentina, Gilberto Freyre in Brazil, and Fernando Ortiz in Cuba. José Vasconcelos in Mexico, more than his contemporaries, celebrated the process of cultural contact: racial *mestizaje* had its apotheosis in the twenties in Vasconcelos' nationalistic concept of *la raza cósmica* (the cosmic race).

The Cuban writer Alejo Carpentier dramatizes this discussion. From his first novel in 1933, he recommends not that cultures struggle against colonialism to remain discrete in their differences, but rather that they recognize cultural otherness and embrace it. His formulation of the *neobarroco* or New World Baroque provides an overarching structure to incorporate European, African and indigenous cultures into a shared Latin American identity. In his 1975 essay "Lo barroco y lo real maravilloso" ("The Baroque and the Marvelous Real"), Carpentier asks:

> ¿Y por qué es América Latina la tierra de elección del barroco? Porque toda simbiosis, todo mestizaje, engendra un barroquismo. El barroquismo americano se acrece con . . . la conciencia de ser otra cosa, de ser una cosa nueva, de ser una simbiosis, de ser un criollo; y el espíritu criollo de por sí, es un espíritu barroco. (Carpentier 1980, 186)
>
> And why is Latin America the chosen territory of the baroque? Because all symbiosis, all *mestizaje*, engenders the baroque. The American baroque develops along with . . . the awareness of being Other, of being new, of being symbiotic, of being *criollo*; and the *criollo* spirit is itself a baroque spirit. (Carpentier 1995, 100)

Carpentier, and following him the Cuban writers José Lezama Lima and Severo Sarduy, understood the irony of engaging the Baroque forms of the Spanish colonizers to construct a postcolonial identity, and they effectively turned the Baroque into an instrument of *contraconquista* (counterconquest.) The Neobaroque is an aesthetics and ideology of inclusion by which Latin American and Latino artists have defined themselves against colonizing structures, and continue to do so.

Before Carpentier and in a more bibliographic mode, Jorge Luis Borges was also to argue that Latin American culture should be open to all influences. In his justly famous essay "The Argentine Writer and Tradition," he declares that "nuestro patrimonio es el universo"—"our patrimony is the universe." This phrase summarizes Borges' advice to his contemporaries, Argentine writers in 1932, and refers more generally to the ongoing project of Latin American literary self-definition. Octavio Paz follows Borges in embracing all possible intellectual cultures and thus defining his own.

Carlos Fuentes, following Paz, Borges and Carpentier, makes trans-culturation the central theme of his fiction. His novels are Carpentierian in their ideology of cultural inclusiveness, Pazian in their understanding of Mexico as the first instance of planetary globalization, and Borgesian in their intellectual reach. Take, for example, his underappreciated novel *Distant Relations*, published in 1981, which dramatizes the transcultural contacts between France and the Caribbean in the nineteenth and twentieth centuries in a region still grounded in indigenous American cultures. A character in this novel is described by the narrator as having "esa característica de los latinoamericanos cultos: sentirse obligados a saberlo todo, leerlo todo, no darle al europeo cuartel ni pretexto, conocer igualmente bien lo que el europeo ignora y lo que considera propio, el Popol Vuh y Descartes. Sobre todo, demostrarle que no hay excusa para desconocer a los demás" (Fuentes 1980, 15) ["that quality so characteristic of cultured Latin Americans: the passion to know everything, to read everything, to give no quarter, no pretext, to the European, but also to know well what the European does not know and what he considers his own, the Popol Vuh *and* Descartes. And, above all, to demonstrate to the European that there is no excuse not to know other cultures"; Fuentes 1982, 9–10]. Beyond the individual's engagement of universal culture, this novel dramatizes the assumption that cultures are cumulative despite conquest, colonization, globalization and other disasters of suppression and appropriation: "Todos los pueblos antiguos se niegan a desterrar las formas viejas en beneficio de las nuevas; unas y otras, en vez de expulsarse sucesivamente, se suman en una acreción permanente. Allí, todo está vivo y presente . . ." (Fuentes 1980, 16) ["All ancient peoples refuse to abandon the old ways in favor of the new; rather than being cast aside one after the other, some realities accumulate in a permanent accretion. When this happens, all things are living and present"; Fuentes 1982, 11]. Fuentes's fiction depicts cultures that are indigenous and European and African, colonized and postcolonial, western and otherwise: the ratios and quotients may vary from place to place and novel to novel, but the experience of transculturation does not.

Fuentes was in Rio de Janeiro in March of 2001 at a conference with the intentionally oxymoronic title *Voces universales de la latinidad*; he, along with the Argentine Ernesto Sábato and the Uruguayan Augusto Roa Bastos, spoke about what the Mexico City newspaper *La Reforma* reported as "*el futuro de la cultura latina en un mundo globalizado bajo la hegemonía de los valores anglosajones*" (*La Reforma* C4) ["the future of Latin culture in a world that is globalizing under the hegemony of Anglo Saxon values"]. From this phrase, the debate would seem to have been predecided, but Fuentes sounds quite a different note. Drawing a globalizing comparison, he states: "Así como los griegos sobrevivieron a través del helenismo en los tiempos de dominio del Imperio Romano, los latinos, con su rico imaginario, tal vez se tornen una isla de resistencia ante la estandarización impuesta por la cultura globalizada" (*La Reforma* C4) ["As the Greeks survived the Hellenism of the Roman Empire, so Latin Americans, with our rich imaginary, may become an island of resistence against the standardization imposed by globalization"]. If Latin America is an island, it is a well populated one, where many writers take as their subject the operations and outcomes of cultural contact.

There are, of course, writers who are less sanguine than Borges or Carpentier or Fuentes, and who dramatize the fragility of Latin American culture when confronted with foreign incursions. I think of *Betrayed by Rita Hayworth* by Manuel Puig, and *One Hundred Years of Solitude* by Gabriel García Márquez. Puig's 1968 autobiographical novel traces the impact of "Hollywood" during the 40s on a small town, and a small boy, in provincial Argentina. Long before the term "globalization" was coined, the term "Hollywood" and its multiple adjectives—*hollywoodista, hollywoodesco, hollywoodense*—was the reigning metaphor for U.S. cultural imposition and, by extension, for social and economic inequities in the region. In *Betrayed by Rita Hayworth*, Puig indicts Hollywood's cultural imperialism, and he also indicts Argentina's willingness to be colonized. Communal identity, he shows, cannot be established by imitation.

One Hundred Years of Solitude was written the year before *Betrayed by Rita Hayworth*, in 1967, and it is a cautionary tale from beginning to end—from the moment that the gypsy Melquíades arrives in Macondo with his gadgets to the invasion of the gringos and the ensuing banana company hurricane. Recall the scene in García Márquez's novel where the people of Macondo finally get fed up with cultural imports—here, Hollywood is again at issue—and they destroy the outdoor movie theatre that has recently been constructed:

> Deslumbrada por tantas y tan maravillosas invenciones, la gente de Macondo no sabía por dónde empezar a asombrarse. Se trasnochaban contemplando las pálidas bombillas eléctricas, alimentadas por la planta que llevó Aureliano Triste en el segundo viaje del tren, y a cuyo obsesionante tumtum costó tiempo y trabajo acostumbrarse. Se indignaron con las imágenes vivas que el próspero comerciante don Bruno Crespi proyectaba en el teatro con taquillas de bocas de león, porque un personaje muerto y sepultado en una película, y por cuya desgracia se derramaron lágrimas de aflicción, reapareció vivo y convertido en árabe en la película siguiente. El público que pagaba dos centavos para compartir las vicisitudes de los personajes, no pudo soportar aquella burla inaudita y rompió la silletería. El alcalde, a instancias de don Bruno Crespi, explicó mediante un bando, que el cine era una máquina de ilusión que no merecía los desbordamientos pasionales del público. Ante la desalentadora explicación, muchos estimaron que habían sido víctimas de un nuevo y aparatoso asunto de gitanos, de modo que optaron por no volver al cine, considerando que ya tenían bastante con sus propias penas para llorar por fingidas desventuras de seres imaginarios. (García Márquez 1967, 194)

> Dazzled by so many marvelous inventions, the people of Macondo did not know where their amazement began. They stayed up all night looking at the pale electric bulbs fed by the plant that Aureliano Triste had brought back when the train made its second trip, and it took time and effort for them to grow accustomed to its obsessive *toom-toom*. They became indignant over the living images that the prosperous merchant Bruno Crespi projected in the theater with the lion-head ticket windows, for the character who had died and was buried in one film and for whose misfortune tears of affliction had been shed would reappear alive and transformed into an Arab in the next one. The audience, who paid two cents apiece to share the difficulties of the actors, would not tolerate that outlandish fraud and broke up the seats. The mayor, at the urging of Bruno Crespi, explained in a proclamation that the cinema was a machine of illusion that did not merit the emotional outbursts of the audience. With that discouraging explanation many felt that they had been the victims of some new and showy gypsy business and they decided not to return to the movies, considering that they already had too many troubles of their own to weep over the acted-out misfortunes of imaginary beings. (García Márquez 1970, 211)

In this scene, García Márquez engages the same issue of communal identity as Puig, impugning sources of cultural self-definition that are imposed from outside and thus removed from the community's own experience of itself. His critique of this "new and showy gypsy business" does not imply that cultures should be closed entities (impossible, in any case) but that collective judgments must be exercised, as the residents of Macondo appear to be doing, at long last.

I want to refer to one final example, a novel that I consider the most self-conscious and complex treatments of this subject, Mario Vargas Llosa's *El hablador* (*The Storyteller*, 1987). The novel is set in the fairly recent past in Perú; it condemns U.S. ecological barbarities in the Amazon region, but its principal transcultural drama is an internal one involving a character whose name is Saúl, nicknamed Mascarita. This young man from Lima enters into the ancient culture of the Machiguengas, a nomadic indigenous group in the Amazon region, learning their stories and ultimately becoming one of their storytellers. Because the storytellers are the cultural glue of this fragile prehispanic group, Mascarita's relation to the Machiguenga culture is treated with far more narrative concern than the devastating environmental impact of oil exploration in the region. However, modernity does not overwhelm indigenous culture, as we might expect, but the reverse: Mascarita becomes the premodern other. The narrator, a writer living in Florence, contemplates retrospectively his friend's amazing cultural crossing:

> Porque hablar como habla un hablador es haber llegado a sentir y vivir lo más íntimo de esa cultura, haber calado en sus entresijos, llegado al tuétano de su historia y su mitología, somatizado sus ta-

> búes, reflejos, apetitos y terrores ancestrales. Es ser, de la manera más esencial que cabe, un machiguenga raigal, uno más de la antiquísima estirpe que . . . recorría los bosques de mi país llevando y trayendo las anécdotas, las mentiras, las fabulaciones, las chismografías y los chistes que hacen de ese pueblo de seres dispersos una comunidad y mantiene vivo entre ellos el sentimiento de estar juntos, de constituir algo fraterno y compacto. Que mi amigo Saúl Zuratas renunciara a ser todo lo que era y hubiera podido llegar a ser, para, desde hace más de veinte años, trajinar por las selvas de la Amazonía, prolongando, contra viento y marea—y, sobre todo, contra las nociones mismas de modernidad y progreso—la tradición de ese invisible linaje de contadores ambulantes de historias, es algo que, de tiempo en tiempo, me vuelve a la memoria y . . . desboca mi corazón con más fuerza que lo hayan hecho nunca el miedo o el amor. (Vargas Llosa 1987, 234)
>
> Talking the way a storyteller talks means being able to feel and live in the very heart of that culture, means having penetrated its essence, reached the marrow of its history and mythology, given body to its taboos, images, ancestral desires, and terrors. It means being, in the most profound way possible, a rooted Machiguenga, one of that ancient lineage who . . . roamed the forests of my country, bringing and bearing away those tales, lies, fictions, gossip, and jokes that make a community of that people of scattered beings, keeping alive among them the feeling of oneness, of constituting something fraternal and solid. That my friend Saúl gave up being all that he was and might have become so as to roam through the Amazonian jungle, for more than twenty years now, perpetuating against wind and tide—and, above all, against the very concepts of modernity and progress—the tradition of that invisible line of wandering storytellers, is something that memory now and again brings back to me, and . . . it opens my heart more forcefully than fear or love has ever done. (Vargas Llosa 1989, 244–45)

The final scene is of the narrator walking through the Piazza della Signoria of Florence, celebrating the profusion of cultural differences in "esa multitud variopinta y juvenil" ["this colorful, youthful multitude"]: "conjuntos de maraqueros y tumbadores caribeños, equilibristas turcos, tragafuegos marroquíes, una tuna española, mimos franceses, jazzmen norteamericanos, adivinadoras gitanas, guitarristas alemanes, flautistas húngaros" (235) ["Caribbean maraca players and acrobats, Turkish ropewalkers, Moroccan fire-eaters, Spanish student serenaders, French mimes, American jazz musicians, gypsy fortune-tellers, German guitarists, Hungarian flutists"; 245]. Here, Vargas Llosa reminds us that globalization cannot be reduced to U.S. cultural imperialism, that global energies are now decentered and decentering in ways that cannot be reduced to one more narrative in which the United States is sole protagonist. Decisions about what a culture is, and what it should be, remain the province of those who live in those cultures, not those who would decide from a distance.

To conclude: the cultural specificity of literary fictions may serve as antidote to current processes of cultural homogenization, and to the *perception* of homogenization as propagated from critical centers in the United States and Europe. For it is surprising that literary theorists of globalization refer so infrequently to works of literature to ground their generalizations about the leveling of cultures. As intelligent as their discussions often are, they sometimes seem to me to reiterate familiar colonizing trajectories from the United States and European academic centers to the peripheries: Latin America, Africa, Asia. This, I confess, worries me, for however we choose to structure (or restructure) our approach to the new spaces of global culture, we will need to continue to direct our attention, and our students' attention, to the specificities of literary texts and their comparative cultural contexts. We will, then, be prepared to measure the dialectics of difference in an increasingly "globalized" world. This has always been the aim of our discipline, and in Latin America, at least three centuries of self-conscious transculturation have generated a textual tradition by which we may consider (and reconsider) an array of possible approaches to the question of cultural contact.

Works Cited

Borges, Jorge Luis. "El escritor argentino y la tradición." *Discusión*. 1932. *Obras completas*. By Jorge Luis Borges. Buenos Aires: Emecé Editorial, 1974. Vol. 1, 267–74.

Borges, Jorge Luis. "The Argentine Writer and Tradition." *Labyrinths*. By Jorge Luis Borges. Trans. James E. Irby. New York: New Directions, 1962. 177–85.

Carlson, Andrew M. "The Country Music Television Dispute: An Illustration of the Tension between Canadian Cultural Protectionism and American Entertainment Exports." *Journal of Global Trade* 6 (1997): 585–623.

Carpentier, Alejo. "Lo barroco y lo real maravilloso." *La novela latinoamericana en vísperas de un nuevo siglo, y otros ensayos*. By Alejo Carpentier. Mexico: Siglo Veintiuno Editores, 1980. 111–35.

Carpentier, Alejo. "The Baroque and the Marvelous Real." Trans. Tanya Huntington and Lois Parkinson Zamora. *Magical Realism: Theory, History, Community*. Ed. Lois Parkinson Zamora and Wendy B. Faris. Durham: Duke UP, 1995. 89–108.

Dussel, Enrique. *The Invention of the Americas: Eclipse of "the Other" and the Myth of Modernity*. New York: Continuum, 1995.

Dussel, Enrique. "Beyond Eurocentrism: The World System and the Limits of Modernity." *The Cultures of Globalization*. Ed. Fredric Jameson and Masao Miyoshi. Durham: Duke UP, 1998. 3–31.

Fuentes, Carlos. *Una familia lejana*. Mexico: Ediciones Era, 1980.

Fuentes, Carlos. *Distant Relations*. Trans. Margaret Sayers Peden. New York: Farrar, Straus & Giroux, 1982.

García Márquez, Gabriel. *Cien años de soledad*. Buenos Aires: Editorial Sudamericana, 1967.

García Márquez, Gabriel. *One Hundred Years of Solitude*. Trans. Gregory Rabassa. New York: Avon, 1970.

Herder, Johann Gottfried. "Essay on the Origin of Language" (1770). Trans. F.M. Barnard. By Johann Gottfried Herder, *Social and Political Culture*. Ed. F.M. Barnard. Cambridge: Cambridge UP, 1969. 115–77.

Herder, Johann Gottfried. *On World History: An Anthology*. Ed. Hans Adler and Ernest A. Menze. London: M.E. Sharpe, 1997.

La Reforma. "Debaten intelectuales sobre la latinidad." *La Reforma* (22 March 2001): C4 [Anonymous].

Miyoshi, Masao. "A Borderlesss World? From Colonialism to Transnationalism and the Decline of the Nation-State." *Critical Inquiry* 19 (1993): 726–51.

North American Free Trade Agreement / Tratado de libre commercio (2002): <http://www.sice.oas.org/trade/nafta.asp>.

Spitta, Silvia. *Between Two Waters: Narratives of Transculturation in Latin America*. Houston: Rice UP, 1994.

Suárez-Orozco, Marcelo M. "Globalization, Immigration, and Education: The Research Agenda." *Harvard Educational Review* 70.3 (2001): 345–65.

Taruskin, Richard. "Authenticity Now." *Aspen Magazine* (August 2001): 32–38.

Vargas Llosa, Mario. *El hablador*. Barcelona: Seix Barral, 1987.

Vargas Llosa, Mario. *The Storyteller*. Trans. Helen Lane. New York: Penguin Books, 1989.

Wallerstein, Immanuel. *The Politics of the World-Economy: The States, the Movements, and the Civilizations*. Cambridge: Cambridge UP, 1984.

Zamora, Lois Parkinson. "American Films/American Fantasies: Moviegoing and Regional Identity in Literature of the Americas." *Look Away! Inter-American and Postcolonial Approaches to U.S. Southern Cultures*. Ed. Deborah Cohn and Jon Smith. Durham: Duke UP, forthcoming 2004.

Bibliography of Scholarship in Comparative Latin American Culture and Literature

Sophia A. McClennen, comp.

The objective of this bibliography is to present a resource for scholars engaged in the comparative study of Latin American culture and literature. The bibliography includes general theoretical works that contribute to comparative studies of Latin American culture and literature as well as examples of the practice of comparative cultural studies of Latin America. It also includes works about Latin American literature in exile or in diaspora as well as work that touches upon Latin American literature and culture tangentially. Most items in the bibliography are works in English, Spanish, and Portuguese, but works in other languages are represented as well. A number of websites are included in order to provide scholarly resources available online, which in some cases lead to further bibliographical references.

Bibliographies and Websites

Associação Brasileira de Literatura Comparada (ABRALIC) (2002): <http://www.ufmg.br/abralic/>.

Biblioteca Virtual de Estudos Culturais (2000): <http://www.prossiga.br/estudosculturais/pacc/>.

Buchenau, Barbara, and Marietta Messmer, comp. "Selected Bibliography for the Study of Interculturality in the Americas: Theories and Practice." *CLCWeb: Comparative Literature and Culture: A WWWeb Journal 3.2* (2001): <http://clcwebjournal.lib.purdue.edu/clcweb01-2/biblio(americas).html>.

Fitz, Earl E., comp. *Inter-American Literature and Criticism: An Electronic Annotated Bibliography* (2001): <http://www.uiowa.edu/uiowapress/interamerican/>.

Gac-Artigas, Priscilla. *Reflexiones: Essays on Contemporary Spanish-American Women Writers* (1998): <http://bluehawk.monmouth.edu/~pgacarti/>.

Juan-Navarro, Santiago. *Hispanet: Recursos en Internet para la enseñanza de la Literatura Hispánica* (1999):<http://members.tripod.com/sjuannavarro/>.

Lajolo, Marisa, and João Roberto Faria. *História da literature*: <http://www.unicamp.br/iel/histlist/index.htm>.

Landow, George P. "Contemporary Postcolonial and Postimperial Literatures in English." *Websites Created and Managed by George P. Landow* (2001): <http://landow.stg.brown.edu/post/misc/postov.html>.

LANIC: Latin American Network Information Center: Humanities in Latin America (2001): <http://www.lanic.utexas.edu/subject/humanities.html>.

McClennen, Sophia A. *Cinergía: A Web Site Dedicated to the Study of Spanish, Latin American and Latino Cinema, Film, Movies, and Media for Students and Scholars* (2001): <http://lilt.ilstu.edu/smexpos/cinergia/Cinergia.htm>.

Molloy, Molly. *Internet Resources for Latin America* "The Guide." (2002): <http://lib.nmsu.edu/subject/bord/laguia/>.

Parks, Melissa, and Robin Pruter. *Postcolonialism for Beginners: A Brief Annotated Bibliography* (2002): <http://orion.it.luc.edu/~mparks1/Postcolonial/Bibliography/bib.html>.

Programa Avançado de Cultura Contemporânea (PACC/UFRJ): (1988): <http://acd.ufrj.br/pacc/>.

Puleo, Augustus C., and James F. Crapotta. *Gay & Lesbian Themes in Hispanic Literatures & Cultures* (1994): <http://www.columbia.edu/cu/libraries/events/sw25/case9.html>.

SAIL: Studies in American Indian Literatures (1977–): <http://oncampus.richmond.edu/faculty/ASAIL/sail-hp.html>.

Scharlau, Birgit, Mark Münzel, and Karsten Garscha, eds. *Kulturelle Heterogenität in Lateinamerika. Bibliographie mit Kommentaren*. Tübingen: Narr, 1991.

Siegmund, Marianne. *Film in Latin America: A Selective Bibliography* (1999): <http://www.libs.uga.edu/lais/laisno7.html >.

Tötösy de Zepetnek, Steven. "Postcolonial Literatures: A Selected Bibliography of Theory and Criticism (to 1995)." *CLCWeb: Comparative Literature and Culture: A WWWeb Journal* (*Library*) (1998–): <http://clcwebjournal.lib.purdue.edu/library/poco.html>.

Tötösy de Zepetnek, Steven. "Selected Bibliography of Theoretical and Critical Works about Canadian Ethnic Minority Writing." *CLCWeb: Comparative Literature and Culture: A WWWeb Journal* (*Library*) (1998): <http://clcwebjournal.lib.purdue.edu/library/caneth.html>.

Tötösy de Zepetnek, Steven, Steven Aoun, and Wendy C. Nielsen. "Bibliography for Work in Comparative Cultural Studies (History, Theory, Method)." *CLCWeb: Comparative Literature and Culture: A WWWeb Journal* (*Library*) (2002–): <http://clcwebjournal.lib.purdue.edu/library/comparativeculturalstudies (biblio).html>.

Valdés, Mario J., and Djelal Kadir, eds. *Oxford Comparative History of Latin American Literary Cultures* (2001): <http://www.chass.utoronto.ca/lithist/>.

Velarde, Hector. *Patria Grande* (2002): <http://www.patriagrande.net/>.

Theories and Practice

Achugar, Hugo. "El parnaso es la nación o reflexiones a propósito de la violencia de la lectura y el simulacro." *Esplendores y miserias del siglo XIX*. Ed. Beatriz González Stephan et al. Caracas: Monte Avila, 1994. 53–72.

Adams, Florence. *Latinos and Local Representation: Changing Realities, Emerging Theories*. New York: Garland, 1999.

Adams, Percy G. "The Discovery of America and European Renaissance Literature." *Comparative Literature Studies* 13.2 (1976): 100–15.

Adorno, Rolena. "Cultures in Contact: Mesoamerica, the Andes, and the European Written Tradition." *The Cambridge History of Latin American Literature*. Ed. Roberto González Echevarría and Enrique Pupo-Walker. Cambridge: Cambridge UP, 1996. 33–57.

Agosin, Marjorie. "In Search of Memory: Women and the Jewish Imaginary in Latin America." *Multicultural Review* 8.1 (1999): 36–40.

Agosin, Marjorie, ed. *Passion, Memory, and Identity: Twentieth-Century Latin American Jewish Women Writers*. Albuquerque: U of New Mexico P, 1999.

Agosin, Marjorie, ed. *A Woman's Gaze: Latin American Women Artists*. Fredonia: White Pine, 1998.

Ainsa, Fernando. *Identidad cultural de Iberoamérica en su narrativa*. Madrid: Gredos, 1986.

Albuquerque, Severino João. *Violent Acts: A Study of Contemporary Latin American Theatre*. Detroit: Wayne State UP, 1991.

Aldaraca, Bridget, Edward Baker, and John Beverley, eds. *Texto y sociedad: Problemas de historia literaria*. Amsterdam: Rodopi, 1990.

Aldridge, A. Owen. *Early American Literature: A Comparatist's Approach*. Princeton: Princeton UP, 1982.

Aldridge, A. Owen. "The Enlightenment in the Americas." *Proceedings of the Seventh Congress of the ICLA [International Comparative Literature Association]*. Stuttgart: Kunst und Wissen / Erich Bieber, 1979. Vol. 1, 59–67.

Aldridge, A. Owen. "The Influences of Thomas Paine in the United States, England, France, Germany, and South America." *Proceedings of the Second Congress of the International Comparative Literature Associa-*

tion. Ed. Werner P. Friederich. Chapel Hill: U of North Carolina P, 1959. Vol. 3, 369–83.

Aldridge, A. Owen, ed. *Ibero-American Enlightenment.* Urbana: U of Illinois P, 1971.

Alisky, Marvin. *Latin American Media: Guidance and Censorship*. Ames: Iowa State UP, 1981.

Alonso, Carlos. *The Spanish American Regional Novel: Modernity and Autochthony*. Cambridge: Cambridge UP, 1989.

Altamiranda, Daniel, ed. *Segundas Jornadas Internacionales de Literatura Argentina / Comparatistica*. Buenos Aires: U de Buenos Aires, 1997.

Alva, Klor de. "Colonialism and Postcolonialism as (Latin) American Mirages." *Colonial Latin American Review* 1.1–2 (1992): 2–23.

Alvarez-Altman, Grace. "A Comparative Onomastic Vignette of the Picaresque Novel in Spain and Mexico." *Literary Onomastics Studies* 13 (1986): 183–92.

Amar Sánchez, Ana María. *Juegos y seducción y traición: Literatura y cultura de masas*. Buenos Aires: Beatriz Viterbo Editora, 2000.

Amirthanayagam, Guy. *The Marriage of Continents: Multiculturalism in Modern Literature.* Lanham: UP of America, 2000.

Anderson, Benedict. *Imagined Communities: Reflections on the Origin and Spread of Nationalism*. London: Verso, 1991.

Anzaldúa, Gloria. *Borderlands: The New Mestiza / La Frontera*. San Francisco: Aunt Lute Books, 1987.

Arieli, Yehoshua. *Individualism and Nationalism in American Ideology.* Cambridge: Harvard UP, 1964.

Arnold, James A., Julio Rodriguez-Luis, J. Michael Dash, et al., eds. *A History of Literature in the Caribbean, I: Hispanic and Francophone Regions.* Amsterdam: Benjamins, 1994.

Arnold, A. James. "Caribbean Literature / Comparative Literature." *Semper Aliquid Novi: Littérature comparée et littératures d'Afrique.* Ed. J. Riesz and A. Ricard. Tübingen: Narr, 1990. 39–46.

Arnold, James A., ed. *A History of Literature in the Caribbean*. 3 vols. Amsterdam: Benjamins, 1994. Vol. 1 Hispanic and francophone regions. Vol. 2 English- and Dutch-speaking regions. Vol. 3 Cross-cultural studies.

Asante-Darko, Kwaku. "Language and Culture in African Postcolonial Literature." *CLCWeb: Comparative Literature and Culture: A WWWeb* Journal 2.1 (2000): <http://clcwebjournal.lib.purdue.edu/clcweb00-1/asante-darko00.html>.

Alegría, Fernando. *Walt Whitman en Hispanoamérica.* Mexico City: Fondo de Cultura Económica, 1954.

Antelo, Raúl. "Borges/Brasil." *Boletim bibliográfico, Biblioteca Mário de Andrade* 45.1–4 (1984): 91–102.

Ashcroft, Bill. "Modernity's First Born: Latin America and Postcolonial Transformation." *Ariel: Review of International English Literature* 29.2 (1998): 7–29.

Ashcroft, Bill, Gareth Griffith, and Helen Tiffin, eds. *Key Concepts in Post-Colonial Studies*. London: Routledge, 1998.

Ashcroft, Bill, Gareth Griffith, and Helen Tiffin, eds. *The Post-Colonial Studies Reader.* London: Routledge, 1995.

Ashcroft, Bill, Gareth Griffith, and Helen Tiffin, eds. *The Empire Writes Back: Theory and Practice in Post-Colonial Literatures.* London: Routledge, 1989.

Assmann, Jan. *Das kulturelle Gedächtnis. Schrift, Erinnerung und politische Identität in frühen Hochkulturen.* München: Beck, 1992.

Atwood, Margaret. *Survival: A Thematic Guide to Canadian Literature*. Toronto: Anansi, 1972.

Auerbach, Susan, ed. *Encyclopedia of Multiculturalism.* New York: Marshall Cavendish, 1994.

Balakian, Anna, and M.J. Valdés, eds. *Inter-American Literary Relation.* New York: Garland, 1985.

Balderston, Daniel, ed. *Sexualidad y nación*. Pittsburgh: Biblioteca de América, Instituto Internacional de Literatura Iberoamericana, 2000.

Ballón, José. *Autonomía cultural de América: Emerson y Martí.* Madrid: Pliegos, 1986.

Bammer, Angelika, ed. *Displacements: Cultural Identities in Question.* Bloomington: Indiana UP, 1994.

Barber, Benjamin R. *Jihad vs. McWorld: How Globalism and Tribalism Are Reshaping the World.* New York: Random House, 1996.

Barbosa, Maria José Somerlate. "Life as an Opera: *Dom Casmurro* and *The Floating Opera*." *Comparative Literature Studies* 29.3 (1992): 223–37.

Barkan, Elliott Robert, ed. *A Nation of Peoples: A Sourcebook on America's Multicultural Heritage.* Westport: Greenwood, 1999.

Barth, John. "The Literature of Exhaustion." *Atlantic* (August 1967): 29–34.

Barth, John. "The Literature of Replenishment: Postmodernist Fiction." *Atlantic* (January 1980): 65–71.

Barthold, Bonnie. *Black Time: Fiction of Africa, the Caribbean and the United States*. New Haven: Yale UP, 1981.

Baym, Nina. "Early Histories of American Literature: A Chapter in the Institution of New England." *American Literary History* 1.3 (1989): 459–88.

Bassnett, Susan. *Comparative Literature: A Critical Introduction.* Oxford: Blackwell, 1993.

Beardsell, Peter. *Europe and Latin America: Returning the Gaze*. Manchester, England: Manchester UP, 2000.

Bell-Villada, Gene H. "The Canon is el Boom, et. al., or the Hispanic Difference." *Comparative Cultural Studies and Latin America*. Ed. Sophia A. McClennen and Earl E. Fitz. West Lafayette: Purdue UP, 2004. 1–7.

Bell-Villada, Gene H. *Art for Art's Sake and Literary Life: How Politics and Markets Helped Shape the Ideology and Culture of Aestheticism, 1790–1990*. Lincoln: U of Nebraska P, 1996.

Bell-Villada, Gene H. *Borges and His Fiction: A Guide to His Mind and Art*. Chapel Hill: U of North Carolina P, 1981.

Bell-Villada, Gene H. "Functional Criticism." *Review* 23 (1979): 79–81.

Bell-Villada, Gene H. *García Márquez: The Man and His Work*. Chapel Hill: U of North Carolina P, 1990.

Bell-Villada, Gene H. "Lit. Crit. in Latin America, or the Advantages of Underdevelopment." *American Book Review* 5.6 (1983): 4–5.

Bell-Villada, Gene H. "Two Americas, Two World Views, and a Widening Gap." *Monthly Review* 34 (1982): 37–43.

Bell-Villada, Gene H. "What the Young García Márquez Marquez Learned from the Master Graham Greene: The Case of 'Un Dia de Estos'." *The Comparatist: Journal of the Southern Comparative Literature Association* 24 (2000):146–56.

Bennett, Maurice J. "The Detective Fiction of Poe and Borges." *Comparative Literature* 35.3 (1983): 262–75.

Bercovitch, Sacvan. "America as Canon and Context: Literary History in a Time of Dissensus." *American Literature* 58.1 (1986): 99–107.

Bercovitch, Sacvan, ed. *The Cambridge History of American Literature*. Cambridge: Cambridge UP, 1994.

Berding, Helmut, ed. *Nationales Bewußtseins und kollektive Identität. Studien zur Entwicklung des kollektiven Bewußtseins in der Neuzeit.* Frankfurt: Suhrkamp, 1994.

Berg, Henk de, and Matthias Prangel, eds. *Interkulturalität. Zur Konzeptualisierung eines Leitbegriffs interkultureller Literaturwissenschaft.* Heidelberg: Winter, 1999.

Berg, Walter Bruno. *Lateinamerika. Literatur, Geschichte, Kultur. Eine Einführung*. Darmstadt: Wissenschaftliche Buchgesellschaft, 1995.

Berger, Mark T. *Under Northern Eyes: Latin American Studies and US Hegemony in the Americas 1898–1990.* Bloomington: Indiana UP, 1995.

Bergmann, E. et al. *Women, Culture, and Politics in Latin America*. Berkeley: U of California P, 1990.

Bergmann, Emilie L., and Paul Julian Smith, eds. *¿Entiendes?: Queer Readings, Hispanic Writing*. Durham: Duke UP, 1995.

Bernheimer, Charles, ed. *Comparative Literature in the Age of Multiculturalism*. Baltimore: Johns Hopkins UP, 1995.

Bernucci, Leo. *Historia de un malentendido: Un estudio transtextual de La guerra del fin del mundo*. New York: Peter Lang, 1989.

Beverley, John. *Against Literature.* Minneapolis: U of Minnesota P, 1993.

Beverley, John. "Can Hispanism Be a Radical Practice?" *Ideologies & Literature: A Journal of Hispanic & Luso-Brazilian Studies* 4.16 (1983): 9–22.

Beverley, John. *Del Lazarillo al sandinismo: estudios sobre la función ideológica de la literatura española e hispanoamericana.* Minneapolis: Prisma Institute and Institute for the Study of Ideologies and Literature, 1987.

Beverley, John. "On the Subject of 'Studies': Subaltern, Cultural, Women's, Ethnic, etc." *Journal of Iberian & Latin American Studies* 5.2 (1999): 45–63.

Beverley, John. "Subalternidad/Modernidad/Multiculturalismo." *Revista de Critica Literaria Latinoamericana* 27 (2001): 153–63.

Beverley, John. *Subalternity and Representation*. Durham: Duke UP, 1999.

Beverley, John, ed. *Una Modernidad Obsoleta: Estudios sobre el Barroco.* Los Teques, Venezuela: Ediciones ALEM, 1998.

Beverley, John, and José Oviedo, eds. *The Postmodern Debate in Latin America*. Thematic Issue of *boundary 2* 20.3 (1993).

Beverley, John, and Hugo Achugar, eds. *La Voz del otro: testimonio, subalternidad y verdad narrativa.* Pittsburgh: Latinoamericana Editores, 1992.

Beverley, John, and Marc Zimmerman. *Literature and Politics in the Central American Revolutions.* Austin: U Texas P, 1990.

Beverley, John, Phil Cohen, and David Harvey. *Subculture and homogenization / subcultura i homogeneïtzacio.* Barcelona: Fundació Antoni Tàpies, 1999.

Bhabha, Homi K. *The Location of Culture.* London: Routledge, 1994.

Bhabha, Homi K. *Nation and Narration.* London: Routledge, 1990.

Biron, Rebecca. *Murder and Masculinity: Violent Fictions of Twentieth-Century Latin America.* Nashville: Vanderbilt UP, 2000.

Bissoondath, Neil. *Selling Illusions: The Cult of Multiculturalism in Canada.* Toronto: Penguin Books, 1994.

Block de Behar, Lisa. "Uruguayan Comparative Literature: The Need for a Double Bet." *Comparative Literature World Wide: Issues and Methods / La Littérature comparée dans le monde: Questions et méthodes.* Ed. Tânia Franco Carvalhal. Porto Alegre: L&PM Editores, 1997. 149–72.

Blodgett, E. D. "Towards an Ethnic Style." *Postcolonial Literatures: Theory and Practice / Les Littératures post-coloniales. Théories et réalisations.* Ed. Steven Tötösy de Zepetnek and Sneja Gunew. Thematic issue of *Canadian Review of Comparative Literature / Revue Canadienne de Littérature Comparée* 22.3–4 (1995): 623–38.

Bloom, William. *Personal Identity, National Identity, and International Relations.* Cambridge: Cambridge UP, 1990.

Borges, Jorge Luis. "El arte narrativo y la magia." *Discusión.* Buenos Aires: M. Gleizer, 1932.

Borges, Jorge Luis. "Nathaniel Hawthorne." *Other Inquisitions, 1937–1952.* Trans. Ruth L.C. Simms. New York: Simon and Schuster, 1968. 47–65.

Borges, Jorge Luis. "Note on Walt Whitman." *Other Inquisitions, 1937–1952.* Trans. Ruth L. C. Simms. New York: Simon and Schuster, 1968. 66–72.

Braga, Thomas. "Castro Alves and the New England Abolitionists." *Hispania* 67.4 (1984): 585–93.

Brakel, Arthur. "Ambiguity and Enigma in Art: The Case of Henry James and Machado de Assis." *Comparative Literature Studies* 19.4 (1982): 442–49.

Brathwaite, Edward Kamau. *History of the Voice: The Development of Nation Language in Anglophone Caribbean Poetry.* London: New Beacon Books, 1984.

Bredella, Lothar, and Dietmar Haack, eds. *Perceptions and Misperceptions: The United States and Germany. Studies in Intercultural Understanding.* Tübingen: Narr, 1988.

Breen, T. H. "An Empire of Goods: The Anglicization of Colonial America, 1690–1776." *Journal of British Studies* 25 (1986): 467–99.

Breinig, Helmbrecht. *Interamerikanische Beziehungen. Einfluss, Transfer, Interkulturalität.* Frankfurt: Vervuert, 1990.

Brickhouse, Anna. "Hawthorne in the Americas: Frances Calderón de la Barca, Octavio Paz, and the Mexican Genealogy of 'Rappaccini's Daughter'." *Proceedings of the Modern Language Association* 113.2 (1998): 227–42.

Bronfen, Elisabeth, Benjamin Marius, and Therese Steffen, eds. *Hybride Kulturen. Beiträge zur anglo-amerikanischen Multikulturalismusdebatte.* Tübingen: Stauffenburg, 1997.

Brotherston, Gordon. "Arielismo and anthropophagy: The Tempest in Latin America." *The Tempest and Its Travels.* Ed. P. Hulme and W. Sherman. London: Reaktion Books. 2000. 212–21.

Brotherston, Gordon. *Book of the Fourth World: Reading the Native Americas through Their Literature.* Cambridge: Cambridge UP, 1992.

Brotherston, Gordon. "Bringing It Home in Translation, Marx, Neruda and Chihuailaf." *New Comparison* 29 (2000): 147–59.

Brotherston, Gordon. "A Controversial Guide to the Language of America." *1642: Literature and Power in the Seventeenth Century.* Ed. F. Barker, et al. Colchester: U of Essex, Sociology of Literature Papers, 1981. 84–100.

Brotherston, Gordon. *Image of the New World: The American Continent Portrayed in Native Texts.* London: Thames and Hudson, 1979.

Brotherston, Gordon, ed. *José Enrique Rodó: Ariel.* Cambridge: Cambridge UP, 1967.

Brotherston, Gordon. "The Latin American Novel and Its Indigenous Sources." *Modern Latin American Fiction.* Ed. J. King. London: Faber, 1987. 60–77.

Brotherston, Gordon. "Ubirajara, Hiawatha, Cumandá: National Virtue from American Indian Literature." *Comparative Literature Studies* 9.3 (1972): 243–52.

Brotherston, Gordon. "World Views & Defined Territories." *Mapping the Americas.* Ed. P. Antrobus, V. Fraser, and P. Hulme. Colchester: U of Essex, 1992. 11–17.

Brotherston, Gordon, and Lúcia de Sá. "First Peoples of the Americas and Their Literature." *Comparative Cultural Studies and Latin America.* Ed. Sophia A. McClennen and Earl E. Fitz. West Lafayette: Purdue UP, 2004. 8–33.

Bruce-Novoa, Juan. "Pluralism vs. Nationalism: U.S. Literature." *Council on National Literatures / Quarterly World Report* 6.1–2 (1983): 13–18.

Bruner, Charlotte. "The Meaning of Caliban in Black Literature Today." *Comparative Literature Studies* 13.3 (1976): 240–53.

Brushwood, John S. "Two Views of the Boom: North and South." *Latin American Literary Review* 15.29 (1987): 13–31.

Buchenau, Barbara. "Comparativist Interpretations of the Frontier in Early American Fiction and Literary Historiography." *Intercultural Negotiations in the Americas and Beyond.* Ed. Barbara Buchenau and Marietta

Messmer. Thematic issue of *CLCWeb: Comparative Literature and Culture: A WWWeb Journal* 3.2 (2001): <http://clcwebjournal.lib.purdue.edu/clcweb01-2/buchenau01.html>.

Buchenau, Barbara. *Zwischen Windschattenfahrt und Eigenständigkeit. Vergleichende Studien zum historischen Roman in den USA des frühen 19. Jahrhunderts.* Diss. Göttingen: U of Göttingen, 1999.

Buchenau, Barbara. "'Wizards of the West?' How Americans Respond to Sir Walter Scott, the Wizard of the North." *James Fenimore Cooper: His Country and His Art.* Ed. Hugh MacDougall. Oneonto: State U of New York P, 1999. 14–25.

Buchenau, Barbara, Annette Paatz, Rolf Lohse, and Marietta Messmer, eds. *Do the Americas Have a Common Literary History?* Frankfurt: Peter Lang, 2001.

Buchenau, Barbara, Eva Findenegg, Frank Lauterbach, Beata Weinhagen, and Frank Seemann. "Normative Programs and Artistic Liberties: Inter-American Case Studies in Historical Fiction and the Campaigns for Cultural Dissociation." *Internationalität nationaler Literaturen.* Ed. Udo Schöning, Udo, Beata Weinhagen, and Frank Seemann. Göttingen: Wallstein, 2000.

Buell, Lawrence. "American Literary Emergence as a Postcolonial Phenomenon." *American Literary History* 4.3 (1992): 411–42.

Bush, Andrew. "On Exemplarity and Postmodern Simulation: Robert Coover and Servero Sarduy." *Comparative Literature* 14:2 (1992): 174–92.

Cabezon Doty, Claudia. "Literatura y cine latinoamericanos en dialogo intermedial." *Taller de Letras* 26 (1998): 29–54.

Cagidemetrio, Alide. "'The Rest of the Story'; Or, Multilingual American Literature." *Multilingual America: Transnationalism, Ethnicity, and the* Languages of American Literature. Ed. Werner Sollors. New York: New York UP, 1998. 17–28.

Campos, Maria do Carmo. "Poetics and Contemporary Culture in Drummond and Borges." *Latin America as Its Literature.* Ed. Maria Elena de Valdés, Mario J. Valdés, and Richard A. Young, 1995. 89–104.

Cândido, Antônio, et al. *Hacia una historia de la literatura latinoamericana.* México: Colegio de México, 1987.

Cândido, Antônio. *Literatura e sociedade: estudos de teoria e história literária.* São Paulo: Nacional, 1976.

Cândido, Antônio, et al. "Os Brasileiros e a Nossa América." *Recortes.* São Paulo: Companhia das Letras, 1993. 130–39.

Canovan, Margaret. *Nationhood and Political Theory.* Cheltenham: Edward Elgar, 1996.

Ceaser, James W. *Reconstructing America: The Symbol of America in Modern Thought.* New Haven: Yale UP, 1997.

Carvalhal, Tânia Franco. "Le Brésil et la littérature comparée." *Revue de Littérature Comparée* 66 (1997): 19–28.

Carvalhal, Tânia Franco. "Comparare i comparatismi. La letteratura comparata in Americo Latina." Trans. Anna Trocchi. *Comparare i comparatismi. La comparatistica letteraria oggi in Europa e nel mondo.* Ed. Armando Gnisci and Franca Sinopoli. Roma: Lithos, 1995. 14–26.

Carvalhal, Tania Franco. "Les Images fondatrices: La Question de l'espace geographique et culturel en Amerique Latine." *Proceedings of the XIIth Congress of the International Comparative Literature Association / Actes du XIIe congres de l'Association Internationale de Littérature Comparée.* Ed. Roger Bauer et al. München: Iudicium, 1990. II. 372–77.

Carvalhal, Tânia Franco. *Literatura comparada.* São Paolo: Editora Atica, 1986.

Carvalhal, Tânia Franco. "Literatura comparada na América-Latina: contribuição para novos paradigmas." *Literature Comparada: Os novos paradigmas.* Ed. Margarida L. Losa, Isménia de Sous, and Gonçalo Vilas-Boas. Porto: Afrontamento, 1996. 465–72.

Carvalhal, Tânia Franco. "Literatura e História: A Ficção Latino-Americana." *La Torre: Revista de la Universidad de Puerto Rico* 2.4–5 (1994): 321–29.

Carr, Pat, and Willard Gingerich. "The Vagina Dentata Motif in Náhuatl and Pueblo Mythic Narratives: A Comparative Study." *New Scholar* 8 (1982): 85–101.

Carvalho, Joaquim de. *Panorama das literaturas das Américas.* Nova Lisboa: Edição do Município de Nova Lisboa, 1958–63. 4 vols.

Castillo, Debra A. *Talking Back: Toward a Latin American Feminist Literary Criticism.* Ithaca: Cornell UP, 1992.

Castro-Klarén, Sara. "Locura y dolor: la elaboración de la historia en *Os Sertões* y *La guerra del fin del mundo.*" *Revista de Crítica Latinoamericana* 10.20 (1984): 207–31.

Castro-Klarén, Sara. "Santos and Cangaceiros: Inscription without Discourse in *Os Sertões* and *La guerra del fin del mundo.*" *Modern Language Notes* 101 (1986): 157–64.

Castro-Klarén, Sara, Sylvia Malloy, and Beatriz Sarlo, eds. *Women's Writing in Latin America.* Boulder: Westview P, 1991.

Chamberlain, Bobby. "Through Eagle Eyes: U.S. Brazilianists and Their Relationship to Brazilian Literature." *Hispania* 74.3 (1991): 604–9.

Chamberlain, Bobby J. "Frontier Humor in *Huckleberry Finn* and Carvalho's *O Coronel e o Lobisomem*." *Comparative Literature Sudies* 21.2 (1984): 201–16.

Chanady, Amaryll. "The Origins and Development of Magic Realism in Latin American Fiction." *Magic Realism and Canadian Literature: Essays and Stories.* Ed. P. Hinchcliffe and Ed Jewinski. Waterloo: U of Waterloo P, 1986.

Chanady, Amaryll, ed. Latin American Identity and Constructions of Difference. Minneapolis: U of Minnesota P, 1994.

Chapman, Arnold. "Pampas and Big Woods: Heroic Initiation in Güiraldes and Faulkner." *Comparative Literature* 11.1 (1959): 61–77.

Chapman, Arnold. *The Spanish American Reception of U.S. Fiction: 1920–1940.* Berkeley: U of California P, 1966.

Chevigny, Bell Gale. "Teaching Comparative Literature of the United States and Spanish America." *American Literature* 65.2 (1993): 354–58.

Chevigny, Bell Gale, and Gari Laguardia, eds. *Reinventing the Americas: Comparative Studies of Literature of the United States and Spanish America.* Cambridge: Cambridge UP, 1986.

Chevrel, Yves. *Comparative Literature Today: Methods and Perspectives.* Trans. Farida Elizabeth Dahab. Kirksville: The Thomas Jefferson UP, 1995.

Chinweizu, Onwuchekwa Jemie, and Ihechukwu Madubuike. *Toward the Decolonization of African Literature: African Fiction and Poetry and Their Critics.* London: KPI, 1985.

Clifford, James. *Routes: Travel and Translation in the Late Twentieth Century.* Cambridge: Harvard UP, 1997.

Christ, Ronald J. *The Narrow Act: Borges' Art of Allusion.* New York: Lumen Books, 1995.

Cisneros-Lavaller, Alberto. "Old Wine in New Bottles: An Essay on the Study of Inter-American Relations." *New Scholar* 8 (1972): 267–88.

Cobb, Martha K. *Harlem, Haiti and Havana.* Washington: Three Continents P, 1979.

Cohn, Deborah. "'He was one of us': The Reception of William Faulkner and the U.S. South by Latin American Authors." *Comparative Literature Studies* 34.2 (1997): 149–69.

Cohn, Deborah H. *History and Memory in the Two Souths: Recent Southern and Spanish American Fiction.* Nashville: Vanderbilt UP, 1999.

Colás, Santiago. *Postmodernity in Latin America: The Argentine Paradigm.* Durham: Duke UP, 1994.

Colás, Santiago. "Of Creole Symptoms, Cuban Fantasies, and Other Latin American Postcolonial Ideologies." *PMLA* 110.3 (1995): 382–96.

Collier, G., Dieter Riemenschneider, and Frank Schulze-Engler, eds. *Postcolonial Theory and the Emergence of a Global Society.* Frankfurt: Acolit, 1998.

Collmer, Robert G. "When 'Word' Meets 'Palabra': Crossing the Border with Literature." *Proceedings of the Comparative Literature Symposium: William Faulkner, Prevailing Verities and World Literature.* Ed. W.T. Zyla and W.M. Aycock. Lubbock: Texas Tech UP, 1973. 153–64.

Coonrod Martínez, Elizabeth. "The Latin American Innovative Novel of the 1920s: A Comparative Reassessment." *Comparative Cultural Studies and Latin America.* Ed. Sophia A. McClennen and Earl E. Fitz. West Lafayette: Purdue UP, 2004. 34–55.

Cornejo Polar, Antonio. *Escribir en el aire.* Lima: Horizonte, 1994.

Coronil, Fernando. "Challenging Colonial Histories: Cuban Counterpoint / Ortiz's Counterfetishism." *Critical Theory, Cultural Politics, and the Latin American Narrative.* Ed. Steven M. Bell, Albert H. LeMay, and Leonard Orr. Notre Dame: Notre Dame UP, 1993. 61–80.

Costa Picazo, Rolando, and María Alejandra Rosarossa, eds. *Estados Unidos y América Latina: modernismo, posmodernismo.* Buenos Aires: Ediciones del Cifrado, 1999.

Costigan, Lúcia Helena, ed. *O Brasil, a América Hispánica e o Caribe: Abordagens Comparativas.* Special issue of *Revista Iberoamericana* 64 (1998): 1–311.

Cotler, Julio, and Richard R. Fagen, eds. *Latin America and the United States: The Changing Political Realities.* Stanford: Stanford UP, 1974.

Coutinho, Afrânio. *Conceito de literatura brasileira.* Petrópolis: Vozes, 1981.

Coutinho, Afrânio. *Introdução à literatura no Brasil.* Rio de Janeiro: Civilização Brasileira, 1976.

Coutinho, Afrânio. *O processo de descolonização literária.* Rio de Janeiro: Civilização Brasileira, 1983.

Coutinho, Eduardo F. "Cambio de rumbo en la literatura comparada en Brasil." *Revista de Occidente* 197 (1997): 49–62.

Coutinho, Eduardo F. "Literatura comparada na América Latina: do ethnocentrismo ao diálogo de culturas." *Literature Comparada: Os novos paradigmas.* Ed. Margarida L. Losa, Isménia de Sousa, and Gonçalo Vilas-Boas. Porto: Afrontamento, 1996. 133–38.

Coutinho, Eduardo F. "Postmodernism in Brazil." *International Postmodernism.* Ed. Hans Bertens and Douwe Fokkema. Amsterdam: John Benjamins, 1997. 327–34.

Coutinho, Eduardo, and Tânia Franco Carvalhal, eds. *Literatura comparada. Textos fundadores.* Rio de Janeiro: Rocco, 1994.

Cowan, Bainard, and Jefferson Humphries, eds. *Poetics of the Americas: Race, Founding, and Textuality.* Baton Rouge: The Louisiana State UP, 1997.

Dahab, F. Elizabeth. "Visages de la francophonie. Du politique, du littéraire, du sociologique." *Postcolonial Literatures: Theory and Practice / Les Littératures post-coloniales. Théories et réalisations.* Ed. Steven Tötösy de Zepetnek and Sneja Gunew. Thematic issue of *Canadian Review of Comparative Literature / Revue Canadienne de Littérature Comparée* 22.3–4 (1995): 693–705.

Daroqui, María Julia. *(Dis)locaciones: Narrativas híbridas del Caribe hispano.* Valencia: Universitat de Valencia UP d'Estudis Iberoamericans, 1998.

Dash, Michael. "Psychology, Creolization, and Hybridization." *New National and Post-Colonial Literatures: An Introduction.* Ed. Bruce King. Oxford: Clarendon P, 1996. 45–58.

DaMatta, Roberto. *Carnivals, Rogues and Heroes: An Interpretation of the Brazilian Dilemma.* Trans. John Drury. South Bend: U of Notre Dame P, 1991.

Davies, C.B., and E.S. Fido, eds. *Out of the Kumbla: Caribbean Women and Literature.* Trenton: Africa World P, 1990.

Davis, Mary E. "The Haunted Voice: Echoes of William Faulkner in García Márquez, Fuentes, and Vargas Llosa." *World Literature Today* 59.4 (1985): 531–35.

Davis, Mary E. "The Town That Was an Open Wound." *Comparative Literature Studies* 23.1 (1986): 24–43.

de Campos, Haroldo. *De la razón antropofágica y otros ensayos.* México: Siglo Veintiuno Editores, 2000.

de Campos, Haroldo. "Beyond Exclusive Languages." *Latin America in Its Literature.* Ed. César Fernández Moreno, Julio Ortega, and Ivan A. Schulman. Trans. Mary G. Berg. New York: Holmes and Meier, 1980. 221–43.

de Costa, Elena. *Collaborative Latin American Popular Theater: From Theory to Form, From Text to Stage.* New York: Peter Lang, 1992.

de la Campa, Román. "Latin American Studies: Literary, Cultural, and Comparative Theory." *Comparative Cultural Studies and Latin America.* Ed.

Sophia A. McClennen and Earl E. Fitz. Thematic issue of *CLCWeb: Comparative Literature and Culture: A WWWeb Journal* 4.2 (2002): <http://clcwebjournal.lib.purdue.edu/clcweb02-2/delacampa02.html>.

de la Campa, Román. *America Latina y sus comunidades discursivas: cultura y literatura en la era global*. Caracas: Celarg, 1998.

de la Campa, Román. "Latin America and the Advent of Postcolonial Criticism." *Postcolonial Literatures: Theory and Practice / Les Littératures post-coloniales. Théories et réalisations.* Ed. Steven Tötösy de Zepetnek and Sneja Gunew. Thematic issue of *Canadian Review of Comparative Literature / Revue Canadienne de Littérature Comparée* 22.3–4 (1995): 745–71.

de la Campa, Román. *Latin Americanism.* Minneapolis: U of Minnesota P, 1999.

de la Campa, Román. "Latin, Latino, American: Split States and Global Imaginaries." *Comparative Literature* 53.4 (2001): 373–88.

de la Campa, Román. "Mainstreaming Poststructuralist and Feminist Thought: Jonathan Culler's Poetics." *MMLA: Journal for the Midwest Modern Language Association* 23 (1985): 29–27.

de la Campa, Román, Ann E. Kaplan, and Michael Sprinker, eds. *Late Imperial Culture.* London: Verso, 1995.

Dean, James Seay. "Upon These Banks and Shoals of Time: Herman Melville's Whale, João Guimarães Rosa's Crocodile." *Luso-Brazilian Review* 20.2 (1983): 198–212.

Degregori, Carlos Iván. "El estudio del otro: cambios en los análisis sobre etnicidad en el Perú." *Perú 1964–1994. Economía, Sociedad y Política.* Ed. Julio Cotler. Lima: IEP, 1995. 303–32.

Dessau, A. "La Littérature latino-americaine dans la littérature universelle: Historicité, traditions, et universalisme." *Actes du VIIIe Congres de l'Association Internationale de Littérature Comparée / Proceedings of the 8th Congress of the International Comparative Literature Association.* Ed. Béla Köpeczi and György M. Vajda. Stuttgart: Bieber, 1980. Vol. 2, 117–25.

D'Haen, Theo. "Deleuze, Guattari, Glissant and Post-'American' Narratives." *Yearbook of Research in English and American Literature* 13 (1997): 387–99.

D'Haen, Theo, and Hans Bertens, eds. *"Writing" Nation and "Writing" Region in America.* Amsterdam: Rodopi, 1996.

Dharwadker, Vinay. "The Internationalization of Literatures." *New National and Post-Colonial Literatures: An Introduction.* Ed. Bruce King. Oxford: Clarendon P, 1996. 59–77.

Dinnerstein, Leonard, Roger L. Nichols, and David M. Reimers. *Natives and Strangers: A Multicultural History of Americans*. New York: Oxford UP, 1996.

Dixon, John. *Reversible Readings: Ambiguity in Four Latin American Novels*. Huntsville: U of Alabama P, 1985.

Donoso, José. *The Boom in Spanish American Literature: A Personal History*. Trans. Gregory Kolovakos. New York: Columbia UP, 1977.

Dorfman, Ariel. *The Empire's Old Clothes: What the Lone Ranger, Babar, and Other Innocent Heroes Do to Our Minds*. Trans. Clark Hansen. New York: Pantheon, 1983.

Dorfman, Ariel. *Hacia la liberación del lector latinoamericano*. Mexico: Ediciones del Norte, 1984.

Dorfman, Ariel. *Imaginación y violencia en América*. Barcelona: Editorial Anagrama, 1972.

Dorfman, Ariel, and Armand Mattelart. *Para leer al pato Donald*. Havana: Editorial de Ciencias Sociales, 1974.

Dorfman, Ariel. *Patos, elefantes y héroes: la infancia como subdesarrollo*. Buenos Aires: Ediciones de la Flor, 1985.

Dornheim, Nicolas Jorge. "Arturo Farinelli en la Argentina (1927): Un momento estelar de la literatura comparada junto al Rio de la Plata." *Revista de Literaturas Modernas* 25 (1992): 39–52.

Dornheim, Nicolás Jorge. "Germanistik und Komparatistik in Lateinamerika: Aspekte einer fruchtbaren Kontroverse." *Kontroversen, alte und neue*. Ed. János Riesz. Tübingen: Niemeyer, 1986. 95–102.

Dornheim, Nicolás Jorge. "La literatura comparada en la Argentina." *Boletin de literatura comparada* 3.1–2 (1978): 17–47.

Driver, David Miller. *The Indian in Brazilian Literature*. New York: Hispanic Institute, 1942.

Durisin, Dionýz. *Theory of Interliterary Process*. Trans. Jessie Kocmanová and Zdenek Pistek. Bratislava: Slovak Academy of Sciences, 1989.

Eagleton, Terry, Fredric Jameson, and Edward W. Said, eds. *Nationalism, Colonialism, and Literature*. Minneapolis: U of Minneapolis P, 1990.

Earle, Robert L., and John D. Wirth, eds. *Identities in North America: The Search for Community*. Stanford: Stanford UP, 1995.

Edinger, Catarina. "Dona Flor in Two Cultures." *Literature and Film Quarterly* 19.4 (1991): 236–37.

Edinger, Catarina. "Machismo and Androgyny in Mid-Nineteenth Century Brazilian and American Novels." *Comparative Literature Studies* 27.2 (1990): 124–39.

Elliott, Emory, ed. *Columbia Literary History of the United States*. New York: Columbia UP, 1988.

Emberley, Julia. "The Logics of Discovery: Border/Body Disputes." *Postcolonial Literatures: Theory and Practice / Les Littératures postcoloniales. Théories et réalisations*. Ed. Steven Tötösy de Zepetnek and Sneja Gunew. Thematic issue of *Canadian Review of Comparative Literature / Revue Canadienne de Littérature Comparée* 22.3–4 (1995): 603–21.

Engelbert, Manfred. "Apropiaciones de realidad en la novela hispanoamericana a partir de 1968—El post-boom: una novela liberada?" *Apropiaciones de realidad en la novela hispanoamericana de los siglos XIX y XX*. Ed. Hans-Otto Dill et al. Frankfurt: Vervuert, 1994. 400–18.

Englekirk, John E. *Edgar Allan Poe in Hispanic Literature*. New York: Instituto de las Españas en los Estados Unidos, 1934.

Englekirk, John E. *A literatura norteamericana no Brasil*. Mexico City: n. p., 1950.

Essmann, Helga. "Literary 'Universality': Henry Wadsworth Longfellow and American National Literature." *The Internationality of National Literatures in Either America*. Vol. 1: *Transfer and Transformation*. Ed. Armin Paul Frank and Helga Essmann. Göttingen: Wallstein, 1999. 85–106.

Essen, Gesa von, and Horst Turk, eds. *Unerledigte Geschichten. Der literarische Umgang mit Nationalität und Internationalität*. Göttingen: Wallstein, 2000.

Ette, Otmar. "Internacionalizacion e intertextualidad." *Actas: Hacia una historia social de la literatura latinoamericana*. Giessen: Aelsal, 1985. 85–97.

Ette, Otmar. *Modernidad, modernización, postmodernidad*. Toluca: Facultad de Humanidades, Centro de Investigación en Ciencias Sociales y Humanidades, 1994.

Ette, Ottmar. "Transatlantic Perceptions: A Contrastive Reading of the Travels of Alexander von Humboldt and Fray Servando Teresa de Mier." *American Journal of Cultural Histories & Theories* 17 (1992): 165–97.

Faris, Wendy B. "Alejo Carpentier à la recherche du temps perdu." *Comparative Literature Studies* 17 (1980): 133–54.

Faris, Wendy B. "'Desyoizacion': Joyce/Cixous/Fuentes and the Multi-Vocal Text." *Latin American Literary Review* 19 (1981): 31–39.

Faris, Wendy B. "1001 Words: Fiction against Death." *Georgia Review* 36.4 (1982): 811–30.

Faris, Wendy B. "Ulysses in Mexico: Carlos Fuentes." *Comparative Literature Studies* 19.2 (1982): 236–53.

Faris, Wendy B. "Pasos Perdidos, Temps Perdu: Carpentier and Proust." *Journal of Romance Literary Relations* (1982): 20–31.

Faris, Wendy B. "Cities and Towns: The Development of a Collective Voice." *Inter-American Literary Relations*. Ed. Mario J. Valdés. New York: Garland, 1985. 3–13.

Faris, Wendy B. "'Proustitución'?: Una familia lejana de Carlos Fuentes." *De la crónica a la nueva narrativa mexicana: Coloquio sobre literatura mexicana*. Ed. Merlin H. Forster and Julio Ortega. Mexico: Editorial Oasis, 1986. 369–82.

Faris, Wendy B. "Desire and Power, Love and Revolution: Fuentes and Kundera." *The Review of Contemporary Fiction* 82 (1988): 273–84.

Faris, Wendy B. "Marking Space, Charting Time: Text and Territory in Faulkner's "The Bear" and Carpentier's *The Lost Steps*." *Do the Americas Have a Common Literature?* Ed. Gustavo Perez Firmat. Durham: Duke UP, 1990. 243–65.

Faris, Wendy B. "Writing in/of/on the New World: Metafictional Dimensions of Land Use in North and South American Fiction." *Space and Boundaries*. Ed. Roger Bauer and Douwe Fokkema. München: iudicum, 1990. 151–58.

Faris, Wendy B. "Scheherazade's Children: Magical Realism and Postmodern Fiction." *Magical Realism: Theory, History, Community*. Ed. Lois Parkinson Zamora and Wendy B. Faris. Durham: Duke UP, 1995. 163–90.

Faris, Wendy B. "Imaginary Visual Memories: Françoise Sagan Prewrites Fernando Botero." *Das visuelle Gedächtnis der Literatur*. Ed. Manfred Schmeling and Monika Schmitz-Emans. Würzburg: Königshausen and Neumann, 1999. 178–87.

Fayen, Tanya T. *In Search of the Latin American Faulkner.* Lanham: UP of America, 1995.

Fee, Margery. "What Use is Ethnicity to Native Peoples?" *Postcolonial Literatures: Theory and Practice / Les Littératures post-coloniales. Théories et réalisations.* Ed. Steven Tötösy de Zepetnek and Sneja Gunew. Thematic issue of *Canadian Review of Comparative Literature / Revue Canadienne de Littérature Comparée* 22.3–4 (1995): 683–91.

Fender, Stephen, ed. *American and European National Identities: Faces in the Mirror.* Keele: Keele UP, 1996.

Fernández, Pablo Armando. "Dreams of Two Americas." In *Reinventing the Americas: Comparative Studies of Literature of the United States and*

Spanish America. Ed. Bell Gale Chevigny and Gari Laguardia. Cambridge: Cambridge UP, 1986. 122–36.

Fernandez Moreno, Cesar, Julio Ortega, Ivan A. Schulman, and Mary G. Berg, eds. *Latin America in Its Literature*. New York: Holmes & Meier, 1980.

Fernández Retamar, Roberto. *Apuntes para una teoría literaria hispanoamericana*. Havana: Casa de las Américas, 1975.

Fernández Retamar, Roberto. *Caliban and Other Essays*. Trans. Edward Baker. Minneapolis: U of Minnesota P, 1989.

Fernández Retamar, Roberto. "Caliban: Notes toward a Discussion of Culture in Our America." Trans. Lynn Garafola, David Arthur McMurray, and Robert Marquez. *The Massachusetts Review* 15.1–2 (1974): 7–72.

Fitz, Earl E. "Spanish American and Brazilian Literature in Inter-American Perspective: The Comparative Approach." *Comparative Cultural Studies and Latin America*. Ed. Sophia A. McClennen and Earl E. Fitz. West Lafayette: Purdue UP, 2004. 69–88.

Fitz, Earl E. "Ambigüidade e gênero: estabelecendo a diferenç a entre a ficção escrita por mulheres no Brasil e na América espanhola." *Entre Resistir e Identificar-se: Para uma Teoria da Prática da Narrativa Brasileira de Autoria Feminina*. Ed. Peggy Sharpe. Florianópolis: Editora Paraula, a Editora da UFG, e a Editora Mulheres, 1997.

Fitz, Earl E. "The Black Poetry of Jorge de Lima and Nicolás Guillén: A Comparative Study." *Inti: Revista de Literatura Hispanica* 4 (1976): 76–84.

Fitz, Earl E. *Brazilian Narrative Traditions in a Comparative Context*. New York: MLA, 2004 (forthcoming).

Fitz, Earl E. "Caracterização e a visão fenomenológica nos romances de Clarice Lispector e Djuna Barnes." *Travessia* 14 (1987): 135–47.

Fitz, Earl E. "The First Inter-American Novels: Some Choices and Some Comments." *Comparative Literature Studies* 22.2 (1985): 361–76.

Fitz, Earl E. "Gregôrio de Matos and Juan del Valle y Caviedes: Two Baroque Poets in Colonial Spanish and Portuguese America." *Inti: Revista de Literatura Hispanica* 5–6 (1977): 143–50.

Fitz, Earl E. "The Influence of Machado de Assis on John Barth's *The Floating Opera*." *The Comparatist: Journal of the Southern Comparative Literature Association* 10 (1986): 56–66.

Fitz, Earl E. "The Interplay of History, Fiction, and Language in the Development of Colonial Literature in the Americas: Québec and Latin America." *La Nation dans tous ses états: le Québec en comparaison*. Montréal: Harmattan, 1997.

Fitz, Earl E. "Is There a Latin American Literature? The Comparatist's Dilemma." *Council on National Literatures / Quarterly World Report* 4.2 (1981): 5–8.

Fitz, Earl E. "John Barth's Brazilian Connection." *New World* 2.1–2 (1987): 123–38.

Fitz, Earl E. *Machado de Assis.* Boston: Twayne, 1989.

Fitz, Earl E. "Macondo, Yoknapatawpha y Santa Rosa: Una interpretación comparativa de tres perspectivas regionalistas." *Humanidades* 2.1 (1982): 47–60.

Fitz, Earl E. "Metafiction in Latin American Narrative: The Case for Brazil, or, if Brás Cubas were here today, what would he say about Spanish American Fiction?" *Mester* 26 (1997): 43–69.

Fitz, Earl E. "Old World Roots / New World Realities: A Comparatist Looks at the Growth of Literature in North and South America." *Council on National Literatures / Quarterly World Report* 3.3 (1980): 8–11.

Fitz, Earl E. *Rediscovering the New World: Inter-American Literature in a Comparative Context.* Iowa City: U of Iowa P, 1991.

Fitz, Earl E. "The Rise of the New Novel in Latin America: A Lyrical Aesthetic." *Inter-Muse: An Interdisciplinary Journal* 2 (1979): 17–27.

Fitz, Earl E. "Two Baroque Poets in Colonial Portuguese and Spanish America." *Inti: Revista de Literatura Hispanica* 5–6 (1997): 134–50.

Fitz, Earl E. "Whither Inter-American Literature?" *Canadian Review of Comparative Literature / Revue Canadienne de la Littérature Comparée* 18 (1991): 1–13.

Fitz, Earl E., and Judith A. Payne. *Ambiguity and Gender in the New Novel of Brazil and Spanish America: A Comparative Assessment.* Iowa City: U of Iowa P, 1993.

Fogelquist, Donald F. *Españoles de América y Americanos de España.* Madrid: Gredos, 1968.

Fohrmann, Jürgen. *Das Projekt der deutschen Literaturgeschichte. Entstehung und Scheitern einer nationalen Poesiegeschichtsschreibung zwischen Humanismus und deutschem Kaiserreich.* Stuttgart: Metzler, 1989.

Forbes, Hugh D. *Ethnic Conflict: Commerce, Culture, and the Contact Hypothesis.* New Haven: Yale UP, 1997.

Forman, Gabrielle P. "Past-On Stories: History and the Magically Real, Morrison and Allende on Call." *Feminist Studies* 18.2 (1992): 369–88.

Foster, David William. *Cultural Diversity in Latin America.* Albuquerque: U of New Mexico P, 1994.

Foster, David William. *Gay and Lesbian Themes in Latin American Writing.* Austin: U of Texas P, 1991.

Foster, David William. "Spanish American and Brazilian Literature: A History of Disconsonance." *Hispania* 75.4 (1992): 266–78.

Fox, Patricia D. "Fiction, Biography, Autobiography, and Postmodern Nostalgia in (Con)Texts of Return." *CLCWeb: Comparative Literature and Culture: A WWWeb Journal* 1.4 (1999): <http://clcwebjournal.lib.purdue.edu/clcweb99-4/fox99-2.html>.

Fox, Patricia D. "What's Past is Prologue: Imagining the Socialist Nation in Cuba and in Hungary." *CLCWeb: Comparative Literature and Culture: A WWWeb Journal* 1.1 (1999): <http://clcwebjournal.lib.purdue.edu/clcweb99-1/fox99.html>.

Franco, Jean. "Beyond Ethnocentrism: Gender, Power and the Third-World Intelligentsia." *Colonial Discourse and Post-Colonial Theory: A Reader.* Ed. Patrick Williams and Laura Chrisman. New York: Columbia UP, 1994. 359–69.

Franco, Jean. "Pastiche in Contemporary Latin American Literature." *Studies in 20th Century Literature* 14.1 (1990): 95–107.

Franco, Jean. *Plotting Women: Gender and Representation in Mexico.* London: Verso, 1989.

Franco, Jean, George Yúdice, and Juan Flores. *On Edge: The Crisis of Contemporary Latin American Culture.* Minneapolis: U of Minnesota P, 1992.

Frank, Armin Paul. "On the Comparison of Interliterary Configurations." *Intercultural Negotiations in the Americas and Beyond.* Ed. Barbara Buchenau and Marietta Messmer. Thematic issue of *CLCWeb: Comparative Literature and Culture: A WWWeb Journal* 3.2 (2001): <http://clcwebjournal.lib.purdue.edu/clcweb01-2/frank01.html>.

Frank, Armin Paul, and Helga Essmann, eds. *The Internationality of National Literatures in Either America.* Vol. 1: *Transfer and Transformation.* Göttingen: Wallstein, 1999.

Frank, Armin Paul, et al., eds. *Übersetzen, Verstehen, Brücken bauen. Geisteswissenschaftliches und literarisches Übersetzen im internationalen Kulturaustausch.* Berlin: Schmidt, 1993.

Frank, Armin Paul, and Kurt Mueller-Vollmer. *The Internationality of National Literatures in Either America: Transfer and Transformation.* Vol. 2: *British America and the United States, 1770s–1850s.* Göttingen: Wallstein, 2000.

Frank, Armin Paul. "Vorüberlegungen zu einer internationalen Geschichte der anglo-amerikanischen Literatur." *Tangenten: Literatur und Geschichte.*

Ed. Martin Meyer, Gabriele Spengemann, and Wolf Kindermann. Münster: Lit-Verlag, 1996. 27–52.

Frederickson, George. "From Exceptionalism to Variability: Recent Developments in Cross-National Comparative History." *Journal of American History* 82 (1995): 587–604.

Frugoni de Fritzsche, Teresita, ed. *Primeras Jornadas Internacionales de Literatura Argentina/Comparistica: Actas.* Buenos Aires, Argentina: Facultad de Filosofia y Letras, Universidad de Buenos Aires, 1996.

Fuchs, Lawrence H. *The American Kaleidoscope: Race, Ethnicity, and the Civic Culture.* Hanover: Wesleyan UP, 1990.

Galens, Judy, et al., ed. *Gale Encyclopedia of Multicultural America.* New York: Gale, 1995.

Gálik, Marián. "Interliterariness as a Concept in Comparative Literature." *Histories and Concepts of Comparative Literature.* Ed. Steven Tötösy de Zepetnek. Thematic issue of *CLCWeb: Comparative Literature and Culture: A WWWeb Journal* 2.4 (2000): <http://clcwebjournal.lib.purdue.edu/clcweb00-4/galik2-00.html>.

García Canclini, Néstor. *Culturas híbridas: Estrategias para entrar y salir de la modernidad.* Buenos Aires: Suramericana, 1995.

Garcia Pinto, Magdalena, "Anatomia de la revolución en La guerra del fin del mundo e Historia de Mayta de MVL." *The Historical Novel in Latin America.* Ed. Daniel Balderston. Tulane: Ediciones Hispamerica, 1986. 162–68.

Gass, William H. "The First Seven Pages of the Boom." *Latin American Literary Review* 15 (1987): 33–56.

Geist, Anthony, and Jose Monleon, eds. *Modernism and Its Margins: Reinscribing Cultural Modernity from Spain and Latin America.* New York: Garland, 1999.

Gellner, Ernest. *Nations and Nationalism.* Oxford: Blackwell, 1983.

Gérard, Albert S. "Problématique d'une histoire littéraire du monde caraïbe." *Revue de littérature comparée* 62.1 (1988): 45–56.

Gerbi, Antonello. *Nature in the New World: From Christopher Columbus to Gonzalo Fernández de Oviedo.* 1975. Trans. Jeremy Moyle. Pittsburgh: U of Pittsburgh P, 1985.

Gerbi, Antonello. *Dispute of the New World: The History of a Polemic, 1750–1900.* 1955. Trans. Jeremy Moyle. Pittsburgh: U of Pittsburgh P, 1973.

Gibson, Charles. *Spain in America.* New York: Harper Colophon, 1966.

Giesen, Bernhard, ed. *Nationale und kulturelle Identität. Studien zur Entwicklung des kollektiven Bewusstseins in der Neuzeit.* Frankfurt: Suhrkamp, 1991.

Gikandi, Simon. *Writing in Limbo: Modernism and Caribbean Literature.* Ithaca: Cornell UP, 1992.

Gill, Anne. "*Dom Casmurro* and *Lolita*: Machado among the Metafictionists." *Luso-Brazilian Review* 24.1 (1987): 17–26.

Gilroy, Paul. *There Ain't no Black in the Union Jack: The Cultural Politics of Race and Nation.* London: Hutchinson, 1987.

Glasenapp, Jörn. *"Prodigies, anomalies, monsters": Charles Brockden Brown und die Grenzen der Erkenntnis.* Göttingen: Wallstein, 2000.

Glissant, Édouard. *Caribbean Discourse.* Trans. Michael Dash. Charlottesville: UP of Virginia, 1989.

Glissant, Édouard. *Le Discours Antillais.* Paris: Seuil, 1981.

Goldberg, David Theo, ed. *Multiculturalism: A Critical Reader.* Oxford: Blackwell, 1995.

González, Manuel Pedro. *José Martí: Epic Chronicler of the United States in the Eighties.* Chapel Hill: U of North Carolina P, 1953.

González, Patricia E., and Eliana Ortega, eds. *La Sartén por el Mango: Encuentro de Escritoras Latinoamericanas.* Rio Piedras: Ediciones Huracán, 1984.

González Stephan, Beatriz. *La historiografía literaria del liberalismo hispano-americano del siglo XIX.* La Habana: Casa de las Américas, 1987.

González Echevarría, Roberto. "Latin American and Comparative Literature." *Comparative Cultural Studies and Latin America.* Ed. Sophia A. McClennen and Earl E. Fitz. West Lafayette: Purdue UP, 2004. 89–104.

González Echevarría, Roberto. *Myth and Archive: A Theory of Latin American Literature.* Cambridge: Cambridge UP, 1990.

González Echevarría, Roberto. *The Voice of the Masters: Writing and Authority in Modern Latin American Literature.* Austin: U of Texas P, 1985.

González Echevarría, Roberto, and Enrique Pupo-Walker, eds. *The Cambridge History of Latin American Literature.* Cambridge: Cambridge UP, 1996. 3 vols.

Gordon, Avery F., et al., eds. *Mapping Multiculturalism.* Minneapolis: U of Minnesota P, 1996.

Grace, Sherrill E. "Re-Inventing Franklin." *Postcolonial Literatures: Theory and Practice / Les Littératures post-coloniales. Théories et réalisations.* Ed. Steven Tötösy de Zepetnek and Sneja Gunew. Thematic issue of

Canadian Review of Comparative Literature / Revue Canadienne de Littérature Comparée 22.3–4 (1995): 707–25.

Graf, Marga. "Roots of Identity: The National and Cultural Self in Présence Africaine." *Intercultural Negotiations in the Americas and Beyond*. Ed. Barbara Buchenau and Marietta Messmer. *Thematic issue of CLCWeb: Comparative Literature and Culture: A WWWeb Journal* 3.2 (2001): <http://clcwebjournal.lib.purdue.edu/clcweb01-2/graf01.html>.

Greenblatt, Stephen. *Marvelous Possessions: The Wonder of the New World*. Oxford: Clarendon, 1991.

Gugelberger, Georg M., ed. *The Real Thing: Testimonial Discourse and Latin America*. Durham: Duke UP, 1996.

Guillén, Claudio. "Distant Relations: French, Anglo-American, Hispanic." *World Literature Today* 59.4 (1985): 503–07.

Guillén, Claudio. *Entre lo uno y lo diverso. Introducción a la literatura comparada*. Barcelona: Crítica, 1985.

Gunew, Sneja. *Framing Marginality: Multicultural Literary Studies*. Melbourne: Melbourne UP, 1994.

Guthunz, Ute, and Thomas Fischer, eds. *Lateinamerika zwischen Europa und den USA. Wechselwirkungen, Wahrnehmungen und Transformationsprozesse in Politik*. Frankfurt: Vervuert, 1995.

Guy, Donna H., and Thomas E. Sheridan, eds. *Contested Ground: Comparative Frontiers on the Northern and Southern Edges of the Spanish Empire*. Arizona: U of Arizona P, 1998.

Haberly, David. "The Search for a National Language: A Problem in the Comparative History of Postcolonial Literatures." *Comparative Literature Studies* 11.1 (1974): 85–97.

Hagenbüchle, Roland. "Living Together as an Intercultural Task." *Intercultural Negotiations in the Americas and Beyond*. Ed. Barbara Buchenau and Marietta Messmer. Thematic issue of *CLCWeb: Comparative Literature and Culture: A WWWeb Journal* 3.2 (2001): <http://clcwebjournal.lib.purdue.edu/clcweb01-2/hagenbuchle01.html>.

Hagenbüchle, Roland, Josef Raab, and Marietta Messmer, eds. *Negotiations of America's National Identity*. Tübingen: Stauffenburg, 2000.

Hall, Stuart. *Critical Dialogues in Cultural Studies*. London: Routledge, 1996.

Hanke, Lewis. *Do the Americas Have a Common History?* New York: Knopf, 1964.

Harss, Luis, and Barbara Dohmann. *Into the Mainstream*. New York: Harper and Row, 1967.

Hinchcliffe, Peter, and Ed Jewinski, eds. *Magical Realism and Canadian Literature.* Waterloo: U of Waterloo P, 1986.

Hansen, Klaus P. *Kultur und Kulturwissenschaft.* Tübingen: Francke, 2000.

Harney, Stefano. *Nationalism and Identity.* London: Zedbooks, 1996.

Harrison, Keith. "Samuel Hearne, Matonabbee, and the 'Esquimeaux Girl': Cultural Subjects, Cultural Objects." *Postcolonial Literatures: Theory and Practice / Les Littératures post-coloniales. Théories et réalisations.* Ed. Steven Tötösy de Zepetnek and Sneja Gunew. Thematic issue of *Canadian Review of Comparative Literature / Revue Canadienne de Littérature Comparée* 22.3–4 (1995): 647–57.

Hebel, Udo J., ed. *The Construction and Contestation of American Cultures and Identities in the Early National Period.* Heidelberg: Winter, 1999.

Hebel, Udo J., ed. *Transatlantic Encounters: Studies in European-American Relations.* Trier: WTV, 1995.

Henríquez Ureña, Pedro. *Las corrientes literarias en América Hispánica.* México: Fondo de Cultura Económica, 1949.

Henze, Kerstin. *Anglo-hispanische Sprachwege durch New York. Ethnographie der Kommunikation in einer globalisierten Gesellschaft.* Tübingen: Narr, 2000.

Herlinghaus, Hermann and Utz Riese, eds. *Heterotopien der Identität. Literatur in den interamerikanischen Kontaktzonen.* Heidelberg: Winter, 1999.

Herzog, Reinhart, and Reinhart Koselleck, eds. *Epochenschwelle und Epochenbewusstsein.* München: Fink, 1987.

Hess, David J., and Roberto da Matta, eds. *The Brazilian Puzzle: Culture on the Borderlands of the Western World.* New York: Columbia UP, 1995.

Heydenreich, Titus. "Translatio Latinitatis: Aspekte südamerikanischer Italien-Rezeption." *The Internationality of National Literatures in Either America: Transfer and Transformation.* Vol. 1. *Cases and Problems.* Ed. Armin Paul Frank and Helga Essmann. Göttingen: Wallstein, 1999. 166–78.

Hinchman, Lewis and Sandra K. Hinchman, eds. *Memory, Identity, Community: The Idea of Narrative in the Human Sciences.* Albany: State U of New York P, 1997.

Hine, Darlene Clark, and Jacqueline McLeod, eds. *Crossing Boundaries: Comparative History of Black People in Diaspora.* Bloomington: Indiana UP, 1999.

Hobsbawm, E. J. *Nations and Nationalism since 1780: Programme, Myth, Reality.* Cambridge: Cambridge UP, 1995.

Hollinger, David A. *Postethnic America: Beyond Multiculturalism.* New York: Basic Books, 1995.

Huff, Toby E. *The Rise of Early Modern Science: Islam, China, and the West.* Cambridge: Cambridge UP, 1993.

Hutcheon, Linda, Djelal Kadir, and Mario Valdés. *Collaborative Historiography: A Comparative History of Latin America.* New York: American Council of Learned Societies, 1996.

Irwin, John T. *The Mystery to a Solution: Poe, Borges, and the Analytic Detective Story.* Baltimore: Johns Hopkins UP, 1994.

Jackson, Richard. "Remembering the 'Disremembered': Modern Black Writers and Slavery in Latin America." *Callaloo* 13.1 (1990): 131–44.

Jackson, Richard L. *The Black Image in Latin American Literature.* Albuquerque: U of New Mexico P, 1976.

Jackson, Richard L. *Black Literature and Humanism in Latin America.* Athens: U of Georgia P, 1988.

Jackson, Richard. *Black Writers and Latin America: Cross-Cultural Affinities.* Washington: Howard UP, 1998.

Jackson, Richard L. *Black Writers in Latin America.* Albuquerque: U of New Mexico P, 1979.

Jameson, Fredric. *The Cultures of Globalization.* Durham: Duke UP, 1998.

Janik, Dieter. *Stationen der spanischamerikanischen Literatur- und Kulturgeschichte. Der Blick der anderen der Weg zu sich selbst.* Frankfurt: Vervuert, 1992.

Janik, Dieter. *Die Anfänge einer nationalen literarischen Kultur in Argentinien und Chile. Eine kontrastive Studie auf der Grundlage der frühen Periodika (1800–1830).* Tübingen: Narr, 1995.

Jay, Gregory. "The End of 'American' Literature: Toward a Multicultural Practice." *College English* 53 (1991): 264–268.

Jay, Paul. "The Myth of 'America' and the Politics of Location: Modernity, Border Studies, and the Literature of the Americas." *Arizona Quarterly* 54 (1998): 165–92.

Jehlen, Myra. *American Incarnation: The Individual, the Nation, and the Continent.* Cambridge: Harvard UP, 1986.

Jensen, John B. "On the Mutual Intelligibility of Spanish and Portuguese." *Hispania* 72.4 (1989): 848–52.

Jitrik, Noé. "De la historia a la escritura: predominios, disimetrías, acuerdos en la novela histórica latinoamericana." *The Historical Novel in Latin America.* Ed. Daniel Balderston. Gaithersburg: Hispamérica, 1986.

Jozef, Bella. *O Jogo Mágico.* Rio de Janeiro: José Olympio, 1980.

Kadir, Djelal. *Columbus and the Ends of the Earth.* Berkeley: U of California P, 1992.

Kadir, Djelal. "Neruda and Whitman: Short-Circuiting the Body Electric." *Pacific Coast Philology* 8 (1973): 16–22.

Kadir, Djelal. *The Other Writing: Postcolonial Essays in Latin America's Writing Culture.* West Lafayette: Purdue UP, 1993.

Kadir, Djelal. "The Posts of Coloniality." *Postcolonial Literatures: Theory and Practice / Les Littératures post-coloniales. Théories et réalisations.* Ed. Steven Tötösy de Zepetnek and Sneja Gunew. Thematic issue of *Canadian Review of Comparative Literature / Revue Canadienne de Littérature Comparée* 23.1 (1996): 431–42.

Kadir, Djelal. *Questing Fictions: Latin America's Family Romance.* Minneapolis: U of Minnesota P, 1986.

Kadir, Djelal. "The Survival of Theory and the Surviving Fictions of Latin America." *Modern Fiction Studies* 32.3 (1986): 383–96.

Kaminsky, Amy. *Reading the Body Politic: Feminist Criticism and Latin American Women Writers.* Minneapolis: U of Minnesota P, 1993.

Kelemen, Pal. *Art of the Americas, Ancient and Hispanic with a Comparative Chapter on the Philippines.* New York: Bonanza, 1969.

King, Bruce, ed. *New National and Post-Colonial Literatures: An Introduction.* Oxford: Clarendon, 1996.

Klobucka, Anna. "A intercomunicação homem/animal como meio de transformação do Eu em 'Axolotl' de Julio Cortázar e 'O búfalo' de Clarice Lispector." *Travessia* 14 (1987): 161–76.

König, Hans-Joachim, and Stefan Rinke. *Transatlantische Perzeptionen. Lateinamerika, USA, Europa in Geschichte und Gegenwart.* Stuttgart: Hans-Dieter Heinz, 1998.

Kowalczyk-Tarnowski, Kryzisztof. "Southern American Regional Sensibility versus the North." *Intercultural Negotiations in the Americas and Beyond.* Ed. Barbara Buchenau and Marietta Messmer. Thematic issue of *CLCWeb: Comparative Literature and Culture: A WWWeb Journal* 3.2 (2001): <http://clcwebjournal.lib.purdue.edu/clcweb012/kowalczyktwarowski01.html>.

Kramer, Sabine. *Lateinamerika schreiben. Zur Darstellung von kultureller Alterität in deutschen und lateinamerikanischen Texten.* Bern: Peter Lang, 2000.

Kristal, Efraín. "En torno a la historia del concepto de historia literaria hispanoamericana." *Teoría de la historia de la literatura y el arte.* Ed. Pedro Aullón de Haro. Alicante: U of Alicante, 1994. 195–209.

Kristal, Efraín. "Captive in the Wilderness: An Argentine Adaptation of an Anglo-Saxon Image." *The Internationality of National Literatures in Either America: Transfer and Transformation.* Vol. 1. *Cases and Problems.* Ed. Armin Paul Frank and Helga Essmann. Göttingen: Wallstein, 1999. 215–30.

Kroes, Rob, ed. *The American Identity: Fusion and Fragmentation.* Amsterdam: Amerika Instituut, U of Amsterdam, 1980.

Kushigian, Julia A. *Orientalism in the Hispanic Literary Tradition: In Dialogue with Borges, Paz, and Sarduy.* Alburquerque: U of New Mexico P, 1991.

Kutzinsky, Vera M. *Against the American Grain: Myth and History in William Carlos Williams, Jay Wright, and Nicolás Guillén.* Baltimore: Johns Hopkins UP, 1987.

Lamming, George. "Concepts of the Caribbean." *Frontiers of Caribbean Literature in English.* Ed. Frank Birbalsingh. London: Macmillan Caribbean, 1996. 1–14.

Lang, George. *Entwisted Tongues: Comparative Creole Literatures.* Amsterdam: Rodopi, 2000.

Lang, Hans-Joachim. "The Making of Henry James's *The American*: The Contribution of Four Literatures." *Amerikastudien / American Studies* 20.1 (1975): 55–71.

Lauterbach, Frank. "British Travel Writing about the Americas, 1820–1840: Different and Diffentiating Views." *Intercultural Negotiations in the Americas and Beyond.* Ed. Barbara Buchenau and Marietta Messmer. Thematic issue of *CLCWeb: Comparative Literature and Culture: A WWWeb Journal* 3.2 (2001): <http://clcwebjournal.lib.purdue.edu/clcweb01-2/lauterbach01.html>.

Larsen, Neil. *Determinations: Essays on Theory, Narrative and Nation in the Americas*. London: Verso, 2001.

Larsen, Neil. "Latin America: The View from Comparative Literature." *Ideologies and Literature* 4.16 (1983): 144–48.

Larsen, Neil. *Reading North by South: On Latin American Literature, Culture, and Politics.* Minneapolis: U of Minnesota P, 1995.

Lauter, Paul. "The Literatures of America: A Comparative Discipline." *Redefining American Literary History*. Ed. A. LaVonne Brown Ruoff and Jerry W. Ward. New York: MLA, 1990. 9–34.

Leal, Luis. "Native and Foreign Influences in Contemporary Mexican Fiction: A Search for Identity." *Tradition and Renewal: Essays on Twentieth Century Latin American Literature and Culture.* Ed. Merlin H. Forster. Urbana: U of Illinois P, 1974. 102–28.

Leavitt, S. E. *Hispano-American Literature in the United States.* Cambridge: Harvard UP, 1932.

León, Juana Ponce de. "Brazilian Authors, American Readers." *Publishers Weekly* (25 November 1988): 26.

Lester, James D., ed. *Diverse Identities: Classic Multicultural Essays.* Lincolnwood: NTC Publishing, 1996.

Levine, Daniel H. ed. *Constructing Culture and Power in Latin America.* Michigan: U of Michigan P, 1993.

Lienhard, Martin. "Of Mestizajes, Heterogeneities, Hybridisms and other Chimeras: On the Macroprocesses of Cultural Interaction in Latin America." *Journal of Latin American Cultural Studies* 6.2 (1997): 183–200.

Lienhard, Martin. "Kulturelle Heterogenität und Literatur in Lateinamerika." *Iberoamericana* 16.3–4 (1992): 95–110.

Levin, Harry. "Literature and Cultural Identity." *Comparative Literature Studies* 10.2 (1973): 139–56.

Levine, Susan F., and Stuart Levine. "Poe and Fuentes: The Reader's Prerogatives." *Comparative Literature* 36.1 (1984): 34–53.

Lindstrom, Naomi. *Women's Voices in Latin American Literature.* Washington: Three Continents P, 1989.

Lipp, Solomon. "The Popular Novel in Nineteenth-Century Latin America." *Canadian Review of Comparative Literature / Revue Canadienne de Littérature Comparée* 9.3 (1982): 406–23.

Lipset, Seymour Martin. *American Exceptionalism: A Double-Edged Sword.* New York: Norton, 1996.

Losada, Alejandro. "Internationalización de la literatura latinoamericana." *Caravelle* 42 (1984): 15–40.

Luis, William. *Dance between Two Cultures: Latino and Caribbean Literature Written in the United States.* Nashville: Vanderbilt UP, 1995.

Luzuriaga, Gerardo, ed. *Popular Theater for Social Change in Latin America.* Los Angeles: UCLA Latin American Center Publications, 1978.

Mac Adam, Alfred J. "Euclides da Cunha y Mario Vargas Llosa: Meditaciones Intertextuales." *Revista Iberoamericana* 50 (1984): 157–64.

Mac Adam, Alfred. *Modern Latin American Narratives: The Dreams of Reason.* Chicago: U of Chicago P, 1977.

Mac Adam, Alfred J. *Textual Confrontations: Comparative Readings in Latin American Literature.* Chicago: U of Chicago P, 1987.

MacShane, Frank, ed. *Impressions of Latin America: Five Centuries of Travel and Adventure by English and North American Writers.* New York: William Morrow, 1963.

Malamud, Randy. "The Culture of Using Animals in Literature and the Case of José Emilio Pacheco." *CLCWeb: Comparative Literature and Culture: A WWWeb Journal* 2.2 (2000): <http://clcwebjournal.lib.purdue.edu/clcweb00-2/malamud00.html>.

Maree, Cathy. "Theatre and the Struggle of Memory against Forgetting in Spain, Latin America and South Africa." *Journal of Literary Studies / Tydskrif vor Literaturwetenskap* 14.3–4 (1998): 299–321.

Martí, José. *The America of José Martí.* Trans. Juan del Onís. New York: Noon-day P, 1954.

Martí, José. *Martí on the U.S.A.* Trans. Luis A. Baralt. Carbondale: Southern Illinois UP, 1966.

Martí, José. *Our America.* Trans. Elinor Randall, Juan de Onís, and Roslyn Held Foner. Ed. Philip S. Foner. New York: Monthly Review P, 1977.

Martí, José. "El poeta Walt Whitman." *José Martí: Letras Fieras.* Ed. Roberto Retamar. Havana: Editorial Letras Cubanas, 1981. 494–506.

Martin, Gerald. *Journeys through the Labyrinth: Latin American Fiction in the Twentieth Century.* London: Verso, 1989.

Martin, Terence. "From Redskin to Redneck: Atrocity and Revenge in American Writing." *Intercultural Negotiations in the Americas and Beyond.* Ed. Barbara Buchenau and Marietta Messmer. Thematic issue of *CLCWeb: Comparative Literature and Culture: A WWWeb Journal* 3.2 (2001): <http://clcwebjournal.lib.purdue.edu/clcweb01-2/martin01.html>.

Martin, Terence. *Parables of Possibility: The American Need for Beginnings.* New York: Columbia UP, 1995.

Martínez Cuitiño, Luis and Elida Lois, eds. *Actas del III Congreso Argentino de Hispanistas "España en América y América en España."* Buenos Aires, Argentina: El Instituto, 1993.

McClennen, Sophia A. "Comparative Literature and Latin American Studies: From Disarticulation to Dialogue." *Comparative Cultural Studies and Latin America.* Ed. Sophia A. McClennen and Earl E. Fitz. West Lafayette: Purdue UP, 2004. 105–130.

McClennen, Sophia A. "Chilex: The Economy of Transnational Media Culture." *Cultural Logic: An E-Journal of Marxist Theory and Practice* 3.1 (2000): <http://eserver.org/clogic/3-1&2/mcclennen.html>.

McClennen, Sophia A. "Cultural Politics, Rhetoric, and the Essay: A Comparison of Emerson and Rodó." *CLCWeb: Comparative Literature and Culture: A WWWeb Journal* 2.1 (2000): <http://clcwebjournal.lib.purdue.edu/clcweb00-1/mcclennen00.html>.

McClendon, Carmen Chaves. "A Rose for Rosalina: From Yoknapatawpha to Opera dos Mortos." *Comparative Literature Studies* 9.4 (1982): 450–58.

Mead, Robert G., ed. *Iberoamérica, sus lenguas y literaturas vistas desde los Estados Unidos.* México: Ediciones de Andrea, 1962.

Mead, Robert. *Perspectivas interamericanas: literatura y libertad.* New York: Las Américas, 1967.

Megenney, William W. "The Black in Hispanic-Caribbean and Brazilian Poetry: A Comparative Perspective." *Revista/Review Interamericana* 5 (1975): 47–66.

Menton, Seymour. *La novela experimental y la república comprensiva de Hispanoamérica: estudio analítico y comparativo de Nostromo, Le Dictateur, Tirano Banderas y El señor Presidente.* Monterrey: Universidad de Nuevo León, 1960.

Merquior, J.G. "The Brazilian and the Spanish American Literary Traditions: A Comparative View." *The Cambridge History of Latin American Literature.* Ed. Roberto González Echevarría and Enrique Pupo-Walker. 3, 363–82.

Merrim, Stephanie. *Logos and the Word: The Novel of Language and Linguistic Motivation in "Grande Sertão: Veredas" and "Tres tristes tigres."* New York: Peter Lang, 1983.

Messmer, Marietta. "Twentieth-Century American Literary Historiography." *Intercultural Negotiations in the Americas and Beyond.* Ed. Barbara Buchenau and Marietta Messmer. Thematic issue of *CLCWeb: Comparative Literature and Culture: A WWWeb Journal* 3.2 (2001): <http://clcwebjournal.lib.purdue.edu/clcweb01-2/messmer01.html>.

Messmer, Marietta. "Reading National American Literary Historiography Internationally." Comparative Literature 52.3 (2000): 193–212.

Meyer, Doris, ed. *Reinterpreting the Spanish American Essay: Women Writers of the 19th and 20th Centuries.* Austin: U of Texas P, 1995.

Meyer, Doris. "Victoria Ocampo and Alfonso Reyes: Ulysses's Malady." *Studies in Twentieth Century Literature* 24.2 (2000): 307–24.

Meyer, Doris, ed. *Lives on the Line: The Testimony of Contemporary Latin American Authors.* Berkeley: U of California P, 1988.

Mignolo, Walter. *Local Histories / Global Designs: Coloniality, Subaltern Knowledges, and Border Thinking.* Princeton: Princeton UP, 2000.

Milz, Sabine. "Comparative Cultural Studies and Ethnic Minority Writing Today: The Hybridities of Marlene Nourbese Philip and Emine Sevgi Özdamar." *CLCWeb: Comparative Literature and Culture: A WWWeb*

Journal 2.2 (2000): <http://clcwebjournal.lib.purdue.edu/clcweb00-2/milz00.html>.

Moeller, Hans-Bernhard. *Latin America and the Literature of Exile: A Comparative View of the 20th-Century European Refugee Writers in the New World.* Heidelberg: Winter, 1983.

Molloy, Sylvia. "His America, Our America: José Martí Reads Whitman." *Modern Language Quarterly* 57.2 (1996): 369–79.

Montalvo, Juan. "Washington y Bolívar." 1882. *Voces de Hispanoamérica: Antologia Literaria.* Ed. Raquel Chang-Rodríguez and Malva E. Filer. Boston: Heinle & Heinle, 1988. 182–83.

Monteiro, George. "Emily Dickinson's Brazilian Poems." *Revista Inter-Americana de Bibliografia / Inter-American Review of Bibliography* 22.4 (1972): 404–10.

Morales, Mario Roberto. *La articulación de las diferencias o el Síndrome de Maximón (Los discursos literarios y políticos del debate interétnico en Guatemala).* Guatemala: FLACSO, 1998.

Moraga, C. and G. Anzaldúa, eds. *This Bridge Called My Back: Writings of Radical Women of Color.* Watertown: Persephone, 1981.

Moraña, Mabel, ed. *América Latina: agendas culturales para el nuevo siglo.* Pittsburgh: Instituto Internacional de Literatura Iberoamericana, 2000.

Moraña, Mabel, ed. *Angel Rama y los estudios latinoamericanos.* Pittsburgh: Instituto Internacional de Literatura Iberoamericana, 1997.

Moraña, Mabel, ed. *Indigenismo hacia el fin del milenio: Homenaje a Antonio Cornejo-Polar.* Pittsburgh: Instituto Internacional de Literatura Ibero-americana, 1998.

Moraña, Mabel, ed. *Nuevas perspectivas desde, sobre América Latina: el desafío de los estudios culturales.* Santiago: Editorial Cuarto Propio, 2000.

Moreiras, Alberto. "The Villain at the Center: Infrapolitical Borges." *Comparative Cultural Studies and Latin America.* Ed. Sophia A. McClennen and Earl E. Fitz. West Lafayette: Purdue UP, 2004. 131–48.

Moreiras, Alberto. "Elementos de articulación teórica para el subalternismo latinoamericano: Candido y Borges." *Revista Iberoamericana* 62.176–77 (1996): 875–91.

Moreiras, Alberto. *The Exhaustion of Difference: The Politics of Latin American Cultural Studies.* Durham: Duke UP, 2001.

Moreiras, Alberto. *Tercer espacio: Literatura y duelo en América Latina.* Santiago: U Arcis, LOM Ediciones, 1999.

Morejón, Nancy, and Victor Carrabino. "A Cuban Perspective: The Americas of Langston Hughes." Trans. Victor Carrabino. *The Langston Hughes Review* 6.1 (1987): 1–3.

Morency, Jean. "Forms of European Disconnection in Literature of the Americas." Trans. by Nicole Santilli and Barbara Godard. *Topia* 2 (1998): 11–21.

Morse, Richard M. *El espejo de Próspero: un estudio de la dialéctica del Nuevo Mundo.* México: Siglo Veintiuno Editores, 1999.

Morse, Richard M. *New World Soundings: Culture and Ideology in the Americas.* Baltimore: Johns Hopkins UP, 1989.

Morse, Richard. "Triangulating Two Cubists: William Carlos Williams and Oswald de Andrade." *The Latin American Literary Review* 14.27 (1986): 175–83.

Moss, Howard. "The Canada-Brazil Connection." *World Literature Today* 51.1 (1997): 29–33.

Mueller-Vollmer, Kurt. *Translating Literatures, Translating Cultures: New Vistas and Approaches in Literary Studies.* Berlin: Erich Schmidt, 1998.

Mueller-Vollmer, Kurt. "Regionalismus, Internationalismus, Nationalität: Amerikanischer Transcendentalismus und deutsche Romantik." *Kulturelle Grenzziehungen im Spiegel der Literatur.* Ed. Horst Turk, Brigitte Schulze, and Roberto Simanowski. Göttingen: Wallstein, 1998. 299–322.

Mueller-Vollmer, Kurt. "Übersetzungen aus dem Deutschen in den Vereinigten Staaten, 1820–1850. Versuch einer historischen Topographie." *Übersetzen, verstehen, Brücken bauen. Geisteswissenschaftliches Übersetzen im Internationalen Literaturaustausch.* Ed. Armin Paul Frank. Berlin: Schmidt, 1993. 816–33.

Mullen, Edward J. "European and North American Writers in *Contemporáneos*." *Comparative Literature Studies* 8.4 (1971): 338–48.

Nadeau, Carolyn. "Nicolás Guillén and Langston Hughes." *Aleph* 6 (1991): 4–15.

Nasta, Susheila, ed. *Motherlands: Black Women's Writing from Africa, the Caribbean and South Asia.* New Brunswick: Rutgers UP, 1992.

Neubauer, John. "Vargas Llosa's *La Ciudad y los perros* and the European Novel of Adolescence." *Intercultural Negotiations in the Americas and Beyond.* Ed. Barbara Buchenau and Marietta Messmer. Thematic issue of *CLCWeb: Comparative Literature and Culture: A WWWeb Journal* 3.2 (2001): <http://clcwebjournal.lib.purdue.edu/clcweb01-2/neubauer01.html>.

Nitrini, Sandra. *Literatura comparada: história, teoria e crítica.* São Paulo: Edusp, 2000.

Nitrini, Sandra. "La Littérature comparée au Brésil. Un fragment de son histoire." *Comparative Literature: History and Contemporaneity / Littérature Comparée. Histoire et contemporanéité.* Ed. Milan V. Dimic and Steven Tötösy de Zepetnek. *Canadian Review of Comparative Literature / Revue Canadienne de Littérature Comparée* 23.1 (1996): 75–90.

Nitrini, Sandra. "Teoria literária e literatura comparada." *Revista Estudos Avancados.* 22 (1994): <http://www.usp.br/iea/revista/>.

Nunes, Cassiano. "The Characteristics of Modern Poetry in Brazil." *Comparative Literature Studies* 5.1 (1968): 21–39.

Nuñes, Estuardo. "Literatura comparada en Hispanoamérica." *Comparative Literature Studies* 1 (1964): 41–45.

Núñez, Eduardo. "Franklin en Hispanoamérica." *Cuadernos Americanos* 88.4 (1956): 155–68.

Núñez, Eduardo. "Herman Melville en la América." *Cuadernos Americanos* 68.2 (1953): 209–21.

Núñez, Eduardo. "Literatura Comparada en Hispanoamérica." *Comparative Literature Studies* 1.1 (1964): 41–45.

Núñez, Eduardo. "El poeta Chocano en Nueva York." *Cuadernos Americanos* 75.3 (1954): 292–98.

Oberhelman, Harley. *The Presence of Faulkner in the Writings of García Márquez.* Lubbock: Texas Tech UP, 1980.

Oberhelman, Harley. *The Presence of Hemingway in the Short Fiction of Gabriel García Márquez.* Fredericton: York P, 1994.

Oberhelman, Harley. *García Márquez and Cuba: A Study of its Presence in His Fiction, Journalism, and Cinema.* Fredericton: York P, 1995.

O'Gorman, Edmundo. "Do the Americas Have a Common History?" *Points of View* 3 (1941).

O'Gorman, Edmundo. *La invención de América.* México: Fondo de Cultura Económica, 1958.

Onís, José de. "Literatura Comparada como disciplina literaria." *Cuadernos* 56 (1962): 63–69.

Ortega, Julio. "Towards a Map of the Current Critical Debate about Latin American Cultural Studies." *Comparative Cultural Studies and Latin America.* Ed. Sophia A. McClennen and Earl E. Fitz. West Lafayette: Purdue UP, 2004. 149–58.

Ortega, Julio. "Borges sobre el Quijote: Una conferencia recobrada." *Insula—Revista de Letras y Ciencias Humanas* 631–632 (1999): 3–5.

Ortega, Julio. "Diez novelas hispanoamericanas del XX." *Inti: Revista de Literatura Hispanica* 48 (1998): 47–52.

Ortega, Julio. *El discurso de la abundancia.* Caracas: Monte Ávila, 1992.

Ortega, Julio. "Identity, Diversity, and the Humanities." *La Torre: Revista de la Universidad de Puerto Rico* 4.12 (1999): 469–76.

Ortega, Julio. "La lectura en Mexico." *Cuadernos Hispanoamericanos* 617 (2001):109–12.

Ortega, Julio. *Poetics of Change: The New Spanish American Narrative.* Austin: U of Texas P, 1984.

Ortega, Julio. "Postmodernism in Spanish-American Writing." *International Postmodernism.* Ed. Hans Bertens and Douwe Fokkema. Amsterdam: John Benjamins, 1997. 315–26.

Ortega, Julio. *El principio radical de lo nuevo: Postmodernidad, Identidad y Novela en América Latina.* Lima: Fondo de Cultura Económica, 1997.

Ortiz, Fernando. *Contrapunteo cubano del tabaco y azúcar.* Caracas: Biblioteca Ayacucho, 1987.

Owens, Louis. *Other Destinies: Understanding the American Indian Novel.* Norman: U of Oklahoma P, 1994.

Paatz, Annette. "The Socio-Cultural Function of Media in Nineteenth-Century Latin America." *Intercultural Negotiations in the Americas and Beyond.* Ed. Barbara Buchenau and Marietta Messmer. Thematic issue of *CLCWeb: Comparative Literature and Culture: A WWWeb Journal* 3.2 (2001): <http://clcwebjournal.lib.purdue.edu/clcweb01-2/paatz01.html>.

Palencia-Roth, Michael. "Cannibalism and the New Man of Latin America in the 15th- and 16th-Century European Imagination." *Comparative Civilizations Review* 12 (1985): 1–27.

Palencia-Roth, Michael. "Comparing Literature, Comparing Civilizations." *Comparative Civilizations Review* 21 (1989): 1–19.

Palencia-Roth, Michael. "Contrastive Literature." *ACLA: American Comparative Literature Association Bulletin* 24.2 (1993): 47–60.

Palermo, Zulma. "Cultural Articulation of the Comparative Literary Studies: The Argentinian Case." *Comparative Literature World Wide: Issues and Methods / La Littérature comparée dans le monde: Questions et méthodes*. Ed. Tânia Franco Carvalhal. Porto Alegre: L&PM Editores, 1997. 211–31.

Paolucci, Anne. "Multinational Literature and Integration into Existing Programs." *Geolinguistic Perspectives.* Ed. Jesse Levitt. Lanham: UP of America, 1987. 195–202.

Paolucci, Anne. "Multi-Comparative Literary Perspectives." *Comparative Literary Theory: New Perspectives.* Ed. Anne Paolucci. *Review of National Literatures* 15. New York: Griffon House Publications, 1989. 1–29.

Patán, Federico. "No Country Is an Island: Some Aspects of American Literature in Mexico." *As Others Read Us: International Perspectives on American Literature*. Ed. Huck Gutman. Amherst: U of Massachusetts P, 1991. 176–88.

Payne, Johnny. *Conquest of the New Word: Experimental Fiction and Translation in the Americas.* Austin: U of Texas P, 1993.

Payne, Judith A., and Earl E. Fitz. *Ambiguity and Gender in the New Novel of Brazil and Spanish America: A Comparative Assessment.* Iowa City: U of Iowa P, 1993.

Paz, Octavio. *The Labyrinth of Solitude.* Trans. Lysander Kemp. New York: Grove P, 1961.

Paz, Octavio. "A Literature of Foundations." Trans. Lysander Kemp. *The TriQuarterly Anthology of Contemporary Latin American Literature.* Ed. José Donoso and William Henkin. New York: Dutton, 1969. 2–8.

Paz, Octavio. *The Other Mexico.* Trans. Lysander Kemp. New York: Grove P, 1972.

Paz, Octavio. "Reflections: Mexico and the United States." *New Yorker* (17 September 1979): 136–53.

Peavler, Terry J. "Guillermo Cabrera Infante's Debt to Ernest Hemingway." *Hispania* 62 (May–December 1979): 289–96.

Peden, Margaret Sayers. "Knopf, Knopf: Who's There?" *Translation Review* 50 (1996): 27–30.

Peden, Margaret Sayers. "Translating the Boom: The Apple Theory of Translation." *Latin American Literary Review* 15.29 (1987): 159–72.

Peixoto, Afranio. "American Social and Literary Influences in Brazil." *Books Abroad* 9.2 (1935): 3–5; 9.3 (1935): 127–29.

Peixoto, Afrânio. *Noções da História da Literatura Brasileira.* Rio de Janeiro: F. Alves, 1931.

Pereira, Teresinha Alves. "Coincidencia de la técnica de Julio Cortázar y Clarice Lispector." *Nueva Narrativa Hispanoamericana.* 3.1 (1973): 103–11.

Pérez de Mendiola, Marina, ed. *Bridging the Atlantic Toward a Reassessment of Iberian and Latin American Cultural Ties.* New York: State U of New York P, 1996.

Pérez Firmat, Gustavo, ed. *Do the Americas Have a Common Literature?* Durham: Duke UP, 1990.

Perrone, Charles A. *Seven Faces: Brazilian Poetry Since Modernism.* Durham: Duke UP, 1996.

Pescatello, Ann M. *Power and Pawn: The Female in Iberian Families, Societies, and Cultures.* Westport: Greenwood P, 1976.

Phillips, Lynne, and Judith Ewell, eds. *The Third Wave of Modernization in Latin America: Cultural Perspectives on Neoliberalism.* Wilmington: Scholarly Resources, 1998.

Pike, Frederick B. *The United States and Latin America: Myths and Stereotypes of Civilization and Nature.* Austin: U of Texas P, 1992.

Pizarro, Ana. "Sobre las direcciones del Comparatismo en la America Latina." *Casa de Las Americas* 135 (1982): 40–49.

Pratt, Mary Louise. "Comparative Literature as a Cultural Practice." *Profession 1986: The Modern Language Association of America* (1986): 33–35.

Pratt, Mary Louise. "Comparative Literature and Global Citizenship." *Comparative Literature in the Age of Multiculturalism.* Ed. Charles Bernheimer. Baltimore: Johns Hopkins UP, 1995. 58–65.

Pratt, Mary Louise. *Imperial Eyes: Studies in Travel Writing and Transculturation.* London: Routledge, 1992.

Putnam, Samuel. *Marvelous Journey: A Survey of Four Centuries of Brazilian Writing.* New York: Knopf, 1948.

Raab, Josef. "El gran viejo: Walt Whitman in Latin America." *Intercultural Negotiations in the Americas and Beyond.* Ed. Barbara Buchenau and Marietta Messmer. Thematic issue of *CLCWeb: Comparative Literature and Culture: A WWWeb Journal* 3.2 (2001): <http://clcwebjournal.lib.purdue.edu/clcweb01-2/raab01.html>.

Rabassa, Gregory. "A Comparative Look at the Literatures of Spanish America and Brazil: The Dangers of Deception." *Ibero-American Letters in a Comparative Perspective.* Ed. W.T. Zyla and W.M. Aycock. Lubbock: Texas Tech UP, 1978. 119–32.

Rama, Angel. *La cuidad letrada.* Hanover: Ediciones del Norte, 1984.

Rama, Angel. *Transculturación narrativa en América Latina.* Montevideo: Fundación Angel Rama, 1989.

Ramirez, Susan E., ed. *Indian-Religious Relations in Colonial Spanish America.* Syracuse: Syracuse UP, 1989.

Reising, Russell. *The Unusable Past: Theory and the Study of American Literature.* New York: Methuen, 1986.

Robles, Mercedes. "La presencia de The Wild Palms de William Faulkner in Punta de rieles de Manuel Rojas." *Revista Iberoamericana* 45.108–09 (1979): 563–71.

Rodó, José Enrique. *Ariel*. Trans. Margaret Sayers Peden. Austin: U of Texas P, 1988.

Rodríguez Monegal, Emir. *El Boom de la novela latinoamericana*. Caracas: Editorial Tiempo Nuevo, 1972.

Rodríguez Monegal, Emir. "Carnaval, Antropofagía, Parodia." *Revista iberoamericana* 45.108–109 (1979): 401–12.

Rodríguez Monegal, Emir. "The Integration of Latin American Literatures." *Proceedings of the Eighth Congress of the ICLA: International Comparative Literature Association*. Ed. Béla Köpeczi and György M. Vajda. Stuttgart: Erich Bieber, 1980. 2, 111–16.

Rodríguez Monegal, Emir. *Narradores de esta América*. Buenos Aires: Alfa, 1969. 2 vols.

Rodríguez Monegal, Emir. "The New Latin American Literature in the USA." *Review '68*. New York: The Center for Inter-American Relations, 1969. 3–13.

Rojo, Grinor. *Crítica del exilio: Ensayos sobre literatura latino-americana actual*. Santiago de Chile: Pehuén, 1987.

Romera-Navarro, Miguel. *El hispanismo en Norte-América: exposición y crítica de su aspecto literario*. Madrid: Renacimiento, 1917.

Rössner, Michael, ed. *Lateinamerikanische Literaturgeschichte*. Stuttgart: Metzler, 1995.

Rudnyckyj, J. B. "Canadian and Argentine-Brasilian Novels on Ukrainian Pioneers." *Proceedings of the Seventh Congress of the ICLA: International Comparative Literature Association*. Ed. Béla Köpeczi and György M. Vajda. Stuttgart: Erich Bieber, 1979. 1, 295–99.

Running, Thorpe. *The Critical Poem: Borges, Paz, and Other Language-Centered Poets in Latin America*. London: Associated UP, 1996.

Sadow, Stephen A., ed. *King David's Harp: Autobiographical Essays by Jewish Latin American Writers*. Albuquerque: U of New Mexico P, 1999.

Sagrera, Martín. *Los racismos en las Américas*. Madrid: IEPALA, 1998.

Said, Edward W. *Culture and Imperialism*. New York: Knopf, 1992.

Saldívar, José David. *Border Matters: Remapping American Cultural Studies*. Berkeley: U of California P, 1997.

Saldívar, José David. "The Limits of Cultural Studies." *American Literary History* 2.2 (1990): 251–66.

Saldívar, José David. *The Dialectics of Our America: Genealogy, Cultural Critique, and Literary History*. Durham: Duke UP, 1991.

Sánchez, Luis Alberto. *Historia comparada de las literaturas americanas*. Buenos Aires: Losada, 1974. 4 vols.

Santiago, Silviano. *Latin American Literature: The Space In Between.* Trans. by Stephen Moscov. Buffalo: State U of New York at Buffalo and the Council on International Studies, 1973.

Santiago, Silviano. *The Space In-Between: Essays on Latin American Culture.* Trans. Ana Lucia Gazzola. Durham: Duke UP, 2002.

Sayers, Raymond. "Contemporary Brazilian Criticism." *Comparative Literature Studies* 1.4 (1964): 287–304.

Scharlau, Birgit, ed. *Lateinamerika denken. Kulturtheoretische Grenzgänge zwischen Moderne und Postmoderne*. Tübingen: Narr, 1995.

Schipper, Mineke. Towards an Intercultural Comparative Study of Critical Texts." *Toward a Theory of Comparative Literature.* Ed. Mario J. Valdés. New York: Peter Lang, 1990. 195–208.

Schipper, M., ed. *Unheard Words: Women and Literature in Africa, the Arab World, Asia, the Caribbean and Latin America.* London: Alison and Busby, 1985.

Schulman, Ivan A. "Social Exorcisms: Cuba's (Post)Colonial (Counter) Discourse." *Hispania* 75.4 (1992): 941–49.

Sedycias, João. *The Naturalistic Novel of the New World: A Comparative Study of Stephen Crane, Aluísio Azevedo, and Federico Gamboa.* Lanham: UP of America, 1993.

Seed, Patricia. "Colonial and Postcolonial Discourse." *Latin American Research Review* 26.3 (1991): 181–200.

Seed, Patricia. "More Colonial and Postcolonial Discourses." *Latin American Research Review* 28.3 (1993): 146–52.

Seixo, Maria-Alzira, Graca Abreu, John Noyes, and Isabel Moutinho, eds. *The Paths of Multiculturalism: Travel Writings and Postcolonialism.* Lisboa: Cosmos, 2000.

Senst, Angela M. "Regional and National Identities in Robert Frost's and T.S. Eliot's Criticism." *Intercultural Negotiations in the Americas and Beyond.* Ed. Barbara Buchenau and Marietta Messmer. Thematic issue of *CLCWeb: Comparative Literature and Culture: A WWWeb Journal* 3.2 (2001): <http://clcwebjournal.lib.purdue.edu/clcweb01-2/senst02.html>.

Shohat, Ella, and Robert Stam, eds. *Unthinking Eurocentrism: Multiculturalism and the Media.* London: Routledge, 1994.

Shouldice, Larry. "Wide Latitudes: Comparing New World Literature." *Canadian Review of Comparative Literature / Revue Canadienne de la Littérature Comparée* 9 (1982): 46–55.

Simpson, Amelia S. *Detective Fiction from Latin America.* Cranbury: Fairleigh Dickinson UP, 1990.

Sims, Robert L. "The Question of History and the Postmodern Debate in Latin America." *The Comparatist: Journal of the Southern Comparative Literature Association* 22 (1998): 145–67.

Slater, Candace. "Brazil in the Poetry of Elizabeth Bishop." *World Literature Today* 15.1 (1977): 33–36.

Slatta, Richard W. *Comparing Cowboys and Frontiers.* Norman: U of Oklahoma P, 1997.

Smith, Paul Julian. *The Body Hispanic.* New York: Oxford UP, 1989.

Smith, Peter H. *Latin America in Comparative Perspective: New Approaches to Methods and Analysis.* Boulder: Westview P, 1995.

Sollors, Werner, ed. *Multilingual America: Transnationalism, Ethnicity, and the Languages of American Literature.* New York: New York UP, 1998.

Sollors, Werner. *Beyond Multiculturalism.* Berlin: John F. Kennedy Institut fur Nordamerikastudien, 1997.

Sollors, Werner. *Theories of Ethnicity: A Classical Reader.* New York: New York UP, 1996.

Sollors, Werner. *Beyond Ethnicity: Consent and Descent in American Culture.* Oxford: Oxford UP, 1986.

Sommer, Doris. *Foundational Fictions: The National Romances of Latin America.* Berkeley: U of California P, 1991.

Sommer, Doris. *Proceed With Caution, When Engaged by Minority Writing in the Americas.* Cambridge: Harvard UP, 1999.

Sommer, Doris, ed. *The Places of History: Regionalism Revisited in Latin America.* Durham: Duke UP, 1999.

Sousa, Ronald W. "Re-evaluation of Luso-American Popular Literature." *New Canadian Review* 2.1 (1989–90): 47–63.

Spencer, Sharon. *Space, Time and Structure in the Modern Novel.* New York: New York UP, 1971.

Spillers, Hortense J., ed. *Comparative American Identities: Race, Sex, and Nationality in the Modern Text.* New York: Routledge, 1991.

Spitta, Silvia. *Between Two Waters: Narratives of Transculturation in Latin America.* Houston: Rice UP, 1995.

Stam, Robert. *Tropical Multiculturalism: A Comparative History of Race in Brazilian Cinema and Culture.* Durham: Duke UP, 1997.

Stavans, Ilan. *The Hispanic Condition: Reflections on Culture and Identity in America.* New York: Harper Collins, 1995.

Steele, Cynthia. "The Fiction of National Formation: The 'indigenista' Novels of James Fennimore Cooper and Rosario Castellanos." *Reinventing the Americas: Comparative Studies of Literature of the United States and Spanish America*. Ed. Bell Gale Chevigny and Gari Laguardia. Cambridge: Cambridge UP, 1986. 60–67.

Sterne, Richard C. "Hawthorne Transformed: Octavio Paz's 'La hija de Rappaccini.'" *Comparative Literature Studies* 13.3 (1976): 230–39.

Stoddard, Ellwyn R. *Comparative U.S.–Mexico Border Studies*. El Paso: Border-State U Consortium for Latin America, 1970.

Tannenbaum, Frank. *Slave and Citizen: The Negro in the Americas*. New York: Random House, 1946.

Taylor, Diana, and Juan Villegas, eds. *Negotiating Performance: Gender Sexuality and Theatricality in Latin America*. Durham: Duke UP, 1994.

Taylor, Patrick. *The Narrative of Liberation: Perspectives on Afro-Caribbean Literature, Popular Culture, and Politics*. Ithaca: Cornell UP, 1989.

Tiburski, João Carlos, ed. *Continente Sul/Sur* 1 (1996): 1–252.

Todorov, Tzvetan. *The Conquest of America*. Trans. by Richard Howard. New York: Harper and Row, 1987.

Tourino, Christina Marie. "Anxieties of Impotence: Cubans in New York City." *Comparative Cultural Studies and Latin America*. Ed. Sophia A. McClennen and Earl E. Fitz. West Lafayette: Purdue UP, 2004. 159–77.

Tötösy de Zepetnek, Steven. "From Comparative Literature Today toward Comparative Cultural Studies." *Comparative Literature and Comparative Cultural Studies*. Ed. Steven Tötösy de Zepetnek. West Lafayette: Purdue UP, 2003. 235–67.

Tötösy de Zepetnek, Steven. "From Comparative Literature Today toward Comparative Cultural Studies." *CLCWeb: Comparative Literature and Culture: A WWWeb Journal* 1.3 (1999): <http://clcwebjournal.lib.purdue.edu/clcweb99-3/totosy99.html>.

Umphrey, George U. "Spanish American Literature Compared with That of the United States." *Hispania* 26 (1943): 21–34.

Valdés, María Elena de. "Guadalupana Syncretism and Postcolonial Literature in Mexico." *Postcolonial Literatures: Theory and Practice / Les Littératures post-coloniales. Théories et réalisations*. Ed. Steven Tötösy de Zepetnek and Sneja Gunew. Thematic issue of *Canadian Review of Comparative Literature / Revue Canadienne de Littérature Comparée* 22.3–4 (1995): 729–44.

Valdés, María Elena de, Mario J Valdés, and Richard A Young, eds. *Latin America as Its Literature*. Whitestone: Council on National Literatures, 1995.

Valdés, Mario J. "A Historical Account of Difference: A Comparative History of the Literary Cultures of Latin America." *Comparative Cultural*

Studies and Latin America. Ed. Sophia A. McClennen and Earl E. Fitz. West Lafayette: Purdue UP, 2004. 178–97.

Valdés, Mario J. "Collaborative Historiography: A Comparative Literary History of Latin America." *Neohelicon: Acta Comparationis Litterarum Universarum* 24.2 (1997): 85–93.

Valdés, Mario J. "Cultural Intertext as an Alternative to the Concept of National Literatures." *Differential Multilogue: Comparative Literrature and National Literatures*. Ed. Gurbhagat Singh. Delhi: Ajanta, 1991. 79–88.

Valdés, Mario J. "From Geography to Poetry: A Braudelian Comparative Literary History of Latin America." *La Formation de l'imagination / Constructing the Imagination*. Ed. Mario J. Valdés. Thematic cluster of *Canadian Review of Comparative Literature / Revue Canadienne de Littérature Comparée* 23.1 (1996): 199–205.

Valdés, Mario J. "Hermenéutica de la representación fílmica de la mujer: *La Regenta, ¿Qué he hecho yo para merecer esto? y Danzón*." *Revista Canadiense de Estudios Hispánicos* 20.1 (1995): 69–80.

Valdés, Mario J. "The Hermeneutics of Historical and Literary Remembering." *La Torre: Revista de la Universidad de Puerto Rico*. 2.4–5 (1997): 209–22.

Valdés, Mario J. *Hermeneutics of Poetic Sense: Critical Studies of Literature, Cinema, and Cultural History*. Toronto: U of Toronto P, 1998.

Valdés, Mario J. *La interpretación abierta: Introducción a la hermenéutica literaria Contemporánea*. Amsterdam: Rodopi, 1995.

Valdés, Mario J. "Relational Literary Theory and Comparative Literary History." *Neohelicon: Acta Comparationis Litterarum Universarum* 13.2 (1986): 45–60.

Valdés, Mario J., ed. *Toward a Theory of Comparative Literature*. New York: Peter Lang, 1990.

Valdés, Mario J. "Why Comparative Literary History?" *Comparative Literary History as Discourse*. Ed. Mario J. Valdés, Daniel Javitch, and A. Owen Aldridge. Bern: Peter Lang, 1992. 3–20.

Valdés, Mario J. *World-Making: The Literary Truth-Claim and the Interpretation of Texts*. Toronto: U of Toronto P, 1992.

Valdés, Mario J., and Linda Hutcheon. *Rethinking Literary History Comparatively*. New York: American Council of Learned Societies, 1995.

Valdés, Mario J., and Djelal Kadir, eds. *The Oxford Comparative History of Latin American Literary Cultures*. New York: Oxford UP, 2000–03. 3 vols.

Valdés, Mario J., and Owen Miller, eds. *The Identity of the Literary Text.* Toronto: U of Toronto P, 1985.

Valdés-Cruz, Rosa E. *La poesía negroide en América.* New York: Las Américas Publishing Company, 1970.

Vargas Llosa, Mario. *Making Waves.* Trans. John King. New York: Farrar, Straus & Giroux, 1997.

Vargas-Llosa, Mario. *A Writer's Reality.* Ed. Myron I. Lichtblau. Syracuse: Syracuse UP, 1991.

Vega-González, Susana. "Memory and the Quest for Family History in *One Hundred Years of Solitude* and *Song of Solomon.*" *CLCWeb: Comparative Literature and Culture: A WWWeb Journal* 3.1 (2001): <http://clcwebjournal.lib.purdue.edu/clcweb01-1/vega-gonzalez01.html>.

Véliz, Claudio. *The New World of the Gothic Fox: Culture and Economy in English and Spanish America.* Berkeley: U of California P, 1994.

Veríssimo, José. *Cultura, literatura e política na América Latina.* Ed. João Alexandre Barbosa. São Paulo: Brasiliense, 1986.

Vidal, Hernan. "The Concept of Colonial and Postcolonial Discourse: A Perspective from Literary Criticism." *Latin American Research Review* 28.3 (1993): 113–19.

Vidal, Hernan, ed. *Cultural and Historical Grounding for Hispanic and Luso-Brazilian Feminist Literary Criticism.* Minneapolis: Institute for the Study of Ideologies and Literature, 1989.

Villegas, Juan. *Para la interpretación del teatro como construcción visual.* Irvine: Ediciones de GESTOS, 2000.

Walcott, Derek. "The Caribbean: Culture or Mimicry?" *Journal of Inter-American Studies and World Affairs* 16, no. 1 (1974): 3–13.

Wasserman, Renata R. Mautner. *Exotic Nations: Literature and Culture in the United States and Brazil, 1830–1930.* Ithaca: Cornell UP, 1994.

Wasserman, Renata R. Mautner. "Mario Vargas Llosa, Euclides da Cunha, and the Strategies of Intertextuality." *PMLA* 108.3 (1993): 460–73.

Wasserman, Renata R. Mautner. "Re-Inventing the New World: Cooper and Alencar." *Comparative Literature* 36.2 (1984): 130–45.

Watters, R. E. "A Quest for National Identity: Canadian Literature vis-à-vis the Literature of Great Britain and the United States." *Proceedings of the Third Congress of the ICLA: International Comparative Literature Association.* Ed. W.A.P. Smit. Gravenhage: Mouton, 1962. 224–41.

Ween, Lori. "Family Sagas of the Americas: *Los Sangurimas* and *A Thousand Acres.*" *The Comparatist: Journal of the Southern Comparative Literature Association* 20 (1996): 111–25.

Weiner, Deborah. "Difference That Kills / Difference That Heals: Representing Latin America in the Poetry of Elizabeth Bishop and Margaret Atwood." *Comparative Literature East and West: Traditions and Trends.* Ed. Cornelia Moore and Raymond A. Moody. Honolulu: U of Hawaii P, 1989. 208–19

Wellek, René. *The Attack on Literature and Other Essays.* Chapel Hill: The U of North Carolina P, 1982.

Welsch, Wolfgang. "Transculturality: The Changing Form of Cultures Today." *The Internationality of National Literatures in Either America: Transfer and Transformation.* Vol. 1. *Cases and Problems.* Ed. Armin Paul Frank and Helga Essmann.Göttingen: Wallstein, 1999. 287–308.

West, Cornel. *Beyond Eurocentrism and Multiculturalism.* Monroe: Common Courage-P, 1993. 2 Vols.

Whitlock, Gillian. "From Prince to Lorde. The Politics of Location in Caribbean Autobiography." *History of Literature in the Caribbean.* Ed. A. James Arnold. Vol. 3. Amsterdam: John Benjamins, 1997. 325–38.

Williams, Stanley T. *The Spanish Background of American Literature.* New Haven: Yale UP, 1955. 2 vols.

Williams, William Carlos. *In the American Grain.* New York: Albert and Charles Boni, 1925.

Wilson, Robert Rawdon. "On the Boundary of the Magic and the Real: Notes on Inter-American Fiction." *Compass* 6 (1979): 37–53.

Wing, Adrien Katherine, ed. *Global Critical Race Feminism: An International Reader.* New York: New York UP, 2000.

Zamora, Lois Parkinson. "'A Garden Inclosed': Fuentes' *Aura*, Hawthorne's and Paz's 'Rappaccini's Daughter,' and Uyeda's *Ugetsu Monogatari.*" *Revista canadiense de estudios hispanicos* 8 (1984): 321–34.

Zamora, Lois Parkinson. "Magical Romance / Magical Realism: Ghosts in U.S. and Latin American Fiction." *Magical Realism: Theory, History, Community.* Ed. Lois Parkinson Zamora and Wendy B. Faris. Durham: Duke UP, 1995. 497–550.

Zamora, Lois Parkinson. "Quetzalcóatl's Mirror: Reflections on the Photographic Image in Latin America." *Image and Memory: Photography from Latin America 1866–1994.* Ed. Wendy Watriss and Lois Parkinson Zamora. Austin: U of Texas P, 1998. 300–84.

Zamora, Lois Parkinson. *Writing the Apocalypse: Historical Vision in Contemporary U.S. and Latin American Fiction.* Cambridge: Cambridge UP, 1989.

Zamora, Lois Parkinson. *The Usable Past: The Idea of History in Modern U.S. and Latin American Fiction.* Durham: Duke UP, 1990.

Zamora, Lois Parkinson, and Wendy B. Faris, eds. *Magical Realism: Theory, History, Community.* Durham: Duke UP, 1995.

Zapf, Hubert. "National Literary Historiography from a Transnational Perspective: On the Conception of the *Amerikanische Literaturgeschichte* (Metzler, 1997)." *REAL: Yearbook of Research in English and American Literature.* Ed. Brook Thomas. Tübingen: Narr, 1998. 287–315.

Zapf, Hubert, ed. *Amerikanische Literaturgeschichte.* Stuttgart: Metzler, 1997.

Zavala, Iris M. *Colonialism and Culture: Hispanic Modernisms and the Social Imaginary.* Bloomington: Indiana UP, 1992.

Zubizarreta, John. "Darío, Stevens, and Paz: The Modernist Connection." *South Atlantic Review* 56.1 (1991): 47–60.

Zyla, Wolodymyr T., and Wendell M. Aycock, eds. *Ibero-American Letters in a Comparative Perspective.* Lubbbock: Texas Tech UP, 1978.

Contributors

Gene H. Bell-Villada teaches Romance languages at Williams College, Massachusetts. His many publications encompass various genres of writing, including literary essays, general-interest criticism, political polemic, satires, short stories, and a novel. His books include *Borges and His Fiction: A Guide to His Mind and Art* (1981, 2000), *García Márquez: The Man and His Work* (1990), *The Carlos Chadwick Mystery: A Novel of College Life and Political Terror* (1990), and *The Pianist Who Liked Ayn Rand: A Novella and Thirteen Stories* (1998). His *Art for Art's Sake and Literary Life: How Politics and Markets Helped Shape the Ideology and Culture of Aestheticism, 1790–1990* was a 1997 National Book Critics Circle Award finalist.

Email: <gene.h.bell-villada@williams.edu>

Gordon Brotherston (<http://www.stanford.edu/dept/span-port/people/faculty/jgbrothe/>) teaches in the Department of Spanish and Portuguese at Stanford University. After receiving his doctorate from Cambridge University in 1965, he taught at King's College, London, and then at the new University of Essex, where he was involved with the Department of Literature and the Latin American program. He has since held posts at universities in the United States, Canada, Mexico, and Brazil. He has published over ten books and more than 120 articles and has lectured throughout Europe and the Americas, as well as in North Africa, Hong Kong, and Australia. His research and teaching interests include the cumulative history of Native and later American literature, the Mexican codices, and the intellectual interface between the Old and New Worlds, poetry and narrative in Latin America, and translation.

Email: <jgbrothe@stanford.edu>

Elizabeth Coonrod Martínez teaches Spanish and Latin American literatures at Sonoma State University. Her research interests include the nature of the intersection between literature and culture and the relation between gender and artistic identities. Coonrod Martínez's publications include "Recovering a Space for a History Between Imperialism and Patriarchy" in *Thamyris* (1998) and "Crossing Gender Borders: Sexual Relations and Chicana Artistic Identity" in *Melus: The Journal of the Society for the Study of the Multi-Ethnic Literature of the United States* (2002), and her book, *Before the Boom: Latin American Revolutionary Novels of the 1920s*, was published in 2001.

Email: <elizabeth.martinez@sonoma.edu>

Lúcia de Sá (<http://www.stanford.edu/dept/span-port/people/faculty/lusa/ index.html>) teaches in the Department of Spanish and Portuguese at Stanford University. She holds a B.A. and an M.A. from Universidade de São Paulo, Brazil, and a Ph.D. from Indiana University. Her research interests include the intertextual relationships between indigenous narratives and twentieth-century literature in Brazil and Spanish America, the literary shaping of a national discourse in Brazil, discourses of identity in Latin America, Brazilian avant-garde poetry, and Brazilian popular culture. Sá's new book, *Reading the Rain Forest: Indigenous Texts and their Impact on Brazilian and Spanish American Literatures* (University of Minnesota Press, 2004), is forthcoming, and she has published articles on Brazilian poetry and fiction, Peruvian fiction, censorship in Brazil, and Brazilian popular culture.

Email: <lusa@stanford.edu>

Román de la Campa (<http://www.sunysb.edu/hispanic/faculty.htm#roman>) teaches Latin American and comparative literature at the State University of New York, Stony Brook, where he also chairs the Department of Hispanic Languages and Literature and the Program in New American Studies. De la Campa has published numerous books and articles in the United States, Latin America, and Europe, including *Late Imperial Cultures,* co-edited with Michael Sprinker and Ann Kaplan (1995), *America Latina y sus comunidades discursivas: Literatura y cultura en la era global* (1998), *Latin Americanism* (1999), and *Cuba on My Mind: Journeys to a Severed Nation* (2000).

Email: <rvdelacampa@notes.cc.sunysb.edu>

Earl E. Fitz (<http://www.vanderbilt.edu/AnS/spanport/fitz.htm>) teaches Portuguese, Spanish, and comparative literature at Vanderbilt University, where he is also director of Vanderbilt's Program in Comparative Literature. At Vanderbilt, Fitz is engaged in building a major inter-American dimension to Vanderbilt's Program in Comparative Literature (graduate and undergraduate) and he is helping to plan the creation of Vanderbilt's new Center for the Americas, a multi-million dollar initiative that will encourage inter-American teaching, research, and study, including an emphasis on both Canada and Latin America. Fitz has published extensively on comparative approaches to the study of Latin America, including *Rediscovering the New World: Inter American Literature in a Comparative Context* (1991) and (with Judith Payne) *Ambiguity and Gender in the New Novel of Spanish America and Brazil* (1993). In his current book project, Fitz compares the development of narrative in the United States, Brazil, and Spanish America.

Email: <earl.e.fitz@vanderbilt.edu>

Roberto González Echevarría teaches Hispanic and comparative literatures at Yale University, where he is also chairman of the Department of Spanish and Portuguese. One of the early editors of *Diacritics* and *The Yale Journal of Criticism*, González Echevarría is the author of many books on Spanish and Latin American literatures. His *Myth and Archive: A Theory of Latin American Narrative* (1990) won awards from the Modern Language Association of America and The Latin American Studies Association. His *The Pride of Havana: A History of Cuban Baseball* (1999), which also won an award, is González Echevarría's contribution to cultural studies. In the Spring of 2002, González Echevarría delivered the De Vane Lectures at Yale on the topic of his next book: *Love and the Law in Cervantes*. He is the recipient of several honorary degrees, the most recent a doctor in letters *honoris causa* from Columbia University in May of 2002.

Sophia A. McClennen (<http://www.personal.psu.edu/users/s/a/sam50/>) teaches comparative American cultural studies in the Departments of Comparative Literature and Spanish at the Pennsylvania State University, where she is also affiliated with the Program in Women's Studies. Her first book, *The Dialectics of Exile: Nation, Time, Language, and Space in Hispanic Literatures,* is a comparative study of exile literature from Spain and Latin America in the series *Books in Comparative Cultural Studies* from Purdue University Press, 2004. Her second book, *Ariel Dorfman: An Aesthetics of Hope*, is forthcoming from Duke University Press in 2005. McClennen has published widely on comparative cultural studies and Latin America in journals such as *Revista de estudios hispánicos* (2002), *The Review of Contemporary Fiction* (2000), *Cultural Logic* (2000), *Mediations* (1999), and *CLCWeb: Comparative Literature and Culture* (2000). She is currently working on a book on gender and politics in Latin American cinema. McClennen also serves on the advisory board of *CLCWeb: Comparative Literature and Culture* <http://clcwebjournal. lib.purdue. edu>.

Email: <sam50@psu.edu>

Alberto Moreiras teaches Romance studies and literatures at Duke University. A prolific scholar, his many publications include *Interpretación y diferencia* (1991), *Tercer espacio: Literatura y duelo en América Latina* (1999), *The Exhaustion of Difference: The Politics of Latin American Cultural Studies* (2001), and, as co-editor with Nelly Richard, *Retrazos de la transición* (2001). Moreiras is co-editor of the *Journal of Spanish Cultural Studies.*

Email: <moreiras@duke.edu >

Julio Ortega teaches Latin American literature and directs the Trans-Atlantic Project at Brown University. His research interests include twentieth-century Spanish

American literature and culture and literary theory. He is the author of a number of books in Spanish, among them *Una poética del cambio* (1994) and *El principio radical de lo nuevo* (1997). Currently in English translation are *Poetics of Change: The New Spanish-American Narrative* (1986) and *García Márquez and the Powers of Fiction* (1989), and forthcoming is his new book, *After Wonder: Post-Colonial Writing and Transatlantic Readings* (2002).

Email: <julio_ortega@brown.edu>

Corey Shouse teaches Spanish and Latin/o American studies at St. John's University in Minnesota. His areas of interests and publications include Colombian literature, postmodern fiction in the Americas, cultural studies, and Latin American cinema. He is currently researching the testimonial sublime in contemporary Colombian cinema.

Email: <cshouse@csbsju.edu>

Christina Marie Tourino teaches English, U.S. ethnic minority writing, Latin American literatures, and feminist theory at St. John's University in Minnesota. With a recent Ph.D. from Duke University (2000), Tourino's dissertation—*Sex and Reproduction in Contemporary Ethnic Literature*—is about contemporary ethnic texts of the United States. In her work, Tourino analyses U.S. ethnic texts comparatively, based on the premise that such texts are about the problematics of ethnic reproduction in a hostile environment. Tourino recently published on Kogawa's *Obasan* in *Frontiers: A Journal of Women Studies* (2002), and she is at work on a project about Latin and Mediterranean masculinity.

Email: <ctourino@csbsju.edu>

Mario J. Valdés has taught comparative literature and Spanish at the University of Toronto since 1963 and holds the Chair in Iberoamerican Studies at the University of Toronto. His interests and publications encompass the ontology of literary texts, comparative literary history, and the hermeneutics of poetics. His many publications include *Death in the Literature of Unamuno* (1964, 1966), *The Identity of the Literary Text* (1982), *A Ricoeur Reader: Reflection and Imagination* (1991), *World-Making: The Literary Truth-Claim and the Study of Literature* (1992), and *Hermeneutics of Poetic Sense* (1998). Valdés is editor, with Djelal Kadir, of *The Oxford Comparative History of Latin American Literary Cultures* (Oxford University Press, forthcoming in 2004).

Email: <m.valdes@utoronto.ca>

Lois Parkinson Zamora teaches at the University of Houston in the departments of English, History, and Art. Zamora's main area of specialization is contemporary fiction in the Americas, and her many publications include *Writing the Apocalypse: Historical Vision in Contemporary U.S and Latin American Fiction* (Cambridge University Press, 1989), *Image and Memory: Photography from Latin America 1866–1994* (University of Texas Press, 1998), and *The Usable Past: The Imagination of History in Recent Fiction of the Americas* (Cambridge University Press, 1997), and she co-edited with Wendy B. Faris *Magical Realism: Theory, History, Community* (Duke University Press, 1995). *Image and Memory* was named the Best New Art Book of 1998 by the Professional/Scholarly Publishing division of the Association of American Publishers. Currently, Zamora is working on a book about the visual arts and their relation to Latin American literatures, tentatively entitled *The Inordinate Eye*. Zamora served as Dean of the College of Humanities, Fine Arts, and Communication at the University of Houston, 1996–99.

Email: <lzamora@uh.edu>

Index